Routledge Revivals

Bath, 1680–1850

First published in 1981, *Bath, 1680–1850* reveals the changing structure of society and its social values as shown in the expansion of the city. The book examines the lives of men and women who lived in Bath and who, as consumers and producers, transformed it from a small Cotswold town built in the vernacular style, into a uniquely spacious Palladian city devoted to the well-being and leisure activities of the wealthy. In doing so, it explores how the changes in Bath emerged in response to the needs of commerce, industry, and its growing working class, and presents the city as a microcosm of the social transformation brought about by the development of capitalism in England.

Bath, 1680–1850 will appeal to those with an interest in social and cultural history.

Bath, 1680–1850

A Social History or A Valley of Pleasure, yet a Sink of Iniquity

By R. S. Neale

First published in 1981
by Routledge & Kegan Paul Ltd.

This edition first published in 2019 by Routledge
2 Park Square, Milton Park, Abingdon, Oxon, OX14 4RN

and by Routledge
605 Third Avenue, New York, NY 10017

Routledge is an imprint of the Taylor & Francis Group, an informa business

© R. S. Neale 1981

All rights reserved. No part of this book may be reprinted or reproduced or utilised in any form or by any electronic, mechanical, or other means, now known or hereafter invented, including photocopying and recording, or in any information storage or retrieval system, without permission in writing from the publishers.

Publisher's Note
The publisher has gone to great lengths to ensure the quality of this reprint but points out that some imperfections in the original copies may be apparent.

Disclaimer
The publisher has made every effort to trace copyright holders and welcomes correspondence from those they have been unable to contact.

A Library of Congress record exists under LCCN: 80042033

ISBN 13: 978-0-367-65059-9 (hbk)
ISBN 13: 978-1-003-12764-2 (ebk)

BATH 1680–1850
A SOCIAL HISTORY
OR
A VALLEY OF PLEASURE, YET A SINK OF INIQUITY

R. S. NEALE
PROFESSOR OF ECONOMIC HISTORY
UNIVERSITY OF NEW ENGLAND, NEW SOUTH WALES

ROUTLEDGE & KEGAN PAUL
LONDON, BOSTON AND HENLEY

TO THE PEOPLE OF BATH

*First published in 1981
by Routledge & Kegan Paul Ltd
39 Store Street, London WC1E 7DD,
9 Park Street, Boston, Mass. 02108, USA, and
Broadway House, Newtown Road,
Henley-on-Thames, Oxon RG9 1LN*

*Phototypeset by
Input Typesetting Ltd, London SW19 8DR*

© *R. S. Neale 1981
No part of this book may be reproduced in
any form without permission from the
publisher, except for the quotation of brief
passages in criticism*

British Library Cataloguing in Publication Data

Neale, R. S.
Bath 1680-1850.
1. Bath (Avon) – Social life and customs
I. Title
942.3'98   DA690.B3   80-42033

ISBN 0-7100-0639-X

CONTENTS

	Acknowledgments	xi
1	By way of introduction	1
2	The company and the size of the market	12
3	The labouring population	49
4	Landowners and peasants	95
5	Stockjobbers and entrepreneurs	116
6	Ideology and utopia	171
7	Property and absolute self-interest	226
8	Social structure and economic welfare	264
9	The consciousness of the people: 1680–1815	302
10	A radical utopia: 1812–47	329
	Appendices	383
	Notes	431
	Name index	453
	Subject index	459

FIGURES

1 The King's and Queen's Baths at Bath, 1672, Thomas Johnson (British Museum) 14
2 Map, building in Bath 1700–96 43
3 'Prior Park', seat of Ralph Allen Esq., 1752, Anthony Walker (Photo: Science Museum, London) 57
4 Removal order on James Hayes, 1836 (private collection) 78
5 The City of Bath, 1694, Joseph Gilmore (Bath Reference Library) 97
6 A plan of the parish of Walcot, 1740, Thomas Thorp (Bath Reference Library) 105
7 St John's Hospital, 1694 – detail from Gilmore's map (Bath Reference Library) 132
8 a) Chandos's accounts with Wood. b) Part of Anne Phillips's account for furnishing Chandos Buildings (ST12, vol. 4, pp. 46–9, 157; the Huntington Library, San Marino, California) 142
9 Richard Jones, Ralph Allen, Robert Gay and John Wood the elder, attributed to William Hoare (c 1707–92) (Bath Preservation Trust) 152
10 Plan of Queen Square, from John Wood, *Essay towards a Description of Bath* (1765), with Vitruvian Figure from Cesariano's edition of Vitruvius (Como, 1521) 194
11 Queen Square, Bath, 1784, Thomas Malton (Victoria Art Gallery, Bath) 195
12 Plan of the Grand Parade, from John Wood, *Essay towards a Description of Bath* (1765), with Vitruvian Figure (Leonardo's version) 197

FIGURES

13 South Parade, 1775, Thomas Malton (Victoria Art Gallery, Bath) 198
14 North Parade, 1779, Thomas Malton (Victoria Art Gallery, Bath) 198
15 Plan of the King's Circus, John Wood (City Archives, Bath) 200
16 The King's Circus, J. R. Cozens (Victoria Art Gallery, Bath) 200
17 A Plan of the City of Bath, 1735, John Wood (British Museum) 202
18 The Royal Crescent, 1769, Thomas Malton (Victoria Art Gallery, Bath) 208
19 Map, the City of Bath: distribution of houses according to rate assessment 1766 212
20 Pulteney Bridge (Victoria Art Gallery, Bath) 236
21 John Eveleigh's drawings of proposed buildings at Grosvenor Gardens to be financed by an Equitable Trust in 1794 (author's collection) 244
22 Improvement Proposals for the City Centre, 1789 (City Archives, Bath) 254
23 Bath in 1900, the Parish of St James in the foreground (author's collection) 272
24 Street plan of the Lower Town, the Parish of St James. Source: Ordnance Survey Map (1888) 273
25 Avon Street, nineteenth century (Bath Reference Library) 275
26 Coat of Arms of Bath Fire Office. A unique depiction of two of Bath's labouring population in 1769 (author's collection) 296
27 The middling class in relation to other classes 301
28 Anti-Roebuck election poster, 1832 (Bath Reference Library) 351
29 John Arthur Roebuck (1801–79), MP for Bath 1832–7 and 1841–7 (Victoria Art Gallery, Bath) 352
30 Roebuck's voting card, 1832 (private collection) 353
31 Old Bath Chairs, 1907 (author's collection) 381
Endpapers A map of the principal buildings and places in Bath circa 1840 (adapted from E. F. Tew, *A Map of Bath* and from *A New and Accurate Plan of the City of Bath*, Taylor & Meyler, 1976)

TABLES

2.1	The number of houses, population, and weekly coach services in Bath, 1700–1850	44
3.1	Cost of apprenticeship in selected trades in the city of Bath, 1765–76	52
3.2	Occupations of apprentices enrolled in the city of Bath, 1724–69	54
3.3	Richard Marchant's loans	62
3.4	Places of origin or settlement of applicants for poor relief, Bath. Selected years, 1763–1824	71
3.5	Applications for poor relief in Bath and Walcot, 1763–74 by sex	72
3.6	Earnings and real wages, non-agricultural labourers in the city of Bath, 1780–1817	86
3.7	Economic conditions, crime, and poor law decisions, Bath, 1777 and 1787–93	88
3.8	Cases of assault brought before Quarter Sessions in Bath, 1777 and 1787–93	90
4.1	The Doddington survey, 1713	102
4.2	Leases granted by Bath Corporation by type and duration, 1585–1769	109
5.1	The accounts of James Brydges, First Duke of Chandos, with his brokers in England, 1711–34	122
5.2	Selected items in Chandos's account with Sir Matthew Decker, June 1715 to June 1719	124
5.3	Moses Hart's trading in South Sea stock for Chandos, 24 November 1719 to 23 March 1720	126

TABLES

5.4	Number of leases according to occupation of sub-lessee in building developments in Bath, 1761–92	154
5.5	The number and value of houses in developments by John Wood and Son, 1728–87	156
5.6	House values in Wood's developments, 1786–1827	165
6.1	Distribution of houses in Bath in 1766 by parish, according to contribution to rates under the Bath Act, 1766	213
7.1	Building leases granted on the Bathwick estate, 1784–93	238
7.2	Expenditure by improvement commission and net produce of the tolls, 1790–1815	258
8.1	Intercensal rates of population change, 1801–51	267
8.2	Occupations in Bath, 1831	268
8.3	Number of females per 100 males, Bath 1821–51	276
8.4	Employment of women in Bath, 1851	276
8.5	Widows in Bath Union, 1842	281
8.6	The charge per week for keeping a poor man, wife and two children with nothing superior to gaol allowance	282
8.7	Earnings and real wages, non-agricultural labourers, in the city of Bath, 1812–44	286
8.8	Average age of death in families in three classes in selected towns, 1841	287
8.9	Deaths from cholera and diarrhoea in Bath, 1848–9 and from smallpox in 1837	291
8.10	Mortality rates per 1,000 living 0–5 years, 1838–44	293
8.11	Distribution of subscribers to the Bath Fire Office, 1767	298
8.12	Distribution of Bath subscribers to the Equitable Trust for Grosvenor Gardens and Hotel, 1794	299
10.1	Percentage of voters on the roll, according to parish, voting for J. A. Roebuck, 1832	354
10.2	Votes of shoemakers in the parishes of Walcot and St James in 1847 according to estimated gross rental of houses and property	357
10.3	Estimated gross rental of houses occupied by plumpers in the parish of Walcot in the Bath election, 1841	360
10.4	Estimated gross rental of houses occupied by plumpers in the parish of St James in the Bath election, 1841	361
10.5	Political allegiance of councillors, 1835	365

APPENDICES

A Economic activity in Bath, 1700–1832   383
B Peaks in building activity, 1700–1800, and rates of interest
   and Corporate Debt in Bath, 1700–1800   395
C Number of houses in Bath according to contribution to
   rate in shillings as levied by the Act, 1766   397
D Food price indices, Bath, 1812–44   405
E Wages and real wages in Bath, 1780–1814   411
F Mortality in Bath, 1838–44, compared in 21 healthy and
   32 unhealthy statistical districts   419
G Ratios of poor law offences, 1777, and 1787–93   424
H Estimated rent of houses in the parish of St James in the
   1830s   426
I Population in Bath and its suburban parishes, 1801–51   428

ACKNOWLEDGMENTS

I carried out my first piece of research on Bath in the summer of 1952; its result is recorded in two lines in this book. Subsequently, as I found that the history of Bath as written afforded no material through which to illustrate the major themes of English Economic and Social history as I taught it to students at Bath Technical College, it became apparent that I would have to write my own history of Bath – a history that would comprehend Bath within the mainstream of eighteenth- and nineteenth-century history. As I began to write this history, slowly and sporadically at first and more intensively over two periods from 1958 to 1962 and from 1971 to the present, I incurred many obligations which I now acknowledge. The first is to Philip Hopkins, one time Labour candidate for Bath and lecturer in the Extra-Mural Department at Bristol University. It was he who sowed the seed of the idea that what I had prepared for my teaching might usefully be put in the form of a further degree. My next is to Professor W. Ashworth who accepted my application to work part-time for an MA at Bristol University and left me pretty much alone to work on my study of Bath in the early nineteenth century in my own way. But I could only work at all with the willing co-operation of Jim Webber, then Head of the Department of General Education at Bath Technical College. He allowed me to timetable my own 'free time' so that I could work on the material housed in Bath Reference Library. In those days in Bath this was a hard-won concession for although we taught general studies to workers on day-release from industrial enterprises and government offices the notion of 'day-release' for teachers still lay very much in the future.

ACKNOWLEDGMENTS

In the course of my research I was given the free run of the basement stacks in the Bath Reference library and for that I will always be grateful to John Kite who was then reference librarian as well as a colleague in offering a course on History from the Local Record which we taught in the Reference Library. In more recent years both old and new members of the staff of Bath Reference Library have continued to give unflagging help in tracking down sometimes elusive material.

The creation of the new county of Avon, which finally took away the local autonomy of the city which in the period of this book did so much for itself, created many problems for the location of archival material, problems which may affect the location of some of my references, and in 1971 and 1978 I became greatly indebted to John Bryant, city archivist, who with the barest of facilities and resources gave me unstinted service and co-operation. But, for a city apparently caring for its historic heritage and benefiting from the high level of rates that heritage helps to maintain, Bath council treats its archives with scant respect and maintains the worst research facilities I have encountered in writing this history. It seems that in their preference for appearance modern councillors are no different from their eighteenth-century counterparts. The one difference is that the eighteenth-century Corporation was a closed one and its members irremovable at least until the Act of 1835. But who in Bath cares about archives?

Fortunately there are many outside Bath who do care about archives and I acknowledge my debt to the library staffs of other libraries and repositories where care is taken of them; the Somerset County Record Office, Taunton, the Bristol Archives, the British Museum, the Public Record Office, the British Transport Commission Archives, London, the St Bartholomew Hospital Archives, London, the National Library, Canberra, and the Huntington Library and Art Gallery, San Marino, California.

Then I thank those many individuals who have helped me with references, frequently directing me to new sources or allowing me to use their own work; Klaus Loewald, John Chartres, Hugh Torrens, Jane Linden, Patricia Croot, Sylvia McIntyre, John Kite, Leslie Presnell and, especially, Christopher Chalkin.

Since I have tested my ideas on Bath on other people before finally committing myself to the pages of this book my thanks must also go to those institutions and groups of people who have provided

ACKNOWLEDGMENTS

a forum for those ideas: *Economic History Review*, *Victorian Studies*, *Business History*, *Somersetshire Archaeological and Natural History Society*, *Our History* and the David Nichol Smith Seminar in Canberra in 1973; Seminars at the Universities of New England, Tasmania, Melbourne, Exeter, Leeds, Bristol, The Australian National University, The London School of Economics and Birkbeck College from 1975 to 1978; The Van Dyck Society at Bristol University and a one-day WEA School on the history of Bath at Bath in 1978. To all the people involved, my thanks. But especially to Stephen Beck who over the years has been my model representative of those to whom this book is addressed – he has already heard much of it in one way or another, the rest I hope he will accept as a substitute for the letters I never wrote.

I acknowledge, too, the help given to me by the University of New England whose arrangements for study leave gave me two years in England in 1971 and 1978 and time in August and September 1977 to work at the Huntington Library in California. I am also much indebted to the Trustees of the Huntington Library for the grant of a Visiting Fellowship for that period and to Eugène Kamenka and The Australian National University for a Visiting Fellowship at the History of Ideas Unit from November 1973 to March 1974 which enabled me to work on eighteenth-century material held at the National Library of Australia. My work also benefited from two year-long periods spent with the Department of Economic History at Bristol University, the first as Visiting Fellow in 1971, the second as Visiting Professor in 1978.

I am also pleased to acknowledge the generous financial assistance towards the publication of the book granted by the Publication Committees of the Universities of New England and Bristol, and the willing co-operation of all those institutions which at short notice gave their permission for the reproduction of the illustrations as follows: Figures 1 and 17 are reproduced by courtesy of the Trustees of the British Museum; Figure 2 by permission of the Science Museum, London; Figures 5, 6, 7, 25, 28 courtesy of Avon County Library (Bath Reference Library); Figure 8 by permission of the Huntington Library, San Marino, California; Figure 9 courtesy of the Bath Preservation Trust; Figures 13, 14, 16, 18, 20, 29 by permission of the Victoria Art Gallery, Bath City Corporation; Figures 15, 22 courtesy of the Bath City Council. Parts of chapter 9 appeared in my *Class in English History, 1680–1850* (1980) and are

ACKNOWLEDGMENTS

included in the present work by permission of the publishers, Basil Blackwell of Oxford.

Although the final typescript was produced under the direction of Alison Affleck and my secretary Jenny Weissel, and I thank them for it, my greatest debt is to my wife Margaret who, throughout 1978, toiled away typing various drafts of the book when she could have been enjoying the beauty of Branscombe in Devon and the pleasures of Vicarage Cottage where the book was written.

CHAPTER ONE

BY WAY OF INTRODUCTION

There is no secret about the received social history of Bath. It is architectural first, medical and literary next, and all about Bath as a social melting pot. Above all it is about architects and their architecture, much of which is still there for everyone to see. All kinds of historians have described, mapped, drawn and photographed it. Indeed, so much has this been done that historians might well be forgiven for supposing that what has been written about architecture in Bath is in fact an objective representation of the city as it existed in the eighteenth century; that the stones, as it were, as well as the facts, speak for themselves and leave very little else for anyone else to say. However, to write about eighteenth-century Bath is to write about eighteenth-century England. About both there is still much to be said. In this book I offer a new perspective on the social history of Bath in the eighteenth century. In it I set out to reveal the changing structure of society and its social values as shown in the social organisation of its space and its social movements; aspects of life in Bath generally so well hidden by the city's apparent survival as an objective reality. Moreover, I illustrate this perspective by reference to historical materials not customarily incorporated into social histories of Bath, even though that history has been re-told every four or five years since the end of the Second World War. Furthermore, I try to face up to the fact that I can only report my experience of Bath through the inadequate metaphor of a language which compels me to write seriatim even though I can sometimes see the Bath I write about as an historical gestalt. What I would like to do is write this piece of social history

BY WAY OF INTRODUCTION

in the way Picasso painted Kahnweiler, whereas I can scarcely manage to do it as Hogarth painted Captain Thomas Coram. Thus the manner of its writing may cause as much disquiet as what is included in it and omitted from it. The book does not simply start in 1680 and march ruthlessly on to its predetermined end in 1850. It starts and stops and starts again, frequently returning to its original starting point or close to it – and not only in Bath itself – and ending at some other point before or after its first stopping. Thus what narrative there is is continually interrupted and the chapters sometimes cover the same ground several times. But, I am strengthened in my resolve to proceed thus by Laurence Sterne's brilliant, although fictional, exposition of an historian's task:[1]

> Could a historiographer drive on his history, as a muleteer drives on his mule – straight forward; – for instance, from Rome all the way to Loretto, without ever once turning his head aside either to the right or to the left, – he might venture to foretell you to an hour when he should get to his journey's end; – but the thing is, morally speaking, impossible: For, if he is a man of the least spirit he will have fifty deviations from a straight line to make with this or that party as he goes along, which he can no ways avoid. He will have views and prospects to himself perpetually soliciting his eye, which he can no more help standing still to look at than he can fly; he will moreover have various
> Accounts to reconcile:
> Anecdotes to pick up:
> Inscriptions to make out:
> Stories to weave in:
> Traditions to sift:
> Personages to call upon:
> Panegyrics to paste up at this door;
> Pasquinades at that: All which both the man and his mule are quite exempt from. To sum up all; there are archives at every stage to be looked into, and rolls, records, documents, and endless genealogies, which justice ever and anon calls him back to stay the reading of: In short, there is no end of it; – for my own part, I declare I have been at it these six weeks, making all the speed I possibly could, – and am not yet born: – I have just been able, and that's all, to tell you when it

BY WAY OF INTRODUCTION

happened, but not how; – so that you see the thing is yet far from being accomplished.

And my starts and stops and deviations are all necessary and deliberate. I am unable to use any other way to convey the structure and density of action in historical time and the passing of varieties of linear time and to draw out the sense of the drama of successive generations, yet keep the main lines of analysis sharp and clear. But, to traverse old ground a second or third time is a way of seeing old friends anew and of seeing them differently, each time recalling in memory what they were like or how they were drawn first time round. Of course I may fail in this. Therefore, this account of the context and overview of the book might help to hold the argument together and dispel some of the disquiet potential readers might feel about it.

The pre-industrial city of which Bath is a late example, was as much a human invention as the fast-breeder reactor. Like the reactor it too grew out of the economic and social conditions of its time. These conditions included an ecological base and an advanced technology able to guarantee an agricultural surplus, and a complex social structure marked by a concentration of power in the hands of an élite, which was either literate itself or able to command the services of those who were literate, and which appropriated that surplus. Yet, even after the first invention of the city in Mesopotamia about 3500 BC and their second invention in Meso-America, cities spread only unevenly and erratically throughout the world. This is not surprising. The social organisation and technology available to sustain them were indeed fragile. And it is only in the last 200 years that the predominance of the city as a place of production and residence in advanced societies has been assured by the achievements of industrial capitalism. Even in Europe at the end of the seventeenth century, cities were few and only a very small proportion of any region lived in them. Moreover, they fulfilled only a limited number of useful functions, mainly military, administrative, religious, and commercial ones. Therefore, the innovation in the early eighteenth century of a pre-industrial city almost entirely devoted to the leisure activities of the ruling élite, such as was Bath, is a most remarkable fact.

The physical presence of Bath in the second half of the twentieth century, although only as a partial survival, provides overwhelming visual evidence of the ability of the ruling class of agrarian capitalists and their satellite classes in the eighteenth century to extract and consume a very high proportion of well-established agricultural and commercial surpluses. Moreover, as a social product resulting from social action structured by relationships between classes, the city of Bath is also a manifestation of the way space was socially organised in the eighteenth century. As such it is the result of social structures largely hidden from view, at least at first sight, and of social relationships flowing from them.

Usually, however, Bath appears in history as the product of creative acts carried out by individual architects, developers and builders. Indeed, this is how it appears in the writings of architectural historians – even the best of them. Yet, these acts will be seen to be but unconscious expressions of particular social points of view. This is so because, in the economic and social context of town building in the eighteenth century, no architect or builder could force upon his customers an organisation of space not congenial to their needs and the demands of the market. Thus, while it is true that builders built apparently as autonomous agents, it was the market that determined which acts of production and creativity would be allowed to survive to fulfil the intent or aspirations of their builders. Therefore the social organisation of space which was Bath may be thought of as a manifestation of collective or class consciousness – knowledge in a society about itself – expressed in stone and arrangements of space and available to us in these forms as a basis for our own knowledge about that society.

But, any city is more than the social organisation of space either as artefact or expression of class consciousness. It is also the people who organise that space – a few more constructively and deliberately than the many – and those who occupy it. Of course, most residents of a city are mere occupiers. For them the social organisation of its space is a given fact. They simply use what is left over after the wealthy and powerful have taken their shares. Their place in it is allocated to them and it forms for them the spatial conditions of their consciousness. Such consciousness becomes manifest in social movements rather than in building. Bath in the eighteenth and early nineteenth centuries was no exception.

This history will explore both aspects of consciousness; that displayed in building and the organisation of space and that manifest in social movements. The theoretical grounds for such a juxtaposition I find in this extract from Jordis Borja:[2]

> The analysis of the urban phenomenon suffers, in its theoretical formations, from a particular difficulty in explaining *both* the urban structure and the urban movements. . . . The rupture, idealist in origin, between structures and practices paralyses dialectical analysis and develops an analytical dichotomy between a *theory of reproduction* ('the city of capital') and a *theory of change* of a historicist type (the city transformed by 'urban social movements'). The dialectical analysis conceives any structure as a contradictory reality in continuous change. These objective contradictions give rise to social conflicts that appear as *immediate agents* of change. There are no structures that are not something other than an ensemble of contradictory and conflicting social relations, more or less crystallized, but always in process of change. And there are no urban movements, in which all the social classes participate to different degrees, that are not situated within structures, expressing them and modifying them constantly.

Accordingly – although in this social history there is mention of Beau Nash and concerts and balls; Ralph Allen and Fielding and Pope; John Wesley and the Countess of Huntingdon's Chapel – these myriad aspects of the social life of the company at Bath are but the starting point of a more powerful drama – the production of the city itself and the transformation in consciousness of its producers in the 'act' of production. Which 'act' is, of course, merely the notional sum of countless numbers of individual acts many, perhaps most, of which are lost to recorded history. Here I can only describe some of them. The reader's mind must do the rest.

The subject matter of what generally passes for the social history of Bath, with a little more besides, which earned it the title, a Valley of Pleasure, Yet a Sink of Iniquity, is outlined in the chapter on the Company and the Size of the Market. It is in this chapter that we meet with John Wesley and Beau Nash, Sarah Scott and pretty Miss Braddock, Philip Thicknesse and the gentleman who dropped dead after dancing thirty-three couple in the Assembly Rooms, and pornography and prostitution. Since all the services and commodities that Bath could supply had their price and since markets are about prices this chapter considers them and, although it finds them lacking and inadequate for serious study concludes that consumption expenditures must have been very great indeed for them to have generated house-building with a capital value of over £3,000,000, which was about the same as that invested in fixed capital in the cotton industry during the eighteenth century.

The chapter on the labouring population adds a new dimension to the social history of Bath. In it I tell all that I can of the men and women who were born in the city and who lived and worked in its trades and professions, or who flocked to it seeking work as servants and labourers. It contrasts the different experiences of natives and immigrants, particularly early in the eighteenth century, and contrasts the lives of those who were successful, like Richard Marchant and Ralph Allen, with those of unknowns, like Prudence Brown and Thomas Roberts, who were failures. Then it has much to say about the decline of that corporate paternalism or corporatism, which characterised much of life at Bath early in the eighteenth century when its Burrough Walls enclosed a mere 335 households. It contrasts this with the rise of free trading interlopers and successful entrepreneurs and the consequential stirrings of organised labour in 1765. In this chapter I take the story well into the nineteenth century in an attempt to assess the effect on the economic welfare and social experience of the bottom stratum of society of nearly 150 years of economic development in the city which, at the time, had a population of 50,000. It is a preliminary survey only and is pessimistic; urban labourers in Bath had no share in the benefits of the goods and services their work supplied – in terms of average life expectancy they were dead at 25. Their masters and the consumers of their products had another thirty years to run.

The chapter on Landowners and Peasants begins in the late seventeenth century with Williams's invasion, the battle of Wincanton, and the ideology of absolute property. It describes a social structure in the villages around Bath, notably Walcot and Bathwick, somewhat different from that in Bath itself but, like it, destined to be swept away as conditions were created for the development of the city. It demonstrates the importance of capitalist-minded landlords in the production of Bath. These men, determined to eliminate numerous small tenants occupying land on lifehold tenancies in order to consolidate holdings to let at a rack rent, included proprietors of large acreages in Walcot Lordship and Barton Farm and

BY WAY OF INTRODUCTION

in the manor of Bathwick as well as numerous smaller landowners like George Trymme, a member of Bath Corporation who is credited with starting the first development of a new street outside the Burrough Walls. Within the walls the Corporation was the major landowner but, in the first half of the century, it was not set on the maximum possible development of its property. In fact, throughout this early period and in spite of the favourable conditions of the market, development was piecemeal and sporadic. The dynamic capitalist producers of Bath were only warming up.

In the chapter on Stockjobbers and Entrepreneurs, I show how the production of Bath got under way in the mid-1720s. And that is where the story starts again with the partnership between the Duke of Chandos, England's biggest financial tycoon, and John Wood, an unknown and struggling surveyor digging dirt in the Avon Navigation just outside Bath. Although the chapter starts in Bath it starts again with the life and doings of James Brydges, First Duke of Chandos. This is so because Chandos's life and his employment of Wood in a major building speculation in Bath reveals at the outset the dependence of the production of Bath on the intricate development of local, national, and international webs of credit. It shows how a society saturated with credit was as important for the production of the city as one built on landed property. These two things – credit and land – were, of course, two aspects of absolute property. And, absolute property, a necessary condition for the growth of the market was also a necessary condition for production for it; together these two 'necessary' conditions were virtually sufficient for the whole experience of Bath from 1700 to 1850. But, after starting again with the life of Chandos the chapter starts once more with Wood's development of Queen Square after 1728. This new start takes the details of the financial story through to the financial ruin of Wood's son in 1781. The chapter ends with the claim that Bath was both product and symbol of the success of agrarian capitalism – an existential expression of the economic and social structure of society and its dominant, agrarian-capitalist, ideology. But, just as the growth of Bath destroyed the existing social structure of the villages and transformed labour in the city, the very success of its entrepreneurs and the growth of the city threatened the social relations existing between those for whom Bath was a luxury consumption-good and those for whom Bath was a place of work and production; relations between consumers and producers. Thus, Bath, as it was known to the eighteenth century, was doomed by the very success of its capitalist citizens and the expansion of civil society.

In the chapter on Ideology and Utopia I look in detail at this hidden contradiction and attempt to show how it was reflected in the townscape itself. So, the discussion moves from the history of money and credit to the history of art. At the outset I raise the question of meaning in art and in architecture and, therefore, in architecture in Bath. But, the chapter is not about the history of architecture in Bath: Ison's *The Georgian Buildings of Bath* has yet to be surpassed in this field. The chapter starts at the beginning of the eighteenth century with an account of the role of the Corporation in development and its growing commitment to the development ethos. It traces successive stages in its influence upon the townscape in Bath. Therefore it makes claims about the effect of the Corporation's resistance to change as well as the consequences of its growing commitment to it. This discussion of the role of the Corporation takes the story into the period 1750 to 1765. Then the chapter begins again, this time in 1728, to tell the parallel story of John Wood. Only this time we look at him as creative artist rather than as developer and dynamic entrepreneur. The origin of the polemic signs in Wood's work is outlined and I show that his creativity as an architect was constrained by the very society which provided him with his opportunities and which, through his work as developer, he helped to change even as he built to inhibit change and isolate his customers from change. The dynamic aesthetic quality given to his work by this contradiction and the tension arising from it transformed the city in appearance, pulling it up the lower slopes of Lansdown Hill. Wood's perception of how space in a city should be organised also appealed to the company at Bath. This is not to say that they shared all his values but that for them his buildings and spatial arrangements satisfied their feeling for separation from and domination over the individualistic world they had conjured up; his work reassured them of their security and status.

Subsequently Wood's work also shaped and influenced the work of his successors such that large masses and spaces of the townscape can be thought of as a total social organisation of space, embodying Wood's religious utopian imagery and the company's demand for separation and status. It is, therefore, expressive of a utopia at odds with the world for which he produced and which produced him; a Utopia which would become less realisable in reality the more he and other architects and developers, developed. This part of the chapter takes the story up to 1789 and shows that just at the point when the Corporation made its commitment to development, turning its back on corporatism in favour of individualism, Wood's architecture called men back from unrestrained individualism and the absolute self-interest inherent in absolute property.

Then the chapter starts again in 1764. This time to work out the final success of absolute property and absolute self-interest in the city, marked by the building of the New Assembly Rooms two years before the publication of *The Wealth of Nations*. However, as its citizens sought to place limits on absolute property and self-interest in the guise of morality and social order, Bath, like *The Wealth of Nations* itself, retained its hidden contradictions. Throughout this chapter memories of earlier chapters, particularly the chapter on The Labouring Population, are called upon to relate changes at the level of art to the humbler experiences of men.

In the chapter on Property and Absolute Self-Interest, I argue that all the elements favourable for the building explosion, which added new spatial dimensions to the townscape and 42 per cent to the number of houses, were present. This was particularly true in the case of the development of Bathwick. Some aspects of this development already discussed arise again since this chapter also starts in 1726. It also recalls some aspects of the Corporation's growing commitment to development and plunges back into the world of money and credit written about in the chapter on Stockjobbers and Entrepreneurs but now come to maturity in a world of architects and developers completely in tune with their market. It is an easy and straightforward story to tell – a sort of placid plateau for a society sure of itself in every way, comfortably at ease in the pages of Jane Austen, in spite of recurring signs of social conflict. But, it ends in disaster. Contradictions in the world of money and credit, accentuated by war, precipitate a great crisis in building and confidence. Then changes in patterns of leisure, provoked in part by the very success and expansion of Bath, result in a virtual cessation of the social organisation of space as hitherto described.

The next three chapters describe the transformation of social structure and the generation of social movements antithetical to the continued domination of a class of privileged agrarian capitalists –

a domination in Bath made more visible by the very structure of the city itself. In the chapter on Social Structure and Economic Welfare I touch upon the final destruction of peasant society around Bath and on the final demise of corporatism within it. But I pass rapidly to a discussion of population and its physical and social distribution in the fifty years from 1800 to 1850 and of the growth of manufacturing in the city. This leads to a detailed consideration of the experiences and welfare of the different social classes. Thus it takes up again a theme touched upon in the chapter on The Labouring Population but amplifies it to explore in detail more about the urban structure and social relations of Bath than is revealed in the discussion in the chapter on Ideology and Utopia.

In the chapters on The Consciousness of the People and A Radical Utopia I start again in the seventeenth century to show how developments in consciousness in Bath were intimately bound up with the growth of social movements in the country as a whole. However, by the early nineteenth century there were very significant local factors that for a time pushed the political aspects of social movements in Bath to the forefront of national politics. The ideology of the successful movement, Philosophic Radicalism, was a logical outcome of that absolute property and absolute self-interest which had built the city and transformed the local environment and, paradoxically, left it as a monument to and repository of a social class which now sought to inhibit any further developments likely to erode its own power and status. The central objective of the Philosophic Radicals was, however, to do just that. J. A. Roebuck, MP for Bath, was their very mirror. Under his inspired leadership the middling-class in Bath sought to re-make the world in their own image. The temporary capture of this Radical movement by Chartism and its control by working-class leaders born of long travail both in and out of Bath and their demise in Bath provide the theme of the final dénouement. The economic and social structure of Bath as well as the Philosophic Radicals and the Chartists were overtaken by events. Bath's social structure changed again. It lost its artisans and became predominantly a city of old retired women, female domestic servants and unskilled labourers. In England generally, the centre of gravity of the economy and working-class movements was by now fairly settled in the north of England. Thus Bath continued for another hundred years; a repository for members of the old society attracted to it by the physical structures and amen-

BY WAY OF INTRODUCTION

ities of an earlier age, that is, by its social organisation of space. Fortunately for them the worst excesses of Victorian urban development passed it by. Bath's new residents had it both ways; they enjoyed the economic fruit of absolute property and absolute self-interest in a social organisation of space produced by perceptions of urban living at odds with the economic and ideological basis of their wealth. Bath remained a world in which neither the occupant of a Bath Chair nor the privileged labourer who pulled and pushed it challenged the economic structure which determined their social relationships. Bath was a valley of pleasure still and, for the poor, a sink of iniquity.

Therefore, the theme of this book is the influence of consumption on the production of Bath and the influence of production on consciousness as shown in its social organisation of space and in its social movements. Since production is the link between consumption and consciousness, and since property is the key to production, it also has much to say about property, land, labour, money, credit and business enterprise, and about contradictions between different kinds of property and between those with and those without property. It is a social history of Bath.

CHAPTER TWO

THE COMPANY AND THE SIZE OF THE MARKET

I should be glad to send you some news, but all the news of the place would be like the bills of Mortality; Palsey four, Gout six, Fever one. – Indeed, the only thing one can do one day one did not do the day before is to dye.

Elizabeth Montague to the Duchess of Portland, 4 January 1740.

I

At the beginning of the eighteenth century Bath, although an ancient city, was neither beautiful nor rich. According to one of its many anonymous visitors:[1]

Tis neither Town nor City, yet goes by the Name of both: five Months in the Year 'tis as Populous as London, the other seven as desolate as a Wilderness . . . 'tis a Valley of Pleasure, yet a sink of Iniquity; Nor is there any intrigues or Debauch Acted in London, but is Mimick'd here.

Yet, five months of popularity, soon to be spread over two seasons in the spring and autumn, shows that 'The Bathe', for all this lowly reputation, was a place to go to. In 1714 it so endeared itself to Alexander Pope that he wrote to his friend Martha Blount:[2]

If Variety of Diversions and new Objects be capable of driving our Friends out of our minds, I have the best excuse imaginable for forgetting you. For I have Slid, I can't tell how, into all the

Amusements of this Place: My whole Day is shar'd by the Pump-Assemblies, the Walkes, the Chocolate houses, Raffling Shops, Plays, Medleys, etc.

If Pope could be so easily distracted by Bath lesser men and women may be excused for having found in it so many alluring attractions: eating and drinking, shopping and chit-chatting, dancing and card-playing, revelling and horse-racing, bathing and reading, gambling and whoring – couple them as you will, the visiting company certainly coupled and combined them in many ways. And the sheer spectacle they made of life at Bath was another of its attractions – a view nowhere more clearly shown than in Thomas Johnson's drawing of The King's and The Queen's Baths at Bath in 1672 (Figure 1). The Baths were simply another piece of theatre. Indeed, the mélange of attractions and pleasures Bath had to offer is so rich that it is best, perhaps, to let some of the company speak for themselves about themselves and about their fellow visitors.

One thing about Bath that attracted and pleased so many men and women of property and wealth was the easy optimism of its doctors and apothecaries who claimed to be able to protect the health of the rich against their own worst excesses and the dangers endemic to living. Mary Chandler, one of Pope's contemporaries and one of Bath's many moralising poets, put the problem this way:[3]

> Fatal Effects of Luxury and Ease!
> We drink our Poison, and we eat Disease;
> Indulge our Senses at our Reason's cost,
> Till Sense is Pain, and Reason's hurt, or lost.

Consequently doctors of physick and apothecaries flocked to Bath to ease pain and restore reason. In this enterprise they gained much by the primitive state of medicine and the great faith people had in the power of their nostrums and potions. At least one of them, Dr Oliver, was an astute businessman able to attract rich customers to Bath by persuading them, for their health's sake, that they should take its waters, warm as they were, both inside and out. Once captured in Bath he placed his patients on a strict diet and invented the 'Oliver' biscuit for their jaded appetites. Like other doctors, he bled his patients frequently and prescribed as if he knew what the

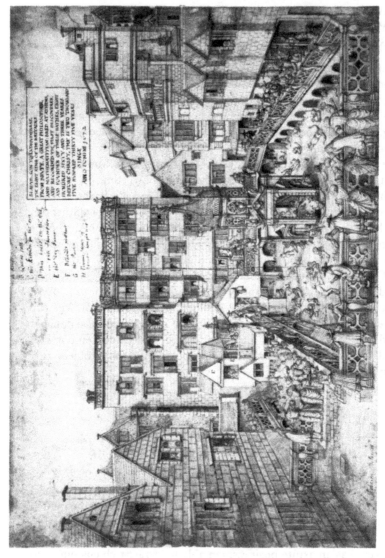

Figure 1 The King's and Queen's Baths at Bath, 1672, Thomas Johnson

waters could do. 'I don't frequent the same Pump that the company does,' wrote one of his patients, 'for having had a violent cough since my illness Dr Oliver ordered me to drink the waters at another pump which are less heating to the lungs, till my cough should leave me.'[4]

In advertising the benefits of Bath waters Dr Oliver, like Henry Chapman, Thomas Guidot, and Robert Peirce before him, told what his patients suffered from and what their worst fears of pain and sickness were. According to Dr Oliver the Bath waters would cure those suffering from: gout, rheumatism, palsies, convulsions, lameness, colic, consumption, asthma, jaundice, scurvy, the itch, scab, leprosy, scrofula, gravel as well as coldness and pain in the head, epilepsies, most diseases of the eyes, deafness and noise in the ears, running of the ears, palpitation of the heart, sharpness of urine, wounds, ulcers, piles, numbness, in any part, and all the special diseases of women, including infertility.[5] But it was Dr Peirce more than Dr Oliver who exploited the claim about the treatment of the special diseases of women, particularly infertility. The attractiveness of this claim turned upon the need by women to live authentically as their age informed them they must. This was to breed. Accordingly Peirce produced many case histories to 'prove' his point.

Fertility generally required and followed marriage, especially where property was concerned. But marriage, too, depended upon health at least as much as upon fortune, and a certain barrier to marriage was undoubtedly the 'Virgin-Distemper' or the 'Green Sickness'. Who, in his right mind and without the compensation of very large fortune, would marry Mistress Elizabeth Wayte at age 20?

According to Dr Peirce, Elizabeth:[6]

> look'd pale, yellow, and black under the eyes, etc. with Green Sickness: she seemed also to have the Jaundice, Scurvey, and Dropsie (for her feet and legs swell'd) and she had itchings upon her arms and legs, was short breath'd, had distended Hypochonders (especially the right) was hot and dry, inclining to a Hectick. Upon any disturbance (from little sudden things) apt to Tremblings and Palpitations of the Heart, and Giddiness in the Head, etc. This illness began five or six years before, not being well purg'd after the Smallpox. She could not now walk

the length of her chamber without panting, and sinking under the burden of her own emaciated body. She greatly complain'd of the Palpitation of the Heart, a symptom incident, more or less, to all that labour under this Virgin-Distemper, and indeed all Cochexies, and great Obstructions; whether in men or women; whether young or old.

Indeed,[7]

This young gentlewoman was so dispirited by her long continued illness, that she could hardly bear the working of a gentle Purge, which was given her as a preparation for drinking the waters, and bathing.

Although she would have done better eating a dish of turnip tops, Elizabeth decided to follow Peirce's course of treatment in the Bath waters and began by drinking them and then:[8]

bathed in the Cross-Bath, and took Deoppilatives and Anticochecticks, and improv'd so well upon them, that in five or six weeks time she could walk the town, and into the meddows, and at length recover'd a good stomach, and a fresh colour in her face, and some flesh upon her bones, and all her swelling fallen. Seeing her a year or two after, I found her as plump and as brisk, as any of her sisters, which were all comely young women.

Peirce does not tell us whether the cure produced husband, fortune and pregnancy as well as plumpness and colour. His book, an advertisement for Bath waters, includes many other case histories.

Although the nuptial outcome of Elizabeth Wayte's visit to Bath is unknown, the strong Jacobite element in the city could have taken pride in a known success. This was the conception of a son by Maria Beatrice, the wife of James II, during their joint visit to Bath in September 1687. (The same citizens may also have regretted the sharpening of focus it brought about in the minds of the King's opponents.) Certainly the reported success of the waters in the case of Maria Beatrice seems to have outweighed their failure in the case of Queen Anne – a failure plain for all to see in the reign of George I – and, well into the eighteenth century, people professed a belief in the special powers of the waters in the case of women. 'Mrs. Langton is here', wrote Elizabeth Montague from Tunbridge, 'in hopes of an heir by these waters, which I think an affront to the prolifick streams of the Bath Waters.'[9] Her sister even thought they might work wonders on men. Writing ironically of her brother's flagging love affair she said, 'I am afraid he will never have courage to ask her the question. I made him drink a great deal of Bath water in the hopes it might make him a warmer lover.'[10]

Sadly for infertility many of the gentlemen visitors to Bath were a good deal warmer for love than Elizabeth's brother appeared to be. The result, the dissemination of the pox, which was probably the real cause of much infertility. That, too, said Dr Oliver, the waters would cure. 'If they can't be cured by drinking and bathing here', he wrote, 'they will never be cured anywhere.'[11] But, there was the rub. Bathing at 'The Bathe', if not the drinking of its waters, was sweetened by the knowledge that it was accompanied by amatory dalliance, sexual titillation, and open prostitution. The plain fact was that for a gentleman to visit the place was as like to bring on the pox as cure it. For gentlewomen, too, the sexual stakes were very high, relief from the Green Sickness and infertility were but two of them; life at Bath was suffused in sexuality. And a calico shift worn in the Cross Bath, 'more fam'd for Pleasure than cures' was only one of its manifestations. It was said that at the Cross Bath were:[12]

> perform'd all the wanton dalliances imaginable; celebrated Beauties, panting breasts, and curious shapes, almost exposed to public view; languishing eyes, darting killing glances, tempting amorous postures, attended by soft musick, enough to provoke a vestal to forbidden pleasure, captivate a saint, and charm a Jove. . . . The ladies with their floating Jappan bowls, freighted with confectionary, knick-knacks, essences and perfumes, wade about like Neptune's courtiers, supplying their industrious joynts. The vigorous sparks, presenting them with several antick postures, as sailing on their Backs, then embracing the elements, sink in rapture.

Yet, it is a remarkable fact about Bath today that mention of its name, unlike that of Brighton, summons up neither libertine imagery nor salacious interest. Rather, it evokes a sigh! In the early eighteenth century they seemed to know better. Even respectable young gentlewomen of easy circumstances, like the sisters Elizabeth and Sarah Robinson, seemed to know better. Sarah eventually settled in Bath, translated French novels and, as Sarah Scott, became author of the first Utopia written by a woman. Elizabeth, as Elizabeth Montague, became well known as one of the leading 'Blue Stockings'. From the late 1730s through to the 1750s they wrote interminably and seriously to each other and their friends. They wrote about headaches and stomach pains, the merits of Quin and Garrick, the fate of the Patriots, Gothic Architecture, Greek Gods and Goddesses, and the best time to wean Elizabeth's first baby. But when they turned their attention to thinking and writing about Bath they dwelt inevitably on items of sexual interest and it was in a vein of down-to-earth, knowledgeable, and slightly bawdy chastity that they wrote to each other and their friends about sex and marriage at Bath. Few sources can show better the attractions and repulsions of the place than their letters.

At 14, in 1734, Elizabeth was precociously sceptical about the powers of the Bath waters and aware of the gullibility of mankind about them. At 20 she was bored with Bath. It was a hospital. She wrote to the Duchess of Portland:[13]

> I wish your Grace would consider Bath water is no Helicar and affords no inspiration and that there is no place where one stands in greater need of something to enliven the brain and inspire the imagination. I hear every day of people pumping their arms or legs for the rheumatism, but the pumping for wit is one of the hardest and most fruitless labours in the World. As my own invention is like to fall short of a sheet of paper I should be glad to send you some news, but all the news of the place would be like the bills of Mortality; Palsey four, Gout six, Fever one . . . Indeed, the only thing one can do one day one did not do the day before is to dye.

The men she found very stupid and ignorant. And the women. The women, well, there were many sorts. 'We have all characters,' she wrote, 'the impertinent, the stupid, the absurd, and the comical.' They included:[14]

> Some laughing Hoydens, who set up for aggreeable creatures as they call one another. Then we have some affected, simpering dames who are pretty sort of women. There are likewise half a dozen grinning women who are the best naturdest creatures, a few ugly women, who are all good housewives and not

at all Coquet, for they would not have the men follow them for the world, and with great truth they say they always keep 'em at a distance.

Then she wrote about the races. There a young girl came into her own since she could both exploit and enjoy her sensuality and keep her reputation:[15]

> My Dear Sally,
> Your going to the Races cannot give you more pleasure than it does me. I was much grieved at the prudence of those who intended to deprive you of the Pleasures of killing Squires in their new buckskin breeches. Oh the pleasures of seeing them look at one almost as much as they do at the distance Post and rival Thunderbolt and the Ratcatcher more in their affections. The mighty Roman Conquerors were pleased with Ovations as well as triumphs so a fine Lady may now and then be content with the petty trophies of Conquest. Good falconers delight not in the quarry but the flight, it is remarkable that the best shooters seldom Love Partridge.
> Yours etc.

Then there was her suitor:[16]

I wish you could see him . . . he speaks me in the Romantick stile and tells everybody I am divinely fair. This my Damelas you must know is a great wit in his own conceit and a very drole Man in other peoples opinion. He fills the capacity of fool and jester very well. He has convinced me that Love is a jest and a Lover is a fool. I was pretty well fixed in that opinion before but he has quite determined me.

Three years later it was Sarah's turn to write from Bath:[17]

If I should get many lovers my reputation will not be in much danger, for most of my acquaintances are old enough to preserve it . . . Mrs. Coles is the greatest Prude in Bath. Positively there is not a married woman here behaves as well. She has got into such a grave set that the men I believe have scarce found out she is pretty. She passes quite for a sober matron.

In response to her sister's query about her love life at Bath, she wrote:[18]

I can't bring you a great list of conquests nor will my admirers make a good figure in description. When they are about me I look like the best beloved nurse at an hospitall and they all seem to be sueing for my care and attendance. They on their crutches come and may almost all be comprized under the three heads of the song; the halt, the blind, the lame. The wofull picture of the young woman giving an old man with a long beard suck through a grate is not half as good an image of the respect due to old age as I am almost every night.

Yet, in spite of the cynicism, the image of a young woman giving suck to an old man and her perception of herself as a nurse in a hospital stayed with Sarah for most of her life. It was to be the very basis of her Utopia.

Even Elizabeth's cousin, an impecunious young man of the cloth with a brand new wife, regaled her with the latest sexual gossip:[19]

> Anthony Henley is here, and become Sir Anthony. He is actually now at law with the Mayor for having sent a Lady of Pleasure he keeps to Bridewell.
>
> Lord and Lady Noel are as happy here as Day and Night can make them, and we hear the Duke and Duchess are got into one house again. Languishing Mr. Warburton is to be maryed to a Young Lady of £15,000 who dies for those eyes. I'm told they marry tomorrow. I think I wrote you word that a Countryman of his run off from hence with a Girl from a Boarding School. The fellow was a common Pedlar but was Irish enough to keep the Girl three days without marrying her or making her unfit for anyone else to Marry. So the Parents hearing where she was fetched her home and sent him to Bridewell. This is much such an affair as Mr. Lowes I think. The agreeable Mr. Oha . . . continues to charm the Ladys with the fluency of his Rhetorick and the tightness of his Stockings.

Certainly everybody seemed to know what everybody else was doing, sexually as well as socially and politically and thought it proper to express a view about it. Sarah wrote to Elizabeth:[20]

> Lady Jane Bertie, a sister of the Duke of Ancaster was yesterday married to a son of Governor Matthews. They went out of Church into the rooms and at night her ladyship danced, but being asked to drink tea she said she could not stay out so late

that night, which occasion'd some surprise, as she had before assured the whole company that she and Mr. Matthews had agreed not to consummate till they got to London, but had married to prevent opposition.

Thirty-two years old and a mother, Elizabeth was still bored with Bath. She thought of herself as superannuated and unable to keep up with the modern vivacity of behaviour. 'It is,' she said, 'hard to be superannuated so early but I had rather give up the cause than take such pains to be lively.'[21] One can sympathise with her because a later generation in Bath told the story of the young gentleman who dropped dead after dancing thirty-three couple in the Assembly Rooms. According to the story his partner fainted but was at it again after being revived by, 'Spirit of Hartshorn and Tincture of Fiddler'.[22] Elizabeth, however, needed to take the waters for her cough and all her aches and pains which never seemed to go away. While she preferred Tunbridge to Bath, as more convenient to London, Sarah found Bath more congenial. On one occasion, when Elizabeth was in Tunbridge, she wrote to Sarah in Bath warning her of a mutual acquaintance who was on her way to Bath flaunting a lesbian relationship. Mrs Lyttleton had taken up with a certain Miss R. who had recently been dropped by another gentlewoman. She wrote:[23]

> Mrs. Lyttleton has taken her Miss R. to live with her, which I must confess I am sorry for, as it will add to the jests the men make on that friendship and I own I think those sorts of reports hurt us all and fall in their degree on the whole sex. And really if this nonsense gains ground one must shut oneself up alone, for one cannot have men intimates and at this rate the women are more scandalous. So we must become Savages and have no friendships of connexion.

But, the connections people made, in Bath and on their way to it, were remarkably varied. There was something for everybody. Anthony Henley, the languishing Mr Warburton, Mrs Lyttleton and Miss R. we have already met. They were joined by the Duke of Bolton who visited openly with Mrs Beswick and all their illegitimate children and by James Woodforde. Woodforde, a Fellow of New College Oxford and Mr Fisher from University College, on their way from Oxford to Bath, took up with two servant maids and at the Bull Inn, Cirencester, 'The two maids supped and spent the evening with us'.[24] On another occasion in Bath, Woodforde, now curate of Castle Cary wrote:[25]

> After tea this evening I took a walk in the Fields and met in my walk two girls, the eldest about 17, the other about 15, both common prostitutes even at that early age – I gave 'em some good advice to consider the end of things. I gave them 0–1–0.

Fifty years later things had not changed except that on that occasion it was the Vicar of Camerton who recorded in his diary: 'I was not a little astonished, as I walked through Bath, to observe the streets so crowded with prostitutes, some of them apparently not above 14 or 15 years of age.[26]

Even Elizabeth was not immune to flirtation. According to Sarah, she did not always live by her own convention that women could not have men intimates. Travelling home with a man friend after a flying visit to Bath she provided material for Sarah's liveliest fantasy:[27]

> I fear you and your fellow traveller were a little time in the dark, and certainly should be under most allarming apprehensions if I did not trust in that profound respect which always accompanies a sincere and tender passion; were his regard for you no other than what generally gives rise to a flirtation so natural and universal in such gay young Men, I should have feared the light de Berger as much as the heure de Berger, for I apprehend the lustre of the twinkling stars and glimmering Moon to have languishing effects, and who knows what consequences might have arisen from being between the blankets together. A less respectful lover might have forgot the difference between Woollen and Linnen, or like a true Englishman, have preferred the Woollen manufacture to anything· flax can produce.

Or was it all a mere prelude to a joke about the textile industry? Whether fantasy or joke, this letter and the rest support the view that while gentlemen visitors to Bath could take their sexual pleasures in brothels and private apartments, gentlewomen enjoyed a largely vicarious sexual life; in Bath as elsewhere. According to Steele, a sober and sexually modest man in Bath was looked upon by women as well as by other men as an 'unfashioned fellow of no

Life or Spirit'. Rather it was expected, 'for a man who had been drunk in good company, or passed a night with a wench, to speak of it next day before women for whom he had the greatest respect.' Every woman was then expected to reprove him with an 'Oh Fy!' or with the blow of a fan, but to keep a look in her face of apparent approval. He was to be called, 'a strange wicked fellow, a sad wretch; And he was to shrug his shoulders, swear, receive another blow, swear again he did not know he swore, and all would be well.'[28]

In addition to this living and re-living of illicit sexual encounter at 'The Bathe' there was, possibly for those who preferred to live vicariously, a supply of obscene writing published there. This kind of writing grew and blossomed in England between 1660 and 1745 during the period in which agrarian capitalism came to predominate and in which Bath experienced its first substantial period of growth.[29] Towards the end of this period, in 1740, James Leake, Bath's leading printer and bookseller, printed a book by Thomas Stretzer called *A New Description of Merryland*. This book was purported to be written by a 'Roger Phfuquewell, with the addition of Esq., descended from an ancient Family in Ireland, remarkable for their being Red-Headed, of great Note and of long standing in that Country'. Merryland, a 'Paradise of Pleasure, and Garden of Delight' was a woman's body. Its form and sexual attractions were described in the manner of a serious work of topographical discovery. It goes without saying that it was a fruitful country, marred only by the inconvenience and expense of managing too fruitful a crop. As a result the people had discovered birth control. It was said that a certain kind of sponge was to be found in Merryland which, 'They use not only as a cleanser, but also as an Antidote against the bad effects of the Juice above mentioned.'[30] And so on.

By 1742 the book reached its tenth edition. As a sequel to its success Stretzer also wrote and published under Leake's Bath imprint in 1741 an illustrated version, *Merryland Displayed*. This was probably that book described as containing 'A Compleat Set of Charts of the Coasts of Merryland where-in are exhibited all the Ports, Harbours, Creeks, Bays, Rocks, Settings, Bearings, Gulphs, Promontories, Limits, Boundaries, etc.'[31] James Leake probably printed these books for his father, John Leake, a London printer and publisher who was committed to Newgate for printing other works regarded as obscene including *Aretinus Redivivus* and *The School of Venus*. In 1741 James Leake also printed another pamphlet by Stretzer, purporting to attack *A New Description of Merryland*. In fact it was a marketing device. *Merryland*, it said, has:[32]

> occasioned the re-publishing and selling several other Pamphlets of the same Stamp, which had long been neglected and forgot: For the Booksellers perceiving the taste of the Age, by the great demand for this Pamphlet, saw it was a proper Season to reprint all the smutty stuff they could think of to humour the prevailing Gout of the Town, and scratch the callous Appetites of their debauched readers.

What was more, it had become the book of the Season, talked about by women as well as by men. 'Over a Tea Table,' wrote Stretzer, 'some of them make no more Scruples of mentioning Merryland, than any other part of the Creation.'[33]

Since James Leake was also the proprietor of Bath's first and most successful circulating library, the resort of men of respectable reputation like Ralph Allen and Bishop Warburton, the conjunction of fashion is noteworthy. It is particularly so since James Leake's sister Elizabeth was married to Samuel Richardson and Leake was much involved with the printing and selling of Richardson's books. According to Richardson, the first of these, *Pamela*, was a highly moral book which 'Attempted to steal upon the world reformation, under the notion of amusement ... pursuing to their closets those who fly from the pulpit.'[34] But, the plain fact was, where books were concerned, Leake was always more renowned for business acumen rather than literary taste. He simply responded to the demands of the market. It was said of him, 'He is the Prince of all the Coxcomical fraternity of booksellers; and not having any learning himself, he seems to have resolved to sell it as dear as possible to others.'[35]

The possibility that somewhere on the shelves or in the storerooms of Leake's bookshop in The Terrace Walk copies of Richardson's *Pamela* and *Clarissa* and of Mary Chandler's *The Description of Bath* nestled side by side with Stretzer's *A New Description of Merryland* or an edition of *The School of Venus* should be taken as a reminder that the market for Bath embraced the whole spectrum of the tastes of the consuming classes in eighteenth-century England. As Dr Cheyne put it Leake's was, 'One of the finest bookshops in Europe' and a guinea subscription to it, 'the very best money laid out in the Place, for those who go for Pleasure or Amusement only.'[36]

By the end of the century there were ten bookshops with circulating libraries in Bath, one of which had more than 500 monthly subscribers and, over a seven-year period, provided books for nearly 200 members of the aristocracy. If we are to judge by the booklist of another of the libraries, books like those appearing under Leake's imprint were then uncommon, the total stocks of books on divinity and sermons outweighed that of plays, novels and romances combined.[37] Whether they were outweighed in the reading is another question to which there seems to be no answer.

Gambling, however, was what everybody did: young, old; rich, poor; men, women; rakes, whores. It was so popular that from 1712 to 1720 government revenue from cards and dice increased threefold while, during Marlborough's wars, informed men placed bets on the likely outcome of battles and sieges.

In Bath the most popular game of skill was whist but it was games of chance like Ace of Hearts, Pharaoh, Basset, Hazard, and Faro, all of which were stacked in favour of the Bank that attracted most passion and money and made Bath an international centre for gambling. It was so popular in 1706 that fifty known gamesters and sharpers were reported to have arrived in Bath from London. 'They want cullies,' it was said, 'and are forced to devour each other'.[38] Generally, however, there were dupes enough, even among the most unlikely people.

'I am sorry for another of our Acquaintance,' wrote Lady Mary Wortley Montague to Lady Mar:[39]

> whose follys (for it is not possible to avoid that word) are not of a kind to give Mirth to those who wish her well. The discreet and Sober Lady Lechmere has lost such Furious sums at the Bath that 'tis questioned whether all the sweetness that the Waters can put into my Lord's blood can make him endure it, particularly £700 at one sitting, which is aggravated with many astonishing Circumstances. This is as odd to me as Lord Tenham's shooting himself, and another Demonstration of the latent Fire that lyes under cold Countenances. We wild Girls always make your prudent Wives and mothers.

Whatever the truth in Lady Mary's homespun philosophy it was certainly true that *wild Girls* did not always become wives and mothers, at least, not in Bath. Take the case of pretty Miss Braddock. She, enamoured of a lover, spent most of £6,000 in paying his debts and lost both money and lover. In 1726 she lost the rest of her fortune in the excitement of Bath's gaming houses and in 1727 became a decoy for Dame Lindsey, the keeper of one of the casinos. There she drew down upon herself the odium of her being a whore. Rescued by Nash she rented part of John Wood's house in Queen Square where, in 1731, she hanged herself from a closet door, having scratched on her window the following lines:[40]

> O Death, thou pleasing End to human woe;
> Thou Cure for Life! thou greatest Good below;
> Still may'st thou fly the Coward and the Slave,
> And thy soft Slumbers only bless the Brave.

Some writers believe that gambling was the real basis of Bath's popularity. Certainly it was the occasion for the first and most successful attempt to organise its attractions. In 1704 Captain Webster was Bath's Master of the Ceremonies charged with bringing some order into its social life. But, Webster was a gambler. Caught up in the spirit of the times and the lawlessness that accompanied gambling he was challenged by one of his victims at play and killed in a duel in the Orange Grove. His place was taken by Richard Nash. Nash, too, was a gambler. A large vain man with a coarse wit he could yet see that the best of people would be deterred from visiting Bath by too great a rustic coarseness at the public entertainments and too free a use of the sword in the gaming house. He drew up a code of behaviour for the entertainments, including a ban on women displaying that emblem of prostitution, a white apron, and sought to ban swords and duelling from the card table and from the city streets in general. This has led some writers to argue that Nash's organisation of gambling and associated social functions was the cause of the growth of Bath and that he himself was the driving force behind the provision of public amenities such as the Bath Turnpike in 1707. In short they argue that Nash was the sufficient cause for the growth of the City in the eighteenth century and of its attraction to its visitors.

It is the theme of this chapter, however, that there were many elements in early eighteenth-century society shaping the market for Bath; ill-health, amatory dalliance, sexual titillation, gambling, and organised public functions among them. It is another of the themes of this book that the market was but a necessary condition for the production of the City and for the social organisation of its space. By itself the market, even with the help of Beau Nash, determined nothing. What really mattered in the production of the city were the myriad response to the market by thousands of obscure and little known persons and the social and economic milieu in which they moved. While Nash undoubtedly had a part to play in creating a favourable social climate in Bath, the part he played was merely one of many. Nash, like everyone, was as much a symptom as a cause of his times. It is well to remember what Goldsmith wrote about him in order to place him in perspective.[41]

> Had it been my design to have made this history more pleasing at the expense of truth, it had been easily performed, but I chose to describe the man as he was, not such as imagination could have helped in compleating his picture; he will be found to be a weak man, governing weaker subjects, and may be considered as resembling a monarch of Cappodocia, whom Cicero somewhere calls, the little king of a little people.

In 1754 when this *'little king'* claimed to have no more than £200 a year and sought assistance from the public, Sarah Scott expressed her views about him. Such a small sum, she said, was 'full equal to his merits, whether one considers them as moral or entertaining.'[42] But, there he was and there was gambling.

Concern about the possible effects of James Leake's obscene publications led to the prosecution of his father, and growing public concern about the consequences of gambling resulted in sporadic attempts by the Mayor and Justices to regulate its worst effects. In 1713, Thomas Tirrell was convicted and fined 40 *s.* for keeping 'A Common House of Gameing with Cards and Dice unlawfully.' Tirrell refused to pay the fine and was sentenced to the city gaol until he paid and had also found sureties not to keep such a house any more. In the same year John and Philip Ditcher were fined £2 2*s.* each for running a game called New Invention, the pieces of which were not stamped or marked according to law. The next recorded action against gambling was not until 1731. In that year the Mayor and Justices meeting in Quarter Sessions twice issued proclamations against Faro and other games and resolved to: 'assemble and meet together as often as there shall be occasion to take and use such lawful means as may be most effectual for preventing any unlawful games within the said City.'[43] There is no further record of what they achieved.

Then, in 1739 Parliament passed an Act to prevent fraudulent and excessive gambling, and to suppress all private lotteries and the games of Faro, Basset, Hazard, Ace of Hearts and Pharaoh. This was indeed a blow to the gambling fraternity. One of them, Toney Aston, a devotee of Pharaoh and Ace of Hearts, broke out into verse;[44]

> Fare well Bath, and hie for Scarborough;
> Bath's as dull as Market Harborough.

Others, to avoid the Act, devised new games such as *'Passage'*. Then, in 1740, all games of chance with dice and involving numbers were declared illegal. When that happened gamesters invented more new games such as 'Roly Poly', 'Marlborough's Battles' and 'Even and Odd', more familiarly known as E.O.

E.O. was brought to Bath by Nash who went into business with the proprietors of the two Assembly Rooms at Bath. In return for his authority and protection both proprietors paid him 20 per cent of the takings from E.O. until they felt powerful and greedy enough to do without him. When Nash sued to recover his share of the profits he lost the case. Finally, in 1745, all games of chance were declared illegal and subsequently public gambling was ferociously dealt with by the Mayor and Justices in Quarter Sessions. For example, in 1787, two men, Twycross and Wetenhall, were charged with keeping a gaming house. Twycross was fined £100, Wetenhall £450. Because Wetenhall could not find the money his goods and chattels were distrained by order of the court.[45]

The ups and downs of the fortunes of Bath resulting from evasions of the Law against gambling from 1739 to 1745 are, no doubt, reflected in the fluctuations of the revenue from cards and dice. They are probably revealed most clearly in the 57 per cent increase in the takings of the Avon Navigation and in a 250 per cent increase in Corporation expenditure between 1740, when E.O. was invented, and 1743. Gambling always did attract people to Bath and whist was perennially popular with the company.

This aspect of Bath's history and Nash's part in it are, perhaps, best recaptured by the Earl of Chesterfield's comment upon the full length statue of Nash in the Pump Room set between busts of Newton and Pope.[46]

> The Statue placed, the busts between,
> Adds to the satire strength;
> Wisdom and Wit are little seen,
> But Folly at full length.

John Wesley, as might be expected, was more scathing. His view of the people of Bath was, 'that by nature they were all children of wrath', and 'that all their natural tempers were corrupt and abominable.'[47] Possibly because of the challenge Bath offered, he made eighty visits[48] to the city to combat there, as elsewhere, the threefold threat from Calvinism, Deism, and sheer irreligion. He did so by preaching his own version of the doctrine of assurance as he adapted it from Arminius and the Moravians. According to this doctrine salvation was not dependent upon pre-selection by God nor did it require hard intellectual application. Rather, experience of God mediated by an appeal to one's own enlightened consciousness was considered sufficient to grant assurance of God's grace to any man or woman.

It seems that the market appeal of Wesley's message was greater for the producers and labourers of Bath than for its visiting company. Thus, a Wesleyan class list for 1757 shows only seventeen members, most of whom were artisans or women without skills of any kind. All but three of them lived in Avon Street,[49] already on its way to becoming the place of residence for the lowest class of Bath's working population. Perhaps, because of Wesley's appeal to the lower orders, Nash, on Wesley's third visit to the city, challenged his right to preach there and on his next he was asked by the sheriffs not to preach there again. Undaunted, Wesley visited the city many more times until, in the end, the local authorities, as they realised the benefit of his work for the moral ease and quiet of the place, were won over to him and his doctrines. In 1780 a member of the Corporation presented him with a roasted ox!

As far as the visiting company was concerned it was Whitfield's Calvinism that appealed to them more than Wesley's Arminianism and when Lady Huntingdon opened her chapel she did so under Whitfield's rather than Wesley's influence. Even so it must be doubted whether many of the company found Bath more attractive merely on account of Lady Huntingdon's Chapel or the frequent appearance of John Wesley.

Other writers have claimed that eighteenth-century Bath was a centre and fountain of letters and the sciences and that they were an important component in the attractions of Bath. Accordingly, in 1826, the Rev. Joseph Hunter read to the Bath Literary and Philosophical Association a paper entitled, 'The Connection of Bath with the Literature and Science of England'. The purpose of the paper was to show, 'That the city of Bath has ever had, and deserved to have, a name in the literature and science of England.'[50] It sought to show that this feature of Bath began in the tenth century with one Elfege, who was born in Weston, became Abbott of Bath Abbey and Archbishop of Canterbury, and resulted in a great flowering of culture in the eighteenth century. Twenty-six years later, inspired by Hunter's paper, G. Monkland Esq., read an essay to the Bath Literary Club called 'The Literature and Literati of Bath'. In this essay Monkland sought to improve on Hunter's claims by proving 'That many gifted individuals and literary characters have either been born in Bath, or have made it their residence, and that many savants have been in the constant habit of resorting to it.'[51] He might also have added that many others who were neither born nor lived there, died there!

Monkland listed eighty-four authors born between 1584 and 1811 who either visited or lived in Bath. He included many of the great names of the eighteenth century: Pope, Chesterfield, Fielding, Sarah Fielding, Johnson, Walpole, Smollett, Burke, Goldsmith, Herschel, Boswell, Sheridan, Malthus, Wordsworth, Walter Scott, Jane Austen. In the text Monkland also referred to the actors: Quin, Garrick, Miss Linley and Mrs Siddons and to the artists: Hoare, Gainsborough, the two Barkers, and Lawrence. It has since been the fashion for historians of Bath to write about its significance for the world of literature and the arts. Perhaps the most celebrated of these authors is A. Barbeau in his *Life and Letters at Bath in the Eighteenth Century* in which he wrote:[52]

> It is because of these last, indeed the writers, who claim the largest share of our attention, that the city and society of Bath have a perennial interest for all students of English letters. It is no exaggeration to say that English literature owes something

of Smollett, Sheridan, and Jane Austen to the city and this society.

Even more recently it has been argued:[53]

> Il y eut donc une vie littéraire à Bath et à Bristol: active, comme le prouvent les textes des auteurs cités, autonome, ne devant rien à d'autres centres littéraires.

According to the author, this Bath School of Literature sprang into being when the man we have already met as a publisher of obscene books, James Leake, opened his bookshop:[54]

> Il semble que le moment où James Leake ouvrit boutique de libraire, aux environs de 1724, marque un tournant dans la vie littéraire à Bath. Il devint rapidement célèbre et publia beaucoup pour l'époque.

Some of which, of course, is true. Performers and writers and artists and scientists did come to Bath and some of them lived at least part of their lives there. Many of them found inspiration in Bath; Pope's long association with Ralph Allen and Prior Park found its way into his social poetry and Allen's benevolence plus Mary Chandler's own couplet on him prompted Pope to write his own well-known lines:[55]

> Let low-born ALLEN, with an awkward Shame,
> Do good by stealth, and blush to find it Fame.

And, in 1741, Pope wrote much of *The New Dunciad* at Prior Park. In the realm of Art, Bath was Gainsborough's training ground. He painted there from 1759 to 1774 charging half the price of Reynolds at a time when the number of people wanting their portraits painted seems to have been greater than at any other time in the eighteenth century. It was in Bath, too, in 1760, that Gainsborough painted his first full length portrait. It was of Miss Ford, the future Mrs Thicknesse. In commenting upon it, Mrs Delany also expressed the sexual prejudices of her age:[56]

> I saw Miss Ford's picture, a whole length with her guitar, a most extraordinary figure, handsome and bold; but I should be very sorry to have anyone I loved set forth in such a manner.

These instances of literary and artistic inspiration in Bath could be multiplied many times but they have to be weighed in the balance with the inspiration of other artists and writers who saw in the company at Bath reason only for caustic and ribald comment upon the coarseness, gluttony and sheer philistinism of most of them. For most of its company culture was a sort of theatre.[57] Rowlandson painted them and Smollett wrote about them:[58]

> Every upstart of fortune, harnessed in the trappings of the mode, presents himself at Bath. Clerks and factors from the East Indies, loaded with the spoil of plundered provinces; planters, negro-drivers, and hucksters, from our American plantations, enriched they know not how; agents, commissaries, and contractors, who have fattened, in two successive wars, on the blood of the nation; usurers, brokers and jobbers of every kind; men of low birth, and no breeding, have found themselves suddenly translated into a state of affluence ... all of them hurry to Bath, because here, without any further qualification, they can mingle with the princes and nobles of the land. Even the wives and daughters of low tradesmen, who like shovel-nosed sharks, are infected with the same rage of displaying their importance; and the slightest indisposition serves them for a pretext to insist upon being conveyed to Bath, where they may hobble country dances and cotillons among lordlings, squires, counsellors and clergy ... such is the composition of what is called the fashionable company at Bath.

Other writers were aware of how thinly spread were people like themselves; in Bath as elsewhere. Even when, like Philip Thicknesse, they originally found Bath congenial for its intellectual comfort, they could also abruptly be made aware of their cultural isolation. In 1773 Thicknesse had written from Bath:[59]

> A man of sentiment cannot live where sentiment is not to be found: here (for here I would have you live) I can go to the Coffee House and spend two hours from seven to nine, I can look round me and see seven or eight men all of general knowledge and many skilful in some particular, and suit my present mood with the conversation I feel most inclined to partake of: Age or youth, fun or gravity. The Manager of the Theatre has given me the run of his House; so I take sometimes a bit of our friend Shakespeare's wit. Add to this for five shillings each

subscription (three in the year) there is a good Library, well furnished with books and well warmed with fires, where you may always find men of sense, cloathed either in Woollen or Calfskin. I might add the Balls, the Concerts etc., but I seldom go to either but have often made music at home. Now my Dear Sir life is short.

By 1780, things had changed. Thicknesse was never an easy man to get on with and his *Valetudinarian's Bath Guide* had upset many people. In the guide, he had written about opium. He claimed that it was not the only treatment for prolonging life and ensuring good health. Instead he had recommended the partaking of the breath of young virgins and wrote:[60]

> There is no place else in Britain where the prescription is so easily made up; to be so repeatedly had, nor where it may be so conveniently conveyed by the most lovely of the sex,

than at Bath. Also he used the Bladud myth of the origins of Bath to mock the pretensions of the place. Then he also upset many patriots by intervening with a press gang on behalf of a man pressed for service. So he had provided a dual motive for those who excited the local mobs to attack him. 'It was,' he wrote, 'the Bath not the Bathampton Mob who was excited to assault me and that not about the pressed man but the Bath Guide which presses the Gamblers and the trading part of the town . . . and though I have been hung in Effigies I don't swallow the worse for it, nor sleep the worse neither.' Finally he wrote, 'I have had my share of Anger and Scolding thro' this life and wit not, if possible, and it so, London alone is the place where a man's House is most secret and his person (except for footpads) least liable to insult.[61]

If a resident like Thicknesse could in a few years pass from a sense of intellectual comfort to real experience of cultural isolation, visitors to Bath could spend a season there without even gaining entrée into the limited world of writers and artists. Indeed, like George Lichtenberg, Professor of Physics at Göttingen University, they could pass their time at Bath not knowing that that world existed! In 1775 when Lichtenberg visited Bath he was 33 and William Herschel 39. Herschel had worked at Bath for nine years as music master, organist and conductor of the orchestra at the New Assembly Rooms. During the same time he had built telescopes and worked incessantly at the observations which resulted in 1781 in the discovery of the planet Uranus. I quote Lichtenberg's letter to Herschel to show that while the historians of Bath can point to the fact of Herschel's life in Bath they may not claim from that fact alone that his life there had any effect on life at Bath:[62]

> My God! if only I had known in October 1775, when I spent several days at Bath, that such a man was living there! I am no friend of Tea-rooms (*in English*) and card games and dances, I was much bored there and finally spent part of my time on the tower with my telescope. I still remember with delight the answer of a boy whom I had with me on the tower when I asked him: whether there were no people in Bath who knew something of books and who stood out in other ways and of whom he had heard more than of others. I did it for fun, and was properly rewarded: He knew of nobody but his Schoolmaster (*in English*).

To this it might be replied that had Lichtenberg arrived in Bath four years later he would have found a different scene for, in 1779, the Bath Philosophical Society was founded. With twenty members, including Dr Joseph Priestley, who was then living at Calne before moving to Birmingham in 1781, and William Herschel as its most famous and active member, it was a very lively society. But, when Herschel also left Bath in 1782, it declined. After languishing a few more years it died in 1787 with the death of its founder and secretary Edmund Rack. Subsequently it revived in 1801 but was not fully resurrected until 1819.[63] The very briefness of the life of the Philosophical Society together with the fact that its small membership was mainly made up of medical men, teachers, ministers of religion and tradesmen is evidence enough that neither the company at Bath nor the mass of its producers was touched by its existence. Had Lichtenberg arrived in Bath only a dozen years after he did he would have found the same void as he found in 1775 and Herschel would have been better remembered locally for his contribution to the entertainments at the New Assembly Rooms!

There are, perhaps, two areas of science in which Bath might be regarded as giving a lead. First, geology. But, even in this case the work of early local natural historians such as John Walcott in the late 1770s went largely unremarked by local society. And it was only through the development by William Smith of his system of identifying strata after 1791 that Bath gained a place in science as the 'so-called cradle of English Geology'. And that only from 1827 and through its particular value in the hunt for coal.[64] The second science is Economics. In 1799 Ricardo, who was then a successful dealer on the Stock Exchange and himself an amateur geologist, was staying in Bath for the benefit of his wife's health. Whiling away the time in one of the town's circulating libraries he happened to take up a copy of Adam Smith's *Wealth of Nations*, and turning over a page or two ordered it to be sent to his house.[65] According to his brother Moses and John Cam Hobhouse, the book so pleased him that he counted that day as the beginning of his interest in political economy. It is, surely, a sobering thought that the mind from which sprang, on the one hand, modern positivist economics and, on the other, one strand in Marxist socialism, received its original stimulus to take up the study of political economy through Mrs Ricardo's belief in the magical power of Bath's hot springs and in her husband's frequenting a bookshop that might well have been Leake's old shop in the Terrace Walk! Yet, as the rest of this book will show, the connection of Bath with political economy did not begin and end with Ricardo. In fact, the history of Bath from 1680–1850 will suggest that as men in it lived their lives they, too, shaped their own minds and contributed their individual mites to the creation of a social and cultural milieu conducive to the generation of both strands in post-Ricardian political economy. One might say that the lightning of Ricardian thought took fire only because of the prior transformation in economy and society. Further, in that transformation the building and growth of Bath was as much an integral part as the much later, and in a sense, consequential growth of the cotton industry.

While that is as it may be, there can be little doubt that Bath's chief contribution to literature, art and science was not that the demands of the company or the activities of its citizens created a school in any one of them, not even in the painting of miniatures nor in the output of the numerous petty poets and writers referred to by Lamoine – mere numbers do not constitute a school – but that in itself Bath provided the object and material of art and literature and, thereby, the material and object of social description and criticism of it. As an object of description it was meticulously delineated in the novels of Jane Austen, *Persuasion* and *Northanger Abbey*. In these works it served as backdrop for the concerns of the society of the propertied, who walked and rode through the city oblivious of the changes taking place around them, of which the building of Bath was itself an early example. As Charlotte Brontë put it, 'Jane Austen's business is not half so much with the human heart as with the human eyes, mouth, hands, feet.'[66] There was plenty of scope for all of these in Bath.

However, in the 1790s, Jane Austen's Bath was already old. For all its similarities to its earlier self it was not the Bath of Elizabeth Montague and pretty Miss Braddock. Indeed, Monkland's list of authors connected with Bath includes very few early eighteenth-century writers. Although Pope is mentioned, it does not include any of the great men of England's Enlightenment: Newton, Locke, Shaftesbury, and Hume – although Hume, like Burton and Berkeley, did visit the place in passing and remained unnoticed. In the early eighteenth century eminent men seemed to have stayed away from Bath in large numbers. It even failed to attract the attention of Hogarth. Moreover, although in 1775 Lichtenberg had regretted the absence of men of learning in Bath, fifty years earlier, Lord Hervey, the most intelligent fop in England, seemed only to regret its lack of '*quality*'. Replying to an inquiry from Lady Mary Wortley Montague he wrote:[67]

> I come to this place but yesterday, from which you may imagine I am not yet sufficiently qualify'd to execute the Commission you gave me, which was to send you a list of the Sojourners and Inmates of this Place; but there is so universal an affinity and resemblance among these individuals that a small paragraph will serve amply to illustrate what you have to depend on. The D. of Marlborough, Congreve, and Lady Rick are the only People whose Faces I know, whose names I ever heard or who I believe have any Names belonging to them.

The conclusion of this brief survey of the attractions of Bath – of the composition of its market – is an unsurprising one. Bath, like life itself, appeared differently to different people and to different sets of people. It attracted them for diverse reasons. As well Bath appears differently to historians according to their choice of perspective and evidence. Its portrayal in their work also depends on how much weight they give to opinion rather than behaviour. On this question John Wood was perceptive. He wrote:[68]

The Amusements of Bath so insensibly engross the Time of the Strangers Resorting to the City, that nothing is more common than for the graver sort of People to declare that they do nothing while they are at Bath, and yet can find no spare Time for the least Employ: Amusements so Sweet and Alluring must therefore be beyond the Power of a particular Description, even for the Space of a single Day, much less of a whole Year, or Number of Years: so that from what I have already said, every Body must form their own Ideas of what necessarily passes between real and apparent People of Rank and Fortune, when they meet together in the Baths, Pump Rooms, Coffee Houses, Assembly Houses and other Places of general Resort, as well as when they Meet in select Parties, or on mutual Visits.

Since so many people went to Bath leaving their record of what passed between them it is small wonder that a single simple answer to the question of the attraction of Bath is not to be found. As we have said, every perspective is necessarily a partial one, whether it be that of a participant or an historian. Such perspectives are not necessarily false in consequence. Yet, one perspective may be better than others because of the comprehensiveness of coverage it affords, and because its vantage point may be such as to enable its panorama to incorporate those generated from several other points of perspective. For example, in spite of disclaimers such as Barbeau's, that at Bath scandalous anecdote and allusion, 'are conspicuous by their absence',[69] and in spite of claims that Bath was a conservatoire of good manners and a crucible of social fusion, there is evidence to show that both claims are only partially true. Bath *was* a microcosm of eighteenth-century society; as it was when the century began and as it changed with time, and there can be no doubt that it was resorted to by members of all the groups alluded to in this chapter. Therefore, one can see that 'good manners' was a flexible concept. It was able to incorporate the giving of a lecture and a shilling to a 15-year-old prostitute as well as every aspect of the sexual double standard. One might also see that the crucible of social fusion, even as described by Smollett, was a very small pot indeed. Regarded, as it will be in this book, from a standpoint offering a wider angle of social vision, which has yet to be described, one might come to see how any social fusion wrought among men of property in Bath was itself a component in generating class conflict in the early nineteenth century.

What might properly be said about the attraction of Bath is that for men and women of property and wealth it offered brief moments of social communion wrapped in a cocoon of pleasure in pleasant surroundings remote from the competitive reality of the economic life of property and wealth. It *was* a valley of pleasure and, in the autumn of 1765, as many as 148 persons of quality were numbered among the visitors. The list included three princes, four dukes, four duchesses, one marquis, two marchionesses, twenty-four earls, twenty-two countesses, fourteen viscounts, forty-three viscountesses, twelve barons, twelve baronesses, one ambassador, one archbishop and five bishops.[70]

Surely, as a pre-industrial city devoted almost entirely to the leisure activities of the rich and the ruling élite, Bath was a most remarkable invention.

II

All the goods and services supplied in Bath had a price. Lodgings for visitors were as much as 10*s.* a week in the 1720s and 5*s.* twenty years later. Full board, of course, cost more; in 1727 Dr Arbuthnot paid 15*s.* a week in Mrs Phillips's lodgings. As the city developed, it became more fashionable to take a whole house for the season; in the 1750s such a letting for one of the best houses on the Grand Parade was £130 per annum. Later, a house on the east side of Gay Street could be had for as little as £40, on the west side it would cost £60. In the Royal Crescent house rent was about £130 per annum while in the King's Circus it varied between £80 and £140 per annum.

Then there were the things to do. The journey to the Baths in a Sedan chair from any place within the walls cost 6*d.*, the bath itself about 2*s.* Those who thought the water worth taking away could buy a dozen bottles of it for 12*s.* After the day's treatment the visitor could enjoy an evening at the Theatre Royal for between 2 and 5*s.*; a ticket to a stimulating performance of the Messiah directed by William Herschel could only be had at the higher price. To borrow freely from a circulating library cost between 5*s.* and 10*s.* 6*d.* a year. To join the Bath Philosophical Society cost £1 19*s.* Even a duel had its price; £1 6s. 8d., the amount of fine levied on James Brown in 1739 for sending a challenge to fight with sword and pistol. Gambling, as we have seen, was very expensive; £700 a night in the 1720s, a fine of £450 for keeping a gaming house in the 1780s, and suicide for pretty Miss Braddock. Prostitution was cheaper, the fine for keeping a bawdy house was £1 and the price of a moral conversation with a young prostitute 1s. Labour was cheaper still, a servant girl could be hired for the week for as little as 2s. 6d. and a labourer for 8s.

Prices of other commodities in the early part of the eighteenth century were: wheat per bushel, 5s.; water supply for Jane Degge's lodging house, 6d. each week; a closet stool box, 9s.; a white closet stool-pot, 1s. 8d.; a periwig block, 2s. 6d.; an easy chair, £3. We even know that the cost of feathers used in fitting out Jane Degge's lodging was £104 15s. 0d. and that the price of three skewers and a lark spit was 1s. The catalogue of market prices is endless. Yet, while it is possible to precisely identify the prices of hundreds of individual items available for sale in Bath it is not possible to produce continuous series of any of them. Nor is it possible to offer more than the most general estimate of total expenditure at any one time, as the following paragraphs show.

When, in mid-June 1668, Samuel Pepys visited Bath with his wife Elizabeth, his distant niece Betty Turner, and his two servants, Deb and Will, he stayed for only two days. Happily he left a detailed record of his expenses. His stay at the inn, including tips to servants, cost £1 11s. 0d. for five persons. His other expenditures, including donations to the poor and a coach to Bristol for £1 6s. 0d., totalled £3 3s. 0d. Therefore his daily costs per person were: accommodation, 3s. 2d.; other, 6s 4d. If one makes the heroic assumption that all visitors to Bath at the end of the seventeenth century who stayed at inns spent only at the same rate as Samuel Pepys it is possible to arrive at a guess as to their total expenditures. This is possible because in 1686 the War Office, under the direction of William Blathwayt, later MP for Bath, set in motion a survey of accommodation for men and horses then available at all the inns in the country. According to this survey the inns of Bath could provide 324 beds and stabling for 451 horses.[71] This compares with six beds and twelve stables at Beckington and 1013 beds and 1377 stables at Bristol, which was probably ten times as populous as Bath. The six beds noticed at Beckington in 1686 explain why, in 1668, when

Pepys and his party arrived there on their way to Bath, a pedlar asleep in a room had to be disturbed to make room for Pepys and his wife, and why Betty Turner and Deb slept together in a truckle-bed. They also suggest that the War Office figures were not far off the mark. On the assumption that the 324 beds were occupied for 182 days during the season by customers who spent at the rate of Samuel Pepys in 1668, one can show that inns would earn £9,282 per annum and that their customers would disburse a further £18,575 on other services provided in the town. If one assumes that the population was about 2,000, the total annual expenditure of £27,857 was worth nearly £14 per head to the resident population. Of course there are many defects in such a calculation. For example, there is uncertainty about price, the general level of expenditure, and the level of occupancy of beds. There is also the fact that the number of beds in inns was only a fraction of the accommodation available in Bath; in 1694 there were twenty-nine lodging houses there. These facts alone might be held to prevent any further worthwhile calculation of expenditure in the city for this period.

Nevertheless, it is possible to suggest that earnings from lodging houses in the 1720s probably brought as much again into the city as was earned by the proprietors of inns. Two independent sources show that in the 1720s the standard rate for a room was 10s. and for a kitchen or a garret, 5s. per week. Furthermore, the accounts of the Duke of Chandos in his dealings with his landladies in his Chandos Buildings development provide the basis for an estimate of the cash flow into the city to be expected from a substantial lodging house. One of Chandos's lodging houses, worked by Mrs Phillips, contained forty rooms, seventeen garrets, and seven kitchens. At the weekly rates indicated, capacity weekly earnings would have been £26; takings for a twenty week season, £520. According to Chandos's own estimate Mrs Phillips could have expected to clear at least £400 in the season. He also estimated a further £100 for out-of-season earnings. Thus, both our own and Chandos's estimate suggest a level of earnings in the vicinity of £500 per annum. Chandos also anticipated similar returns on a second lodging house run by Mrs Degge but he found that it never cleared more than £300 per annum. However, since his whole development included a third house let for £80 per annum and Carey's Wine Vaults let for a little over £74 it is safe to assume that the cash flow generated by the development of Chandos Buildings was not far off £900 per annum.[72]

Whether the twenty-nine lodging houses in the early eighteenth century generated £500 or £300 each per annum, or some smaller amount is impossible to say. At £300 each they would have brought a further £9700 into the city as well as generated additional expenditures on other services. One might guess, I think, that at the turn of the century visitors to Bath staying at its inns and lodging houses brought close to £60,000 per annum into Bath and generated an average income of about £20 for each of the citizens (supposing the population to have risen to about 3000 by the early 1700s). Compared with Gregory King's figures for the country as a whole for 1695 this figure would have given the average citizen of Bath, including men, women and children, nearly three times the annual income of the average person in the country. But one should not be too carried away by these calculations for there is a high margin of error in all the figures used.

Moreover, in Bath as elsewhere, income was very unevenly distributed, and there is no way of knowing what share of this high average income was retained by the various social groups. Moreover, Bath was not a closed economy and there is no way of telling how much of the income earned in Bath was transferred elsewhere in the form of rents, profits and interest on mortgages.

Even this figure of £60,000 represents a guess at only part of the income generated in Bath by the provision of accommodation for visitors. This is because early in the century and especially from 1727, much building took place to provide a stock of houses to let to the company both in and out of season. By 1766 there were 1,711 houses in Bath, 574 or 33.5 per cent of them, in the newly-developing parish of Walcot. By 1775 the number of houses had grown to 2,335 – 1,114 of which, or 48 per cent, were in the parish of Walcot. In this latter year the Walcot houses generated an income from house rent alone, excluding rents to landlords and fee farm rents to developers, in the region of £19,000. In 1782 house rents for the whole of the city came close to £32,000. On the other hand, accommodation in inns seems to have declined. Thus, a War Office Survey in 1756 shows only eight inns with 229 beds but with stabling for 545 horses. This decline in beds and increase in stabling since 1686 reflects not only the changing pattern of accommodation in the city but also the increase in weekly vehicular traffic to it. This had grown, for example, from 17 weekly coaches from London to Bath in 1740 to 23 in 1757. By 1793 there were 154 weekly coaches to the city.[73]

Unfortunately, there are no continuous series of the number of inns and lodging houses nor of the supply of beds that might be used as indicators of changes in the size of the market for which Bath catered. It would be fruitless, therefore, to attempt to guess further the annual income earned in Bath through the seasonal migration to it by the propertied and consuming rich, and it is necessary to turn elsewhere for evidence of the growth of demand for the services the city supplied.

Perhaps the best indirect indicator of such changes in the size of the market is to be found in the tolls earned on the Avon Navigation between Bath and Bristol. These are continuous from 1729 to 1799.[74] Used in conjunction with other indicators, such as those for Corporation expenditure and debt and counts of additions to the stock of houses,[75] they suggest that Bath grew in four great waves of building resulting from periodic surges in demand for its services. These figures are shown in tables in Appendix A. The periods of greatest increase in building and, possibly in demand for Bath were: 1726–32, 1753–8, 1762–71, 1785–92. The stock of houses and population grew accordingly. These figures are shown in table 2.1. The population figures in the table for the period up to 1793 are calculated by assuming the same ratio of houses to people as shown in the first census in 1801, excluding Bathwick. From 1801 the figures are as in the Census Reports and include figures for the parishes of Bathwick and Lyncombe and Widcombe. The doubling of the number of houses from 1700 to 1743 is assumed. (There is no firm evidence to work with.) The growth of Bath is also represented graphically in graphs 2.1 and 6.1 and diagrammatically in Figure 2.

All the evidence suggests that Bath almost trebled in size in the first sixty-five years of the eighteenth century. However, most of that growth was undoubtedly concentrated in the forty years after 1725. Thereafter, from 1766 to 1801, it grew by about 250 per cent. Indeed, as a comparison between the years 1780 and 1793 will show, 30 per cent of the housing stock (1,173 houses) was built during the fourth great wave of building in the city which was concentrated in the years 1785–92. As we shall see the rate of growth of building in this boom greatly outstripped the rate of growth in visitors to the place, at least as measured by tolls on

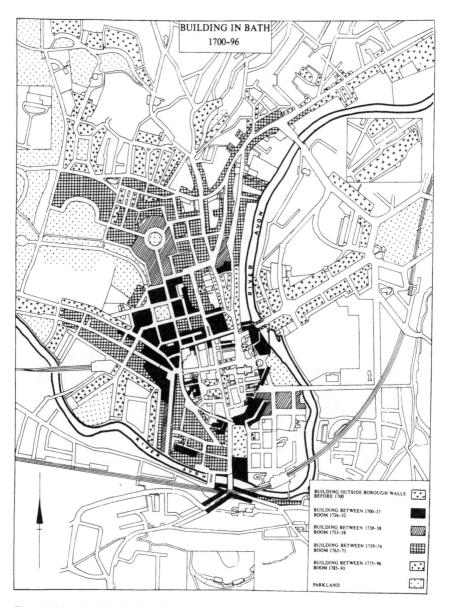

Figure 2 Map, building in Bath 1700–96

TABLE 2.1 The number of houses, population, and weekly coach services in Bath, 1700–1850

	Number of houses	Population*	Weekly coach service from London
1700	669 (assumed)		
1743	1,339 (Wood's estimate)	10,000	17
1766	1,711	13,000	27
1771	2,030	15,000	46
1775	2,335	17,000	45
1780	2,576	19,000	90
1789	2.897	22,000	101
1793	3.749	26,000	154
1801	3,946	33,000	147
1811		38,000	215
1821		47,000	
1831		51,000	
1841		53,000	
1851		54,000	

* The population figures from 1743 to 1793 are based on the number of houses multiplied by occupancy rates by parish as in Census 1801 to the nearest 1,000. But note, the application of this multiplier to the assumed number of houses in 1700 would give a population roughly double that in the Hearth Tax returns which suggest a population of about 2,000 in the 1680s. The fact is there are no reliable population figures before 1801. The figures from 1801 onwards are taken from the *Census of Population*, 1801–51.

Source: *Bath Rate Books, Census of Population 1801–51*, and Sylvia McIntyre, 'Towns as Health and Pleasure Resorts, Bath, Scarborough and Weymouth 1700–1815', DPhil thesis, Oxford, 1973.

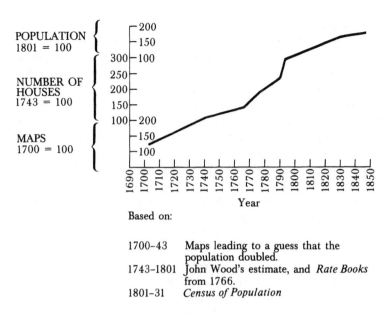

Graph 2.1 The growth of Bath, 1700–1850

visitors collected by the Bath turnpike. The rate of growth of building is not, therefore, a satisfactory measure of the growth of the visiting company's demand for Bath in these years. Nevertheless, as the census of population figures show, there was a continuing influx of people into Bath in the first two decades of the nineteenth century. As a result Bath grew almost fourfold between 1766 and 1821. This pattern of growth is shown in almost all the indicators available. Thus, coach services from London to Bath grew nearly eight times between 1766 and 1811. Such a growth pattern suggests that while Bath was invented as a pre-industrial leisure city its growth was also bound up with the industrial transformation of England from the second half of the eighteenth century.

It is interesting to note that this growth pattern was not wholly reflected in the annual number of licenses granted to alehouses.[76] These rose from 58 in 1704 to 150 in 1749. This increase is roughly in keeping with the growth of the city and indicative of a sustained demand for beer, but the number of licensed alehouses then fell sharply to 1752. Subsequently their number recovered to 136 in 1760. In the third wave of building, from 1762 to 1771, the number of licensed alehouses scarcely changed; 120 in 1762 and 129 in 1772. During the following depression in building the number of alehouses grew to reach a peak figure of 163 in 1780. In the fourth building boom the number of alehouses actually fell; 163 in 1780 to 100 in 1789. Nearly twenty years later in 1806 there were still only 116 licensed alehouses in the city, only twice as many as a hundred years earlier. Consequently over the century the ratio of alehouses to houses fell, 1:10 in 1743, 1:16 in 1780, 1:31 in 1806. Like the decline in the number of inn beds from the end of the seventeenth century to the 1750s, this decline in the number and ratio of licensed alehouses, particularly marked after 1780, also points to change in the nature of the demand for the services of Bath. Taken in conjunction with the heavy fine levied on Wetenhall and Twycross for keeping a gaming house in 1787 it suggests that although, after the 1780s, the company at Bath was more numerous, it had grown less public, less approving of public drinking and more private and sedate in its search for pleasure.

Indeed this study of licensed alehouses shows very clearly how volatile and competitive the market for Bath's services was. Thus, of 130 licensed alehouses, for which the name and street are clearly identified in 1776, 12 had disappeared by 1780, a further 66 had a different licensee, and only 52 out of the original 130 survived over the five-year period with the same licensee. There were also 45 new alehouses in 1780. By 1806 only 64 of the original 130 licensed alehouses had survived. Of the 45 alehouses newly-licensed by 1780, only 10 remained in 1806.

As to the size of the company at Bath nothing very precise can be said. Wood did estimate in 1749 that some 12,000 visitors came to Bath every year and in the light of the number of inn beds available, 118,260 annual bed nights according to the 1686 estimate, or 83,585 according to the 1756 estimate, this seems a plausible figure. In the light of what has been said about the growth of the town and the number of houses by 1800 it is probably safe to assume that the number of visitors was then in the region of 40,000 a year. Assuming an average stay of four weeks for a twenty-week season, this would mean an average weekly attendance of 8,000 visitors.

THE COMPANY AND THE SIZE OF THE MARKET

At the end of the eighteenth century the population of Bath, excluding the parish of Lyncombe and Widcombe, was 30,406, including that parish it was 33,196, and it was among the dozen largest cities in the country. It was bigger than Nottingham, Leicester, Coventry, Swansea, Paisley, Stockport and Sunderland and half the size of Bristol, Liverpool, Manchester and Birmingham. And a very different place it was. Walcot parish, the site of most of the eighteenth-century residential development, was, according to estimates of the annual value of real property made in 1815, the ninth wealthiest parish in the country. Measured in per capita terms it was second only to St George's Hanover Square; the average per capita annual value of real property was St George's £12.14, Walcot £8.56. For England and Wales the average was £5.98.[77] It is little to be wondered at that Bath was said to be fit to be the capital of a small kingdom.

The result of the growth of the market for Bath and of expenditure as estimated above over a period of about 100 years was the production of the city and of a social organisation of space which distinguishes the place even now. All in all at least £3 million was invested in domestic building in Bath. This is a sum roughly equal to the fixed investment in the cotton textile industry by the end of the eighteenth century. As subsequent chapters will show, such a growth of the market and induced investment in Bath meant that financial claims on Bath people were worth holding as it attracted labour, enterprise, and loanable funds to it.

In short, throughout the eighteenth century, Bath was the epitome of Mandeville's *'Spacious Hive Well stocked with Bees'*, where:[78]

> Vast Numbers thronged the fruitful Hive;
> Yet those vast Numbers made 'em thrive;
> Millions endeavouring to supply
> Each other's Lust and Vanity.

Except that, when it all began in Bath at the turn of the century, the millions were but a few. In all some 335 households totalling, perhaps, 2,000 persons serviced the twenty-nine lodging houses, the 324 inn beds, the fifty-eight licensed alehouses, the assembly room, the pump room, the theatre and the five small open baths which supplied most of the lusts and vanities of all its company. At the start of the century Bath was, indeed, a modest invention. At the end of it with a population closer to 33,000, it was a modern city, very beautiful and extremely rich.

CHAPTER THREE

THE LABOURING POPULATION

> That Joseph Perry one of the Wardens of the Company . . . called on him and informed him that he would be sued by the Company if he continued to exercise his trade in the City. . . . That he has been called on by three several successive Masters to pay forfeitures for exercising his trade but was always excused paying on account of his poverty.
>
> Evidence of Charles Knight, Tailor, 1765.

Most of the 335 households whose labour supplied the needs of the company at Bath in the 1680s lived within the town walls. These formed an irregular five-sided enclosure, each side about 400 yards long. This little block of land, incorporating thirty-two acres and fifteen streets, was isolated on a peninsula of land made by a loop of the Bristol Avon. To the north and west lay the cliff face of Beacon Hill and the steep slopes of Lansdown. To the south lay the river and Beechen Cliff so that in wet weather the town was approachable only from the London side. Consequently some thought it a:[1]

> place standing in a hole; on a quagmire; impenetrable to the very beams of the sun; and so confined by inaccessible hills, that people have scarce room to breathe in the town, or to come at it without danger to their lives.

Certainly the town was cramped. North of the east-west line of Westgate Street and Cheap Street conditions were not too crowded for there the streets followed the regular north-south alignment of the old Saxon town plan. But in the southern half of the town, in the parish of St James and southwards from the Abbey Church and the baths, there was a jumble of streets, open places, and narrow meandering alleys. Houses were clustered outside the North Gate, in Walcot Street and Broad Street, and outside the South Gate in Horse Street almost as far as the Old Bridge and the River Avon.

The best of the inns and lodging houses in which many people worked were stone-built and tiled and lay in the central and northern part of the town. They were all built in the vernacular style – mostly three storey buildings with casement and mullioned windows set in large decorated bays, attics, and high gables which, year in and year out, much to the discomfort of pedestrians, poured their storm waters on to the streets they fronted. These buildings were all architectural flourish and asymmetrical. Lacking proportion and harmony they were a collection of mere houses. According to report even those accommodating the visitors were inconvenient and uncomfortable. Doors were slight and thin, windows were incapable of keeping out the least puff of wind, interior walls were rarely wainscotted, chimney pieces and hearths were generally whitewashed every day, and floors were darkstained with a mixture of soot and small beer. Furnishings were equally rustic and spartan. Curtains and hangings were mostly of coarse Kidderminster stuffs while the linen was either corded dimity or a coarse fustian. It was rooms so furnished that let at 10*s*. a week.

In the southern part of the town houses were generally smaller and more slightly built with thatch in place of tiled roofs. Dominating them all was the Abbey Church of St Peter and St Paul. By the early eighteenth century the Abbey was so hemmed in by houses that they seemed to act as buttresses to its structure; take them away and the Abbey and its central tower would collapse like a chimney stack in the hands of a demolisher. The only other building of any size was the squat freestone town hall, built it is said by Inigo Jones and set over the open market in the High Street. During the day, the building served the Corporation for their '*Halls*' or meetings at which they took many small decisions to husband their meagre resources without the help of double-page book-keeping. In the evening it became the resort of the rich for their eating and dancing. On these occasions the door was guarded by two beadles 'to keep out the Mobility'.

At the turn of the century the heads of the families who lived and worked in the town sought to place their sons, and the sons of near relatives, in trades servicing the demands of the visitors to the place.[2] For many years, from 1697 to 1776, they and their descendants recorded the names and trades of boys apprenticed in order later to prove title to the Freedom of the city, since such a title was a condition for practising any of those trades in it. During the first half of the century the number of boys enrolled rose from 48 in the years 1697–1700, to 101 in 1720–3, and to 150 in 1750–3. This threefold increase in the first fifty years of the century roughly confirms what has already been said about the growth of the city.

Of the 150 apprentices enrolled in 1750–3, and of the 113 for whom a place of origin was recorded, 80 were noted as living in Bath and another 30 as coming from the neighbouring counties: Somerset, Wiltshire and Gloucestershire. Only seven came from further afield, from Dorset, Essex, Leicester and South Carolina. Since, ten years later, the number of newly apprenticed boys living in Bath was 65 out of 107, with another 30 from Somerset and Wiltshire, it seems that until the 1760s the citizens of Bath kept control of employment pretty much in their own hands and that Bath, with some help from its neighbouring counties, produced its own skilled labour force.

These boys were apprenticed to some sixty-eight different trades ranging from apothecary to wheelwright, or according to the cost of such apprenticeship, from surgeon to cabinetmaker. Thus, in the 1760s the cost of apprenticing William Thomas to Henry Wright, surgeon, was £262 10s. but the fee for apprenticing a boy to a cabinetmaker was waived in consideration of 'Natural Love and Affection'. Sometimes, as in the case of the apprenticing of James McDougall to Joseph Phillott, innholder, the fee was waived in return for 'work and labour'. The normal cost of an apprenticeship in the various trades at a time when a labourer's wage was about 6s. per week is shown in table 3.1.

Apprenticeship to a skilled trade in Bath was no mere formality, and whatever else the Mayor and Justices might have done when they met in Quarter Sessions they took care to record complaints about the changes in apprenticeship agreements.[3] Moreover, they generally solved problems and complaints with a good deal of sense and humanity. Between 1699 and 1715 they dealt with twenty-four cases of apprenticeship needing some change in the terms of agreement. For example, in 1704 Charles Waters, an apprentice barber, complained that his master, Samuel Lansdown,

TABLE 3.1 Cost of apprenticeship in selected trades in the city of Bath, 1765–76

Apothecary Linendraper	£100 to £105	
Plumber	£70	
Mercer Haberdasher	£50	
Jeweller	£40	
Watchmaker	£31	
Cabinetmaker Brazier Saddler Painter Wheelwright	£20 to £25	
Baker	£10 to £30	
Carpenter	£5 to £20	although frequently less than £10
Tailor	£12 to £20	although often as low as 1s.
Periwig maker Cordwainer	£6 to £10 Up to £10	
Gardener	£1. 1s. 0d.	

Source: *Enrolment of Apprentices Book*, GAB.

hath not taken care of his apprentice either for meat, drink, lodging or for the instructing him in his trade.

The Mayor and Justices decreed that the apprentice be reassigned so that he might complete his training and be admitted a Freeman. Two years later John Collins, apprentice to a baker, Thomas Atwood,

often times disobeyed and affronted the said Thomas Atwood.

His indentures, too, were reassigned to another baker. In 1709 Richard Combes, who had been apprenticed to a farrier, asked to be discharged from his apprenticeship on account of a weakness in his eyes and allowed to be re-apprenticed to Thomas Baker, a joiner. This was permitted. A year later Richard Combes pleaded that he could not complete his time with Thomas Baker. Consequently he was discharged from his apprenticeship and Baker was ordered to return £5 of the £10 paid to him to take Combes as apprentice. At the same time the Mayor and Justices took it upon themselves to decide on Combes's future career. Apprenticeship in a small community like Bath was taken very seriously and regarded as part of the paternal and caring function vested in the city's Corporation.

The occupations to which these boys were apprenticed show clearly the nature of the place as a centre of production. In table 3.2 the figures are shown in seven categories and for four periods. First, 1724–37, a period including the first real building boom in the city. Second, 1738–50, a period of relative depression in building activity and including the depression years 1740–1 and 1745–6. Third, 1751–60, a period of general prosperity and expansion in the city with twin peaks in 1754–5 and 1758–9. Four, 1761–9, initially a period of slump followed by recovery after 1761–2.

Table 3.2 shows three outstanding characteristics. First, the very high proportion of boys entering the workforce who went into the clothing trades throughout the whole period. Second, the almost equally high proportion who, particularly in periods marked by a high level of building activity, went into the building trades. Third, the increasing proportion who, over time, entered other trades in the manufacturing sector; as the city grew in size from 1724–37 to 1,761, the proportion entering the building trades fell from 23 per cent to 17.6 per cent while the proportion entering other trades in the manufacturing sector rose from just over 11 per cent to just over 25 per cent. The slight fall in the proportion entering the clothing trades and the much greater fall in the proportion entering shoemaking is probably best explained by the changing organisation of these trades in circumstances of mass demand rather than interpreted as a reflection of the declining importance of those trades in the economy of the city. But more of this later. The broad conclusion that employment opportunities became more diversified as the city grew in size is not surprising.

TABLE 3.2 Occupations of apprentices enrolled in the city of Bath 1724–69

	1724–37	1738–50	1751–60	1761–9
Carpenter & Joiner	41	19	39	23
Mason	22	11	17	1
Plasterer	13	5	12	3
Painter	0	0	3	2
Plumber	0	2	2	1
Glazier	1	1	5	0
Total in building	77	38	78	30
Merchant Taylor	17	9	16	6
Tailor	20	20	30	11
Staymaker	7	8	7	3
Mercer	4	0	1	0
Feltmaker	3	0	0	0
Draper	2	0	0	0
Haberdasher	2	0	0	1
Woollen Draper	2	1	1	0
Linen Draper	1	3	1	6
Clothier	1	1	0	0
Milliner/Lacemaker	0	1	11	0
Mantua Maker	0	1	3	0
Hoop & Petticoatmaker	0	0	1	0
Glover	0	0	1	0
Currier	0	0	0	1
Barber & Periwig Maker	24	21	19	13
Total in clothing	83	65	91	41
Cordwainer/Shoemaker/Heelmaker				
Total in shoemaking	54	36	34	13
Butcher	11	3	5	0
Baker	7	12	20	11
Poulterer	5	3	1	0
Pastrycook	2	1	1	0
Victualler	1	1	9	3
Grocer	1	0	2	1
Cheesemonger	0	0	2	1
Vintner	15	3	2	0
Malster	4	1	1	0
Distiller	1	3	0	0
Innholder	0	1	9	9
Brewer	0	0	1	0
Teaman	0	0	1	0
Total in food and drink	47	28	54	25

	1724–37	1738–50	1751–60	1761–9
Blacksmith/Farrier	7	1	0	0
Cooper/Winecooper	6	2	5	1
Saddler	6	2	2	1
Tallow Chandler	5	4	4	1
Watchmaker	3	2	2	2
Upholsterer	2	2	2	4
Cutler	2	0	0	0
Brazier	1	2	7	4
Cabinet Maker	1	1	14	10
Pipemaker	1	1	1	2
Ropemaker	1	3	1	0
Jeweller	1	4	7	8
Silversmith	1	0	0	0
Brightsmith	1	1	4	0
Goldsmith	0	0	0	1
Tanner	1	0	0	0
Gunsmith	0	0	2	0
Collar Maker [Harness]	0	1	1	3
Coachmaker	0	1	1	0
Wheelwright	0	0	3	2
Brushmaker	0	2	2	2
Locksmith	0	0	1	0
Carver	0	0	0	1
Musician/Instrument Maker	0	1	3	1
Total in other trades	39	30	62	43
Apothecary	22	11	16	16
Surgeon	0	0	3	1
Total in medicine	22	11	19	17
Gardener	6	1	2	1
Ironmonger	3	0	0	0
Carrier	0	0	1	0
Toyman	1	0	2	0
Bookseller	0	1	0	0
Stationer	0	0	1	0
Total miscellaneous	10	2	6	1
TOTAL	332	210	344	170

Percentage distribution of enrolled apprentices

	%	%	%	%
Building	23.2	18.1	11.6	17.6
Clothing	25.0	30.9	26.5	24.0
Shoemaking	16.3	17.1	9.9	7.6
Food & Drink	14.2	13.3	15.7	14.7
Other	11.7	14.3	18.0	25.3
Medicine	6.6	5.2	5.5	10.0
Misc.	3.0	1.0	1.7	0.6
	100.0	99.9	99.9	99.8

Source: *Enrolment of Apprentices Book*, GAB.

For the whole period, 1724 to 1769, the most popular of the individual trades within these broad categories were: shoemaker 137, carpenter 122, tailor 81 (including merchant taylors the total is 129) barber and periwigmaker 77, apothecary 65, mason 51, baker 50. This order of popularity shows the importance for Bath of clothing its visitors, literally from head to foot, of housing them, of preparing their potions and of feeding them.

For all its accuracy this kind of statistical record can tell us little about the work experiences or life history of the boys apprenticed in response to the demands being made on the city's labouring population. And it is only occasionally that the record can be slowly pieced together to clothe this barest of statistical skeletons. But it can be done. Generally, it is done only for those who were most successful, and in histories of Bath it is Ralph Allen and sometimes John Wood who are singled out for special attention. The first was an obscure boy of 17 from Devon, who came to Bath in 1710 to work in the Post Office. Subsequently he succeeded, first as farmer of the cross and bye-post, then as quarry owner and developer in Bath. Then he became a friend of men of letters such as Alexander Pope and Samuel Richardson and, it is said, was the model for Henry Fielding's Squire Allworthy. His work on the cross and bye-posts is reputed to have saved the government £1,500,000 over forty years while at his height his income was about £12,000 per year. The gravity operated tramway he built in 1730 to carry stone from his quarries on Combe Down to his wharf on the Avon was one of the earliest and most efficient of its kind (Figure 3). It was, too, an architectural feature in its own right and the subject of the earliest known railway print in the world. The second, was probably the son of a mason and a local boy who became a surveyor. He returned to Bath in 1727 at the age of 22 to build the city, so it is said, almost on his own or at most with some help from his son.[4] Of course there is a good deal of truth in these stories and John Wood's will be told in some detail when we come to look at the production of the city itself. But, as I have said, their lives were exceptional, they throw no light on the fortunes of a boy apprenticed to a trade there, nor upon the effects of urban development upon the life chances or work experiences of a boy who never left the place. It is fortunate, therefore, that sufficient fragments of evidence remain from which to reconstruct the outlines of the life and labour of just such a boy, Richard Marchant. Marchant's whole life reflected, indeed was

Figure 3 'Prior Park', seat of Ralph Allen Esq., 1752, Anthony Walker

bound up with, many of the most important facets of the production and growth of Bath in the first three quarters of the eighteenth century; it also touched the lives of Ralph Allen and John Wood. Like theirs, Marchant's story too, was one of success.

Richard Marchant was born in 1703.[5] His father, also Richard Marchant, was a member of Bath's most powerful company, the Company of Merchant Taylors, to which he had been admitted for a fee of £10 in March 1688. Richard Marchant the elder was a Quaker. Whether he was so in 1688 when he was admitted to membership of the Merchant Taylors is not known. Certainly none of the authorities on Quakers refer to him, neither do they refer to a Bath society of Quakers, even though it is reported that in nearby Bristol the society of Quakers experienced severe repression in 1683. Although he probably was a Quaker he appears not to have courted imprisonment or fine for refusing to pay tithes although between 1696 and 1736 107 other Somerset Quakers did so.[6] The date of his admission to the Company and, thereby, to the Freedom of the city, suggests that he may have taken advantage of James II's Declaration of Indulgence whereby James used his dispensing power to suspend the Penal Laws and the Test Act:

> that all my subjects may be at ease and quiet, and mind their trades and private concerns . . . having been ever against persecuting any for conscience's sake.[7]

Richard Marchant the elder certainly minded his 'trades and private concerns'. In the year of his son's birth, before the days of Nash, Allen and Wood, and in partnership with a woolstapler of Devizes, he advanced £900 on mortgage to the owners of the New Inn in Stall Street. Since one of these owners was George Trymme, gentleman clothier, member of the Corporation, and, in 1707, developer of Trymme Street, Marchant was clearly already involved in supplying financial support to men of an entrepreneurial frame of mind as early as 1703. He was also a building entrepreneur in his own right.

In 1709 Marchant purchased from John Hall of Bradford-on-Avon the remainder of a lease to nineteen acres in the Ham. The Ham was an area of meadow lying just outside the south-eastern wall of the town. Traditionally it provided common pasture for Mr Hall's tenants in both summer and winter. The lease was probably a lease for three lives or 99 years and had 98 years to run. It cost Marchant £40. In 1710 he extinguished these tenants' common rights, sub-let two six-acre enclosures at £6 13*s*. 4*d*. each, and contrary to covenant, erected several houses and paved streets and courts in the area subsequently known as Marchant's Passage. Although there is no record of contemporary protest by his tenants against Marchant's action, Kingston's agent (Kingston came into possession in 1710) wrote in 1745:[8]

> Upon the most diligent enquiries amongst the old people at Bath who have known the Ham from their childhood there is no one to be found that can remember the enjoyment of any separate properties in the Ham but all agree that Mr. Hall's several tenants occupied the Ham both summer and winter.

As we shall see, what the father began in the Ham the son was to develop.

In 1714 Richard Marchant the elder took his 11-year-old son Richard as apprentice and enrolled him as such in the Corporation's enrolment book. In due course, in 1721, Richard Marchant the younger was admitted as a Freeman of the City. What his apprenticeship involved is difficult to tell. No doubt it included instruction in money management and in what his father probably regarded as fair practice. But, what the Marchants might have regarded as fair practice was regarded in 1721 by at least one of their customers as sharp practice. The letter in which the charge was made, redolent with outrage, records the destruction of customary and good neighbourly relations, relationships which Marchant also helped to destroy in the Ham in 1710. The charge against Marchant was made by Mrs Frances Vaughan in a letter to John Sommerset in London:[9]

Bath Jan. 27th 1721

> But I have for this many years don him and his famale severall kindnessis and very grat ones to without ever desireing any return from him and Mr. Vaughan did the same and indeed all my famale has don all soe but tis like him and his wife availling against everybody thinking that thayer folts will

not be seen soe much. But tis the same he has don by me as he don by all his other frands in the bisness as he writ of me was a designed thing to try to make me doe what I was resolved I wood not. When I furnished my hous last summer I was over parswaded to have things from that Quaker as in his he namd. A letell while after I gave him a bill of a hundred and fifty pounds to receive for me which if he had sent it then it wod a bin pd. but he cept it above a month prommising me to send to receive it every day and at last did not doe soe. By that delay I have not redeemed it nor I can't when I shall. But I have a tennant at brisellton near bristol as is a quaker one of his acquantons and his life is in my farm and he wod fain put to lives more in the farm or to by it and I will not neither sell nor put lives and for this very reason marchant take this way to work thinking to fors me. I tould him I was disappointed in receiving money and that I was willing to give him a bond and I being a strainger to him I did not take it ill on him to have another in the bond tho I ofered them both more plate and other things than the mony was.

This letter clearly shows Richard Marchant the elder engaged in supplying furnishings for houses and in dealing in inland bills of exchange. He also seems to have been using an unpaid debt to secure a title to ground at Brislington. No doubt instruction in these matters and in the right way to handle tenants on the Ham constituted part of his son's apprenticeship. No doubt, too, other aspects of Richard's education showed him how to square these activities in Bath, the home of gaming, sporting, carding, dicing, dancing and comedies, and the breeding ground for quarrelling, fighting, swearing, routing, revelling, lightness, vanity, wantonness and obscenity, with the principle tenets of his Quaker faith which publicly and enthusiastically condemned outright all such behaviour as contrary to the spirit and glory of God![10]

As Marchant prospered he also served as one of the first surveyors appointed under the Turnpike and Improvement Act of 1707, as a collector of donations for the building of the General Hospital in Bath, and as agent for a London victualler taking up a £500 mortgage on three houses in Trymme Street, that new development outside the walls begun by George Trymme in 1707 and continued for several years thereafter. Richard Marchant, the elder, died in

1727 leaving an apparently thriving business to his son. It is possible that Marchant's career was exceptional and that his son enjoyed advantages denied to others. However, it was not unusual; another branch of the Marchant family sprang from Edward Marchant, a successful rough mason, and other leading families in eighteenth-century Bath with origins in the Company of Merchant Taylors include the Attwoods, Collibies, Chapmans, Wiltshires, Cogwells, Hartfords and Ditchers.

Even before his father died, Richard Marchant the younger was clearly engaged in business either on his own or on his father's account. He was also married and living in the parish of St James. Although apprenticed as a Merchant Taylor, he seems never to have practised as one, and although he never seems to have accepted deposits, was generally described as a banker. In 1726 he was so well known locally that James Brydges, the First Duke of Chandos, possibly the most successful stockjobber of his day, employed him as his local agent in an urban redevelopment project early in the first big building boom of the century in Bath. The full story of this development will be told later. Here it is sufficient to say that, in addition to acting as Chandos's agent, Richard Marchant was the only substantial local financial intermediary in Chandos's development. From 1727 to 1731 he facilitated the development by discounting bills drawn on Chandos to the amount of £1,700. Marchant subsequently advanced £1,000 to the Duke of Kingston, became agent for the Sun Fire Insurance Office, acquired property in the city, built Marchant's Court and put out considerable sums on mortgage.

In 1745 the profitability of the ruthless and illegal act carried out by Richard Marchant, the elder, in 1710, became abundantly clear. As part of John Wood's development of the Parades, Richard Marchant, the younger, granted one-sixth of an acre of the Ham to John Wood. This piece of ground was so necessary to Wood that he paid a fine on entry of £12 10s. and an annual rent of £2 10s. When one remembers that Richard Marchant, the elder, had to pay a fine of £40 for the whole of the Ham and had let the land at just over £1 an acre in 1710, it becomes clear that Marchant's gain was very great; the rent itself represents almost a fifteenfold rise in ground rents in thirty-five years – a rise brought about by extensive building development throughout the city. Since Wood's development was on Kingston's ground and carried out with his consent, Richard

Marchant also sought additional compensation for the loss of herbage for 320 sheep which he considered involved in the transaction. At which Kingston's agent expostulated:[11]

> I have not mentioned the excessive gains Mr. Marchant and his father have reaped by destroying the herbage of the Ham and converting it to the purposes above mentioned. They are much more than such a common as he claimeth can possibly be valued at, Ten times over.

The record does not show whether Marchant was so compensated.

Subsequently, Marchant financed the activities of many persons in and around Bath and, in 1757, during the building of the King's Circus, he made his first recorded loan to John Wood the younger. By 1771 his outstanding advances on mortgage to Wood totalled £4,115 and, by way of outright purchase of ground rents, he had supplied him with a further £1,500. During the early stages of building the Royal Crescent, Wood settled his outstanding debt with Marchant and renegotiated a loan of £8,000 from Marchant and Harford Lloyd, a partner in the Bristol Old Bank.

What can be summarised of Marchant's long-term investments, mostly in land and building, before 1771 is shown in table 3.3.

TABLE 3.3 Richard Marchant's loans

	£ s. d.	
To John Wood, the younger, Bath, by 1771 (for building)	4,115. 9. 0	@ 4½%
To Alexander James, Charterhouse, by 1759	1,650. 0. 0	
To Duke of Kingston, by 1736	1,000. 0. 0	
To James Browne, on his Manor at Street, by 1762	1,400. 0. 0	
To Richard Jones, Ironmonger and Deal Merchant, Bath, by 1766 (for building)	1,000. 0. 0	
To Lunatics Account, Chippenham, by 1766	770. 0. 0	@ 4%
To Henry Dixon, House and Shop at Bath, by 1736	350. 0. 0	@ 5%
To Rev. Walter Chapman, Bath, by 1760	200. 0. 0	

Source: See Note 5.

When Richard Marchant died in 1774 he seems to have possessed personal and real estate worth at least £30,000, including all his property in Bath, his loans to Wood, and a £6,000 share in the Bristol Brass Company. His obituary in the *Bath Chronicle* declared:[12]

> Saturday last died at Redland, near Bristol, in the 72 year of his age, Mr. Richard Marchant, of this city, one of the people called Quakers; greatly regretted by his very numerous circle of friends and acquaintance. His many amiable and good qualities are too publicly known to need repeating, but for the sake of example and imitation: he was an affectionate, endearing husband and parent; humane and generous to the distressed; hospitable to his friends; and was constantly employed in rendering acts of benevolence to those who stood in need of assistance.

Marchant's career as land speculator, building developer, lender on mortgage, discounter of bills of exchange and as agent for others engaged in investment in urban redevelopment was undoubtedly a function of the demand for the pleasures of Bath. His career also shows the advantage he gained by never practising as a Merchant Taylor. This freed him from dependence upon the corporate power of the Company of Merchant Taylors and left him free to act in economic matters in any way he chose. In this respect his life was very different from that of other apprentices who became journeymen and then members of the city's Companies. As masters and members of Companies these men looked to the Corporation and the Companies to protect them against competition from outsiders and from unfair practices. As the account of the enrolment of apprentices shows, they were largely successful, although only within the limited confines of the city itself and until the 1760s. The fact was that most of the apprentices enrolled after the mid-1720s, who were contemporaries of Richard Marchant, had to face increasing competition from outsiders. Furthermore, these outsiders were to benefit increasingly from the extension of the city beyond the city walls which was carried out by men like Marchant and Trymme who were also members of the city's Companies. Consequently, the life and work experiences of most of these apprentices were not like those of Richard Marchant. They may only be dimly perceived in official records like those of the Company of Merchant Taylors.

The Company of Merchant Taylors, drawing strength from its

constitution and rules drawn up in 1628, was the most influential of the city's Companies.[13] In the last third of the seventeenth century it had increased its membership from twenty-one in 1666 to thirty-nine in 1688. After a reduction in membership to thirty-seven in 1700, it increased again to forty-eight members in 1735. Since, between 1724 and 1760, 13 per cent of enrolled apprentices were enrolled as merchant taylors or tailors, the affairs of the Company and the attempts it made to protect the interests of its members as the city grew, touched a significant proportion of the city's labouring population. Their story is almost certainly also the story of artisans employed in other trades.

The rules of 1628 decreed that no stranger should practice within the city unless first allowed to be a workman by the Master of the Company, made Free of the city, and served an apprenticeship. They also decreed that apprentices should be made Free of the city and pay 5s. to the Company before setting up shop. Furthermore, no ready-made work was to be brought into the city unless the material had been previously sent to a country tailor by the owner of the material. Journeymen who were not shopkeepers were prevented from taking in private work. Shops were not to open on Sundays or holy days. Master tailors were not to entice each other's workmen nor employ a workman who had not completed his apprenticeship. Widows of tailors who were also shopkeepers were allowed to continue in the trade taking one apprentice and one journeyman. Penalties for breaches of these rules ranged from 3s. 4d. to 6s. 8d.

In their struggle to preserve and protect their interests, the Company of Merchant Taylors used the legal powers which they believed had been granted to them by their incorporation in 1628. Accordingly, in 1734, they added to the list of penalties a fine of 20s. on any member entering into a partnership with a non-Freeman and, between 1734 and 1737, the Company successfully prosecuted five separate individuals for practising the trade when not Free of the city. Two of the men prosecuted eventually paid £10 for their Freedom and the other three left the city. These actions by the Company, plus the vigilance of the officers of the Company in tracking down offenders, served to maintain the conviction among tailors that they could not practice without first purchasing the Freedom of the city. Charles Knight, a 70-year-old tailor in the early 1760s, who had served his apprenticeship at Batheaston and not in Bath, recalled that during the apprenticeship he:[14]

> has carried cloths made up at Batheaston into Bath and has generally brought them into Bath by stealth or in a secret manner – that he has carried cloths often made up on his own account into Bath – to his own customers there and has oftentimes, put the clothes on himself to avoid being seen or suspected carrying them in the City as a Tailor . . . that Joseph Perry one of the Wardens of the Company about two years after his being in the City and exercising his trade called on him and informed him that he would be sued by the Company if he continued to exercise his trade in the City whereupon he removed out of the City into that part of Walcot as is without the City and there exercised his trade for about half a year and then returned back to Ladymead . . . That he has been called on by three several successive masters to pay forfeitures for exercising his trade but was always excused paying on account of his poverty.

He added that in his judgment in Bath

> there is and had been since time immemorial a custom that no person should exercise the trade of Tailor without being free of the City.

Charles Knight's testimony was supported by that of the 24-year-old John Butler who had served his apprenticeship at Monkton Farley and by sixteen other tailors.

During the building boom of the 1750s, Corporation expenditure increased. In an attempt to produce a matching increase in income, the Corporation raised the fee for the purchase of the Freedom of the city to twenty guineas for men and ten for women. They also encouraged all the unorganised trades in the city to form themselves into Companies. Encouraged by this, and in the belief that the Corporation would enforce its by-laws of 1736 imposing a penalty of 40$s.$ on any non-Freeman selling goods in the city and its 1752 by-law against non-Freemen practising any trade in it, many Freemen formed or re-formed Companies for: Barbers and Peruke Makers, Mercers and Drapers, Grocers, Chandlers and Soapboilers, Carpenters and Joiners, Tylers and Plasterers, Masons and Bakers.

These actions by the Corporation also strengthened the resolve of the Company of Merchant Taylors to take even firmer measures to protect the interest of its members and prevent competition. Accordingly, in 1751, the Company re-stated its rule preventing partnerships with non-Freemen and in 1755 twenty-seven members of the Company entered into an agreement to fix the rate of wages and not to entice journeymen tailors from each other. Then, in 1759, the Company began its case against William Glazby for practising as a tailor without having gained the Freedom of the city and, in 1763, before that case reached a decision, the Company reaffirmed the rules as set out in 1628 with the addition of a heavier penalty of £5 for refusal of office, and a fine of £5 5s. 0d. for paying wages to journeymen in excess of the agreed rates, which were 11s. per week in winter and 12s. in summer. At the same time the enticement of journeymen was severely condemned.

The words used by the Company in its condemnation of enticement and their action in setting up a committee to investigate and prosecute strangers suggest that they were already submerged in the new world of free competition – the world of Richard Marchant. They said:[15]

> Whereas it has been too frequently practised by some of the members of the said Company to entice, seduce, employ or draw away another member's Journeymen Tailor or Journeymen Tailors from such members' service or work and the better to conceal the motives thereof such Journeyman or Journeymen have or hath frequently left or departed from the said City of Bath for a day or some short time and then have or hath returned again to the said city and have or hath gone to and been employed by such member of the said company so prevailing on such Journeyman or Journeymen to quit the former member's service and by such and various other methods of seduction of the Journeymen . . . (They) have been the cause of much strife and uneasiness among the said Company as also very prejudicial to them in their regular carrying on their lawful business.

In an attempt to prevent such competitive bidding for labour the Company imposed a fine of 6s. 8d. for each offence.

The Company also successfully prosecuted several non-Freemen including, in 1764, John Cosgrove. Cosgrove had incurred fines totalling £10 12s. 4d. for breaches of the Company's rules. He also owed the Company £7 9s. 3d. for legal costs awarded against him. Since Cosgrove's only assets were debts owing to him of £7 16s. 10d., he was held in gaol as a debtor to the Company and was still there in February 1765. By this time the Company had also begun a prosecution against John Idle for practising as a tailor without being a Freeman. However, before this case had got very far, a decision was finally brought down in their case against Glazby. Since this decision marked a significant shift in the attitude of the Corporation to the city's Companies the details are worth noting.

William Glazby's career as a tailor in Bath began in 1756 when he took a lease of a property in the Parish of St Peter and St Paul previously occupied by a recently deceased tailor, Samuel Elkington. There he practised as a tailor, having taken Elkington's 17-year-old son as apprentice with a guarantee that he would take him into partnership. When Elkington's term of apprenticeship came to an end, Glazby's legal right to run the business (he was not a Freeman) also came to an end. Glazby then entered into an agreement with George Evill, a poor member of the Company of Merchant Taylors. Under this agreement Evill acted as nominal head of the firm while Glazby appeared as a foreman earning 25s. per week. This arrangement was discovered by the Company in 1759. Thereupon Glazby agreed to pay the Company £30 for membership of the Company but baulked at paying a further £20 for the Freedom of the city. Against the advice of their attorney the Company then sued Glazby for practising as a tailor without the Freedom of the city and for refusing to pay fines totalling £18 3s. 4d. imposed by the Company. The case dragged on for many years. When the decision was finally brought down the judge, on a point of law, directed against the Company and laid down that the power of levying fines for practising as a non-Freeman rested with the Corporation, not with the Company of Merchant Taylors, yet the plea against Glazby had been made by the Company. The significance of this decision was clear and, in September 1765, the Company wrote to the Corporation in the following terms:[16]

> When we consider this (the evidence assembled in the case against Glazby) coupled together with your own late Public Acts, declaring and loudly avowing the same, by your not only obliging a multitude of persons to purchase their freedom of

the City, to enable them to carry on their Trades, whereby several thousands of pounds were raised, but also your forming and uniting so many members or citizens of the City, at a large expense to them, into Companies on the real assured ground and foundation to them of having and enjoying this peculiar privilege we hope that you will for the sake of your fellow citizens and of the trust reposed in you as Guardians of the City not let this Ancient Privilege be lost or trodden underfoot through the dictum or opinion of a single judge.

The Corporation records show no sign that the Corporation received or noted this letter nor do they record any subsequent action by the Corporation on behalf of the privileges of the Merchant Taylors or of any other of the Companies formed or reformed at their behest.

The effect of the decision against the Merchant Taylors was dramatic. After 1765 the City Companies never again paraded their privileges through the streets and there was only one enrolment of an apprentice Merchant Taylor in the city. That was in 1768. Thereafter, they ceased altogether. The enrolment of apprentice tailors also shrank to one every two or three years. By 1774 the number of enrolled apprentices in all the trades in Bath, which in 1752 had totalled 63, had shrivelled to two. In 1776, the year of the *Wealth of Nations* and the American Declaration of Independence, the enrolment of apprentices as a condition for securing the privileges of established companies in Bath ceased altogether.

The advantage to the Corporation of its attempts to enforce Freedom of the city as a condition for practising a trade in it is clear. At £20 per Freedom, it could substantially augment the Corporation's income. The advantage to the members of the Companies was also thought to be clear and certain. It was believed that the Companies' trading privileges would limit competition and that their restricted membership would enable a handful of employers of labour effectively to fix wages and resist wage demands. The evidence suggests that it was this latter consideration that was uppermost in the minds of the members of these Companies as they sought incorporation in the 1750s. We have already seen how twenty-seven members of the Company of Merchant Taylors entered into an agreement not to entice labour and to fix wages in 1755 and how concerned the Company was to restate and enforce these principles in 1763. Behind these protective moves one may see clearly the role of organised labour in bringing pressure on employers by demanding higher wages. For example, in September 1763 during the early stages of Bath's third period of expansion, it was a wish to resist the demands of a combination of journeymen tailors which led a group of Merchant Taylors to initiate the restatement of the rules and the enforcement of the Company's wage principles in that year. It is a measure of the Company's weakness in 1775, that the journeymen tailors in combination stood out for 25 per cent more than the 12s. maximum weekly rate agreed by the Company in 1763.[17] Even earlier, in 1752, the rules of the Company of Masons had also included a clause aimed at preventing the enticement of labour. In that year, too, the Company of Tylers and Plasterers saw the question of wages as so vital to its members' interests that, as well as imposing a penalty of 6s. 8d. for enticement and requiring a week's notice of withdrawal of labour, the Company also decreed that wages should be fixed by the Mayor and two Justices of the Peace and that any breach of the wage agreement would result in the dissolution of the Company.[18]

Clearly, the buoyancy of demand in Bath, particularly during periods of expansion in building, not only provided avenues of success for men like Marchant, Wood, Allen and Nash, and for interlopers like Glazby, Cosgrove and Idle, but also led to conflicts between capital and labour and created opportunities for organised as well as unorganised labour to seek and get higher wages. It was surely this collectivity of opportunities that lay behind the breakdown of attempts at regulation of economic life by the Corporation and the Companies. The Glazby decision in 1765 merely gave legal recognition to what was happening in fact. Thereafter, there was no pretence but that in the economic life of the labouring population in Bath it was a free-for-all. Consequently, organised workers sought even more forcefully to protect their own interests. The clearest example of this was in 1784, when three tailors, William Sloan, William Bennet and William Jones, with many other unidentified tailors, took steps to maintain their wages by compelling cut-price workmen to leave the city. In doing so they broke the windows of one journeyman tailor and beat and bruised him, and when another journeyman, Daniel Ryan, refused the offer of 7s. 6d. to leave the city, William Sloan held a pistol against his head,[19] telling him that he would shoot the said Daniel Ryan and all the men who worked underprice like Rabets.

Although the journeymen tailors struck again and gained 21*s*. a week in 1802, their organisation was weak and they were still struggling to establish their right to combine and to enforce standard wage levels in the second decade of the nineteenth century. It seems that early attempts at organisation by skilled artisans were doomed to failure because of the abundance of cheap labour, both skilled and unskilled, that was attracted to Bath as the city grew.

Just as the experiences of Wood, Allen and Marchant were not those of the majority of boys apprenticed to trades in the city, the experiences of these same apprentices, relatively secure in their skills, at least until 1765, were not those of the mass of the unskilled *'servants'* from whose ranks came the labourers, horsekeepers, waggoners, stay makers, basket makers, coach and post-chaise drivers, inn servants, housekeepers, servants and maids-of-all-work who flocked to the city either in work or in search of it. Their lives, too, can only be approached obliquely. On this occasion through the record of examinations by Justices of the Peace of applicants for poor relief. These examinations were carried out to establish the parishes where applicants had legal settlements and where, therefore, they were entitled to receive assistance from the parish poor law authorities. For a rapidly expanding city like Bath, these examinations were very important, and when they were carried out thoroughly, provide brief biographies of many of the urban poor. This account is based on an analysis of nearly 500 of them in selected years between 1763 and 1824.[20]

Table 3.4 contains a summary of one aspect of this analysis. In contrast to the birthplace or place of origin of boys apprenticed to skilled trades in the years before 1769, it shows that many more of the applicants for relief came from outside Bath. Of the number for whom a birthplace or last place of settlement was recorded (354) only 67 or 19 per cent were born or had a settlement in Bath. The table also shows that a further 199 or 56 per cent came from the neighbouring counties of Somerset, Wiltshire and Gloucestershire and the city of Bristol. The remaining 25 per cent came from other parts of the country, including London and the Home Counties, Wales, Ireland and Scotland. There was also one from Denmark, one from America and one born at sea in the English Channel. The

TABLE 3.4 Places of origin or settlement of applicants for poor relief, Bath. Selected years, 1763–1824

Authority and date	1 Number	2 Number recorded	3 Number from Bath	4 % from Bath	5 Number from Bath, Bristol, Som., Wilts. and Glos.	% in Column 5
Bath 1763	55	28	8	28%	21	75%
Walcot 1766–7	155	94	22	23%	77	82%
Bath 1772–3	98	71	14	20%	55	77%
Walcot 1816–20	93	91	9	10%	65	71%
St Michael 1811–20 St James 1823–4	74	70	14	20%	48	68%
Total	475	354	67	19%	266	75%

Source: Examinations before Justices of the Peace for Bath, and the parishes of Walcot, St Michael and St James, GAB.

majority, therefore, of these applicants, including those described as labourer or servant, were mostly rural immigrants to the city who claimed settlement and relief by virtue of service in it.

Records of Catholicism in Bath in the twenty years 1760–80 also provide evidence of substantial immigration, including long distance migration from Ireland, into Bath. Of the 165 adult Catholics shown in the 1767 return, only three are shown as Bath born. Of the rest, more than 100 had arrived since the start of the decade and most of the others had arrived since the mid-1730s. By 1785 their number had more than doubled to total over 400 adult Catholics, more than a quarter of whom were Irish. Probably this rate of increase of Catholic population roughly matched the rate of growth of the population generally but the growth rate of the Irish Catholics among them, starting from a negligible figure, was far more rapid.[21]

A striking characteristic of the applicants for poor relief, shown in table 3.5, is that two-thirds of them were women, and about half of these were young, pregnant, single women, or deserted wives in their late 20s or early 30s. Indeed, it would be no exaggeration to say that in the third quarter of the eighteenth-century the typical applicant for relief was a young female servant, either married a few years and abandoned with the care of two or three children, or recently pregnant by a man no longer living in the city, or an elderly widow too sick to be moved. In almost every case the woman probably began her working life as an apprenticed servant in a rural household in Somerset or Wiltshire at the age of 8 or 9 for a yearly wage of £2–£5. After completing her initial service she went through several positions as servant until she was either married or made pregnant before marriage, and in the course of time had arrived in Bath. For example, in 1763, Elizabeth Best, from Brighton in Sussex, was married at age 19 to a tenant farmer in Marshfield, Gloucestershire. For some five years her husband rented a farm worth £64 a year, then he rented another smaller farm for a further three years and one day walked off the farm leaving Eliza-

TABLE 3.5 Applications for poor relief in Bath and Walcot, 1763–74 by sex

	1 Total	2 Women	3 Pregnant single women or single mothers	4 Abandoned wives	5 Columns 3+4 as % of Column 2
Bath 1763	55	37 (67%)	19	0	51%
Walcot 1766–7	155	101 (65%)	39	8	46%
Bath 1772–4	98	63 (64%)	26	11	59%
Total	308	201 (65%)	84	19	51%

Source: Examinations before Justices of the Peace, GAB.

beth with two small children to care for. In 1773 she was 29 and applying for poor relief from one of the Bath parishes. Or there was Margaret Selby. Margaret was born a bastard in the poor house at New Sarum in Hampshire and apprenticed as a servant in Avon Street, Bath at age 12. After completing her period of service she returned to her mother's house in New Sarum where she worked at weaving, but had left home some three months before she applied for poor relief in Bath because she was pregnant. In 1766 Prudence Brown, after a lifetime of service, also applied for poor relief. She claimed her settlement in the parish of St James in Bath because when she arrived in the city in 1739 she had worked for seven years for £5 a year for Richard Marchant whose own life story we also know. Sarah Wheeler also worked for one of the leading developers in Bath, Thomas Jelly, carpenter and builder. Sarah was born in 1741 in Burford in Oxfordshire. At the age of 16 she had been apprenticed servant to William Hale of the Tything at Warleigh in Bathford. She served four years with Hale and then spent a further three years in Bathford. Then, when she was 23, she went to Bath to work for Thomas Jelly at £4 a year. After three months she quarrelled with a fellow servant and left Jelly's employ without telling him and went to work for a Mrs Watson. Jelly, however, sought her out and after one week she went back to work for him for a further ten months. On 12 January 1767, she made a claim for relief on the ground of her pregnancy by Thomas Collett, one of Jelly's apprentices.

These life stories were always simply and briefly recorded. Sometimes, however, they were more completely told than at others and they possess an authenticity and poignancy which tells something of the dignity and despair of the applicant in words that appear to be her own. Take the case of Martha Abraham, the daughter of a substantial tenant farmer at Chew Magna. In 1774, at the age of 28, she told her life story:[22]

> Martha Abraham now residing in the Parish of St. James in the said City Singlewoman Make oath that she was born in the Parish of Chew Magna in the County of Somerset and is now about eight and twenty years old. That she lived at home with her parents Oliver Abraham and Hester Abraham till she was about twenty years old. That her father was settled there by being renter of a large farm. That she, when she left her

parents, went to Whitchurch and hired herself a servant to Mr. Whippey a Gentleman of fortune at the yearly wage of five pounds and lived there almost a twelvemonth. That she, when she left Mr. Whippey's service, she came to Bath for her health and stayed there three quarters of a year. That when she recovered her health she went back to Chew Magna and hired herself a servant to Mr. Doyling a Gentleman of fortune at the yearly wage of six pounds and lived under that hiring two years and lodged and boarded in her Master's house. That she went to the Hot wells in the Parish in Clifton in the County of Gloucester and lived three years at Parson Budges a Lodging House as a housemaid but under no agreement for wages yet had her lodging and board there the whole time. That she then came from the Wells to Bath and hired herself to young Mr. Nightingale in Orchard St. in the Parish of St. James in the said city at the yearly wage of five pounds a year and lived under that hiring three quarters of a year and lodged and boarded in her Master's House all that time. That when she quitted Mr. Nightingale's service she hired herself to James Mullaway in the said Parish of St. James, Wine Merchant at the yearly wage of eight pounds. That she lived under that hiring fifteen months and lodged and boarded in her Master's House all that time. That in October last she quitted that service and went into the country to her friends at Chew Magna for a week only and returned to Bath and hired herself a servant to Mr. John Bryant Soap boiler in Walcot St. in the Parish of St. Michael in the said city at seven pounds a year and under that hiring lived only one quarter of a year and a fortnight.

She also deposed that the father of the child with which she was pregnant was her previous master, James Mullaway the wine merchant.

Mary Bank's story, told forty-three years later, is shorter but equally poignant. Mary was born at Batheaston in 1797. When she was 17 she left home to work as a yearly servant in the Bladud's Head in Ladymead, Walcot. After a year's service she was put off a few days before Christmas by the landlady because,[23]

> she was afraid she (Mary) would come to some harm in her house and said that she was a good servant and would give her a good character when she could find a situation.

Although she would have preferred to stay in service, Mary was paid £5 for her year's service and ceased working. Mary never did get another situation and in 1817 she was pregnant and likely to be a charge on the Parish of St Michael and removable to Batheaston, the place of her birth. She was then 20 years old.

Just as the Mayor and Justices acted in a paternal and caring way, in their handling of apprentices and their problems, they also took some pains to ensure that known fathers acted responsibly in relation to their children. They regularly made detailed Bastardy Orders and appear to have been able to enforce some of them. On at least one occasion they exercised their powers under the Act of 1602 to impose legal obligations on the grandparents of children whose father had absconded. This was in 1725 when John Bally, one of the city's chairmen, absconded leaving his wife and two children as a charge upon the poor law. The Mayor and Justices thereupon imposed a levy of 1s. 3d. a week each upon Bally's father, also a chairman, and his wife's father Christopher Margerum, victualler. This sum was to be payable to the Overseers of the Poor in the Parish of St James until the children were seven years old. The first payment was to begin immediately upon a penalty of 20s. and the threat of distraining upon the goods of the grandparents in order to pay the fine.[24] However, even when the town was small, such rulings were rare. When it was so much bigger in the second half of the century, they seem never to have occurred at all and abandoned wives and pregnant spinsters were often thrown upon their own or the parish resources.

Although two-thirds of new applicants for poor relief were females, there were 107 male applicants for relief in Bath and Walcot in the years analysed. The occupations of 104 were recorded. The figures show that forty-eight or nearly half of them, were either labourers or servants. The rest were drawn from a variety of occupations ranging from hawking and lamp-lighting to musicianship. Some were skilled workmen, for example, eight shoemakers or cordwainers, seven masons, and five carpenters. Other trades produced no more than three applicants each and it is, perhaps, the measure of the demand for skilled personal services such as tailoring, as well as of the effectiveness of the organisation of journeymen tailors, that in six years only one tailor applied for poor relief. Nevertheless, these examinations of male applicants do hint at several aspects of the social transformation of England in the second half of the eighteenth century.

Like the women, most of the male applicants came from rural areas in the neighbouring counties and some of their life stories illustrate the social effect of the development of capitalist relations in the countryside. For example, in 1764 Andrew Hillary had rented a farm in East Pennard for £25 a year. In the next year he rented only half of it for £12 but after six months his landlord, Elizabeth Lacey, distrained and seized his stock with the result that in 1767 he was a mere labourer in Bath and an applicant for poor relief there. Lawrence Painter, who was born the previous year (in 1766), was the son of a farmer renting a farm worth £10 a year at Ditcheat but, in 1818 he was also a labourer seeking poor relief in Bath. And so it was with George Groves. In 1788 Groves, who was then 7 years old, was apprenticed to a farmer with whom he stayed until he was 20 years old. But, at 60, he was an urban labourer in Bath. In the 1760s George Bolwell, too, was apprenticed to a farmer at Hinton Charterhouse for 4s. 6d. a week as a waggoner. He tried to apply for poor relief in Bath in 1820. In this same year, Samuel Collins also applied for relief from the Parish of St Michael. He reported that he had been born in Avon Street in 1792 but that when he was 7 or 8 years old his father had gone to London and left him to work at Mr Bamford's factory at Twerton where he:[25]

> lodged and boarded in the factory aforesaid for the space of three years when he enlisted in the Artillery.

He added,

> that he had no regular wages from Mr. Bamford but was paid a farthing an hour for the time he worked over the usual hours of work.

At 28 and retired from the artillery, he was an applicant for poor relief.

Among skilled men with rural origins there were James White and Thomas Roberts. James White was born at Wincanton in 1763. At 20 years of age he bound himself to a local mason for three years without indentures to learn the trade. In his first year he was paid 4s., in the second 5s. and in the third 6s. a week. Subsequently he went to Bath where he found work as a mason. At 54, with a wife and dependent child, he was unemployed and an applicant for poor relief. Thomas Roberts's story is even more remarkable as an example of the cheapness of labour with which Bath was built. Roberts was born in Monmouthshire and apprenticed in 1781 to an ironfounder at Lydney in Gloucestershire. According to his account he completed five year's service with his master and was a qualified ironfounder. In 1792, he went to Bath where he agreed with Richard Hewlett, carpenter, and one of Bath's leading speculating builders, to work for him for three years in order to learn the trade of carpenter without formal apprenticeship. In the first year, when he was 26 years old, he was paid 4s. and in the other two, 5s. a week.[26] Since the weekly wage of an unskilled labourer in Bath was then in the region of 9s. a week and even agricultural labourers in Somerset and Wiltshire could earn between 7s. and 8s. a week, the price Thomas Roberts paid for the privilege of working for Richard Hewlett must have been almost unbearable. At the age of 50 Roberts had a wife and four children and was an applicant for poor relief.

In these circumstances, marked by inward migration, persistent poverty and recurring periods of unemployment, many of Bath's labouring population left the city also in search of work. In fact, before 1816 the overseers of the parish of St James regularly apprenticed the parish's pauper children to workers in the textile trades of the neighbouring counties whilst voluntary emigrants from the city frequently went further afield. Sometimes they also failed to succeed economically away from the city and were returned to the care of the parish authorities. Indeed, in the twenty years from 1797 to 1817, sixty-three persons were returned under removal orders to one parish alone. Their stories also tell something of the desperation of the urban poor. In March 1815, William Sims and his family of five were returned to the parish of St James from Bristol. In November 1816 the four children were returned alone from Brighton where they had been taken by their father who was, by then, a soldier. Their mother was probably dead. In 1823, Priscilla Mitchell, wife of a corporal in the Foot Guards, and her three children were removed to St James from London. Three years later she went off to London again only to be removed to St James in 1830. On this second occasion she had six children. The local record for removal was held by Samuel Shell who tried three times to get away from poverty in the parish of St James. In 1821 he, his wife and two children were removed from London; in 1826, he, his

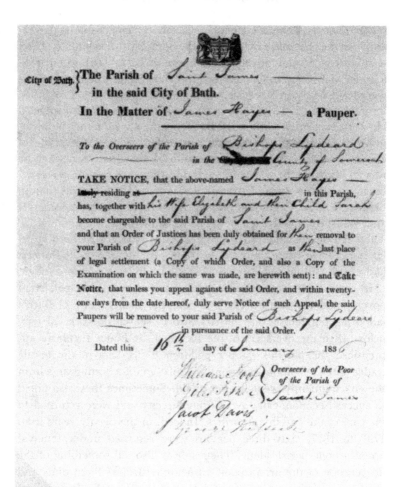

Figure 4 Removal order on James Hayes, 1836

wife and four children were removed from Bristol; in 1833, he, his wife and six children were again removed from Bristol (Figure 4).[27]

Without the work of this largely immigrant and geographically mobile labouring population, Bath could not have been built. Nor could it have been serviced. Yet, it is not possible to measure labour's contribution to the growth of the city, in building, for example, nor even to guess at its economic value for much of the eighteenth century. Indeed, there are records of only two attempts to use labour more efficiently and both were made early in the century. John Wood tells us that he introduced the use of the spade to Bath in 1726–7 and thereby increased labour productivity by cutting earth-moving costs by two-thirds, and in the 1730s Ralph Allen reduced the price of stone by cutting the wage rates of masons but increased their earnings by securing a more regular supply of work.[28] Throughout the century generally, particularly after the Glazby decision in 1765, there seemed no urgent need to use labour efficiently nor to economise in its use, it was in abundant supply. Consequently, money wages paid to labourers at the end of the century were generally low, rarely more than 8s. per week and sometimes as low as 4s. 8d. A further consequence of the abundant supply of labour during the period of high prices at the end of the century was that real wages fell by half between 1780 and 1801. In short, there was abundant labour in Bath; it was cheap and getting cheaper.

The sort of evidence about prices and wages that could help to provide a more detailed description of the changing economic experiences of various types of labour, such as skilled workers in the building trades and service industries and women in domestic service and unskilled labour generally, is difficult to come by and even harder to interpret. Consequently it is not possible to describe the experiences of workers during the booms and slumps that accompanied the building of the city. Only a little can be scraped together about prices and rather less about wages, relating to the experiences of general unskilled labourers, and that only for the last twenty years of the eighteenth century. The following discussion brings together most of that evidence.[29]

According to the accounts of the Assize of Bread recorded in the Quarter Sessions Books for the eighteenth century, the cost of bread in Bath at mid-century was as high as when first recorded in 1718. It was then 5s. 6d. a bushel. In between times, in 1729, the price was as high as 7s. In 1721, 1722, 1731 and 1737 it was as low as 5s. As I have already said, the lack of wage data prevents any discussion or conclusion about living standards in this period. However, evidence for the years 1780 to 1844 suggests that after 100 years of urban development in the city, by which time Walcot was the second wealthiest parish in the country, unskilled general labourers were as precariously balanced on the razor's edge of death through starvation as their rural ancestors had been at the time they became immigrants to Bath. Since general labourers were about 20 per cent of the adult male workforce in the early nineteenth century in Bath, their wage experience was important for a substantial segment of Bath's labouring population. It may also be taken as characteristic of the material standard of life of all those in Bath regularly earning 8s. or 9s. a week in the 1780s, and as superior to those like Thomas Roberts who earned 4s. per week in 1792 and those thousands of itinerant workers whose only experience in Bath was in the Refuge for the Destitute in Avon Street where, in the 1840s, they were relieved with seven ounces of bread, a pint of pea soup, a sack of straw and a quilt for a bed.

During the last twenty years of the eighteenth century the weekly wages of general labourers in Bath were higher than those in neighbouring counties – by as much as 2s. per week in 1795. They fell below the level of wages in those counties by the 1830s. Thus the weekly wage in Bath was 8s. in the 1780s, 9s. 6d. in 1801 and 7s. 7d. in 1837. Also important for estimating the level of real wages are the prices of the items most commonly consumed. In the 1830s these were bread, beer and cheese. Indeed, the basket of goods for a family of four which would have provided a diet equivalent to that of a pauper, would have contained: 33½ lb of bread, 1 lb 11 oz of meat, 1 lb 1 oz of bacon, 4½ lb of cheese and 6 lb of potatoes. At the lowest prices in Bath market in 1837, these items would have cost 8s.10¾d. Since this basket of goods omits any allowance for rent, fuel, clothing, shoes, soap, candles and beer, which would have added another third to the weekly cost of living, the discrepancy between the weekly wage in 1837 of 7s. 7d. per week and the cost of survival was considerable. It shows the degree to which a general labourer was unable to maintain life for his family without extra earnings from his wife and children and assistance from charity and poor relief. My guess is that about one-third of families in Bath were in this condition. Earlier still, in 1799 – 1801, the real wage of a labourer in Bath was about one-third lower than it was in 1837. To show what this meant, I describe in detail life in those years.

In 1799 England's war economy had boomed and the general level of prices had risen. As a result there had been very little building carried out in Bath since the crash of 1793. Additionally, in the harvest month of September 1799, Bath had 8.8 in. of rain. This meant that wheat, which had been 82*s*. per quarter in January 1800, had risen to 160*s*. by the end of June. In Bath the weight of the penny loaf fell from 5oz to 2½oz, at which time bread in Bath cost five times as much as in 1779. In the same period weekly wages for labourers had increased by less than 20 per cent. During July imports from abroad, wheat from Europe, flour and rice from America kept the price of wheat at 86*s*. and led to a rise in the weight of the penny loaf to 4.4oz. But from August prices began to rise sharply. In February 1801 the price of wheat stood at 184*s*. per quarter. In March the price of the quartern loaf was 1*s*. 11*d*. It was then ½*d*. dearer than in London and 5*d*. more than a day's pay for a general unskilled labourer whose wage of 1*s*. 6*d*. a day had remained unchanged since 1792. At these levels of prices and wages, 10,000 people, a third of the city's population, could only survive by consuming some four tons of rice weekly provided by the hastily formed Provision Committee. The *Bath Herald* acknowledged the severity of the situation with the following piece of doggerel:[30]

> Here's Bone and Skin
> Two millers thin
> Would starve the town or near it.
> But be it known
> To Skin and Bone
> That Flesh and Blood can't bear it.

Others among the labouring population acknowledged it more forcefully. In March 1800, after a 50 per cent rise in wheat prices in two weeks, a brewery on Broad Quay was destroyed by a fire said to be caused by a deliberate act of arson by some of the hungry population. The owners lost 20,000 bushels of malt and 1,400 barrels of beer worth £10,000. This event, followed by threats to destroy the property of the mayor and an actual, but unsuccessful, attempt to fire the property of Mr Stothert, ironmonger, led to regular citizens' nightly patrols of the city and the offer of a £500 reward for information leading to an arrest. But there was no end to the riots and violence. In May 200 women attacked dealers in the market forcing them to open sacks of potatoes and sell cheaply. Next, they demonstrated outside the house of a man buying up large stocks of potatoes and rampaged through the city on their way to Larkhall where they attacked a gardener and carried off sacks of potatoes. Finally the Yeomanry had to be called in to disperse them. In October another mob of women stopped the waggon of a Bathwick miller. They used his waggon and horses to carry off fourteen sacks of flour. In the same month eight women attacked Ann Adams of Englishcombe and robbed her of fourteen pounds of butter. Throughout the period of high prices garden robberies and poaching continued on a large scale.

The men of property and the Corporation were utterly confused by such a disastrous turn of events. Some placed the blame on the servant class who were said to be using their masters' money to pay unlimited prices for foodstuffs. Others thought the fault lay with forestallers and regraters, and some that the fixing of prices by the Assize of Bread prevented competition and forced up prices. After the passing of the Brown Bread Act in 1801, it was said that the poor were themselves to blame for preferring bread made of the best wheaten flour to coarser and cheaper brown bread.

Such different diagnoses were matched by different remedies. In March 1800 the wealthy were asked to substitute potatoes for bread and to eat bread only when it was two days old. In December some of their servants gave up eating tea. Then in February 1801 the Assize of Bread was suspended and country bakers were offered free stalls in the market and forestallers and regraters were denounced and gaoled. Newspapers, too, were helpful. Throughout the first six months of the year they published recipes for making bread and other dishes out of rice, and praised rice as highly desirable and nutritious. At the same time they reminded the poor that in all they did they owed the rich:[31]

> respect, gratitude and obedience; as to those whom God in his wisdom has been pleased to make the rulers though not the tyrants of Society.

And they sternly informed the labouring population:[32]

That idleness, discontent and riot, will make things worse; and that industry, patience under adversity, and a perfect reliance that the same almighty power, who had now forbid the grass to grow and the grain to rise will again, if we profit by the lesson, send his refreshing showers and genial heat, and perhaps make the blessings of plenty the harbingers of peace.

Fortunately for the labouring population of Bath and for the preservation of a residue of social stability, much demanded and talked about by men of property, even as they acted to destroy it in building the city itself, the administrative framework of the caring society, which had marked some aspects of life in Bath 100 years earlier, was still available for use in 1799. As a result the provision of poor relief by the parishes of Walcot and St James increased by half between 1799 and 1801. It totalled more than £8,000 in each of the years 1800 and 1801. Nevertheless, these years were marked by high rates of inflation and much of the increase in expenditure was absorbed by rising prices. Since rate payers, too, were adversely affected by inflation they were reluctant to go on paying such high rates of relief to the poor. In August 1800 a select committee examining the accounts of the joint poor house of the Parishes of St Peter and Paul and St James reported:[33]

> Mr James Attwood's accounts were examined for the last 9 weeks when it appeared that the average expense of each pauper amounted to the enormous sum of 5/8 a week, which in the opinion of the Select Committee calls for an immediate alteration in the mode of supplying the Poor within the House.

Since, at the beginning of 1801, the average wage of a labourer in Bath was 9s. 6d. a week, the cost of relief at 5s. 8d. a *person* indicates both the plight of the labourer's family and the extent to which payments for indoor relief exceeded the wages men could earn by their own efforts. Following the investigation, Mr Attwood entered into a new contract in October for 4s. 3d. a head to cover meat, drink, fuel and light. The Parish agreed to pay for tobacco, snuff, cloth and worsted repairs. Yet, in April 1801 it was necessary to compensate Attwood for losses incurred through rising prices by a cash grant of thirty guineas. By the end of the year Mr Attwood was dead. The contract was then let to a new man at 3s. 6d. a head.

The low wages and high prices in the years 1799–1801, plus the high cost of relief, and the existence of a mass of unrelieved poverty meant that parish relief alone could not cope with the starvation conditions in Bath in these years. If bread riots were not to turn into something worse other measures of relief were needed. One such scheme was started by the proprietor of the Twerton textile mill, Bamford and Company. The firm bought flour wholesale and baked bread to sell to their workers at 1*s.* 4*d.* the quartern loaf at a time when the normal retail price was 1*s.* 9*d.* But, the most concerned effort to alleviate the situation and avoid mass starvation was begun by a group of wealthy citizens who believed that 'To the poor the rich owe countenance, protection and support.'

Accordingly, they set up a Provision Committee similar to many set up in other cities throughout the kingdom in December 1799. Very quickly this Committee raised £1,000 for the purchase of food and coal which, in order to prevent relief carrying the stigmata of charity, it resold to the poor at low prices. Repeated appeals for donations raised the amount of money available to the Committee and, by June 1800, 1900 families, about one-third of the population, received weekly relief totalling 5,600 pounds of rice and 5,000 quarts of soup. At the end of its first nine months of providing relief the Committee had supplied: 60,000 quarts of soup at 1*d.* per quart without potatoes, and 1½*d.* per quart with two pounds of potatoes, 200 barrels of rice at 3*d.* to 4*d.* per pound and 317 tons of coal at 8*d.* per hundred weight.

As prices continued to rise in the winter of 1800 and 1801 the Committee raised a further £2,033. By January 1801 it was regularly distributing four tons of rice each week to 3,000 families or nearly half the city's population. Even this figure does not reflect the full measure of need because only some of the poor were allowed to buy from the Committee at reduced prices. This was a privilege reserved for those who could get a written recommendation from a subscriber to the Committee stating the applicant's name and address and size of family. For those who were eligible, rice was rationed according to the following scale and sold to them at half price:

> Two in family 2lbs of rice per week
> Two to five in family 4lbs of rice per week
> Six or more in family 6lbs of rice per week
> Soup could be bought by anyone.

Relief was also provided by old-established charities like the Black

THE LABOURING POPULATION

Alms and Bellotts Hospital and by newly formed societies like The Society for the Relief of Lying-in Women (1792) and The Strangers Friend Society (1790). Altogether fourteen societies for the relief of the poor were created between 1790 and 1811. A generous estimate of the amounts spent on poor relief and distributed by charitable organisations in the year 1801–2 is £14,000. This was worth 6*d*. or 1.3 lb of bread per person per week for one-third of the population. For a general labourer's family of four it meant the addition of 2*s*. each week on a weekly wage of 9*s*. 6*d*. which was barely enough to bring the family to the merely adequate level of 1837. A similar amount was also spent in 1809–10 and £20,000 was distributed in each of the years 1816–17 and 1819–20. Charity such as this, even when used to supplement poor relief, was only a palliative and both charity and poor relief were uncertain and arbitrary in their incidence. They were also inadequate. Therefore, in spite of apparently generous payments, the living standards of general labourers in Bath probably fell between a half and a third between 1780 and 1801 and remained close to this low level in the first two decades of the nineteenth century. The evidence for this is in table 3.6.

The mood of life in Bath for these generations of the labouring population: artisans, labourers and women servants is difficult to assess. Unlike their customers in Bath, they wrote no books and any admirers of the labouring population who might have written about them took their secrets with them; in the literature of the time they are shadowy figures. Moreover, when they are written about it is never done so subjectively through their own perceptions and experience. Indeed, older historians of Bath thought there was no labouring population in Bath while modern ones, although they do occasionally notice the poor, do so only in a fragmentary way; they see them either as the massed hangers-on to social reform movements, or as the remnants of arcadian worlds and older ways. Even those lives recorded in the poor law records and described earlier in this chapter are isolated ones and possibly atypical. Moreover, as biographies, such records are always incomplete and there are never enough of them. Except, perhaps, in the records of business before the Mayor and Justices of the Peace and at Quarter Sessions.

Fortunately, three volumes of such business survive covering the years 1777 and 1778 and the period from 1787 to 1793. These volumes show how the Mayor and Justices were kept in almost

TABLE 3.6 Earnings and real wages, non-agricultural labourers in the city of Bath, 1780–1817 (1780 = 100)

Year	Average weekly earnings	Sch./G.* Consumer goods	Price of quartern loaf	Real wage
1780	100	100	100	100
1781	92	105	–	88
1782	102	105	–	97
1783	83	117	–	71
1786	101	108	–	94
1787	100	106	–	94
1788	96	100	–	86
1789	96	106	–	91
1790	95	112	–	85
1791	108	110	100	98
1792	114	110	–	104
1793	101	117	–	86
1794	102	123	–	83
1795	114	133	–	86
1796	118	140	–	84
1800	–	192	300	–
1801	119	207	278	55
1802	120	158	154	76
1803	113	142	141	80
1804	119	146	146	82
1807	120	169	175	72
1808	125	185	191	67
1809	117	192	229	61
1812	117	215	303	53
1816–17	112	172	208	65

*Schumpeter Gilboy
Source: Highway accounts, Walcot, and for 1816–17 Widcombe district accounts vol. 143.
Elizabeth Boody Schumpeter, 'English Prices and Public Finance 1660–1822', *Review of Economic Statistics*, XX (1938).

daily attendance at the Guildhall dealing with the social problems of urban life. They show, too, something of the responses of hundreds of Bath's citizens to their experience of it.[34]

In 1777 the Mayor and Justices dealt summarily with over 700 individual cases. As they did so they set a price on the service they offered or the penalty they awarded: a summons for an assault cost 1s., a bailable writ for debt from 2s. 4d. to 3s. 4d. and an examination on a matter of settlement cost the parish in question 5s. The summary fine for drunkenness was 2s., the punishment for vagrancy was a whipping, the fine for selling tea unentered was 5s. 3d. By 1790 the number of judgments on matters relating to offences against persons and property, to the administration of the poor and bastardy laws, and to the supervision of apprenticeship was well over 1,000. By 1793 the total was further swollen by the inclusion of 253 men attested soldiers.

The principal items of business in these years are shown in table 3.7 which also includes the Avon Navigation tolls as a measure of economic activity and an index of real wages as an indicator of economic welfare. The main problem in interpreting these statistics is the lack of population figures. The second problem is the impossibility of analysing them for different social strata.

The problem of population is particularly important because the period covered by table 3.7, 1787 to 1793, is just that period in which Bath grew most rapidly during the eighteenth century. Consequently some effort has to be made to relate the absolute totals of offences and decisions to that growing population. The way used here to try to solve the problem is to assume that the rate of growth of the population was a function of the rate of addition to the stock of houses as shown in the rate books for selected years. Calculations based on such an assumption show the population to have been of the magnitude shown in table 2.1 in chapter 2 and annexed to table 3.7. By relating the numbers of summons for assault to the population as calculated for the years 1787 to 1793, it is possible to show how the rate of assaults varied from year to year to reach a peak rate of 1:49 (20:1,000) of the population in 1790. Because some of the assaults recorded were multiple assaults, this figure suggests that something like one person in twenty of the total population or, one person in fourteen of the adult population, was involved either as complainant or defendant in an assault for which a summons was issued in 1790. Also, the indicators of economic activity and welfare show that while 1790 was undoubtedly a good year for building in Bath, high prices associated with the onset of the boom reduced real wages to the lowest level for the whole seven-year period. Moreover, the subsequent rise in real wages in 1791 and 1792, accompanied as it was by a fall in the rate of summons for

TABLE 3.7 Economic conditions, crime, and poor law decisions, Bath, 1777 and 1787–93

| Year | OFFENCES AGAINST PERSONS | | | | | | Population | Ratio of offences against persons to population* | Ratio of summonses for assault only | Index of ratio of summonses for assault 1777=100 | Economic welfare (Index of real wages) 1780=100 | Economic activity (Tolls on Avon Nav.) | POOR LAW DECISIONS | | | | Arrested soldiers | OFFENCES AGAINST PROPERTY | | | | | |
	Summons for assault	Breach of peace	Riot	Drunkenness	Other	TOTAL							Settlement examinations	Removals	Examination of passes	Bastardy examinations		Felony, theft receiving fraud	Detaining property	Damage to property	Bailable writs (Debts)	Non-Payment of rates	TOTAL
1777	286	10	—	32	20	348	18,900	1:54	1:66	100	104	3	84	21	—	20	1	18	—	1	123	—	142
1787	255	65	—	4	—	324	21,600	1:67	1:85	80	94	767	91	22	40	48	40	7	—	2	20	6	35
1788	358	81	—	1	—	440	22,000	1:50	1:62	107	86	1051	115	19	50	45	26	7	4	—	24	7	42
1789	392	19	—	1	3	425	22,300	1:53	1:57	117	91	1118	106	13	34	40	18	4	8	2	13	16	43
1790	488	28	9	—	3	528	24,000	1:45	1:49	133	85	1134	124	21	64	45	69	8	52	16	14	25	115
1791	356	20	—	—	—	376	25,600	1:68	1:72	93	98	1325	83	9	93	34	15	2	23	3	20	16	64
1792	357	73	—	—	—	430	27,300	1:63	1:76	87	104	1425	78	14	51	43	22	14	20	14	26	17	91
1793	305	30	—	—	5	340	29,000	1:85	1:95	70	86	1293	115	37	12	48	253	23	9	5	26	15	80

*Population for 1777, 1780, 1789 and 1793 calculated by multiplying the number of houses in parishes according to the rate of occupancy as shown in the 1801 Census. The figures for other years extrapolated. This procedure probably overestimates the population for 1790.

Source: *Business Before the Mayor and Justices*, GAB.
The Avon Navigation Accounts, British Transport Historical Records, London.
Table 3.6 above.

assault shows that, while personal violence was a general characteristic of life among the labouring population in Bath, its incidence rose and fell with fluctuations in real wages and the general level of economic activity; although fluctuations in these two indicators did not always coincide. Indeed, other ratios reported in Appendix G show that the low level of real wages in 1790 was not only accompanied by the highest ratio of summons for assault, but also by the highest ratio of offences against property, non-payment of rates and settlement examinations. This low level of real wages was also associated with the second highest ratio for removal orders and examinations for bastardy. Nevertheless, in spite of the low level of real wages, the year 1790 was also marked by an increase in the ratio of examinations of the removal certificate of immigrants to the city who were presumably attracted to it by its booming economy.

In spite of the up-turn in economic activity, 1790 was a bad year for many of Bath's workers. Nevertheless the boom in building which continued through to 1791 and 1792, did give them two years of better economic conditions; by 1792 the index of real wages had risen to 104 and the number of new applicants for relief was lower than at any time in the period 1787 to 1793. This rise in real wages was paralleled by a fall in the ratio of summons for assault.

The boom finally broke early in 1793, leaving many unfinished buildings and bankrupt builders. Real wages also fell to a level only slightly higher than that reached in 1790. Conversely new applications for relief and the number of removal orders increased significantly but the sharp fall in the number of passes examined suggests that many fewer workers came to Bath looking for work. Nevertheless the downward trend in the ratio of summons for assault was not reversed. In 1793, the worst year of slump and low real wages, the ratio of summons for assault was the lowest recorded. Perhaps the explanation is that some of the most depressing consequences for the labouring population of the depression were mitigated by the euphoria of war and the fact that 253 men were recruited into the army!

Very few of the offences brought before the Mayor and Justices were brought forward at Quarter Sessions. Of the 2,511 summons for assault in the period 1787 to 1793 only 362, or 14 per cent, came before Quarter Sessions and of those only 11, or 0.44 per cent of total summons, produced a conviction. Table 3.8 separates these summons into four categories. It shows that three-quarters of them

TABLE 3.8 Cases of assault brought before Quarter Sessions in Bath, 1777 and 1787–93

Year	Men on men	Men on women	Women on women	Women on men	Total	Convictions	Convictions men on women
1777	31	13	24	2	70	3	2
1781	28	10	4	5	47	0	0
1788	27	9	4	1	41	0	0
1789	16	7	5	1	29	1	0
1790	19	15	9	6	49	2	1
1791	22	16	6	3	47	1	1
1792	14	6	4	0	24	4	1
1793	27	18	8	2	55	3	0
Total	184 (51%)	94 (26%)	64 (18%)	20 (6%)	362	14	5

Source: *Business Before the Mayor and Justices*, GAB.

were taken out against men and that of those about one-third were taken out by women against men. This proportion (26 per cent of the total) is rather higher than the proportion of total summons taken out by women against men, which was 21 per cent.

Compared with the number of summons for assault issued by the Mayor and Justices the number of actions initiated for offences against property (particularly felony), theft, receiving and fraud were very few indeed. Only bailable writs for the recovery of payments due and for debt and offences under the title, Detaining Property, which included such crimes as detaining work, tools, clothes, money and dogs belonging to others, reached any great number. The number of these latter offences was high only in the bad year, 1790.

In short, the record of business before the Mayor and Justices and at Quarter Sessions seems to point to the conclusion that life among the poorest social strata in Bath was permeated by hostility and aggression manifested in assaults committed by whole groups of persons and families as well as by individual citizens against individuals and other groups and families. The evidence also suggests that as conditions of living deteriorated so violence increased.

Sometimes this general hostility and aggression broke out as breaches of the peace and riot, and group assault was tranformed into mob violence. This happened in 1778 when a mob of fifty people armed with sticks and stones gathered around the house of John Vincent in St James Parish. There, with 'a pair of Gilder Horns commonly called Rams Horns',[35] they drummed upon his door for upwards of half an hour. It happened twice in 1780. The first time when Philip Thicknesse suggested that the breath of virgins in Bath could prolong life and ensure good health and also intervened on behalf of a pressed man. On this occasion the mob hung Thicknesse in effigy.[36] The second time, the occasion of the Gordon Riots, was much more terrifying.

On the afternoon of Friday, 9 June John Butler, a Bath footman employed in the Royal Crescent, led a large and vociferous mob accompanied by the music of a fife towards the newly built Roman Catholic chapel near St James Parade. On the way they met a Catholic priest. They insulted and abused him. They chased him all the way from Stall Street to the Guildhall, where he was refused admission. Rather than stay trapped outside the Guildhall door, he dashed for sanctuary to the nearby White Lion. From there he escaped through a back door and across the river. Frustrated and angry, the mob turned back to St James Parade. There they approached the Roman Catholic chapel. One of them shouted, 'Come tumble in boys' and with a wave of his hat urged them forward. They broke into the chapel, threw everything movable into the street and burned it. Then came the Bath Volunteers – to disperse the mob. A pistol shot was fired. Arthur Brooke, one of the rioters, fell dead. Maddened, the mob fired the chapel and several newly-built houses belonging to Roman Catholics. They got into the cellars and broke open barrels and bottles and kept the fires blazing all night. When the Queen's Dragoons and the Herefordshire Militia from Wells and Devizes converged on Bath the next morning they could see their objective from the high ground by its flames. Not only the Irish and the Catholics, but the whole of Bath was in terror. Too many incidents like this and the visiting company would visit no more.[37]

Another riot occurred in 1784 when the journeymen tailors used force and the threat of a pistol shooting to intimidate non-union tailors and to force them to leave town. In 1793 yet another case of union activity led to the appearance of nine men charged with conspiracy and combination.[38]

These cases show that while the tailors used violence in their own economic interests and while there were bread riots in the early 1740s and in 1765, the mob generally vented its anger in explosive outbursts against socially approved targets; adulterers, obscene writers, Roman Catholics. Even at the end of the century, in 1799, the mob who repeatedly rioted over rising prices and attacked property, mainly expressed their rage against socially approved scapegoats such as forestallers and regraters. Only rarely did they destroy property as in the Gordon Riots, and they never attacked the system of property. Rather, as the number of summons for assault shows, life for the lowest social classes in Bath generated a sort of impotent rage amongst them. Rather than venting their anger against the system of property which structured their lives, making them rootless and anxious about matters of day to day living, such as poor relief, settlement and bastardy, they took to assaulting each other.

As the assault on the Catholic chapel shows, assault could turn to riot and riot could turn to murder. Yet known murders were few. In all, there were six in the years 1778 to 1798. To this number must be added eleven known cases of infanticide. However, given the annual number of examinations for bastardy – an average of 43 for the years 1787 to 1793 – it seems likely that the number of recorded cases of infanticide must represent but the tip of an iceberg. Also there were the thirty-five known cases of suicide. At the rate of 1.66 a year for an average population of 22,000 for the period 1778–98, the suicide rate of 7.5 per 100,000 was comparable to the rate for England and Wales, 1972–6, of 7.72 per 100,000. Of the thirty-five cases, twenty-three were by men and twelve by women and all but six of them were members of the servant and labouring classes. As well there were thirty drownings, including eight caused by drunkenness.[39]

Even so, our sources permit us to create a very incomplete picture of the lives of the labouring population. Indeed, even the figures cited here could be looked at from a different angle to add another dimension to that picture. For instance, it is clear that many more people refrained from assaulting others than those who did, or, if they did experience an assault, refrained from taking out a summons about it. By the same token most people were not sued for debt and most people remained sober. In fact most people harmed no-one. Although they lived their lives in poverty some by dint of hard work and some through talent achieved a modest competence. Some, like John Wood and Ralph Allen, did very well indeed, while Ralph Allen's workmen possibly lived comfortably in their new cottages on Combe Down. Even in Avon Street some men and women sought and won relief in Methodism rather than in drunkenness and violence, while later in the century the Baptists provided a community of peace for many others. The alehouses, too, provided company and ease, not merely drunkenness as a prelude to a violent assault or a death through drowning. And the Avon, where the drownings usually occurred, gave pleasure too; men bathed and washed in its waters and children picked wild flowers along its banks. In the upper town servants were especially advantaged. Sometimes, in the evenings, they could be seen at the theatres dressed in their mistresses' clothes while at the balls in the Assembly Rooms servants sometimes sat in the best seats. At least they did so until 1766 when Derrick, the bohemian master of the ceremonies, requested subscribers not to give subscription tickets to servants, 'either to maid or manservant, as it is evident they are seated every night to advantage while people of very high distinction are obliged to stand'.[40] Although this request for self-effacement was treated with contempt, a subsequent ruling by Derrick reserved the front benches for peers and peeresses. It seems that even the pleasures of the labouring population were reduced with the passing of time! Yet, some pleasures were timeless. Even Martha Abraham must have enjoyed moments of sharing and pleasure in her twenty-eight years; if not with James Mullaway, at least with her friends in Chew Magna when she went on 'holiday' for a week.

Nevertheless, the amount of recorded violence in Bath: assaults, breaches of peace, riots, murders, infanticides, drownings and suicides experienced by the labouring population does point to the existence of a culture of deprivation and violence. Further, if this amount of violence was recorded, how much went unnoticed because it was unremarkable, part of the accepted way of things? There is certainly reason to suppose that the record of violence and of migration points to the absence of community among the labouring population in Bath and suggests that they were a mere shifting agglomeration of people. Ill at ease with themselves and each other, most of them seemed unable to understand their own predicament and unable to help themselves. Certainly a very high proportion of them seemed bent on the physical abuse of their neighbours and some turned against themselves. I am tempted to claim that, trapped as they were in low-paid occupations and subjected to the vagaries of the market and to decisions made by men of substance such as the Mayor and Justices of the Peace, they turned their rage upon themselves in acts of self-destruction. But I take up again the theme of the development of consciousness in the final chapters.

Although the general history of labour in Bath in the eighteenth century might be expanded to include more statistics and illustrative examples, the general picture would remain much the same. There was the virtual monopoly of skilled labour held by the citizens of Bath in the early years of the century; the break-up of this monopoly by the mid-1760s; the influx of cheap rural labour into unskilled trades such as labouring and personal service, mainly from the neighbouring counties of Somerset, Wiltshire and Gloucestershire; the success stories of some of these apprentices and immigrants such as those of Allen, Wood and Marchant; the failure to succeed economically of very many others; the beginnings of labour organisation in the 1760s; and the specially dependent and exploited position of women, both natives and immigrants from rural counties. In the last years of the century this whole society seemed suffused with anxiety about employment, poor relief, settlement and bastardy which generated within the labouring population feelings of impotence and rage so generalised and diffused that they frequently turned against themselves, as well as their superiors, with acts of common assault and other forms of social violence. Beautiful and rich as the city was and a valley of pleasure, it was also and necessarily squalid and poor. It was a sink of iniquity in a sense never intended by the author of the term.

CHAPTER FOUR

LANDOWNERS AND PEASANTS

WALCOT LORDSHIP

Two Lives	Rent	Value over Rent
Widow Sanders two daughters	140 acres £2. 5. 6	£110. 0. 0

I desire twenty years to raise all to the value and to treat for the lives in the (leases).

The Survey of Walcot 1683

When Samuel Pepys visited Bath that midsummer evening in June 1668 he had found the battlements intact and the view from the walls pleasing. A few years later Henry Chapman, one of the town's leading citizens and its mayor described that view:[1]

> In such a narrow Compass is this ancient, famous, little, pretty City contained; which being in such a Bottom, had such a Variety of Prospects and Landskips, that few Places parallel it; whereas, Places scited on levels, seldom please the Eye for, deprived by the Interposition of the next Pole, Wall, or Hedge, whereas, this, raising itself higher than the adjoyning Gardens and Meadows, had full and free Passage; nor do the Hills so

streighten the Prospect, but that the Eye may ever surfeit itself with Variety of Objects (in some Places) for at least three Miles, at once beholding the Meander Avon Semi-circling the City; then the low Meadows, in several small and great Partitions; the Pasture Grounds above them; then the Corn-Fields; so gradually ye come up to the *Downs*, on which, particularly *Lansdown* is an excellent Course of above two Miles.

This description of Bath aided by a close look at Gilmore's map of 1694 (Figure 5) should help us to see the site of the city as it appeared before building began. Enclosed within its walls with only a finger or two of houses pointing north-east towards London and south towards Wells, the city was virtually surrounded by a thinly populated hilly countryside patterned with small fields, gardens and orchards. To the north, west and south-west it was bounded by the parish of Walcot. To the east by Bathwick and to the south by the parish of Lyncombe and Widcombe. It was cut off from both these latter parishes by the great loop of the Avon and connected to them only by ferries and the Old Bridge. On the northern and London side of Walcot the ground, sloping steeply upwards to the heights of Lansdown and Beacon Hill, was parcelled up into numerous small fields, each perhaps two or three acres in extent. The lowlying ground in Bathwick, too, was divided into small parcels of land. Only on the town's western and southern sides, where the ground fell away from Lansdown to the river on a more gentle slope, did the ground appear more open. There lay the ninety-two acres of the Town Common, the eighty-five acre Barton farm and some ground in Kingsmead, all in large enclosures. Bath appeared to be like any other Cotswold town, an urban, perhaps urbane enclave surrounded by a simple and rustic countryside. It seemed a place where an industrious bourgeoisie was surrounded by a sea of peasants. Yet, many of its citizens, especially the worthiest among them, were themselves small landowners or occupiers of land and the division between town and country was not as great as the strength and durability of the town walls and the view from them seemed to suggest.

Underlying the appearance of the ground around Bath were the legal relation of private and corporate property. Although the large open expanse of the Town Commons had distant origins it was also firmly rooted in Nicholas Hyde's award of 1619. This award vested

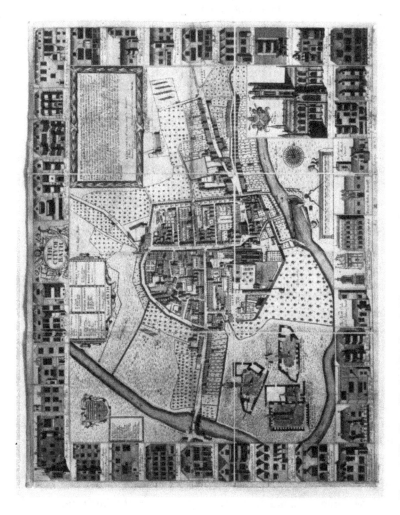

Figure 5 The City of Bath, 1694, Joseph Gilmore

the use and benefit of the commons in the Freemen of the City and appointed the Corporation of the City as trustees. As might have been expected this division of property rights led to differences between the Freemen as beneficiaries and the Corporation as trustees of the Commons. As a result the Commons remained a permanent feature of the landscape around Bath for well over 200 years. The Corporation also collectively held land outside the walls in its own right, in Milsom's Garden, the Town Acre, the Town Garden and Rack Close. Individual members of the Corporation, either as freeholders or leaseholders, also held land: Messrs Saunders, Axford, Attwood, Chapman and Howse among them. Other citizens, like Richard Marchant, were also holders of land outside the city walls. Chief among the larger, mostly absentee, landowners were Robert Gay in Walcot (1699), the Duke of Kingston in the Parish of St James (1710), the Earl of Bath in Bathwick (1726) and Ralph Allen in Lyncombe and Widcombe (1728).

It was the relationships of these landowners and occupiers with their trustees and their tenants as well as their relationships with building developers and working builders that were to fix the location, sequence and financing of building in Bath and, therefore, to structure the social organisation of space in the City. Richard Marchant's tenancy of the Ham in 1709 was a case in point and his attitude to the customary claims of others of Kingston's tenants was characteristic of his time. Marchant's story shows, like other instances yet to be mentioned, that beneath the apparently idyllic and limpid surface of the 'Prospects and Landskips' to be seen from the city walls there was a toing and froing of economic change and development that was soon to break down the walls themselves. As well as being a response to the demands of the visiting company, this burgeoning economic activity was rooted in the institution of private property and in notions of absolute property. Consequently, it was the product of political and legal developments determined within a national context and in no way peculiar to Bath.

In the year in which Richard Marchant the elder had laid the foundations of his and his son's fortune by gaining admission to the Company of Merchant Taylors, Prince William descended on England. Although, like the bourgeoisie generally, Marchant stayed at home, he must have heard tell of the battle of Wincanton on 10 November.[2] (He might even have rejoiced secretly at the outcome.) On that day a party of the King's Horse rode into Wincanton, a small market town about twenty-five miles south of Bath on the road between Exeter and Salisbury. They were ambushed at the eastern approaches of the town by an advance party from William's invading army. As the King's men rode into the town the men in ambush fired at least four volleys almost point blank into the ranks of the 120 horses packed into the narrow lane. About forty men were killed before the King's men broke off the engagement and retreated towards Salisbury. The rest is well known. The King's generals, including John Churchill, later the Duke of Marlborough, defected, the King retreated towards London, and the Prince became King, illegally, and by force of arms.

For men like Marchant and his son, William's victory was also a condition of their own achievements, the grounds of which were spelled out for them in 1690 in John Locke's *Two Treatises of Government*. In this work Locke defended the growth and concentration of large private property, justified revolution against a sovereign whose actions threatened the sanctity of that property and justified the property-owner's right to do what he wished with his own, to the extent of destroying its product. Locke, too, was a Somerset man born at Pensford some eight miles from Bath.

This right to do what they would with their own had been sought by English landowners holding land on military tenures since the time of the Conquest.[3] Their desire for it had led to unremitting legal contest with the Crown over the burden of the feudal incidents required by the military tenures under which they held land from the Crown. They felt particularly oppressed by the arbitrary but lawful claims on the revenues from their lands, particularly those created by the Crown's rights of wardship and marriage. Since these feelings were shared by most landowners, irrespective of political or religious persuasion, the abolition of these military tenures, carried out by Parliament in 1642, was also confirmed at the Restoration in 1660. This meant that all landowners who had held land under these tenures were now secure in law against the claims of the Crown. This security appeared threatened by James II's increasing exercise of his dispensing power. As a result, the Revolution of 1688 was seen by many landowners as an affirmation of their absolute right to property.

During the second half of the seventeenth century it was also coming to be accepted that private claims to land should outweigh either customary or common claims to it. The upshot was that landowners successfully employed their attorneys and the courts, particularly Chancery, to develop a system of land law entirely in their own dynastic interests. Above all, they perfected the settled estate in which, in its classic form, the nominal possessor was in fact only a life tenant and was, therefore, restricted in his freedom of action in regard to his lands. At the same time other members of the family were often granted clear legal claims to a share in the income from those lands. Moreover, with the development of the law relating to mortgages, those in possession of land who were also mortgagors were deemed merely to have an estate in land. And it was established that their mortgagees, with little claim on the land itself, had a legal claim to a share in the income from it for the payment of the interest on their mortgages. The result was that entailed estates, encumbered with many kinds of legal titles to shares in their revenues were protected by law and almost certain to remain intact for several generations. Therefore, settled estates and conveyances by way of lease flowing from them were to prove good mortgage investments at least as safe as government stock. In Bath they were to prove a sure foundation for a system of credit without which the city could never have been built. But, all this could only have been so in the absence of absolute monarchy. Hence the importance for the beginning of the expansion of Bath and of the role of men like Richard Marchant in it, of the Revolution in 1688, the battle of Wincanton and John Locke.

Another characteristic of the land law in the west country also influenced the progress and shaped the pattern of development in Bath. It did so in the sense that only on land where the characteristic did not exist or was removed could space in Bath be organised as it was. This characteristic was the persistence of the practice of granting land on long leases usually for three lives and in small quantities. Under this system of lifehold tenancies, landowners took their income from their lands mainly in the form of lump sum fines paid on inserting a new life or lives into the leases rather than from the annual rents they charged. Accordingly, the annual rents charged were generally nominal ones fixed in the past when the original leases were drawn. Where the fines and the practice of inserting new lives were governed by a firmly established custom of the manor a lifeholder was virtually confirmed in full possession of his small amount of land. This meant that, like Richard Marchant, he could then appropriate almost the full value of its product while the nominal landowner sometimes gained little from possession. Indeed, in valuing the capital value of lifehold land for purposes of sale or mortgage, the custom in Somerset was to multiply the annual value by fifteen or sixteen. Since this was half the multiplier generally used when capitalising the value of land let at a rack rent, it shows very clearly the different valuations placed on land let according to these different systems of leasing. The survival of these lifehold tenancies into the eighteenth century reflects the relatively slow penetration of large scale capitalist agriculture into Somerset.

To illustrate these points table 4.1 represents an analysis of six manors held by George Doddington on the northern edge of the Quantocks in 1713, totalling 2,642 acres.

It shows that of 113 separate holdings listed, 52 per cent were less than twelve acres in extent, and only 13 per cent were larger than fifty acres. The table also shows that 59 per cent of the land was still held on leases for lives and that the other 41 per cent let at rack rents, was all let in lots of more than 100 acres in extent. Surveys of four other manors for 1775 and 1781, two of which were at the base of the Mendips, show a similar pattern except that only in Rodney Stoke was the percentage of land let at rack rents nearly as high, and there it was only 30 per cent. On three other manors closer to Bath; Keynsham, Saltford and Weston, where the total annual rent of land in 1773 was £2,305, only 40 per cent was from land let at rack rents, and all of that was at Keynsham.[4]

Closer still to Bath was Walcot, bordering on the northern and western boundaries of the town. In 1638, only 13 per cent of 574 acres was let at rack rents and that on long leases. The proprietor of this land, who was probably the heavily indebted William Syngges of Bath, calculated the true annual value of 301 acres in Walcot Lordship at £343. Syngges also recorded that it was actually let in sixteen separate parcels of between 5 and 140 acres in extent on a variety of life-hold tenancies for £10 3s.10d. p.a. Only on the 273 acres of Barton Farm, worth £297 p.a. and let in eight separate parcels for £154 12s.10d. did Syngges obtain anything approaching the full annual value of his land. He wrote that his object was to raise all the rents to their full value and to treat for the lives in the leases. In 1638 he expected that this would take him twenty years! No doubt his problems were many; the custom of the manor in specifying fines for the renewal of lives, the small amounts of land covered by any one lease, and the fact that any one piece of ground

TABLE 4.1 The Doddington Survey, 1713

	Total holdings	Cottages & gardens less than 1 acre	No. of holdings under 12 acres	% of holdings under 12 acres	No. of holdings 12-50 acres	% of holdings 12-50 acres	No. of holdings 50-100 acres	% of holdings 50-100 acres	No. of holdings over 100 acres	% of holdings over 100 acres	Total acres	Acres in holdings under 12 acres	% of acres in holdings under 12 acres	Acres in holdings 12-50 acres	% of acres in holdings 12-50 acres	Acres in holdings 50-100 acres	% of acres in holdings 50-100 acres	Acres in holdings over 100 acres	% of acres in holdings over 100 acres	Acres at Rack Rent	% of acres at Rack Rent
Doddington cum Membris	24	9	13	54	7	29	1	4	3	13	853	61	7	131	15	91	11	570*	67	689	80
Williton	10	8	6	60	3	30	1	10	—	—	145	23	16	53	37	69	48	—	—	—	—
Stogursey and Durborow	36	—	24	66	11	31	1	3	—	—	335	89	27	196	59	50	15	—	—	12	4
Lilstock	16	3	3	18	9	56	3	19	1	6	654	7	1	284	43	203	31	160*	24	184	28
Pawlett	18	3	9	50	7	39	1	6	1	6	323	24	7	143	44	56	17	100*	31	100	31
Loxton	9	1	4	41	2	22	2	22	1	11	332	27	8	67	20	137	41	101*	30	101	30
Total	113	21	59	52	39	35	9	8	6	5	2642	231	9	874	33	606	23	931*	35	1086	41
Miscellaneous Surveys for the Duke of Chandos 1775 and 1781																					
Rodney Stoke (1781)	60	11	35	58	21	35	3	5	1	2	1235	198	16	462	37	203	16	372**	30	372**	30
Compton Martin (1781)	30	14	15	50	11	37	2	7	2	7	715	87	12	296	41	116	16	216	30	—	—
Huntspill de la Hayes (1775)	21	0	12	57	8	38	2	5	—	—	301	77	26	167	55	57	19	—	—	—	—
Catcott (1775)	48	19	28	58	18	38	1	2	1	2	757	110	15	446	59	60	8	150	20	—	—
Total	159	44	90	57	58	36	7	4	4	3	3008	472	17	1371	46	436	15	738	25	372	12
Walcot Survey 1638																					
Walcot (1638)	22	3	10	45	10	45	—	—	2	9	574	79	14	173	30	—	—	322	56	76	13

*All at rack rent; **Estimated acreage of Rodney Stoke Farm; o Not shown.

Source: Stowe Collection, Huntington Library, California and the Survey on Walcot, Somerset County Record Office.

could be held through several leases which could also specify different lives. Although we have no details of these problems for Walcot, the 1781 survey for Rodney Stoke shows that of the 71 separate holdings only 57 were held on whole leases. The rest were on multiple leases or on half or one-third leases (for example, John Amey's nine acres was held on six leases). In all there were 185 leases for the 71 holdings.[5]

Where lifeholders were entrepreneurially minded and, like the Marchants, ruthless to boot, they could extract considerable value from their holdings. In the neighbourhood of Bath, they could even venture into building development on them. However, as table 4.1 shows, most lifeholders occupied quite small acreages. The average size of holdings on the 301 acres of Walcot Lordship, even including the 140 acres held by Widow Sanders, was 20 acres. Without Widow Sanders' holding, the average size of the remaining fifteen holdings was a mere 12 acres. Indeed, on the whole 574 acres in the Walcot Survey 45 per cent of holdings were of less than 12 acres. These holdings were also generally fragmented in fields two or three acres in extent. Generally, these lifeholders could not exploit their holdings by any other than traditional means, that is by farming. But in farming they were trapped by the smallness of their holdings, even though they might produce for the market they had to practice small-scale agriculture. On the other hand landowners could neither consolidate their lands nor maximise revenues from them. And one can well imagine the high sense of injustice the 'owner' of Walcot Lordship and Barton Farm must have experienced every time he passed the farm house of Widow Sanders on her 140 acre farm held on a lease for the lives of her two daughters for which she paid £2 5s. 6d. p.a. instead of the estimated full annual value of £112 5s. 6d., especially if he had occasion to remember that she also held twenty acres of Barton Farm on a lease for three lives at £3 6s. 8d. p.a. instead of its full value of £25.

Whether the then owner was able to achieve his rationalising objective is not clear although one suspects that he did not, for in 1687 the Walcot estate, or part of it, was sold to William Saunders, Gentleman, who appears to have resolved some of the problem by selling land to small farmers. In this way, perhaps, he turned some lifehold into freehold tenancies. This is suggested by the fact that in 1745 Nicholas Hooper, Yeoman, of Walcot possessed about fifteen freehold acres previously bought by his father from William

Saunders.[6] The Walcot Survey in 1740 shows that Hooper held his fifteen freehold acres in six separate pieces.

In 1699 a substantial part of Saunders's Walcot estate, by the marriage of his daughter Mary, passed to Robert Gay, a prosperous barber-surgeon in London. Gay later became MP for Bath from 1720 to 1722 and 1727 to 1734. Gay may have been even more successful than Saunders in turning lifehold tenancies into freehold tenancies or leases for years because, by 1740, much of the estate, especially Barton Farm, was let in consolidated blocks on leases that were easily extinguishable. The rest of the parish was parcelled up into more than 150 small fields, between two and three acres in extent, that were either freehold or let on leases for terms of years. Certainly in 1740 the number of lifehold tenancies was negligible[7] (see Figure 6).

Another way in which lifehold tenancies held by small peasant farmers changed their character during the seventeenth century is suggested by Patricia Croot.[8] Her work on the lowland area of Somerset between the Poldens and the Mendips to the west of Wells shows that there was a growing tendency towards the purchase of the reversion of lifehold tenancies by men outside the farming community. It is her view that by the early eighteenth century, copyhold for lives had moved out of the world of the peasant farmer into that of landed property and land speculation. While this cannot be conclusively shown for all the manors around Bath, especially Bathwick, there is evidence to show that, in Walcot and in that part of the parish of St James outside the city walls, much land was in the hands of non-farmers either as tenants or freeholders by the early eighteenth century. Several examples have already been given, including Richard Marchant, the Corporation, the Freemen, and several individual members of the Corporation. Other non-farming landholders included George Trymme, master clothier, the widow of Thomas Robins of Newton St Loe, who held sixteen acres in 1740 and Constant Trease, a London tailor who held a quarter acre orchard in 1700.

The system of holding land in small parcels on lifehold tenancies and the subsequent fragmentation of landholding probably inhibited efficient and profitable land use. These bars to efficient use became particularly noticeable once the town began to expand. As we shall see, the kind of planned urban development started by John Wood on land belonging to the Barton Farm in 1727 would

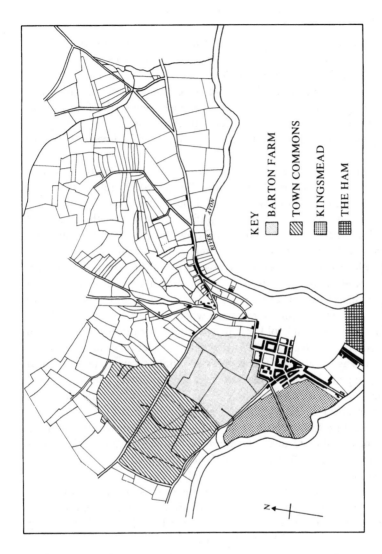

Figure 6 A plan of the parish of Walcot, 1740, Thomas Thorp

have been virtually impossible without the prior extinction of lifehold tenancies and, therefore, without the final extinction of the peasantry in this corner of Somerset. Some of the problems he would have encountered are illustrated by the long negotiations involved in the transfer from Marchant of one-sixth of an acre in the Ham in 1745 and in the delay in the transfer of another piece of ground caused by the need to wait for Ann Collibee and Hester Stone to die.[9]

Landowners were very conscious of this problem of economic rationality. This has already been illustrated by reference to the concern shown by the owner of Walcot Lordship and Barton Farm as early as 1638. It is best exemplified, however, by the actions of the Earl of Bath in the Manor of Bathwick which covered some 600 acres on the river flats on the eastern side of Bath.

Bathwick Manor was in the possession of the Earl of Essex until 1726 when it was acquired by William Pulteney, later the Earl of Bath, in return for £12,000 of a £19,000 debt owed by Essex to Pulteney. At that time almost the whole of the 600 acres was let in small parcels on lifehold tenancies.[10] Pulteney resolved to grant no renewals of the leases and, as they fell in, to let them only for terms of years as leaseholds. The process, inevitably a slow and piecemeal one, replaced one social structure by another and eventually changed the face of the whole area. The first phase, the transformation of the social structure, was well advanced by 1768. In that year all but 160 of the 600 acres had been changed from lifehold tenancies either to direct farming by Pulteney or let out for terms of years. The result was that 440 acres, part of which was let out on leasehold, brought in rents worth £724 per annum while the remaining 160 acres on lifehold tenancies brought in just over £11 per annum. Pulteney's successor, William Johnstone Pulteney, estimated that this 160 acres could eventually be let for £200 to bring in a total rent of £950 for 600 acres.

The second phase which was to change the face of the area through building on a grand scale, to bring the rent roll to over £1,300 on only a fraction of the 600 acres, will be described later. In the meantime we can only imagine the reaction of lifeholders in Walcot and Bathwick, who, like the Widow Sanders in Walcot, saw their livelihoods hanging precariously on the threads of lives growing older and frailer. And we can add our evaluation of their experiences to our other evaluation of the response of the tenants of the Duke of Kingston when they discovered that the new tenant on the Ham, Richard Marchant, had destroyed their rights to herbage on it. But even this might have to be tempered by the realisation that some holders of life tenancies like Nicholas Hooper possibly became freeholders and that if they did they, too, could have shared in the gains to be made by high land prices and speculative building. This is all that we can do because the lives and experiences of most lifeholders, like those of the hundreds of apprentices and the poor of the city, are not in the record. Yet the manner and timing of the extinction of these lifeholders in Walcot and Bathwick was to play an important part in fixing the very shape of the city itself.

While lifehold tenancies appear to have been extinguished in Walcot by 1740 and in Bathwick by the late 1760s, they still predominated in Twerton in the mid-1770s and remained very common in the city itself. There were many small landowners in the city although the Corporation, drawing 46 per cent of its income from rents, an average of £651 per annum in the years 1733–8, was the biggest single landowner. It held four-fifths of all property in the city.[11] Other landowners included public charities such as St John's Hospital and, after 1710, the Duke of Kingston. But there were many others besides. That leases granted by these urban landowners were also leases for lives is illustrated by the fact that in 1716 the Countess of Kingston let the Abbey House and part of Abbey Green to Pierre A Court on a lease for three lives. A Court paid 700 guineas for the lease and agreed to pay a fine of £150 for the addition of further lives. In 1762, when the same site was leased for the development of Kingston Buildings, the lease was for 99 years at £150 per annum. Other examples are the leases purchased by the Duke of Chandos from the Corporation and St John's Hospital in 1726, these were clearly lifehold leases. Other building leases let on lives included John Hall's lease to Thomas Harrison for the building of the first Assembly Room in 1708, this was on four lives at 40s. per annum with a 40s. heriot payable on the death of each life, and George Trymme's leases to various builders after 1707, these were leases for three lives with modest annual rents around 15 to 20s. per annum.[12]

As is shown by the change in the leasing arrangements for the Abbey House ground between 1716 and 1762, there was a tendency for leases for lives to be replaced by straightforward building leases for 42 or 99 years. Since landowners generally had an interest in encouraging building development on their ground, these leases frequently incorporated a clause waiving any claim for rent for one or more years. Indeed, in the case of Kingston's development of Kingston Buildings, the Duke of Kingston received only a peppercorn rent for the first three years. Since the rent of the site was eventually to be £150 per annum it might well be claimed that Kingston had made a direct investment of £450 in the venture. Nevertheless, leases on existing houses granted by the Corporation and St John's Hospital continued to be leased on three lives throughout the eighteenth century. For example, on 19 April 1784 a lease on ground with a frontage of 44 feet on Horse Street was drawn for 99 years or three lives with a fine of £400 and an annual rent of 14s. 4d.[13]

Table 4.2 summarises evidence about the type and duration of leases granted by the Corporation between 1585 and 1769. The persistence of lifehold tenancies within the walls meant that most building and rebuilding was done piecemeal.

Because of its substantial holdings within the city the Corporation clearly had an interest in maintaining and, indeed, in increasing its income from rents and fines within the city itself. It also wished to increase rateable values and to preserve its jurisdiction as, for example, in the matter of the Companies described in chapter 3. Therefore, at the start of the eighteenth century, the Corporation as a body was reluctant to encourage building outside the Borough Walls or to see developed that part of Walcot outside its jurisdiction. This was so despite the fact that the Corporation was itself a substantial landowner outside the walls. In the late eighteenth and early nineteenth centuries it might be said that in the matter of the town commons this reluctance to develop was especially marked and even tinged with outright hostility. This was because property rights were divided. The Corporation, as trustee, administered the affairs of the commons while the use and product of the commons was divisible between all those with Freedom of the city. Any development of the commons therefore, would have enriched several hundred Freemen, possibly at the expense of the Corporation itself. This division of property rights was a constant source of irritation between Corporation and Freemen.

It was not only the development of the town commons that was prevented by the Corporation acting in its own interest as land-

TABLE 4.2 Leases granted by Bath Corporation by type and duration, 1585–1769

	Total	99 years and three lives		Years absolute														
		No.	%	100	99	80	78	77	69	61	60	42	40	39	21	14	11	7
1585–1620	43	23	53	3	–	2	1	1	1	1	3	4	1	–	3	–	–	–
1685–9	90	50	55	–	–	–	–	–	–	–	1	32	–	–	5	–	1	1
1725–9	110	63	57	–	1	–	–	–	–	–	–	34	–	1	12	–	–	–
1765–9	120	114	95	–	–	–	–	–	–	–	–	–	–	–	4	1	–	1

Source: *Lease Book*, GAB.

owner. John Wood's account of how, in 1725–6 the Corporation rejected his grandiose plans for the development of the town is well known. Perhaps less well known is his claim that the Corporation manipulated the rates chargeable by the city's chairmen to influence the siting of new development. He wrote:[14]

> Experience had now convinced the Corporation of Bath that my Scheme for extending the City was far from being Chimerical; their Eyes were sufficiently open in Respect of the West Side of the Town, but they contemned the Design for the East side, as there were no Ways of any Consequence to the Ground; as the Land itself naturally lay low; and as great Part of the Abbey Orchard, by old Motes and Ponds appeared little better than an unfathomable Bog: that Body of Citizens therefore applying to Parliament the latter End of the Year 1738, for a Renewal of the Act mending the Roads leading to the City, for paving, cleaning and lighting the Streets, and for regulating the Chairmen, they, with the Assistance of the Bathonian Monarch, got the Rates of Chairs so settled, that the Fare between the Assembly Houses and New Buildings was double to what it was between those Houses and the Extremities of the old Part of the City; the Effect of which was, that it restrained the progress of Building to the Westward, and encouraged it to the Eastward, to the very utmost of my Wishes.

Since Wood had already made up his mind to build on the east side of the city it is not possible to be sure about the real effects of the Corporation's decision on the rates chargeable by Chairmen. Certainly there does seem to have been a halt to building westwards from Queen Square until the mid-1760s. Against this must be set the fact that the period from 1737 to the early 1750s was generally characterised by a low level of building activity in Bath. After the completion of Wood's development in the Parades in 1749 and of Galloway's Buildings, begun and finished in 1749–50, there were no new major starts until 1754–5 when Wood began the King's Circus and Princes Buildings and the Corporation started Bladud Buildings. Nevertheless, it would be true to say that until 1755 the weight of the Corporation's influence as a landowner was directed towards containing development within the Borough Walls. This attitude reinforced other pressures on builders to build and rebuild in a piecemeal manner and according to individual designs.

One other consequence for the organisation of space in Bath throughout the eighteenth century, arising from the institutions of private and corporate property and the entailing of estates, was that land was rarely sold, and almost never sold in small amounts for purposes of building. It is true that whole estates changed hands; Walcot Lordship and Barton Farm were sold to William Saunders in 1687 and, through marriage, passed to Robert Gay in 1699; the Kingston family came into their Bath estates in 1710; in 1726 the Manor of Bathwick passed into the hands of the Earl of Bath, in payment of a debt; and in 1728, Ralph Allen became a landowner when he bought 135 acres in Lyncombe and Widcombe from Anthony Buckeridge of Ware in Hertfordshire for £4,000.[15] Following such transactions building could only take place if these big landowners, other smaller proprietors and the Corporation would grant building leases to developers or become undertakers on their own account. The fact that the land market was tight is also suggested by the paucity of evidence relating to land sales for building purposes. Indeed, only three examples of land sales which eventually resulted in building are known to me. The first I have already alluded to. It was the purchase by Nicholas Hooper of some fifteen acres of ground in Walcot from William Saunders, a sale that probably took place before 1699. Part of this land was conveniently close to Bath and in 1770 Hooper's great-grandson, a carpenter, built ten houses on the ground in what was to be called Hooper's Court.[16] This is also an example of a small freeholder turned building developer. The second case provides evidence of the great rise in land values as the city grew. This rise in values was almost certainly another reason why land on settled estates was rarely sold. In 1700 Constant Trease, tailor of London and son of a Bath tailor sold a quarter acre orchard for £20 to Joseph Walters. This piece of ground was intermixed with other ground belonging to the Corporation and later known as Milsom's Garden. In 1720 Walters sold the orchard to Richard Harford, woollen draper and Harry Biggs, apothecary, for £170. In 1735 these two sold it to the parishes of St Michael and St Peter and St Paul for £350. The two parishes then built a poor house on it. In the mid-1750s the site of this poor house effectively prevented Daniel Milsom from starting his major building project and it was not until the Corporation had a change of heart about development that they would do anything about it. However, in 1768 under their new powers granted by the Act of

1766, they acquired the site by arranging a transfer of ground and, in 1779, the Corporation let the site for the building of what was to be called Somersetshire Buildings for £130 per annum.[17] The rise in value of this quarter acre site, from £20 in 1700 to £350 in 1735, when it was still a substantial distance from the main centres of building is an indication of the benefits men of property might hope for by the expansion of the city. The rise matches the gain in rents made by Marchant in the Ham between 1709 and the early 1740s. The third example comes from a later period in Bath's development. In 1804 two-thirds of an acre in Burlington Street was sold for building purposes for £840 and seven acres in Lyncombe and Widcombe with four houses already built fetched £2,350.[18]

The shortage of land available for freehold development meant that sites were conveyed to developers and builders either on building leases, generally for 99 years, or on leases in perpetuity for an annual rent. The importance of such rents for landowner's incomes is indicated by the fact that by the mid-1760s about forty acres of the Gay's estate in Walcot brought in an annual rent of £660 and in 1780 the Duke of Kingston's rents in Bath were worth £2,000 per annum and rose to nearly £2,400 in 1801. At this latter date rents of ground granted under building leases in Bathwick contributed over £1,400 to the income of the Pulteney estate.

In summary, it can be said that land unencumbered by lifehold tenancies or customary rights, favourably situated in relation to the attractions of the city and not marred by divided property rights, as was the town common, nor by corporate conservatism as was Corporation land before 1755, was essential for the growth of Bath. Access to land for building depended on the willingness of the landowner to develop it. Therefore, decisions by existing landowners or landholders like Trymme, Marchant, Haynes, Saunders, Hooper, the Duke of Kingston, the Earl of Bath, the Corporation and Robert Gay were crucial. When existing landowners were reluctant or unable to act, outsiders wanting to develop could find life fraught with opposition.

The significance of a landowner's decision to give his land over to urban development was not that it merely provided a site at no capital cost on which to build houses, important though that was. Such a decision also generated a subdivision of property rights in the form of building leases. These building leases could then be used by builders as security for raising mortgage funds with which to build. Protected by the principle of equity of redemption and the safety of an entailed estate, lenders would be willing to advance money on mortgage, and houses could be built without any need of prior capital accumulation by builders. It was in this way that urban development in Bath can be said to have come out of the past and to depend upon the practice and principle of absolute property as well as upon the flexibility with which that principle was treated to create subdivisions of property rights in the form of rights to a share in the income from such property. While this development can be most clearly traced in building projects begun from the late 1720s it was already apparent in the first two building booms in the century. Developments during these booms also show that the first developers in Bath were local landowners. They were not large aristocratic landowners nor corporate landowners, but men of substance in the city and members of the Corporation who were also occupiers of land either as freeholders or on lifehold tenancies.

The first significant building boom in Bath took place between 1704 and 1707. In these years a theatre was built by subscription at a cost of £1,300, a row of houses was completed in the Gravel Walks, the Corporation built a new pumproom and, in 1708, in spite of opposition from the Corporation, Harrison's Assembly Rooms were built at a cost of £1,000. All these developments, except the Assembly Rooms, took place within the Burrough Walls. Even though there had been some earlier building in the Parish of St Michael outside the North Gate and some outside the South Gate, it was only in 1707 that building outside the walls requiring a new way through the Burrough Walls was begun. This development was Trymme Street built at the initiative of George Trymme, gentleman clothier and member of the Corporation.

Trymme, whom I have already mentioned in connection with Richard Marchant, owned land just outside the north wall and it was on this land that he granted building leases for 99 years or three lives. One of the first to take up one of these leases, a 34 foot frontage at an annual rent of 15s. was George Stevens a carpenter. Although there is no record of how he financed the work he straight away built a house. However, the whole development was some time in building. As late as 1718 Trymme granted a building lease for a piece of ground at the western end of the street with a 46 foot frontage to Benjamin Holloway on a lease for 99 years or three lives. On this ground, for which he paid a ground rent of 20*s*. Holloway built three houses, one for himself and two to rent. Two years later Holloway mortgaged all three houses to his brother, Stephen, a London victualler, for £500. In 1723 the mortgage passed to Richard Ford an apothecary and alderman of Bath. In this transaction Richard Marchant was reported to have acted as representative for Stephen Holloway.[19]

These brief details of the Trymme Street development are worth noting because even at this early date they include all the elements but one that were to make the building of Bath possible. First, land held by a landowner in a consolidated block, albeit a small one, and apparently free of encumbrance such as lifehold tenancies. Second, the initiative of the landowner in granting long building leases and, in this case, negotiating for a way through the Burrough Walls. Third, the leases being taken up by craftsmen and professional men with an interest in speculative building. Fourth, the ability of these men to attract mortgage funds, albeit apparently after the event. Fifth, the presence in the city of men like Richard Marchant acting as agents and quasi-bankers for outside investors. Wanting was someone with an over-all vision and the resources, ability and tenacity to pursue that vision against all opposition. In the absence of such an initiative building in Bath in the first quarter of the century was necessarily piecemeal. Trymme built outside the north wall in 1707, Marchant outside the south-east wall in 1710. In the next boom in building from 1717–18, there was further building in Trymme Street but also in Broad Street outside the North Gate, and Thornburgh began his project on Haynes's ground outside the West Gate.

This project of Thornburgh's was, perhaps, the first substantial development of the new style quality housing in Bath. It is also an example of a novel leasing arrangement designed to overcome the problem of a long, probably, lifehold tenancy, and to facilitate building. The site was a piece of ground between Little Kingsmead and Kingsmead fronting north to the Bristol Road. It was, therefore, almost certainly very close to what became Kingsmead Square. This land, like most of the Kingsmead land, was in the possession of Lovelace Haynes, an absentee landlord living in Wallington in Berkshire. In 1716 it was part of a larger area of land, probably Kingsmead, let for two terms of twenty years to John Saunders who was then Alderman and Mayor of Bath. For the first twenty-year term Saunders paid £20 per annum, for the second he paid a different amount. (The figure in the agreement is undecipherable.) In 1719 Lovelace Haynes entered into an agreement with Saunders to relet a part of Saunders' ground to John Thornburgh for the purpose of building three houses, 'fit and convenient for gentlemen of fortune and condition to inhabit in'. In return for the building lease granted to him Thornburgh agreed to pay Saunders a rent of £15 per annum for thirty-eight years and £6 10s. per annum for two years. In addition Thornburgh agreed to pay Lovelace Haynes a ground rent of 30s. per annum for forty years on condition that at the expiration of the forty years, Haynes would grant a further 99 year lease on the payment of a fine of £580 and an annual rent of £16 10s. On these conditions Thornburgh agreed to lay out £1,500 on building the three houses. After Thornburgh had completed two of the houses the title to the land passed to John Stagg, gentleman of Bath, who completed the work. When Stagg died in 1752 he left instructions for the sale of South Sea Stock to pay the fine and renew the lease.[20]

These two projects, Trymme's in 1707 and Thornburgh's in 1719, as well as Marchant's in 1710, show how Bath was beginning to develop in the first two decades of the eighteenth century. As with other evidence in this chapter, they also point to the importance of private property and of notions about absolute property for that development. They show the importance of developmental decisions made by landowners and occupiers of land. They hint, too, at the existence in Bath of experienced financial intermediaries and of an already working financial system and an easy familiarity with the mortgage. They suggest, that is, that men in Bath already lived in a world well practised in the workings of an economic system based on credit. Since, in chapter 2, I have shown the existence of a growing and varied market for the things Bath could supply one might say that Bath was ripe for development and that it would not be long before Chapman's 'Prospects and Landskips' would be transformed for ever, nor long before the battlements themselves would disappear.

CHAPTER FIVE

STOCKJOBBERS AND ENTREPRENEURS

You are extremely kind to Mr. Wood in assisting him with more money, but I can't see what he wants money for now, he having already received thro' your hands and by the notes I have given you, the whole of what is due to him upon the great House he is building except £250 which is not to be paid until the whole is completely finished.

The Duke of Chandos to James Theobald, 1 July 1729

I

The nature of the market described in chapter 2 meant that merely local factors had little importance in influencing the demand for new building in Bath. As a result, the local building booms early in the century, in 1704–7 and 1715–19, corresponded very closely with the timing of similar booms in the country as a whole.[1] The projects undertaken were also carried out in a piecemeal fashion and over long periods of time; the Trymme Street development took at least eleven years to complete. This sluggishness in building plus the fact that the capital sums involved were generally quite small: £1,000 for Harrison's Assembly Rooms in 1708, £3,000 for a lodging house in 1718, £1,500 for three houses 'fit for gentlemen' in 1719, £500 mortgage on three houses in Trymme Street in 1720, suggests that demand for new housing in Bath was still uncertain and that land and money were only cautiously being invested in urban development.

During this time the Corporation certainly husbanded its resources most carefully. Although it extended the markets, improved the Pump Room, widened the bridge across the Avon, obtained improvement Acts and augmented the water supply its expenditure, which averaged £651 per annum in 1701–5, still only averaged £790 per annum in 1716–21, an increase of only 21 per cent over two decades.[2] All of which suggests, in spite of the favourable conditions highlighted by the start of the Trymme Street development, that building activity in Bath in the first quarter of the century was only at a modest country level and in no way peculiar to Bath.

It was not until the mid-1720s that building began to take on a new vitality in which specifically local influences had a part to play, at least on the supply side. One indication of this, in 1725, was that with calls on capital to the amount of £2,240, work began on the Avon Navigation.[3] Authorised by Parliament in 1711, this scheme was designed to canalise and deepen the Avon between Bath and Bristol to cheapen the movement of goods to Bath. Although power to initiate action on the enterprise had been vested in the Corporation the list of thirty-two shareholders included the name of John Hobbs, a Bristol timber merchant who was probably the driving force behind the enterprise. The shareholders also included seventeen citizens of Bath including Ralph Allen and several members of Bath Corporation: Thomas Attwood, plumber and glazier, and John Saunders, landholder and developer. John Hoare of Newbury was the Company's surveyor and Edward Marchant a Quaker of Bath, was its chief mason and contractor.[4] The start of the Avon Navigation some years after the threefold rise in the government's revenue from cards and dice between 1712 and 1720, mentioned in chapter 2, suggests that the entrepreneurial response to the growth of the market for Bath's services was still very sluggish.

It was as part of this response to the market and in the wake of earlier developments that John Wood, then a young man of 22, began work in Bath in 1726. At that time he had no land and no capital of his own and no access to any form of security for raising credit. Indeed, it was only through the good offices of Ralph Allen, one of the shareholders of the Avon Navigation, that he was offered a contract for digging dirt in the 600 yard cut at Twerton just outside Bath.[5] It was under this contract that Wood claimed to have introduced the use of the spade to Bath and, thereby, to have cut earth moving costs by two-thirds, but he could have made little profit or capital accumulation out of his contract; 1½d. a yard in the cut and 3d. in the lock. Because of friction between Wood and Edward Marchant, the main contractor, the Avon Navigation terminated their contract with Wood in mid-July 1727. The Company's minutes record that:[6]

> Whereas some difficulties are like to arise in relation to the lower part of the cut where the lock is to be it is resolved that in consideration of Mr. Marchant putting men to work in the said lock that Mr. Wood be paid four-pence per yard for what is already dug; and that the remaining part of the cut where the lock is to be, be performed by the Proprietors own workmen at their proper charge.

The Company paid the outstanding balance owing to Wood, £55 12s. in September 1727 and work on the Navigation continued without Wood's assistance. His total earnings could not have been large.

Although the first barge load of timber, lead, and meal arrived in Bath from Bristol in December 1727 there was a shortage of funds and much work remained to be completed on the Navigation. As a result the quay and warehouse were not finished until 1729 and it is only from that date that records of traffic on the Navigation are available. These show that the years 1729 to 1732 were good ones for the company. It paid its first dividend of £20 per share in the year 1731-2, and a further dividend of £24 in the peak year 1732-3. During this boom, too, John Allen significantly improved the supply of stone at Bath by building a tramway nearly two miles long to bring stone from his quarries at Combe Down to the Dolemeads on the River Avon. According to Allen's clerk of works, Richard Jones, this tramway cost £10,000 to build while in these early years 1,800 tons of stone was annually exported from Bath. It is very probable that these improvements in transport, the Navigation and the tramway, did much to reduce the cost of building materials at Bath and had an important part to play in stimulating building in the city from 1726 to 1732.

By mid-1727, Wood had clearly failed to establish himself as a satisfactory contractor for the Navigation. He had also failed, throughout 1725 and 1726, to persuade the Corporation and other local landowners, including the Duke of Chandos, to support his grandiose plans for the development of the city. Therefore, it was fortunate for him, as well as for the future development of Bath that, on 23 January 1727, before the termination of the Navigation contract, he had entered into a building contract with James Brydges, Duke of Chandos.[7] This is so because Wood was still an architectural novice without capital. He needed experience and introduction into the world of money and credit without which, for all his plans and building enterprise, he could never have laid one stone up on another.

The building to be constructed under this contract also contributed greatly to the first major building boom of the century in Bath. The story of its building shows in great detail the workings of that world of money and credit already hinted at and shows that the building of Bath, like the demand for it, was part of the general history of England in the eighteenth century. Therefore, since it is certain that a true history of Bath can never be written within a context defined only by local, architectural, and literary history, but that its comprehension and expression must necessarily be formed out of many apparently unrelated events with origins often remote from Bath itself, this chapter, having already begun, will begin again in Dewall in Herefordshire. From there it will pass rapidly to the Duke of Chandos's world of high finance – this is a necessary preliminary to a more comprehensive discussion of the sources of money and of the role of credit in the building of Bath. From there, it will return to Bath itself.

II

Dewall, in 1674, was the birthplace of James Brydges. His father, the eighth Baron Chandos, in direct descent from a family of landed gentry newly created in 1554, had been for a time ambassador of the Turkey Company at Constantinople. His mother was the daughter of a Turkey merchant. He was educated at New College, Oxford. In 1696 he married Mary Lake of Cannons in Edgware, a woman eight years older than himself. In 1698 he was elected MP for Hereford. It was probably through connections arising from his marriage with Mary Lake and his own search after patronage, and in spite of the fact that his father had been 'Warm against King William's reign', that in 1702 he became Surveyor-General to The Board of Ordnance at a salary of £500 per annum and, in 1703, at the age of 29, one of the Commissioners of the Admiralty. In 1705, with Marlborough's support (Marlborough was Master-General of Ordnance as well as Captain-General) he became Paymaster-General to the Forces Abroad, a post which he held until 1713.[8] During his first six years as Paymaster-General £15,374,689 of public money passed through his hands for the provisioning of Marlborough's armies.[9]

As Paymaster Brydges worked closely with Marlborough's Quartermaster-General, William Cadogan. Their letters to each other show their interest in making a profit from the war. There were several ways open to them. One was to use inside information about the next move of the army and then bet on the results of the campaign or buy and sell stock as the prospect of peace looked good or bad. This was a risky business. Brydges lost money on the capture of Charleroi and Toulon while the results of his holdings of refusals stock in anticipation of a rise with the outbreak of peace in 1711, £91,000 refusals of South Sea, are not recorded.

A more certain method of making money arose from exploiting differences between market rates of exchange for currency and the official rate used when making payments overseas to army colonels and others. The essence of the scheme used by Cadogan and Brydges was to buy foreign currencies and gold cheaper than they would sell it to the army in the form of pay and allowances. According to their own accounts they could make a monthly profit of about 2¼ per cent on each transaction, or, about £600 a month. In this manner Brydges took a percentage from all foreign payments made. Also, with the connivance of St John and Arthur Moore he had supplied inferior equipment to the troops defeated in Spain.[10] As a result of his various financial dealings Brydges is reputed to have retired from office with a fortune of some £600,000 and was, in consequence, one of the main targets of the new Tory majority in the House of Commons. The truth of this story is supported by Brydges's surviving accounts.[11] These show that between 1711 and 1713 his turnover with his brokers totalled £685,831. Additionally Sir Theodore Janssen discounted bills for him to the value of £44,609 and his account with his banker, John Mead, goldsmith, totalled £200,409. Altogether his private financial dealings of one kind or another, including his dealings with brokers in Rotterdam, Amsterdam and Antwerp, in these final years of his term as Paymaster-General, gave him a turnover well over £1,000,000. As far as can be established from Brydges's accounts his personal estate held by James Marye, in 1711, included: £19,937 South Sea, £91,000 South Sea Refusals, £6,000 refusals of Bank Stock, £1,795 African Bonds and twenty-five lottery tickets, a total face value of £114,732. When he retired from his post as Paymaster-General and became Earl of Carnarvon in 1714, he held at least a further £84,253 of stock, mainly South Sea, with three other brokers. When one considers that at mid-century 75 per cent of the holders of the public debt held less than £1,000 each and that Alice Carter identified a very large holding as one of a mere £10,000 or over,[12] Brydges's holdings at this early date mark him out even then as an exceptional investor. Since these accounts do not show Brydges's liabilities as well as his assets they are not in themselves a guide to his net worth, for example, his holding of £91,000 South Sea Refusals was also a liability. They simply point to the magnitude of his operations. He was created First Duke of Chandos in 1719.

Chandos's subsequent dealings as an experienced investor on the London stock exchange, as shown in his total annual turnover with some twenty different brokers, is shown in table 5.1. As well Chandos ran five and six figure accounts with his eight brokers in the Low Countries.

As the size of the National Debt in 1719 was £50 million and by 1737 had been reduced to £37 million the sheer magnitude of Chandos's dealings place him in a class of his own. They show that among the active and experienced investors, many of whom Alice Carter believed to have been London based expatriates of Dutch and French origin, there was at least one native born investor skilled in buying and selling in both the London and European money markets on a scale previously unacknowledged. For example, at the end of 1719, when Thornburgh was contemplating investing a mere £1,500 in housing in Bath, Chandos employed the Amsterdam firm of Van Der Leyden and Drummond to speculate in Actions in France to the amount of £35,763! Furthermore, throughout the period 1711 to 1732, he discounted bills to the value of many thousands of pounds sterling drawn on houses in London, Amsterdam, Rotterdam, Brussels and Antwerp, and, in 1720, transferred money to Amsterdam to buy 10,000 guineas to ship to England for sale at a premium. According to his own report and until the ultimate failure of his speculation in Actions he had always made a capital gain from such transactions except for one other loss of

TABLE 5.1 The accounts of James Brydges, First Duke of Chandos, with his Brokers in England, 1711–34

	£
1710–11	110,089
1711–12	248,163
1712–13	327,579
1713–14	111,332
1714–15	113,963
1715–16	356,120
1716–17	252,683
1717–18	284,597
1718–19	353,363
1719–20	1,432,454
1720–1	1,107,147
1721–2	43,297
1722–3	23,021
1723–4	15,893
1724–5	45,242
1725–6	92,253
1726–7	98,588
1727–8	11,906
1728–9	–
1729–30	45,863
1730–1	1,382,112
1731–2	1,322,885
1732–3	157,554
1733–4	96,753

Source: The Accounts of James Brydges with his Brokers, ST 12 vols 1-4, Huntington Library, San Marino, California.

Notes: 1 Without completely reworking Chandos's accounts it is not possible to guarantee that each year conforms precisely to the customary financial year (old-style calendar). Further, the individual accounts are kept in different form for different brokers. In some instances the account deals with a particular operation which overlaps into a subsequent financial year. However, variations from the customary financial year ending in March have been kept to the very minimum. Consequently, the magnitude of each year's operation would not be seriously altered through a reworking of these accounts.
2 These figures exclude Brydges accounts with his bankers.
3 Total number of brokers in England, 20.
4 The totals include all expenditures and disbursements made by all brokers on behalf of Brydges.

£10,000. He was also able to raise a loan in Genoa for £32,915 and, in September 1720, in the depths of the depression following the collapse of the South Sea Bubble, was able to raise a loan of £68,030 in Brussels. As we shall see he also made a fortune out of the South Sea Bubble.

Compared with sums recorded for the early years of the eighteenth century in the accounts of Bath Corporation: average expenditure, £678, average debt, £1,553 in the years 1701–11, Chandos's wealth was clearly immense. (He also used double page book-keeping.) Such a comparison also illustrates the magnitude of personal monetary wealth, built on war, the national debt and taxation which, along with landed wealth, underpinned the consumption of the things Bath could supply; in the mid-1720s Chandos and his wife were among the company at Bath. Moreover, since Chandos was to be an investor in building development in Bath as well as a consumer of it, his accounts can also be used to set out some of the details of the network of financial institutions and means of credit that early in the century facilitated its production.

Chandos always dealt through brokers. Until 1721 his principal agents in England were Sir Matthew Decker, a director of the East India Company of Dutch origin, Moses Hart alias Hartig, probably of Dutch-Jewish origin and James Marye. In his early years he also dealt substantially with Sir Theodore Janssen, a Dutch immigrant in 1680 who became a director of the South Sea Company and declared and forfeited his estate of a quarter of a million pounds in 1720. At one time or another he also ran six figure accounts with Thomas Watts, Richard Shergold, William Maitland and Edward Adderley, and dealt in stock with his bankers John Mead, Bartholomew Zollicoffre and Andrew Drummond. His principal agents in the Netherlands were André Pels et Fils of Amsterdam and Walter Senserf and Son of Rotterdam. In 1720 he ran a large account with Richard Cantillon of Brussels. Thus, Chandos had his own web of credit. He sat at its centre and inundated his agents with instructions about buying and selling, discounting and transferring, lending and borrowing – the Huntington Library in California holds fifty-seven volumes of his correspondence. As he gave his instructions; buying here, selling there, transferring and discounting he generally made it impossible for any one of his brokers, even Sir Matthew Decker with whom he ran six figure accounts from 1715– 21, to determine the profitability of his undertakings or his net worth. The historian is faced with the same problem. To complicate matters he generally settled outstanding accounts with one broker by drawing bills on another or by transferring stock from one to the other. Additionally, in 1712–13, he used John Mead his banker as a broker, and from 1714–15 used Sir Matthew Decker his broker as his banker.

An indication of the magnitude and complexity of Chandos's dealings before 1719 is set out in table 5.2.

TABLE 5.2 Selected items in Chandos's account with Sir Matthew Decker, June 1715 to June 1719

Income (Sale of stock)	£	Selected payments	£
South Sea	24,064	Francis Beaumont	47,154
Malt Tallys	97,605	Marquis de Trivie	116,950
Benefit Tickets	13,965	Pels and Son	174,039
Army Debentures	11,157	Bildstern & Richter	43,607
Debentures & South Sea (mainly South Sea)	123,954	Baron Sohlentholl in Dutch currency for Divers Bills of Exchange	52,380
Capital Annuities	41,247		
Bank Annuities	187,255		434,130
	499,247		
Transfers from other brokers, etc.			
Pels and Son	140,500		
Moses Hart	30,500		
Bank of England	49,500		
Genoa Loan	32,915		
	253,415		
Other	192,600		
Total	945,262		

Source: See table 5.1.

Occasionally Chandos's accounts with his brokers do enable us to break through the screen of discounting and transferring and to observe the completion and sometimes the details of their dealings on his behalf. For example, Edward Adderley was employed by Chandos essentially for one operation dealing in South Sea Stock from November 1719 to April 1720. In that period Adderley bought £91,000 South Sea for £106,905 and sold £76,000 for £105,786. This left Chandos with a balance to pay of £1,119 and £15,000 of stock. Since, at the end of April, South Sea stood at 350, Chandos's capital gain on this operation can be estimated at £51,381. It may well have been this account which gave rise to the rumour that Chandos had in fact made a gain of £50,000.[13] During roughly the same period covered by the Adderley operation Moses Hart carried out five separate buying and selling operations for Chandos the details of which are set out in table 5.3. In this operation the capital gain on £175,000 bought and sold less brokerage of £465 was £7,601 plus £5,000 stock unsold and £10,000 of stock, with a book value of £18,500 transferred to other brokers at the beginning of April.

Chandos's total dealing in South Sea Stock from June 1719 to June 1721 involved the purchase of at least £616,000 stock at £1,207,539. Most of these transactions were completed before the first spectacular rise to 1050 on 24 June 1720. This suggests that he was among the more judicious investors, possibly with inside information. Certainly in his account with Decker he made £100,000 on stock both bought and sold and had remaining £113,000 of stock. In two years he also withdrew £255,510 in cash from his account with Decker. Since he has left no record of the activities he financed from such large cash withdrawals he has made it even more difficult to gauge his net worth and to guess what he was at.

In spite of his wealth the bursting of the Bubble tested Chandos's web of credit to its limits. As late as June 1721 he was in debt to Decker for £37,586. He also owed Thomas Gibson for the purchase of a large quantity of African Stock. Consequently he wrote on 27 September to Richard Cantillon of Brussels:[14]

> Your remarks upon our S.S. project I fear are but too well grounded, and it is incredible the distraction Mankind is in already upon the fall of the Stocks ... The distress that every person of easy circumstances are at present under is inconceivable and I do assure you there is no premium I would not give

TABLE 5.3 Moses Hart's trading in South Sea stock for Chandos, 24 November 1719 to 23 March 1720

Bought	Sold	Capital gain
24 November 1719	16–18 December	
£60,000 @ 121½–125½	£60,000 @ 125¼–125½	
= £74,050	=£75,212	£1,162
20 December 1719–15 January 1720	19–28 January	
£70,000 @ 126¼–135½	£70,000 @ 127½–135½	
= £92,047	= £93,287	£1,240
4 February 1720	25 February	
£30,000 @ 157	£30,000 @ 173–173¼	£4,825
= £47,100	=£51,925	
also 400 @ 154½ for my lady Duchess @ £618		
7 March 1720	7 March	£438
£10,000 @ 174¼–174½	£5,000 @ 183	(on £5,000)
= £17,437	= £9,150	plus £5,000 shares
(note £5,000 cost £8,712)		
16 March 1720	16 March	
£20,000 @ 181–185	£10,000 @ 185	
= £36,600	= £18,500	£400
	Transferred £10,000 @ 185 to Thos. Gibson = £18,500	(on £10,000)
Total purchases	*Total sales*	
£190,000 @ £267,234	£175,000 @ £248,074	

Source: See table 5.1.

for the use of about £40,000 for two months til this calamity is over, and full security into the bargain ... and therefore if you could find anyone I could draw upon in Amsterdam for £2,000 to be redrawn on me again I would deposit a sufficient security and at the same time give what promises I should be desired. My reason is I owe about £70,000 and I doubt but who I owe it may help me to pay it at a time when the Stocks are so low as that the payment of it would be double as much out of my way, if I have no other way of doing it but by selling.

The result of this letter was that in November Cantillon provided a loan of £68,030 to be settled in three months. But this could only have been because Chandos's credit with his principle broker in the Netherlands, Pels et Fils, was good. All in all his dealings with Pels et Fils in 1719–20 had amounted to 1,282,957 Guilders and had been so successful that an entry for a payment to Pels of 100,000 Guilders had the following note attached to it:[15]

> for his Graces generous present to us in consideration of our management in buying and selling of stocks for account of his Grace.
> For the same to our Book-keepers 20,000.

This suggests that Chandos's operations in the Netherlands as well as in England had been successful. However, his accounts do not lend themselves to a simple calculation of their net result. We have to rely on his own summary. On 18 October 1720 he wrote:[16]

> Six weeks ago I was a clear gainer of above £900,000 and now it will not amount to much above £200,000 that I have profited by it, reckoning at the present low rates, but I hope they'll mend.

Unfortunately they did not mend as well as hoped and in June 1721 he was forced to settle his £37,586 debt with Decker by making over £42,260 of stock!

Chandos also had a substantial interest in the African Company and by 1720 he was a member of its governing body, the Court of Assistants, this gave him a considerable stake in the slave trade. In the 1730s he was involved with the York Building Company and the Charitable Society which was essentially a pawn-broking enterprise.

How then are we to assess the outcome of Chandos's dealings during the period from 1711 to 1720 and particularly those that took place in 1719–20? Principally we have to rely on his own testimony, on our knowledge of the scale of his total operation and on the profitability of some of his particular projects. We have already seen how, in October 1720, he claimed to have made a clear gain of £200,000. A few weeks earlier, when requesting the loan from Cantillon, he had also set out some of the details of his personal estate. Valued at the rates then current (28 September 1720) they were: £47,000 South Sea @ 260, £141,000 India @ 190, £10,000 Bank of England @ 190, £40,000 African @ 65, plus three mortgages in land for £80,000, making a total value at par of

£318,000 or, at book value of £515,100.[17] In addition Chandos held landed estates, some of which were only recently acquired, with a capital value of £300,000.[18] Also there was his great house, Cannons, at Edgware, which represented an investment of another £200,000. The only liability that he acknowledged was a debt of £70,000. However one looks at these figures it is difficult to avoid the conclusion that Chandos in 1720 was close to being a millionaire. And this suggests that in a mere seven or eight years Chandos had almost doubled his fortune and lived at a level of luxury rarely if ever matched in England. As well as spending some £200,000 on Cannons, Chandos employed Handel as his composer in residence and built his own private imitation of the Chapel Royal for the performance of the eleven Chandos Anthems composed for him by Handel. According to Macky in 1722 this chapel:[19]

> hath . . . a choir of Vocal and Instrumental Musick, and when his Grace goes to Church, he is attended by his Swiss Guards, ranged as the Yeoman of the Guards; his Musick also play when he is at Table . . . I must say that few *German* sovereign Princes live with that Magnificence, Grandeur and good Order.

Eight years later Young in his *Imperium Pelagi*, written to commemorate the King's return from Hanover and inscribed to the Duke of Chandos, intoned,[20]

> A *Chandos* shines, when other joys are done,
> as lofty turrets, by their height,
> retain the rays of the declining Sun.

The main point arising so far from the Chandos story is that while Chandos inherited some small estate in Herefordshire he laid the basis of his morally and legally questionable fortune in his eight years as Paymaster-General during Marlborough's wars. Subsequently he increased it through speculation in the national debt, manipulation of the institutions and means of credit, and involvement in the African Company and the slave trade. He also invested heavily in mortgages on land, cleared his own estates of mortgages and purchased more land. Chandos was, surely, the personification of the monied interest and an outstanding example of those whose demands created the market for Bath. As well he was one of the entrepreneurs and financiers who were attracted by the profits to be anticipated in satisfying that market.

In all this buying and selling, discounting and transferring, borrowing and lending relatively little cash changed hands. All that was settled were balances which were generally met by bills drawn on other brokers or by the transfer of stocks. Occasionally there was a cash payment. Sometimes, as in 1719–20, there were massive cash withdrawals by Chandos some of which were presumably used to pay bills and settle balances. However, the fact that in September 1720, when Chandos was possibly a millionaire and had run total accounts in London and the Netherlands of well over £1½ million sterling, he needed a loan of £68,000 to settle outstanding accounts reveals something of the relation between his dealings, his realisable assets and his cash transactions. In short, Chandos's whole existence as the 'Princely Chandos' depended upon his ability to use the web of credit. Moreover, he conducted his affairs with his brokers in such ways as to spread a veil over his own web of credit. Therefore, when we come to investigate the nature of those funds Chandos used for his schemes of urban and industrial development, including the Chandos/Wood project in Bath, we are confronted by the problem of origins.

It would certainly be naïve to claim, because Chandos was a landowner and a Duke, that they represent a direct transfer of surpluses from the agricultural sector by a member of the landowning aristocracy; Chandos's rent roll in 1720 was a mere £9,984, which would scarcely have met his expenses at Cannons. In fact, Chandos was still buying and investing in land and engaged in transferring back into agriculture funds accumulated through war, the national debt, taxation and the colonial system. As well as buying land he also engaged in agricultural improvement, and from 1738 to 1742 he imported 2,925 pounds of clover seed for pasture improvement at a cost of £614.

It would be equally naïve to suppose that the credit which supported and facilitated all his activities was underpinned by savings out of income. Rather it was based on capital gains made on the leading money markets of the time, which owed their vitality and growth to the exigencies of war, and was paid for in the last resort by taxation, particularly the land tax, but also by taxes on consumption and by monopoly profits in colonial trade and slavery. Chandos used these resources to finance many ventures beyond the money market.

Chandos's first recorded trading venture arose out of the circumstances of the London money market in 1709 when he laid out £500 with a Captain Phrips to buy silver in the East Indies. He appears to have made a profit of 1,310 Pagodas on this venture. His next was a straightforward trading voyage to Barcelona involving an outlay of £11,323. The result of this venture is not recorded. From 1713 through to 1720 Chandos was mainly involved in building Cannons and speculating on the European money markets. He also built in Cavendish Square in London. After 1721 and until 1730–2 he virtually ceased trading in stock and turned his attention to urban and industrial development. Perhaps he had been affected more hardly by the collapse of the bubble than he cared to admit and was on the look-out for more solid bases for his expensive life style.

His first project was in Bridgwater in Somerset where he acquired an estate in 1721. The fact that this particular project was eventually a failure does not detract from its significance for the general argument in this chapter about the importance of the web and veil of credit for building in Bath. Chandos laid out at least £9,000 in urban redevelopment in Bridgwater; some £1,200 as a third share in a glass factory, and other, possibly smaller sums, in a soap factory and a distillery. All told, Chandos estimated that he invested £15,000 in the Bridgwater development and earned by it an annual income of about £450. His accounts show that the initial investment, which required the construction of houses and workshops and the supply of materials, was almost entirely financed by his agents in Bridgwater drawing bills on Chandos for small amounts, say £100 to £200, and getting them discounted by at least six local 'discount' houses or 'creditmen' although one of them, Pescod, an attorney, lived as far away as Winchester.

The variety and complexity of the sources of Chandos's wealth, a fraction of which he turned into industrial capital in the Bridgwater venture, has already been described. It would be equally valuable to know something of the source of the wealth used by these local 'creditmen' to facilitate the employment of labour, generate a flow of materials and circumvent the problem of circulation time because in one sense Chandos *was* investor of the *last* resort. Nevertheless, the willingness of these six local 'creditmen' to advance possibly locally generated funds for urban and industrial development was itself conditional upon the wealth and creditworthiness of Chandos. And that, as we have seen, was in turn dependent upon the efficient operation not only of the London money market but also upon his ability to exploit the resources of European markets. Who knows whether the failure to raise £68,000 in Brussels in 1720 would have inhibited Chandos's Bridgwater enterprise from 1721–34 and the stimulus he gave to economic activity and employment to the extent of £15,000? And who knows what effect such a failure would have had on his Bath venture and the employment of John Wood?

By the time Chandos had tired of the drain on his resources of the Bridgwater enterprise he also had a large share in the Sun Fire Insurance Office in 1725, a substantial interest in a timber wharf in Scotland Yard in 1730, £591 invested in copper shares and an unspecified investment in the Scottish Fishery Company in 1731, investment in Scottish mines in 1733 and, in 1732–3, in conjunction with local men Thomas Gilbert and William Thynn, had invested nearly £2,000 in lead-mining in Staffordshire. He also prospected for coal in Keynsham. In 1726, Chandos had already turned his attention to Bath.

III

Among the thousands who visited Bath in the spring of 1726 in search of one or all of its pleasures were the Duke of Chandos and his second wife Cassandra, she, suffering from 'hysteric fits', he with a 'twitching upon his nerves (which) still continues troublesome'.[21] In order to be close to the Cross Bath they took lodgings with Mrs Anne Phillips whose lodgings were in the upper storeys of St John's Hospital. As we well know, in 1726 the town was still largely confined within its medieval walls and its lodgings, with floorboards stained with soot and small beer, seemed to be more suited to the needs of Squire Western than to the tastes of the Duke of Chandos; the contrast between Cannons and Mrs Phillips's lodgings scarcely bears thinking about. Chandos found her lodgings objectionable to a 'person of fashion because they did not afford a dressing room and dining room besides the room he lyes in, especially if he has his lady with him'. The furniture was bad and not one of her windows could 'keep out the least puff of wind'. They were, he wrote, 'old rotten lodgings'.[22] He resolved to do something about it, and in the light of the expanding market, to make money into the bargain.

Chandos's first requirement was a suitable site. The one he chose was the one he knew best, Mrs Phillips's lodgings above St John's Hospital (Figure 7). It seemed a good choice. On its eastern side it was within a few yards of the Cross Bath, perhaps the most fashionable of the baths, westwards it fronted the trees and hedges of Kingsmead and gave an unobstructed view across the meadow and river to Beechen Cliff. Chandos began negotiations for the site in May 1726.

The local milieu into which Chandos proposed to intrude was, by contrast with the financial world he was used to inhabit, so small and inward looking that he thought it best to do so secretly and he selected as his agent Richard Marchant, the young Quaker, banker, and member of the Company of the Merchant Taylors with whose career we are already familiar. Chandos wrote to Marchant:[23]

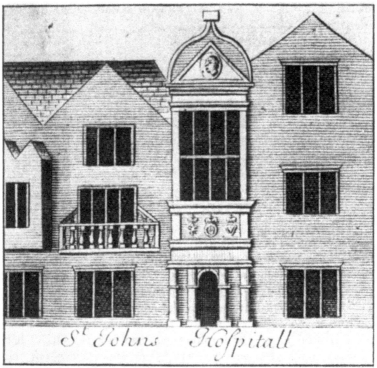

Figure 7 St John's Hospital, 1694 – detail from Gilmore's map

I have, such an opinion of your sincerity and friendship that I shall make no difficulty of letting the assignment be drawn to you. Indeed it is very proper it should be so, and that it should not be known to any one that I am in the least concerned in the purchase, not only by reason of the obstruction which would arise to the buying of this if it were believed to be for me, but like-wise the difficulty I should meet with in buying the other house you mention, and which I have not only had for some time in my thoughts but likewise another that joins to it, inhabited I think by an old Batchelor, and which has the privilege of a Door into the Garden of the house you are now buying. These two houses if I could get in, and live to put into execution the design I have in my thoughts, I should be able to make a very handsome and convenient place of and such a one as would render the Purchase very advantagious.

The fact that Chandos felt obliged to negotiate secretly for the site is additional evidence both of the problem of land and of the importance of subsequent decisions and initiatives by existing landowners including, of course, the Corporation itself. In other letters to Marchant, Chandos indicated that he hoped the main site was all freehold and raised questions about the terms of the leases under which other areas of ground were held, particularly the site of the 'old Batchelor's house'. His letter illustrates the problem of development on ground held on lifehold tenancies. He wrote:[24]

You say the old Batchelor's house is city land, and has 28 years to come off the lease that is upon it; and that at the expiration it is to be renewed for a very small matter. Pray let me know how much that small matter is, whether the fine is limited, or whether it is in the power of the City to demand what fine they please; For if it is there's no doubt but they'll make a demand answerable to the improvement of it. The others you say are full stated, I suppose you mean by this that they have three lives upon them. Pray let me know, whether it would not be easy to get the three lives changed if I should desire it hereafter.

In a further spate of letters Chandos questioned the powers of the Corporation to grant 42-year leases, raised the problem of water supply, and expressed doubts about the ability of local people to draw up the necessary agreements. Finally, in October 1726, Chandos was satisfied and he completed the transfer of several lifehold leases from the Corporation and St John's Hospital for which he paid £3,250.[25]

Chandos's accounts show that £1,000 of the total purchase money was paid through an advance from Charles Stuart, Doctor of Physick and broker of London in October 1726. In return Stuart received a £100 annuity secured on Chandos's property in Bath. Stuart was also Chandos's broker dealing with his holdings in the Sun Fire Insurance Office. In August 1727, as part of the repayment of an £1,800 mortgage on his Bridgwater estate, Chandos also granted an annuity of £80 to Mrs Susanna Tynte of Nempnett in the County of Somerset and shareholder in the Avon Navigation, also to be secured on the Bath property.[26] Since this was payment for a debt already incurred it cannot be regarded as an advance of purchase money for the Bath site. Therefore, £2,250 remains unaccounted for. Such an amount is probably represented by bills concealed in his £98,000 account with his brokers for that year. These annuities also show that even when building Chandos was attracted by a little speculation.

Even before he had completed the purchase of the leases for the site Chandos was on the lookout for, 'a mason on the spot, who is master of his business, and would also undertake the stonework by the great.'[27] He also sought information from Marchant about the day wages of masons, carpenters and labourers and the on-site per foot of stone ready wrought. Although Marchant recommended several local builders such as William Killigrew who built the Blue Coat School in 1722 and St John's Chapel in 1723, and Benjamin Holloway who had built in Trymme Street and in Bridgwater, Chandos finally contracted with John Wood in January 1727.

It is clear from Chandos's correspondence that the over-all concept for the building in Bath was his and that as a contractor Wood had to work to Chandos's specifications and under supervisors appointed by Chandos. Indeed, Chandos's correspondence with one of these supervisors, James Theobald, and with Wood himself make it clear beyond all doubt that everything Wood planned had to be submitted for Chandos's approval. For example, in April 1727 Chandos wrote inquiring the fate of ten water closets he wanted installed and in May he demanded that Wood supply him with, 'a perfect plan of the buildings with the alterations proposed annexed to it.'[28] In August, when the first stage of the project was still unfinished, Chandos issued an ultimatum to Wood:[29]

> I desire therefore you will stay till the whole is finished and keep the men close to their work; for upon the well doing of this will depend in a great measure your being employed in other business hereafter.

Since Wood was desperately in need of employment he did stay with it and Chandos did employ him on the next stage of the project although only after he had rejected Wood's original plans on the grounds that they were too expensive, there was only one staircase for sixteen rooms, the kitchens and pantries took up all the lower storey and, being on the side overlooking the Burrough Walls, blotted out the view, and because:[30]

> You have likewise not contrived one water closet to the whole house, though the want of them is increasingly inconvenient, especially in a house where it is to be supposed there may frequently be lodgers who are out of order and not able to stir far out of their chamber.

When the work eventually got under way Chandos wrote complaint after complaint; work on the first stage was unfinished, window shutters were badly hung, the sewer was scarcely started, rubbish was not cleared, the chimneys smoked, unpinned tiles blew off the roof and the water closets were so badly constructed that after leaking and smelling they had to be removed and outhouses installed in their place. At one stage Chandos wrote to Wood:[31]

> If therefore you do not set about and complete (the alterations) without further loss of time, I will employ some other workman and you shall not receive any more money from me till these are done.

Wood had many excuses. Above all he had labour trouble. His workmen were frequently described as rude, troublesome and noisy. Their workmanship was not always of the best and Wood had difficulty supervising them. On the other hand he was not the most prompt of paymasters; on one occasion he was arrested by the city bailiff, apparently for underpaying a mason, and on another told a mason to whom he owed £50 to write to Chandos for it. On this occasion Wood was firmly told that this was none of Chandos's business, 'His Grace having to do with you only and not with the people employed by you.'[32] Perhaps the main reason for Wood's troubles was that he had taken on too much work; by this time he was also employed by Humphrey Thayer on his Assembly Rooms and by Ralph Allen on extensions to his house near the Abbey Green. Chandos was aware of Wood's other undertakings and expressed the hope that they would not hinder his work on the Chandos project. At the same time, and, no doubt to Wood's uttermost consternation, Chandos appointed John Strahan the *'pirate'* architect, to report upon Wood's work before it was passed for payment!

On the other hand Chandos also pulled strings to facilitate the work. He wrote to the Mayor to seek his co-operation with Wood, particularly in regard to extending the apertures affording light to the basement kitchens and getting consent to carry the sewer along the Burrough Walls into the Bath gout. When Wood was arrested by the bailiff, Chandos threatened to complain to the House of Lords about breach of privilege. He declared, 'I'll move to have this Attorney laid by the heels for his insolence'.[33] Above all, over three long years, he honoured his obligation as investor of the last resort.

As work was passed as complete Wood received periodic payments by drawing bills on Chandos, generally at twenty days, and receiving cash from several discount 'houses' or what Marx referred to as 'creditmen'. In this way he was paid most of a total of £7,875 (Figure 8).[34] One of these 'creditmen' was Richard Marchant. However, although Marchant had been important to Chandos as his agent in negotiations over the site, he played only a small part in facilitating construction on it. In fact he appears to have paid only two bills to the value of £800. Moreover, he charged his 1¼ per cent discount rate to Chandos. Finally, on 16 October 1728, when he refused to accept a bill drawn by Wood on Chandos, Chandos was very annoyed and sought no more accommodation from him for the purpose of building. Earlier in the same year Wood had also received £200 from Humphrey Thayer Esq., the London Commissioner of Excise and property developer for whom he was also working, and £100 from a Mr George.

For all that these men were important to Wood at this early stage in his career, the main agent paying Wood's bills on Chandos was James Theobald. Theobald was a London timber merchant connected with Chandos through his interest in the Scotland Yard timber wharf. All told, over a three-year period, Theobald paid such bills to the value of £5,959. In this same period Theobald also lent Chandos £1,733 and paid out a further £7,177 on promissory notes drawn by Chandos.[35] In view of these figures there can be little doubt that the principal 'creditman' financing and therefore facilitating the Chandos/Wood development in Bath was Theobald. In fact Chandos's letters to Theobald throughout 1729, by which time, to Chandos's consternation, Wood had also embarked on other building, show that Theobald was accommodating Wood at a rate which Chandos thought more than generous. Chandos was particularly upset by some shoddy work, by Wood's inability to install the ten water closets according to specification, and by the fact that the landlady of the first house, Mrs Phillips, wished to have nothing further to do with Wood in the final finishing of the house. He wrote to Theobald:[36]

> You are extremely kind to Mr. Wood in assisting him with more money, but I can't see what he wants money for now, he having already received thro' your hands and by the notes I have given you, the whole of what is due to him upon the great House he is building except £250 which is not to be paid till the whole is completely finished.

But Theobald did more for Wood than guarantee ample and regular payment, important though that was. This whole period of building had been a most vexing time for Chandos; on top of every other irritation Wood greatly annoyed him by living in a small house on the site, which Wood had built for himself without Chandos's authority. It was Theobald who smoothed Wood's path. In face of Chandos's anger Theobald intervened on Wood's behalf to persuade Chandos to keep him at work and even to pay him at all. Chandos himself made this perfectly plain to Wood. His letter, important for the light it throws on Wood's early career and on Theobald's place in it, is also worth reading in full as it illustrates the management function carried out by Chandos throughout the whole building development:[37]

Cannons 23rd November, 1729.

Mr. Wood   Sir,
    It was so long since I heard from you before I received your last of the 19th that I took it for granted something or other

had happened to you and I am glad to find your sickness is pretty well gone off, since I hope you will apply yourself with some diligence to make an end of what remains still to be done about the Buildings. Mrs Phillips is so exceedingly unwilling to have you have anything more to do about hers, that I cannot decline gratifying her in it, and therefore the remaining Business you have to do will be so much the less for I would not have you meddle with any part of her house except the Stone Steps which ought to have been finished long ago, and when I was down at Bath and saw them in that shameful Condition you Promised should be done in three or four days time, I mean the fixing them in Sockets and running them in Lead. I confess when I consider in how scandalous a manner the greatest part of that Work has been performed, I cannot blame her for desiring to have nothing more to do with you. It was this Resolution I had once taken myself, and had it not been for Mr. Theobald I should have imployed other Workmen to have finished what was still left, and have left you to have got the remainder of your money as well as you could. But Mr. Theobald did ingage if I would overlook what has past and give you suitable Encouragement (not withstanding that you could demand no more than what is allowed by your articles) such as the goodness of your work should intitle you to, he would engage you should without loss of time proceed to finish what still remains to be done, and do it in a manner truly workmanlike and to my satisfaction. It was on this promise I allowed him the liberty of supplying you with the last £400 and therefore I think I am very well intitled to what you tell me, that you will not fail to oblige me to the utmost of your power, especially since I desire nothing more than that you'll behave yourself like an honest Man which I cannot say I think you have hitherto done. You tell me Mrs Degge's house is so full she can't suffer your Workmen to come in to finish what still remains upon your contract, but certainly you must be mistaken in this, for besides my Lord Castelmaines's family, I do not know of above one or two lodgers she has. However should that be the Case the Season of the year will quickly make her House empty enough So that this will be no hindrance to you long, but there are several of those works that Mr. Shepherd has put down in his Paper which may be done not withstanding the lodgers being there, as the clearing the two yards of the Rubbish and paving them, and the whitewashing and doing what is necessary to be done about the wall carried up by Mr. Jennings.

I am very well pleased with the hopes you give me of your being able to agree with Mrs Chivers for her Garden. This would be an acceptable Service if it could be brought about and that I could have it for £200, more than which I would not give, but I tell you truly I question very much whether you will be able to effect it, for by what I have seen under her hand She has not such regard for you as gives me Room to hope She would be persuaded by you to come into any such Agreement.

>   I am Sir
>   Yours etc.

In view of all the available evidence the London timber merchant James Theobald must be granted an important place in the history of the building of Bath nowhere acknowledged by Wood and not generally recognised by historians. One might well argue that Theobald's intervention on Wood's behalf and his 'kindness' in supplying him with money over and above that required by Chandos was a crucial, indeed, a necessary condition for Wood's success with Queen Square, which he undertook in 1728 with no capital of his own, and therefore, for his ultimately successful career as the principal architect-developer in the most perfect of Georgian cities.

Of course Theobald's security for giving credit to Wood so lavishly and over so long a period of time and, indeed, for advancing even more to Chandos himself, was undoubtedly Chandos's own position as developer and investor of the last resort; a position itself dependent upon Chandos's whole career as the leading stockjobber of his day dealing in money and accumulating wealth.

There is, therefore, a real problem of identification in any attempt to specify that part of Chandos's fortune which might be thought of as settling Theobald's account and providing the immediate source of Chandos's investment in urban development in Bath. Had he been able to complete the sale to Theobald's father of a farm at South Mims for £1,700 it would have been possible to talk of a substantial direct transfer from investment in agriculture into urban development. Certainly this was Chandos's intent. Unfortunately the sale of the farm fell through because Theobald expressed some doubts about Chandos's clear title to it. As a result Chandos was pressed for money to repay Theobald and he kept him waiting for the balance of his account until the end of December. Chandos wrote:[38]

> I am much concerned I should be anywise instrumental in your being under this difficulty, but I must at the same time say it is chiefly owing to the breaking of the purchase you had agreed to make ... which has very much straightened me by reason of the expense I have put myself to in expectation of that sale's taking effect.

In July 1729, almost as a last gesture to pay in kind, Chandos offered an Advowson at three and a half years purchase to Theobald to settle his account for that year and to pay the balance due to Wood. This, too, was rejected by Theobald.

It is a matter to regret that Theobald's accounts do not indicate the source of the funds eventually used by Chandos to settle his account with Theobald. What they do show is a series of paper transfers to Theobald from several of Chandos's brokers: in 1729, £800 from Thomas Gibson; in 1730 and 1731, £1,086 by bills on Walter Fergusson, probably a land agent or attorney of Bridgwater; £739 by bills on Messrs Nalder and Baily, and £706 by bills on Thomas Watts. All of these men were part of Chandos's web of credit; Thomas Gibson was one of his principal brokers dealing in African Stock, he lent Chandos £22,688 from 1728 to 1731, Thomas Watts was also one of his brokers, from 1729 to 1730 he dealt mainly in York building Stock for Chandos and bought and sold £159,000 stock at £35,328 15s. 0d. for a gain to Chandos of £4,465 8s. 6d. These transfers from these brokers suggest that Chandos settled his account with Theobald by drawing upon his connections, credit, and capital gains made on the London money market.

Consequently, in this fragment of the web of credit the strands were: Theobald, Marchant (and others) to Wood; Gibson and Watt (and others) to Theobald; Theobald to Chandos; Chandos to Theobald, Marchant (and others). Theobald was a London timber merchant, Marchant a banker and merchant taylor, Chandos a successful financier, Gibson, Watt and others were London brokers and bankers, stockjobbers all. Chandos, of course, sat at the centre of this web of credit feasting on capital gains, differences in exchange rates, interest on stock, land rents, and rents on urban property, and sending out bills, promissory notes and cash to all the others and more besides. The act of production he, his 'creditmen' and stockjobbers collectively facilitated at a cost of £7,875 was the construction of two very large lodging houses designed to exploit the luxury trade in Bath. Since Fergusson was a Bridgwater man and Marchant a man of Bath there was, in building as in the purchase of the site, a provincial as well as a London strand in the web of credit.

Furthermore, while the Chandos/Wood project was under way, Theobald also acted as the financial intermediary between Ralph Allen in Bath, and the governors of the newly built St Bartholomew's Hospital in London. In this capacity Theobald also received and held monies due to Allen in Bath.[39] Since, in this case, the investors of the last resort included the Earls of Oxford and Orrery, several members of the banking families of Hoare and Child, as well as Chandos, the web of credit holding together the Chandos/Wood operation in Bath begins to appear as confusing as the pattern of the country roads along which Allen delivered the cross and bye-posts; it would be a brave man, indeed, who would claim to identify the precise source of the funds which, through the web of credit, made possible Wood's first building in Bath.

The third and final stage of the redevelopment was the fitting and furnishing of the newly built lodging houses.[40] The accounts for this stage (Figures 8a and b), detailed by their keepers and tenants, Anne Phillips and Jane Degge, show that here, too, Chandos tried to keep his eye on every penny; $2d.$ for one ladle, $2\frac{1}{2}d.$ for '6 yard of list and half hundred of tacks,' $4d.$ for one 'rowling pin', $5d.$ for blue thread, and $1s.$ for '3 skewers and a lark spit.' The cost of fitting and furnishing Anne Phillips's house, from 1726–30, was £2,315, of Jane Degge's, 1729 to 1731, £986. Total £3,301. Of this £800 was met by bills drawn on Chandos and paid by Marchant, £270 paid by unidentified discount houses, and £50 paid by Andrew Drummond, Chandos's London banker. Of the remainder, £1,649 was paid by various Bath rents payable to Chandos and either collected by or remitted to Anne Phillips and Jane Degge, including either the whole or part of the rents of the lodging houses due to be paid by the two women.

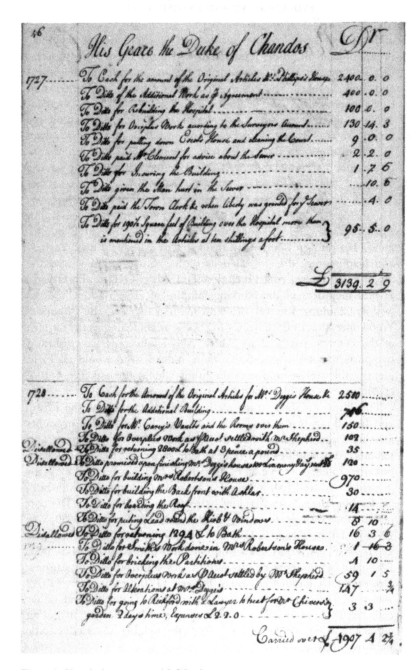

Figure 8 Chandos's accounts with Wood

Pr   Contra   Cr ⁴²

1727	By Cash Received in London	100 . 0 . 0
	By Ditto in D.º	400 . 0 . 0
	By Ditto in D.º	500 . 0 . 0
	By Ditto in D.º	600 . 0 . 0
	By Ditto in D.º	200 . 0 . 0
	By Ditto at Tunbridge	150 . 0 . 0
	By Ditto at Bath	150 . 0 . 0
	By Ditto in London	200 . 0 . 0
	By Ditto in D.º	20 . 0 . 0
	By Ditto in D.º	100 . 0 . 0
	By Ditto in D.º	150 . 0 . 0
	By the old Materials	242 . 16 . 6
	By Deductions for Deficiencys in the Work	15 . 19 . 10
	By Ballance	310 . 6 . 5
		£3139 . 2 . 9

April 13.ᵗʰ 1728

Received of His Grace the Duke of Chandos by the hands of M.ʳ
James Theobald the Sum of Three hundred pounds, being in full of the
Ballance of this Account, and in full of all other Debts Dues & Demands
whatsoever As witness my hand ———— John Wood

1728 June 22	By Cash to Humphry Thayer Esq.ʳ	200
	By Ditto to M.ʳ George	100
	By Ditto to M.ʳ Theobald	700
..g.. 17	By Ditto to M.ʳ Theobald	300
Octob.ʳ 2	By Ditto to M.ʳ Marchant	650
1728/9 Jan.ʳʸ 27	By Ditto to M.ʳ Theobald	200
1729 May 10	By Ditto to M.ʳ Theobald	300
30	By Ditto for a Note of hand	300
July 15	By Ditto to M.ʳ Theobald	150
July 16	By Ditto to Ditto	500
Octob.ʳ 30	By Ditto to Ditto	400
Jan.ʸ 7	By Ditto to Ditto	250
May 15	By Ditto to Ditto	100
June 26	By Ditto to Ditto	150
July 13	By Ditto to Ditto	94
	By Ditto paid by M.ʳ Deggs to any Carpenters	13 . 13
	By Work that remained to finish for M.ʳ Deggs's Water Closets	9 . 15 . 6
	By the Lead of the Water Closets	30 . 7 . 8
	Carried over	4447 . 17 . 2

His Grace the Duke of Chandos... Dr

Brought over £1907 .. 2¾

To Cash for four several Estimates for Houses in London ....

To Ditto for 14 Sq. feet of building in Mrs Phillips's House at 10d ⅌ foot which has not yet been charged in any account ...... } Nil

To Ditto for reducing £2709: 13: 7 to Bath on account of Mrs Phillips's House .... } Nil

To Ditto for making Dark Closets, altering Doors & Windows, & for making several conveniences about Mrs Phillips's House & for Rings to Window Shutters &c cost me ...... } Nil

To Ditto for the Extra Cost of Mrs Phillips's Water Closets, Stone Stairs & Bog houses £31. 10 being the prime Cost ...... } Nil

To Ditto for Ashlar above ground in Mrs Dagge's house, Sash Windows in the Cellar Story instead of two Eight Windows, more windows than agreed for, Dark Closets, Rings to open Shutters &c &c Iron Lead on the House more than agreed for, altogether cost me £62: 3: 6, besides the Rings to ye Doors are better than ye Article & here is 1835: 3 f of London crown Glass in ye Windows, instead of Bristol Glass ye difference in price is 4d ⅌ a foot, comes to 36: 5: 7½ } Nil

To Ditto for better performance of Stairs in Mrs Dagge's House & several other Works in that House, & in Mrs Robertson's House the Stairs, Window Shutters & several other things are much better done than the Article directs .... } Nil

Deduct the 3 Articles disallowed at Supra amounting to ... 171 3 6

August 31. 1730   £1736 .... 0 ¾

I do hereby acknowledge to have received of His Grace the Duke of ...... things in full of all manner of Debts, Dues, & Demands whatsoever due ...... in full of all other Demands whatsoever. And I do hereby acknowledge ...... Shillings & one farthing as a Gratification made me by the said Duke ...... with the treatment I have received from the said Duke I have ...... to ......

Witness R. Allen

Per Contra Cr.

Brought over £ 1447 17 2

By Cash abated upon the ballance of Account for Mr.
Phillip's House 10: 6: 5
Deducted for Deficiency's in Mr. Phillips's House .. 15: 19: 10
                                                    26: 6: 3

Mr. Shepherd's Deduction for Old Doors, Casements,
Sashes & Pantyles for Wainscot that is wanting
for which Basement amounts to .... £ 21: 4: 4
Ill performance in plaistering not above .. 5: 0: 0
                                      26: 4: 4   52 10 7

1730 Aug.t 31   By Ballance paid to John Wood 1500 7 9
                                                                              235 12 11½

£ 1736 ---- 8¾

Received the Sum of Two Hundred Thirty Five Pounds, twelve & Eleven pence halfpenny
to me from the said Duke on account of Work done for His Grace at Bath or elsewhere
I have received of the said Duke the further Sum of One hundred & fourteen Pounds Seven
for my trouble about the said Works. And in witness of my being fully satisfyd
him a General Release, bearing date the same day with this.
                                                                                                      John Wood

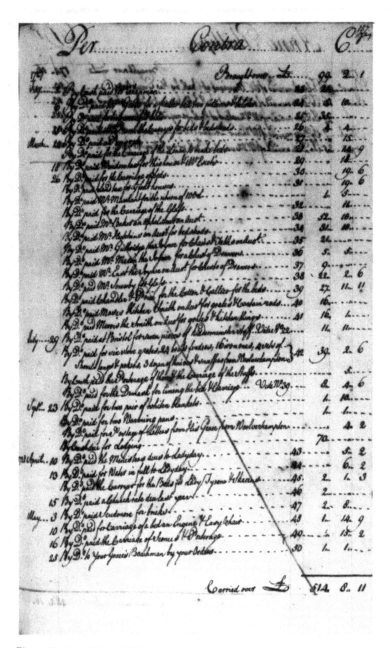

Figure 8b Part of Anne Phillips's account for furnishing Chandos Buildings

The difference between the rent paid to Chandos and the income of the women from lettings was their gross profit. According to Chandos, Anne Phillips, whose rent was £300 per annum, would be able to let forty rooms at 10s. per week each and seven kitchens and seventeen garrets at 5s. per week each. For a twenty-week season she should clear at least £100. Lettings out of season would be all gain to Mrs Phillips. Mrs Degge's rent was also £300.[41]

Since the development also incorporated one other smaller house let for £80 per annum and Carey's house and wine vaults let for £74 10s. 0d. per annum the total rent anticipated by Chandos was £754 10s. 0d. This represents an anticipated return on investment of 5.2 per cent. However, if the two annuities of £180 charged to the properties were to be deducted from the gross income this rate would fall to 3.98 per cent, conversely a higher rate of return would have resulted if both the annuitants had dropped dead the next day. Since a return of 3.98 per cent was 1 per cent better than the yield on Consols and slightly better than the return on Bath Corporation Bonds in 1730 Chandos's notional return was a reasonable one although he could have earned 1 per cent more by putting his money out on mortgages to other speculating builders.

Subsequent developments led to continued wrangling over management with Anne Phillips while Jane Degge's house, much to Chandos's surprise, did not yield £300 per annum. Finally, in 1734, Chandos sold Mrs Phillips lodgings to a London man for £3,800. The cost of this part of the development had been £7,601.

In summary the cost of Chandos's building venture in Bath from 1726 to 1731 was:

	£
Cost of leases of land	3,250
Cost of building	7,875
Cost of building and furnishing	3,301
TOTAL	14,426

Identified direct sources of finance were:	£
Bills paid by Theobald, timber merchant, London.	5,959
Bills paid by other brokers and bankers, mainly London.	770
Bills paid by Marchant, merchant	

	£
taylor, banker, Bath	1,700
Capital sum paid for annuity of £100, Stuart, apothecary, broker, London	1,000
Chandos's note of hand	300
Sundry cash payments	532
Rents remitted in Bath	1,437
Rents collected in Bath	212
Sale of materials	321
Deficiencies in building	42
TOTAL	12,273

Most of these identified direct sources of finance were underpinned by the wealth of Chandos and by the web of credit, provincial, national and international upon which he could draw; the methods of finance integral to his activity in these markets such as, bills of exchange, promissory notes, and annuities; and the accumulation of wealth through war, the national debt, taxation, and the colonial system and slavery upon which these money markets, financial methods and institutions were built. Furthermore, London merchants, bankers, brokers and discount houses were more deeply involved in this development than local men. In fact 66 per cent of the direct sources of finance came from London men.

To the extent that what I have written gives a true account of the Chandos/Wood development, it is probable that the Theobald connection and the liberal way Theobald dealt with Wood gave Wood experience and confidence in the London as well as provincial money markets at a time when he embarked on the Queen Square project with no visible stock of capital of his own. In this connection it is worth noting that it was the lack of £4,000, either as capital or as a fund of credit upon which to draw via bills of exchange, that compelled Wood to begin the project on a sloping rather than a levelled site as he had intended.[42] The fact that from 1727 to 1730, Wood also worked as a contractor for Ralph Allen and Henry Thayer does not weaken this view about Wood's necessary 'apprenticeship' in money matters. Thayer, a London apothecary and property developer also advanced money to Wood by accepting a bill for £200 drawn on Chandos. This advance, too, suggests that

London money-men were important in this early stage of Bath's development. Further, the probability that John Strahan's development of Kingsmead Square, Beauford Square and Avon Street, also begun in 1727, was financed by the Bristol timber merchant, John Hobbs, strengthens the view advanced here about the importance for building development in the first big boom of the century of initiatives and finance external to Bath.

Moreover it is difficult to avoid the conclusion that the Chandos/Wood development in Bath was supported by an elaborate and extensive web of credit. In this respect it was similar to Chandos's Bridgwater development. This web was also a veil of credit. At every linking point were those 'creditmen' described by Marx. These men: Marchant, Theobald, Gibson, Watt and others were links between Chandos as possessor of wealth that was not yet capital and capital proper, and between this form of wealth and building development in Bath. Since Chandos was also a consumer as well as producer in Bath, and dependent upon private property and the structure of credit built on it for his performance in both roles, one might regard him as the epitome of those elements at the heart of England's and, therefore of Bath's development during the eighteenth century; private property, consumption and credit.

To this it might be objected that Chandos was so rare an individual as to be almost unique in his own time both as consumer/producer and as financier. Yet, millionaire that he probably was, the Princely Chandos appears only as a known peak in a range of men of great wealth – Marlborough and the Earl of Bath among them – whose large fortunes were surrounded by other large though smaller fortunes. For example, an incidental but significant aspect of the London money market revealed by Chandos's accounts is that since his accounts with some twenty brokers frequently reached six figures and his total accounts went well beyond the million pound mark in 1719–20 and 1720–1, his London and European brokers, with these six figure accounts as only one of several, must also have operated on a scale rarely if ever acknowledged by historians. We have already seen how Sir Theodore Janssen admitted to an estate worth about a quarter of a million pounds. Yet Chandos's correspondence suggests that André Pels et Fils, at £800,000 was worth almost as much as Chandos himself.[43] The magnitude of the network of credit and wealth implied by these brokers' accounts is very large indeed.

Nevertheless, while it may be that there were some rich men in England almost as wealthy as Chandos, it may still be said that it was the conjuncture of the world of money and urban building highlighted by Chandos's dealings in Bath, that was atypical. Atypical, perhaps, because urban development, like capital accumulation generally, was the achievement of small men using their own resources. According to this argument builders engaged in urban development built at their own expense with little, if any initiative from landowners or involvement with the London or national money markets. This argument has some merit. Nevertheless, it could lead to a blurring of the essential points about Chandos's story. Apart from the question of who was or who was not 'typical' in the early eighteenth century; Chandos, or Marchant, or Theobald, or Allen, or Wood, or any of the scores of other characters in this account of Chandos's building project in Bath, one essential point is that what Chandos did in using the financial institutions available to him and in building his material and economic life on a web of credit was 'characteristic' of his time. How characteristic is shown by the part played in the web of credit by Chandos's brokers, twenty of them; by the six creditmen in Bridgwater; by Marchant in Bath and Theobald in London; by Harrison and Allen; by the Governors of St Bartholomew's Hospital, even by Mrs Frances Vaughan, and in a general way by the drawing of bills worth £2 million as early as 1688–9 (an amount then equal to the notes of the Bank of England in circulation.) Chandos's story simply points to an economic system already built on credit and to a widespread acceptance of it in a society as apparently isolated as Bath at the turn of the seventeenth and eighteenth centuries.

The other essential point about the Chandos story is that it shows how one of Chandos's creditmen, James Theobald, not only persuaded Chandos to keep Wood at work, but also accommodated Wood at a rate beyond that required by Chandos at a crucial stage in Wood's career and in the building of Bath. He, too, was part of that general web of credit. He derives his significance for Wood and urban development in Bath only in that context.

As for the general question of the conjuncture of the world of money and urban development in Bath I hope to show in chapter 7 that what Chandos did in 1727–30 was more than matched by William Pulteney fifty years later. The conjuncture at a more modest level is the theme of the rest of this chapter. I take up the story again at the point where John Wood became an architect-developer on his own account.

IV

The importance to Wood and the Bath townscape of Robert Gay's decision to lease land to him for the development of Queen Square has already been emphasised (Figure 9). So, too, has the fact that the land leased was on that part of Gay's estate, Barton Farm, from which the peasantry had long been removed and on which land appears to have been let in large parcels at rack rents. It was also fortunate that Gay's descendants, none of whom had an interest in setting up as developer on his own account, were greatly interested in increasing their income from the estate. The result was that between 1728 and 1766 they let some forty acres on long building leases to John Wood and his son for annual rents totalling £560. In this manner they gained an eightfold increase in the annual value of their land. Indeed, building in Bath so increased the value of Gay's land that in 1765 the family was able to lease a further five acres of their estate to another group of building developers for £20 an acre.[44]

Gay approached the development of his land by Wood with some caution. The original lease on 30 November 1728 was for an area of ground about one-third of an acre forming the east side of Queen Square. It was let on a 99 year lease for £20 per annum. Subsequently six other leases between June 1730 and October 1734 conveyed another four and a half acres to Wood to enable him to complete the whole site. All of these leases were for 99 years and the total rent for a site of about five acres was £137 per annum. On the strength of these leases Wood granted seventy-five under-leases for a total of £305 1s. 0d. in ground rents. All these under-leases were building leases. The general practice was for the lessees – masons, carpenters and other tradesmen – to use them as security for raising mortgages with which to build houses according to Wood's design, the conditions for which were written into covenants in the leases.

As Wood established himself as a successful developer the terms whereby he leased land from the Gay family improved. Thus the nine-acre site for the King's Circus was leased from Garrard in

Figure 9 Richard Jones, Ralph Allen, Robert Gay and John Wood the elder, attributed to William Hoare (c 1707–92)

1754 at £163 per annum in perpetuity although the final conveyance securing Garrard's rent of £163 on the ground rents of all the houses in Gay Street and on seven in the King's Circus and two in Brock Street was not completed until 1768. The lease for the development of the Royal Crescent in 1766 was also in perpetuity although the final conveyance was still outstanding in 1781. With the security of these leases Wood, who in 1728 had no capital of his own, was able to initiate a great sequence of building carried out by himself and his son with a capital value of £333,000. The first stage of this sequence, Queen Square, probably involved a capital outlay of at least £60,000. Unfortunately there is no list showing the occupations of the men who contracted for the under-leases in Queen Square and no list of those who granted mortgages to them. The earliest of such lists for Wood's buildings is of the thirty-nine lessees in Wood's next development in the Parades which shows the following:[45]

	No. of lessees	% of lessees
Building trades	17	43
Other trades	8	20
Professional and leisured classes	14	36

It is very probable that the Queen Square project was taken up in similar fashion. If this is the case then it seems likely that the professional and leisured classes were more involved in building developments early in the century than evidence for later developments seems to suggest. Nevertheless, other lists relating to building on Corporation land from 1761 to 1778 and in Bathwick from 1788 to 1792 support the view that about 60 to 65 per cent of houses in Bath were built by men in the building trades, 20 per cent to 30 per cent by men in other trades, and the remainder by men from the professions and the leisured classes[46] (see table 5.4).

The majority of these builders, particularly in the earlier years of the century, built on a small scale. For example, in two of Wood's developments – the North and South parades and the King's Circus and Gay Street – the proportion of houses built by builders building one or two houses was 45 per cent and 57 per cent respectively. In the Corporation development of Milsom Street and Edgar's Build-

TABLE 5.4 Number of leases according to occupation of sub-lessee in building developments in Bath, 1761–92

Occupation	Milsom Street, Edgar Buildings, Bennett Street, 1761–78 (Number, 69)	Bathwick 1788–92 (Number, 128)
Building trades		
Architect	–	3
Builder	–	11
Carpenter	15	47
Mason	21	9
Plasterer & Tyler	6	–
Plumber	–	4
Statuary/Carver	3	5
	45 (65%)	79 (62%)
Other trades		
Bargemaster	–	1
Cabinet-maker	4	3
Chemist	–	1
Clothier	–	6
Cloth-worker	–	5
Coal Merchant	–	5
Cooper	6	–
Ironmonger	1	–
Malster	1	1
Mealman	–	16
Musician	1	–
Sadler	1	–
Tailor	1	–
Toyman	–	3
Victualler	–	1
	15 (22%)	42 (33%)
Professional and leisured	9 (13%)	7 (5%)

Source: *Leases*, GAB.

ings the proportion was 54 per cent. In the Bathwick development it was only 21 per cent.

Even in these early years there were some builders who undertook to build more than one or two houses and who, therefore, were responsible for building houses with substantial total capital values. In the Parades (1740–9), which represented a total capital investment of £72,300, eight builders each built from three to six houses with total capital values of more than £3,000. These eight builders were responsible for 55 per cent of the total capital invested. The biggest builder in this development was Ralph Allen with five houses worth £6,900. (According to Allen's clerk of works these houses actually cost £10,000 to build.) In the Circus (1754–8), which represented a total capital investment of £61,650, 46 per cent of the capital value was taken up by five builders each of whom built houses with total capital values of more than £3,000. In this development the biggest builder was Andrew Sproule Esq. who contracted for five houses worth £8,250. In the Milsom Street development (1761–3) 39 per cent of the total capital value was taken up by three builders investing over £2,700 each. The biggest was William Selden, mason, who contracted for eight houses worth £7,200. These principal builders, Allen, Sproule and Selden, were responsible for 9.5, 13.4, and 18.6 per cent respectively of the total capital outlays in the developments in which they were involved.

In table 5.5 I summarise what is known about the annual and capital values of houses built by John Wood and his son between 1728 and 1787.[47] In the developments identified, totalling 346 houses, the Woods initiated building with a capital value of over £330,000. Over one-third of the houses built were worth more than £1,000 and only one-fifth were worth less than £450. The most common capital value was from £765 to £900 and the average was £964. Another valuation of thirty-three newly-built houses in Lansdown Road, Bennett Street, Alfred Street and Saville Row made in the 1780s show an average value of £893. At the same time the average value of twenty-one new houses in Walcot Street, Ladymead and Broad Street was £461; only four of these houses were valued at less than £200. In 1803 the sale of nineteen houses belonging to the builder John Hensley fetched an average sale price of £597. These figures meant that the cost of building even one or two houses was beyond the means of most of the building tradesmen who contracted for building under-leases while some of the bigger

TABLE 5.5 The number and value of houses in developments by John Wood and Son, 1728–87

Development	Starting date	Annual Value £s											Total Houses Number	Total Annual Value £	Total Capital Value £	Average Capital Value £	Percentage over £1000
		0/20	21/30	31/40	41/50	51/60	61/70	71/80	81/90	91/100	101/150	151/200					Percentage
		ESTIMATED CAPITAL VALUES £[1]															
		0/300	315/400	465/600	615/750	765/900	915/1,000	1,065/1,200	1,215/1350	1,365/1,500	1,515/2,250	2,265/3,000					
Queen Square	1728	19	15	5	8	3	2	10	–	9	3	1	75	3,960	59,400	792	31
North and South Parades	1740	–	–	–	9	19	8	18	3	1	7	–	65	4,820	72,300	1,112	45
King's Circus, Gay Street, Brock Street, Stable Lane	1754	9	11	13	11	23	4	25	3	3	3	–	105	6,230	93,600	891	32
Royal Crescent, Rivers Street, Margaret's Court, Catharine Place	1767	1	15	11	11	23	2	1	5	1	19	–	89	6,136[2]	92,040	1,034	29
Queen's Parade	1768	–	–	–	–	–	–	–	12	–	–	–	12	1,080	16,200	1,350	100
Total		29	41	29	39	68	18	54	23	14	32	1	348	22,226[3]	333,540	958	36

Source: Particulars of Fee Farm Rents 1751 – 87 Wood Box, GAB.
[1] Capitalised at 15 times annual value.
[2] Excludes St Margaret's Chapel value, £400, p.a.
[3] Including St Margaret's Chapel value, £22,626.

builders must have been faced with very large capital outlays indeed; when Hensley died he still owned nineteen houses worth £1,910 and the ground rents of fifty-one other houses. Consequently, the general practice was for lessees to raise mortgages on the security of the under-leases. Evidence collected by Christopher Chalkin suggests that between one-half and three-quarters of their mortgagees, who, like Chandos, were investors of the last resort, were men and women from the professions and the leisured classes many of whom gave Bath as their place of residence.[48] Chalkin has also shown that about half the mortgages in a small sample of mortgages were for more than £500. Since many builders built several houses and some built many, even this figure of mortgage debt underestimates the mortgage requirements of many builders. Unfortunately the sources of funds used by Allen, Sproule and Selden to finance their building undertakings are unknown. Nevertheless, the mortgage requirements of some builders are recorded and may be used by way of illustration: Richard Upton needed financial assistance to the extent of £1,800 to build a single house in the Royal Crescent, John Hensley raised a mortgage of £3,000 in Bristol, and John Eveleigh incurred a total mortgage debt of more than £18,000. This practice of raising a mortgage on the security of a building under-lease meant that building tradesmen did not, as is sometimes said, build at their own expense. They built with borrowed money as well as on credit from suppliers. (Builders on Corporation projects were frequently common councilmen or closely associated with men who were. Moreover, they were able to finance this building work by making loans at interest to the Corporation.)

Yet, our quest for the source of funds used in the building of Bath should not stop here. Payment for house-building by contractors and mortgagees alike was generally made in at least three stages; at the completion of the first floor, at the roof level, and after roofing and completion. That payments for work completed were frequently made by the contractor or builder drawing bills on the developer and having them paid by some financial intermediary is well illustrated by Chandos's Bridgwater enterprise and the Chandos–Wood development in Bath. It is also supported by surviving records of Ralph Allen's work as contractor for facing St Bartholomew's Hospital in London with Bath stone in the years 1731–64. Allen, who was Wood's patron in Bath and builder in one of Wood's developments, was paid £7,690 for work on St Bartholomew's. For the third stage of the Hospital he was paid £2,046 18s. 0d. between July 1749 and April 1751. This was done by Allen drawing four separate bills – at the appropriate stages of the building – on the Governors of the Hospital to the order of George Sherlock, his then London agent. In the 1730s he had used James Theobald for the same purpose. In the 1760s Allen also employed a London man, Thomas Pitts, as his intermediary for paying wages to his workmen in London. He did so by drawing bills on several parties and banks payable to Pitts who in turn made weekly cash payment of £5 to £6 to Allen's manager, Richard Biggs. Biggs then paid wages.[49] There is also the evidence of the accounts of John Eveleigh who was engaged in building in Cheapside, Johnson Street and Laura Place in Bathwick. His account with James Cogswell shows Cogswell, generally in conjunction with one or other of the partners in the Bladud Bank, accommodating Eveleigh with £3,212 from July 1792 to February 1793. The total amount was advanced piecemeal by means of notes at two months. Another account for the building of Bailbrook House in 1790 shows John Eveleigh drawing a succession of bills totalling £11,950 on Mr Skeet, the investor of the last resort, and discounting them with Cogswell at a total discount of £180.[50]

Whether payments made by mortgagees to small builders at the appropriate stage in building were also usually paid by the mortgagor, in this case the small builder, drawing bills on the mortgagees and then discounting them is not clear. It certainly appeared to be the method used by the London Banking firm of Elizabeth and Moses Staples in their financing for working-class housing in Half Moon Street in the 1790s. To the extent that mortgage monies were paid in this way the task of isolating the sources of loanable funds in developments such as Queen Square becomes even more difficult. Until we know the extent of payment by bills and the degree of discounting one can only conclude that the question remains an open one and that an elaborate web of credit also supported the work of even the smallest builders in Bath.

Wood's task as a developer was not finished with the completion of the conveyances for the under-leases. Wood, as the developer, had to prepare the site, construct the main sewer, arrange for water supply and supervise building alignments and standards. These activities also required substantial resources. Yet Wood's net income from ground rents in Queen Square was only £168 per annum and was far too small a sum to finance his vital share of the undertaking. Unfortunately, apart from the evidence of Wood's connection with Theobald at this time, there is no evidence to show precisely how Wood did finance this, his first development. Nevertheless, it is possible to get some idea of developers' costs and the problems to be met with in financing them from the records of the Ambury development in 1765.

The Ambury development, sixty houses on a five acre site centring on Thomas Street (St James Street), was begun by three partners: Thomas Jelly, carpenter, Henry Fisher, mason, and Richard Jones,[51] variously described as ironmonger, maltster, brewer and deal merchant. The ground was leased from the Gay family at £100 per annum (£50 for the first two years) and the lease specified that the developers would lay out or cause to be laid out £3,000 in building houses with elevations, 'equal in goodness to those in Gay Street' and that they would not build out the southern aspect in any way that would obstruct or annoy the occupiers. Before the scheme had advanced much beyond the planning stage Jones died leaving the burden and cost of development with Jelly and Fisher. These two surviving partners claimed to have laid out £1,881 19s. 5d. in preparing the site; in erecting vaults, arches, pitching and levelling, and in taking down and setting back Jones' stable. Also, from 1767 to 1772, they paid out £595 3s. 9d. for rent of the ground, £57 3s. 9d. to the Corporation for rent of a section of the Burrough Walls, and £168 7s. 6d. in interest on a £600 mortgage raised to enable the work to proceed. Jelly and Fisher

	£	s.	d.
Stock of ironmongers' goods	711	15	6
Stock of beer, malt casks, vessels, utensils etc.	511	4	6
Stock of deals	992	7	0½
Three houses in Market Place held on 42 year leases from Corporation			
1.	1688	5	9
2.	510	0	0
3	1000	0	0
Stables and coach house in Horse Street	600	0	0
Miscellaneous debts	2069	8	4
	8083	1	1½

claimed that one-third of all these costs should be met by Jones' heirs and executors. As the account of Jones' estate shows, he was not a poor man. Yet it was not easy for his executors to raise their share of the development costs. Jones' worth at the start of the development is shown on p. 159.

In addition Jones was entitled to a third share of Ambury fee farm rents (ground rents) worth £281 8s. 6d. per annum and a third share of sewer money worth £98 10s. 11½d. He was also indebted to the amount of £3,274. Hence his 'wealth', a little over £8,000, was largely in unrealised assets and his debts significantly exceeded the total of debts owing to him; like Chandos he, too, lived in a web and veil of credit. His capital debts incurred between 1739 and 1767, which again show Marchant as a significant figure in the web of credit, were:

	£s
1739 from Hannah Bishop	65
1750 from Richard Wittick	100
1759 from Mary Warr	150
1759 & 1763 from Richard Marchant	1,000
1767 from Joshua and Drummond Smith	1,759 (£1,162 not secured on mortgage)

Because of delays in settling Jones's affairs, Jelly and Fisher only received their final settlement at the end of 1772 when Ralph Allen's son paid £280 to Fisher and Jelly for the purchase of Jones's one-third share in the Ambury ground rents.

In short, on a much smaller site than Queen Square and for a more modest development (£48,000 compared to £59,000), development costs in the first six years were in the region of £2,700, or between £40 and £50 per house. In 1729 Wood's rent for the Queen Square site was £137 and his gross income from ground rent was £305 1s. 0d. The difference, £168 per annum, would have been insufficient to meet his development costs. Even the capitalised value of his net income from the site (the ground rents were sold for £3,150 in 1786) would scarcely have covered them. Hence the importance of the £4,000 economy in not levelling the site and the importance of the fact that Wood was still working for Chandos. Since Wood was still working for Chandos and receiving generous accommodation from Theobald as well as working for Humphrey Thayer, the London Commissioner of Excise, one might well argue that it was the London man, Theobald, who, along with Chandos and Thayer, kept him going until he had developed enough collateral in Queen Square to become a good investment risk himself. This turn of events seems to have happened in 1735, almost at the end of the Queen Square development. In that year, through the patronage of Ralph Allen, he borrowed £1,500 on a mortgage of ground rents from Allen's sister, Mrs Buckeridge, then a widow living in Hertfordshire. Subsequently he borrowed a further sum and, by 1744, was in debt to her for £2,600.[52] Perhaps it was this loan that helped Wood in his next development in the Grand Parade 1740–9. As this project came to a close Wood borrowed again; this time locally; £1,000 in 1747 from Dr Harrington and £1,600 in 1749 from Ann Webb, widow.[53] It was in this project, too, that Wood received considerable further support from Ralph Allen who contracted for the five houses already mentioned. Although not in Chandos's class, Ralph Allen was a man of wealth with a reputed income of £12,000 per annum. He, too, had connections in the London money market and with Theobald.

Wood the elder died in 1754 and his work was carried on by his son, but whether his son paid off outstanding mortgages is not known. What is certain is that between 1757 and 1760 Wood the younger became indebted to Richard Marchant to the extent of £2,400 and that by 1765 this debt had increased to £3,800. By this time, too, Marchant's investment business had expanded both in Bath and in the West Country generally; he had investments in Chippenham, Street and Charterhouse as well as in Bath. In the 1760s Wood also borrowed £800 from Moses Bradley of Clapham and £2,500 from Lewis Clutterbuck of Bath. No doubt most of this borrowing, particularly the £2,500 from Clutterbuck in 1768, was made in connection with the preparation of the site for the Royal Crescent development which was the centre piece of a £92,000 building project.

By 1770 Wood was so heavily indebted that in August a draft agreement was drawn up for the sale of the ground rents in the Grand Parade, Pierrepoint Street and Queen's Parade, to Elizabeth Towers a widow in Bath. These ground rents amounted to

£620 17s. 10d. and in April 1771 Mrs Towers paid £18,626 15s. 0d. for them for a return of 3.3 per cent on her investment. However, only £4,749 14s. 11d. changed hands. The rest, some £13,877, represented debts arising from previous mortgages, £5,000 of which was raised to provide a marriage settlement for Wood's daughter. Even this infusion of funds was insufficient to rescue Wood and in the same year, 1771, he decided to clear several other outstanding mortgages, including the one for £2,500 from Lewis Clutterbuck, and to do so by raising a consolidated loan for £8,000 from Richard Marchant and Harford Lloyd, a partner in the Bristol Old Bank with financial connections with the West Indian and, therefore, the slave trade. This mortgage was secured on the ground rents of properties in Gay Street, the King's Circus, Bennett Street, Miles Court and Brock Street with a yearly value of £450 10s. 0d. Consequently any default on Wood's part would have secured his creditors a return of 5.6 per cent on their investment instead of the 4½ per cent they could expect from the mortgage itself.[54] In 1779 the Marchant–Harford loan was taken over by Love Edridge a widow from Chippenham.[55]

As a result of his attempts to remain solvent, by the early 1770s Wood the younger had disposed of ground rents worth £1,070 per annum in return for a capital sum of £26,626. It is pertinent to note that his ability to raise such a capital sum was based mainly on titles to ground rents generated by his father's development of the Grand Parade. As we have seen this latter development in its turn was made financially possible by the earlier development of Queen Square.

In 1770 Wood was not only worried about the availability of funds but was also concerned about delays in completing the transfer of the ground on which the Royal Crescent was built. This was important because without the transfer there could be no underleases, no ground rents, and no mortgage security for building. Indeed, there had been trouble over the ground rents ever since Wood entered into an agreement with Margaret Garrard for the lease of sixteen acres for a rent of £195 in 1764 with the result that not until December 1766 was a contract finally agreed with Sir Benet Garrard, Margaret having died. In this contract the sixteen acres in the original agreement was increased to match the area of nineteen acres indicated on the plan attached to it and the rent raised from £195 to £220. There was also a proviso in the agreement whereby the final release of the ground would be delayed until Garrard's rent of £220 per annum had been covered by under-leases to builders at ground rents of 4s. a foot, and counterparts of such leases delivered to Garrard. This stage was reached in 1770. In order, therefore, to proceed with proposals to raise funds on the security of the under-leases on the rest of the ground Wood needed the final release. But the Gay family dragged their feet. In these circumstances, in May 1770, Wood wrote to his agent, John Jeffreys, in London:[56]

> The day after you left Bath Sir Peter Gay came to Bath but I did not see him for some days after. I paid him his rent for the Square, stable ground and Queen's Parade home to Lady Day, but as to the balance of the Crescent Rent amounting to upwards of £200: I told him should be paid by you when the Release was executed; that you was in London with the Schedule of the counterpart with you . . . I find Stokes is not concerned for him; and his brother making some hesitation concerning the executing of the Release, I told them plainly I should not let a farthing of the rent be paid till that was done; in consequence they saw me yesterday and seem as anxious as myself to have it done.

Fourteen months later the release had still not been granted and James Rivers was urging William Drake, one of the trustees of the estate, to hurry things up so that the rent could be collected since:[57]

> you know how considerable a share is appropriated for the payment of the annuities charged by Mrs Garrard and Sir Benet Garrard, insomuch that without the regular payment of the £200 a year from the Crescent, there is scarcely a sufficiency to pay them.

How soon after this letter the affair was settled is not known.

In many of these monetary matters Wood now dealt through another of Bath's successful financial intermediaries, John Jeffreys, Attorney at Law. Jeffreys was probably an 'immigrant' attracted to Bath during the early 1750s. His first customers included Richard Marchant and Harford Lloyd and he acted for them in drawing up mortgages and negotiating purchases of land. From experience in this kind of work it was but a short step to acting as an intermediary putting lenders in touch with borrowers. In this way, between 1752 and 1767, he arranged loans totalling £11,000. He also made direct loans himself and negotiated bills of exchange. By the early 1770s he was acting as banker to Wood, negotiating loans to allow building to proceed, providing cash to pay wages and other small accounts, and making long term advances on mortgage. Then, in 1774 when Wood was hard pressed for money for building at Batheaston, he negotiated a £2,000 loan on the security of ground rents in Queen Square to the value of £90 per annum and in 1779 negotiated the ending of the Marchant/Lloyd loan. By 1780 he had himself advanced over £3,000 to Wood to meet his urgent need for funds to pay outstanding rents, wages and bills, and to redeem mortgages.[58]

This was a period of general depression in Bath and Wood's creditors were very pressing. Consequently, early in 1781 various of his properties were conveyed to Philip George, 'to receive the rents and profits and to apply it in keeping down the interest of the several mortgages and also to sell the ... (words indecipherable) and apply the moneys in paying off the mortgages and the residue to Wood.'[59] When Wood died later in the year it would seem that he was heading for bankruptcy, his resources over-extended perhaps in the building of the Royal Crescent, and his need for funds exceeding his ability to obtain them.

It was not only developers who risked failure in building, particularly in an enterprise as expensive as the Royal Crescent. According to estimates of the annual value of houses in the Royal Crescent their capital values ranged from £1,350 to £2,400. This meant that builders taking under-leases needed substantial funds by way of mortgages in order to build. For example, in 1772, one builder, Richard Parker owed fourteen suppliers a total of £249 9s. 0d. While, in the next year, a carpenter, Richard Upton, who had contracted for the next house and raised a mortgage of £1,500 at 4½ per cent from Charles Biggs of Bath, was bankrupt. This house had cost £111 more than the mortgage to build and Upton was in debt to a Bristol timber merchant for £196. The upshot was that Biggs sold the house for £1,400.[60] Surviving records do not show whether other builders and investors also were badly hit by the expense of building in the Royal Crescent.

Nevertheless, while there were risks in building there were also gains; in 1807 a house in the Royal Crescent was sold for £5,000 and in 1813 another was mortgaged for £3,000.[61] Yet these may be seen as gains only in relation to cost prices because a comparison of values between 1786 and 1827 for several houses in the Royal Crescent, the King's Circus, Queen Square and Queen's Parade suggests that over this forty-year period property values in the Wood's developments barely remained stationary (see table 5.6). Nevertheless much house-building may be regarded as a sound investment. As well as paying wages to a speculating builder during construction a house built to let would bring in a gross return of about 7 per cent per annum.[62] Yet, as far as the Woods were concerned Wood the younger seemed little better off after fifty years of building in Bath by himself and his father than his father had been when he began building on his own account as an architect-developer in 1728. Those who appeared to have gained most through building were their financial intermediaries such as Richard Marchant and John Jeffreys.

TABLE 5.6 House values in Wood's developments, 1786–1827

	1786 (15 × yearly value)	1827 (valuation for insurance)	
Royal Crescent			
No. 7	£1,800	£1,800	
13	£1,890	£1,800	
19	£1,950	£ 600	
20	£1,950	£2,000	
28	£1,590	£3,000	
30	£2,400	£5,000	
The King's Circus			
No. 13		£1,100	
21	all houses in	£2,000	Average
26	King's Circus	£2,000	£1,675
S.E. Corner to Bennet St	average £1,344	£1,600	
Queen's Parade			
No. 7	£1,350	£1,000	
4	£1,350	£1,000	
6	£1,350	£1,000	
Queen Square			
No. 9	£1,200	£1,000	
North Side	£1,500	£1,600	

Source: 1768 Particulars of Sundry Fee Farm Rents, Wood Box, GAB. 1827 Bristol Sun Fire Insurance Register Book 1044190 to 1142201.

What, then, may be said by way of summary about the financing of the Wood's developments between 1728 and 1781?

First, John Wood started his career with the financial backing of Chandos, Thayer, and Allen, all of whom had close financial connections with London. All three had made money out of public service: Chandos as Paymaster-General to the Forces Abroad, Thayer as Commissioner of Excise, Allen as Farmer of the Cross and Bye-Posts. Two of them, Chandos and Allen, shared the same London financial intermediary, James Theobald. Second, Theobald was the crucial financial link between Chandos and Wood at the start of the latter's career. At a time when Wood started the Queen Square development without capital resources of his own and when still working for Chandos, Theobald accommodated Wood more generously than Chandos required. Furthermore, Chandos's financial arrangements with Theobald grew out of his connections in the London money market. As a result he settled his accounts with Theobald by transfers from his other London brokers who largely dealt for him in Government Stock. There can be little doubt that the 'monied interest', London money and the London money market were the foundations for Wood's early achievement nor that Theobald was Wood's hidden benefactor.

Subsequently Wood benefited from Allen's connections in Hertfordshire for an infusion of capital until he finally succeeded in attracting local funds into his enterprises.

Wood's son, building on his father's development of new property rights to ground rents in Queen Square and the Grand Parade, was able to attract even more loans from Bath – from Richard Marchant, John Jeffreys, and Lewis Clutterbuck – but also from Bristol and Chippenham. Indeed, funds from these two sources were vitally important in the latter stages of Wood's life. Both Marchant and Jeffreys had extensive financial connections; Marchant in particular ranged as far afield as London (through his connection with Chandos), as well as to Street, Chippenham and Bristol. Through the good offices of Jeffreys and through Marchant's connection with Harford Lloyd of the Bristol Old Bank, loanable funds generated in the West Indian and slave trades also made their way into the Woods development in Bath. As we have seen Wood's borrowings, which were mainly for building, were of the order of at least £26,000. The only obvious ploughback element involved was Wood's use of ground rents as security for mortgages. But these ground rents arose out of decisions by the Gay family not to sell land but to grant leases for building purposes. They were, therefore, the product of a legal contract concerning property and not the result of saving out of income from labour. In fact they originated in various claims to income by members of the Gay family with property rights in the family's settled estate.

There can be little doubt that the Wood's requirements for loanable funds were met through the whole gamut of financial institutions and arrangements available in London and in England generally. They also drew on sources of funds in Bristol and the West Country as well as in Bath itself.

The main instrument for raising long term investment funds was the mortgage, not of the land itself, but of legal titles to shares in the income from it in the form of ground rents. While these mortgages were the principal means of long term investment, the bill of exchange was probably the principal means of payment for work completed and probably the main way of transferring funds from mortgagees to mortgagors. Through the veil of credit thus generated the development of Bath was firmly tied to the general course of economic development in England.

The Wood's share of financing buildings with a capital value of at least £333,000 – about one-eighth of the domestic building in Bath in the eighteenth century – although necessary, in the sense that without it the buildings involved would never have been built, was far from sufficient. Hence the additional importance in Bath as elsewhere of the sub-division of property rights marked by the creation of those building under-leases, whereby builders paid ground rents. The building craftsmen and men from other occupations and the professional and leisured classes who took these under-leases and paid the ground rents, used the titles granted to them by the under-leases as security for mortgage money with which to build. Since, as seems likely, mortgages from £500 to £3,000 were paid by builders drawing bills on mortgagees and either cashing them with a bank or discounting them with some other financial intermediary such as Marchant, Jeffrey and Cogswell, the financing of this aspect of building in Bath also came out of the whole web of credit built on rights to income from property.

Such a web of credit draws a veil over the sources of loanable funds used in urban development in Bath. It strengthens the view advanced here that the mobilisation of such funds involved all the institutions of public and private finance then available in England including the London and even the international money markets. In their turn these were built on the consolidation of property rights, the exigencies of war, the growth of the national debt, and the commercial and trading relations in which England's economy was embedded.

The degree to which, even early in the century, the financing of building activity in Bath was embedded in the national money market can also be shown by the movement of interest rates. Many of the lenders in Bath whether acting as quasi-bankers or in some other capacity as financial intermediaries were professionals; Marchant, Theobald, Jeffreys, Cogswell and many others did not lend simply to do good to neighbours but to make money. Consequently they, as well as their customers, were sensitive to its price. While it is probably true that a low yield on consols was not sufficient to re-stimulate building in Bath in the late 1730s and early 1740s there was a striking coincidence between the major building booms, 1726–32, 1753–8, 1762–71, and 1785–92, and periods of cheap money as shown by the yield on consols, interest rates on local mortgages, and interest rates on Corporation Bonds. While all local interest rates were fairly sticky and certainly did not move freely in steps of half of one percent in tune with movements in the price of consols, it is noteworthy that between 1745 and 1774, when the yield on consols was low, eighteen out of thirty-nine mortgages were at 4 per cent and the Corporation undertook development projects requiring substantial borrowing; £9,450 in 1765–7 and £27,100 in 1776–81. In this period, too, Wood the younger took up his first loan at 4 per cent in 1757.[63] The connection between the fourth boom from 1785 to 1792 and the low yield on consols is, I think, undeniable.

The key factor in this link between building and interest rates was not movements in the yield on mortgages and bonds, these were fairly sticky, but the greater variability in the yield on consols. It seems that when their yield fell to 3 to 3½ per cent, a mortgage on building or a loan to the Corporation at 4 to 4½ per cent was a more attractive proposition – a low yield on consols simply meant that there was more money about. Unfortunately there is no actual record of money being moved from one form of investment to the other in Bath. What is known about interest rates is shown in Appendix B.

The consequence of the whole intricate web of credit, between 1728 and 1781, was that the two Woods were able to create the extensive architectural centrepiece of a remarkable urban landscape. This landscape is also a monument to the credit-raising ingenuity of the eighteenth century and to the sophistication of its property law. In this development the initial decision of Gay, as the landowner of Barton Farm, was crucial. He not only provided the site but, carried along by developments in property law arising out of the confirmation of absolute property, also created conditions for the supply of first class collateral for raising finance from hundreds of investors, both large and small. In this manner the market economy of agrarian capitalism, in which Gay was a mere fragment, as well as determining the strength of demand for the good things Bath supplied and the site and sequence of development, also made it possible to tap reservoirs of loanable funds in such ways as to enable a creative developer like Wood to translate his image of man and nature into architectural forms. Accordingly Bath may be seen as both product and symbol of the success of agrarian and commercial capitalism – an existential expression of the economic and social structure of society and of its dominant ideology.

By mid-century Bath was also the principal resort in England. There, men and women, gentry and bourgeois, shopkeeper and servant aped their betters in a perpetual round of social emulation which served to give some cohesion to a society already fractured by those economic and social developments which were the very conditions of Bath's growth. However, every expansion of the town and of the facilities it provided for emulation widened the area, physically and socially, into which capitalist practice penetrated; the life of Richard Marchant, the case of Glazby versus the Merchant Taylors, and the whole experience of the Woods as architect/developers are only high points in a general process. Every advance of capitalism, or what the eighteenth century referred to as civil society, threatened existing social relations still further and every successful act of emulation pushed the wealthy to seek new ways of putting distance between themselves and their emulators. In the end Bath as it was known to the eighteenth century was doomed by the very success of its capitalist citizens and the expansion of civil society.

In the next chapter I will attempt to show how this contradiction between capitalistic economic development and the need for order in society was reflected in the making of the urban landscape in Bath.

CHAPTER SIX

IDEOLOGY AND UTOPIA

> But yet I preferred an inclosed Square to an open one, to make this as useful as possible: For the intention of a Square in a City is for People to assemble together; and the Spot whereon they meet, ought to be separated from the Ground common to Men and Beasts, and even to Mankind in General, if Decency and good order are necessáry to be observed in such Places of Assembly; of which, I think, there can be no doubt.
>
> John Wood, *Essay Towards a Description of Bath*, Bath 1742, page 345.

I

Men and women have appeared in this history as representatives of classes. Elizabeth Montague and Sarah Robinson as rapporteurs and members of the propertied and consuming rich. The Duke of Chandos as the archetype of the 'monied interest', restlessly making, as well as consuming, hundreds of thousands of pounds. Robert Gay, the Earl of Bath, and Sir William Johnstone Pulteney, as landowners determined to increase rents and maximise revenues. Richard Marchant, Ralph Allen and John Jeffreys as members of the new bourgeois, grown successful in money and trade. John Wood, father and son, as dynamic entrepreneurs, themselves growing to bourgeois status. William Selden, Richard Upton and John Hensley as speculating builders and building craftsmen otherwise too numerous to mention, all anxious to meet the demands of the market. The widow Sanders as a lifeholder threatened in her very life by the effects of the demands of the propertied and consuming rich on all these busy and profit-seeking classes. Thomas Roberts, William Mitchell, Martha Abraham, Prudence Brown and Sarah Wheeler as labourers and servants attracted to the city and uprooted from the countryside to work, fall sick, bear children and die at the expense of the parish in consequence of the demands of the propertied and consuming rich.

These representatives of classes were all born into patterns of social relationships and trapped in a maelstrom of economic and social change not of their own making. As each in his own way grew into his role and acted out his part, he, too, helped shape the course and pace of a fragment of economic and social change in Bath – some more than others. The collective and still partly visible product of their social behaviour and their life's work, intended by none of them, not even by John Wood and others of Bath's architects, was the social organisation of space in the city in the eighteenth century.

This notion about the social organisation of space and the roles played by different classes in it has been succinctly put by Manuel Castells:[1]

> It is scarcely more possible to make an analysis of space 'in itself' than it is to make one of time. Space, as a social product, is always specified by a definite relation between the different instances of social structure, the economic, the political, the ideological, and the conjuncture of social relations that result from them. Space, therefore, is always an historical conjuncture and a social form that derives its meaning from the social processes that are expressed through it.

Accordingly, in histories of building and architecture in eighteenth-century Bath it has sometimes been the practice to raise questions about the social significance or meaning of Bath. This has usually arisen from the belief that architecture, including the architecture of eighteenth-century Bath, is art. For then it becomes proper to ask questions about architecture similar to those asked about other forms of art. And, as art, Bath may be thought of as a kaleidoscope of individual and sometimes collective acts of creativity, rather like the Book of Kells or St Peter's in Rome. It may also be thought of as embedded within an artistic tradition; it could not have been built had not Brunelleschi created the Pazzi Chapel in Florence and Palladio written his *Quattro Libri dell' Architettura*. And so one may ask questions about the meaning of Bath.

Answers to these questions are generally attempted at one or other of three levels, objective, expressive, or, documentary. At the objective level, concerned only with appearance, Bath may easily be identified as an eighteenth-century watering place, and its buildings as lodging houses and places of entertainment and recuperation. So far this is the level at which this book has considered them for that, after all, is what objectively they were. At the expressive level, historians usually refer to the purposes of its architects and builders. Those concerned with this level of explanation generally concentrate on John Wood's expressed desire to recreate a Roman city complete with Forum, Gymnasium and Circus and on an intention, imputed to him, to re-unite urban man with nature; Wood, it is often argued, anticipated the Romantics and modern town planners. At the third level of explanation, the documentary level, historians also point to Bath as some collective thing symptomatic of ideas or concepts outside or beyond the city itself. It is said that the city reflects the Spirit of the Age, Whiggism, or the Age of Reason.[2]

These answers to the questions of meaning at the expressive and documentary levels are frequently asserted as if there can be no doubt about them. Yet, if one pauses awhile to look at the form and structure of the city in the past, to understand the activities, ideas and motivations of men in the historical time in which it was built, as well as the form in which it appears to us today, and to question the real existence of general concepts such as the Spirit of the Age, Whiggism, and the Age of Reason such certainty might be seen to fade. This is also likely to be the case because to ask questions about the meaning of these individual and collective acts of creativity in Bath and their relationship one with another, set as they are in a total organisation of space, is also to pose questions about the role and significance of all the myriad unconnected yet socially related acts in the life work of those classes who appear to us only through representatives and whose work in Bath was not art. Accordingly, my approach to the meaning of Bath is concerned more with trying to reveal the structure of society hidden beneath its organisation of space than with using general concepts, such as the Age of Reason, to explain real phenomena. And my claim is that space in Bath *is* an historical conjuncture and a social form deriving its meaning from the social processes expressed through it. One problem with conventional claims about meaning in art at the documentary level is that art is very rarely the mere representation of an order or structure in society or of a style said to be associated with it. Some art also continuously and anxiously opposes and questions order and structure. Therefore, Bath as architecture, as an organisation of space, may be thought of as possessing a dual function and not existing as a mere reflection of an age, be it called, Rational, Whiggish, Bourgeois or Georgian. And, while Bath may be thought of as simply another example of the Renaissance in England, it may also be thought of as a manifestation of other aspects of eighteenth-century society. Indeed, there is some reason to believe that creative expression and the organisation of space in Bath, in a sense defined by Karl Mannheim, was both ideological and utopian.[3] That is to say that, while it may be true that Bath was the result of collective and personal expressions in building arising out of serving and reaffirming the emergent agrarian capitalist structure of society, and that it was, therefore, an existential expression of the conjuncture of the economic and social structure of society and of an ideology based on absolute property and growing towards one based on absolute self-interest, which one might like to think of as the Spirit of its Age, its architecture and organisation of space also flowed from responses antagonistic to the disorder and anomie of the market economy of civil society in which it was built. According to this view much of the organisation of space in Bath, particularly John Wood's contribution to it, may also be regarded as a statement about the need for a traditional social and moral order; one, perhaps, that would put spiritual bounds around the merely material life of civil society and direct men's thoughts towards God. According to this view the organisation of space in Bath is best thought of as a product of and pointer to the structure of power, therefore, of class relations in eighteenth-century society and of ideological and utopian ideas arising from them. To elaborate this view will call for another halt in the narrative, a return to an earlier starting point and a new journey over ground already covered but traversed here in a new light.

II

At the start of the century power in the city was vested in the Corporation, a closed and self-perpetuating one with a membership ranging from twenty-seven to thirty. Its officers, elected from its members, consisted of a Mayor, two Justices of the Peace, one Chamberlain, two Bailiffs or Sheriffs and two Chief Constables. The Corporation sent two members to Parliament and did so free of all aristocratic or royal patronage. It was also master over the Freemen of the city who had rights to practice trades in it and to a share in the income from the commons but no right to or share in power, except in the administration of the three parishes in the city. The Corporation was proprietor of four-fifths of property in Bath. These property rights and powers had survived virtually intact since the sixteenth century and although, like all property rights they had been confirmed and strengthened as a result of the revolution in 1688, they embodied a traditional view of how society should be composed and held together as a community. In Bath this community then consisted of 335 households earlier described as living in an urban island in what looked like a predominantly peasant society, although inundated for twenty weeks every year by foreigners drawn from geographical regions and social orders somewhat different from those in Bath itself.

In many ways the Corporation acted as the collective head of this small group of households and exercised a paternal function in looking after its own. Through the Companies and its control over the Freedom of the city it controlled production and trade in the interest of the wealthier and more powerful citizens, including those of its own members. Through its control over Freemen and the enrolment of apprentices it sought to provide work for many of the others. Through the power of its Mayor, Justices of the Peace and its parish authorities it provided for the maintenance of the poor, the sick, the aged, and the illegitimate. It took what care it could of its apprentices. At the same time it denied these benefits to strangers, sending them back to their place of settlement. Through its legal powers it sought to control the worst criminal excesses of its citizens and in a desultory way sought to impose a morality sometimes at odds with their economic interests. In all these ways it exercised its responsibility for what has been called the 'moral economy' characteristic of the period. In this context, I shall refer to it as social corporatism. The Corporation's willingness to allow Beau Nash to exercise social control over visitors to the place was in accord with this traditional paternal responsibility.

The Corporation also had an economic function. It was chief landlord within the Burrough Walls and owner of large areas of land outside them. In carrying out its function as landlord it largely worked in its own corporate interest. It is in its role as landlord that the Corporation made its greatest impact on the town and its organisation of space. Its actions under this head, I refer to as economic corporatism. Some of the consequences of the Corporation's corporate self-interest – its economic corporatism – for Bath's architecture and its townscape have already been shown. Its opposition to Wood's chimerical Utopia influenced Wood's choice of site for Queen Square. Its exercise of property rights in the town commons choked off development west of the Royal Crescent and fixed the site of the future Victoria Park. Its regulation of chairmen's rates, to contain development within the walls, influenced Wood's choice of site for the Grand Parade. Therefore, all these significant features of the organisation of space in Bath are partly accidents arising from the exercise of property rights by the Corporation. They are consequences of its economic corporatism. Since two of these features, Queen Square and the Grand Parade, were also made possible only by the supply of land and the web and veil of credit arising out of property rights characteristic of agrarian capitalism, Wood's work was obviously deeply affected by the interest of two orders or classes in society. One, the Corporation, already entrenched in urban society. The other, the 'monied interest', relatively new but with roots deep in the countryside as well as in national and even international money markets. In this way the practice and ideology of local élites was divided; conservative and cautious economic corporatism on the one hand; on the other, aggressive agrarian capitalism and commercial individualism.

But, the Corporation was not homogeneous. Even at the start of the century its members were torn between economic corporatism and individualism. While individual members of the Corporation, Trymme, Allen, Saunders among them, acted energetically as landlords and aggressively as entrepreneurs in their own private interests and in ways that frequently ran counter to the interests of the Corporation, the Corporation only cautiously made improvements in the city and generally husbanded its resources most carefully. Certainly economic corporatism held no brief for Wood's grandiose schemes or for aggressive individualism. In short, the Corporation simply did a customary and conserving job and did so without the aid of modern, sixteenth-century techniques, such as double page book-keeping.

Even the Act of 1707, which established a system of turnpike roads into Bath and provided for the lighting and cleansing of the town, and which has been singled out by earlier historians of Bath as a positive act by the Corporation in response to the initiative of its alleged appointee Beau Nash, seems to have been a tardy and reluctant response to initiatives by others. There appears to be no evidence that Nash was involved in any way. Rather, a petition for a turnpike was presented to Parliament by Messrs Blathwayte and Trotman, MPs for the city. This was followed by the Corporation meeting in camera. At this meeting they decided to proceed to get an Act of Parliament. When it came to acting upon the decision, by sending the town clerk to London to solicit Parliament, there was dissension and six out of twenty-one members voted against.[4] Nevertheless, the town clerk did go to London and the Act was passed. It provided for the improvement of 12½ miles of the main roads leading from Bath to London, Glastonbury, Bristol, Salisbury, Oxford and Bradford-on-Avon. The Trust, a Justice Trust, shifted the financial burden of maintaining these roads from the authorities of the parishes and counties through which they ran and placed them firmly upon the users. Consequently it concerned the parishes around Bath more than Bath itself. The governing body of the trust reflected that interest. It consisted of two Justices of the Peace from each of the three counties, Wiltshire, Somerset, and Gloucestershire and only one or more from Bath. A subsequent Act in 1720 reduced the quorum to six of the Justices from the three counties. These commissioners were granted powers to borrow up to £3,000 on the security of the tolls. The Act decreed that no part of this money was to be used for repairing any of the streets or lanes within Bath itself. Instead, tacked to the Act was one for cleansing, paving and lighting the streets and for regulating chairmen. Even so no action was taken under the Act until May 1709 when the first surveyors for the three parishes were appointed[5] – Richard Marchant was one of the first three appointed for the parish of St James, where, in the same year, he was beginning his first building project.

The turnpike itself did not get off to a good start. In 1709 the investors sought the repayment of their original loans and gained a decree in Chancery giving them a claim upon the profit of the tolls from which they took £600 to the detriment of work on the roads. Consequently further Acts were sought and passed in 1720 and 1739 to each of which was tacked an Act for paving and lighting the city itself. It was not until 1757 that the Corporation obtained an Act not tacked to a Turnpike Act. It is worth emphasising that it was under these Turnpike Acts, the powers of which were largely vested in the Justices of Somerset, Wiltshire and Gloucestershire, that the road from London to Bristol through Bath was completed by 1750. Although the turnpike roads into Bath were a component in the social organisation of space in Bath and a development halving the London–Bath travelling time, the Corporation's role was a minor one. Its main legislative contribution was through the Acts for cleansing and lighting tacked to the Turnpike Acts.

There was, however, one very important aspect of the Act of 1707 that was a portent of things to come. The Act vested powers of compulsory purchase of land in the Turnpike Commissioners, subject only to a decision by a jury. Subsequently, in 1711, similar powers were vested in the Corporation in connection with the then proposed Avon Navigation, and, in 1766, the same powers were granted to the Corporation for its development of the markets and the supply of water to the city. But, more of this later.

The story of the Corporation's minor role in the administration and financing of the turnpike could be matched with accounts of its cautious approach to several other matters relating to the development of Bath in the first half of the eighteenth century, such as water supply and the enforcement of its powers under the Acts for paving and lighting. But, rather than detail the history of each separate activity I prefer to use figures of Corporation expenditure and estimates of its borrowing as the best indicators of changes over time in the Corporation's economic behaviour. The very small growth in the Corporation's economic activity between 1701–5 and 1716–21, as shown by these accounts has already been referred to. These figures are in Appendix A and in graph 6.1. I present the figures and estimates for the period from 1730 to 1832.[6]

The expenditure tables show that Corporation expenditure grew very little during the first half of the eighteenth century. Then after a modest hiccup in the early 1750s, it rose during the last forty years of the century to an average level about five times that during

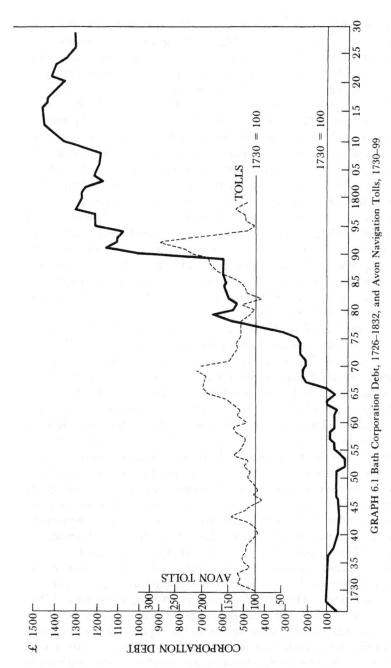

GRAPH 6.1 Bath Corporation Debt, 1726–1832, and Avon Navigation Tolls, 1730–99

Source: See Appendix A.

the first fifty years. In peak years: 1778–9, 1794–5, 1797–8 expenditure was eight to ten times higher. The graph of Corporation debt shows a similar sequence except that when expenditure rose in the early 1750s there was no matching increase in borrowing until after 1762–3, some twelve years after a noticeable increase in expenditure. Before 1762–3 the average level of indebtedness was £2,764. Afterwards it was £27,443. In the last decade of the century the average debt was £54,020, almost twenty times as high as in the first sixty years of the century. A comparison of the two sets of figures suggests that in the first half-century the Corporation rarely undertook activities that could not be financed out of income. Indeed, since accounts were expected to balance year by year, expenditure was limited by a revenue largely derived from rents of property and water, neither of which could be easily or quickly increased. Even projects undertaken in the 1750s, such as improvements to the Pump Room and the rebuilding of the Free School were initially financed out of income although by this time income was augmented by sales of property and the increase of fees for the Freedom of the city mentioned in chapter 2.

By the mid-1750s it was clear that some extraordinary sources of funds would be needed. Consequently, Ligonier, elected MP for the city in 1761, donated £500, William Chapman, the Chamberlain, advanced £600, and Walter Wiltshire gave six £100 drafts drawn on his brother in London and £300 from Mr Ford. Also the annual budget surplus, £829 in 1749–50, was turned into a deficit of £110 by 1752–3. The net result was that the debt, which had stood at £1,100 in 1751–2 rose to £3,900 in 1756–7. Thereafter, although there was a slight reduction in the debt in the depression year 1761–2, the Corporation's building activities, particularly those associated with the construction of a new Guildhall and improvements to the markets in the late 1760s and the improvement of the decayed city centre after 1789, were financed by borrowing. Consequently, whereas in the first two years of the eighteenth century Corporation expenditure averaged £646 and interest charges amounted to a mere 5 per cent of expenditure, expenditure in the last two years of the century averaged £6,863 and interest charges averaged 24 per cent of expenditure. The ratio of expenditure to debt, which before 1762–3 was 1:2.4, rose in the last decade of the century to 1:7.9.

The importance of these figures for the argument about the forces shaping the organisation of space in Bath is that they show very clearly how little the Corporation was involved in development of any kind in the first half of the century. They show, too, that when it did begin to show interest in the 1750s, it did so very cautiously indeed, conscious all the time of the expense involved. When the Corporation was not actively hostile to development it remained largely passive. Its function was still a conservative and conserving one. As a result the effect of economic corporatism on building in Bath in the first half-century flowed more from what the Corporation did not do than from what it did. Moreover, economic corporatism influenced the timing of building and the organisation of space much more than it did the style of building.

Before the Corporation developed sufficient confidence to engage directly in large-scale building on its own account it began to show a change of mind about development as such. The turning point, the building of Bladud's Buildings, came in the mid-1750s. Bladud's Buildings, the first speculative development on Corporation land outside the walls, was designed to increase Corporation revenue and it was probably its success that encouraged the Corporation to go ahead with other improvements in the 1750s without feeling any immediate need for extraordinary sources of income. Since this development also shaped the townscape in the interest of economic corporatism it is worth seeing how it came about and how it grew out of the Corporation's traditional role as landlord of ground outside the city walls.

The first move in the drama was sparked off in 1753 by Daniel Milsom, schoolmaster and member of the Corporation. Milsom was building a school and was also interested in a private building development. To give himself security for this he sought a new lease of ground outside the Burrough Walls, including Rack Close, which had been occupied by him since 1741. He was granted a new lease for 42 years absolute. Later in the year Milsom sought another lease for 99 years absolute on this ground plus the Town Acre at a yearly rent of £100. On this occasion there was much opposition to him and the vote went against him. Instead, the Corporation agreed to let the Town Acre at auction to the highest bidder. It appears that Milsom outbid his competitors for in December the Corporation resolved to grant him a lease for 99 years absolute of the Town Acre and of Milsom's Garden for £100 per annum. By 1754 the agreement was no further forward because all the ground needed for Milsom's development was not included in the lease. Obstructing his proposed line of building was that quarter acre of ground sold off in 1735 for £350 for the site of the poorhouse for the parishes of St

Michael and St Peter and Paul. Consequently Milsom tried to get an abatement of rent on that part of the ground he would be unable to let on building leases and was offered an abatement of £10 p.a. Milsom rejected the offer, kept his original 42-year lease, and the building development lapsed.[7] By the end of 1755 Milsom was dead.

Nevertheless, this business of Milsom's lease and the divisions surrounding it in council seemed to have provoked the Corporation into action. In any case development was in the air. Accordingly, in order to help private developers, the Corporation resolved to pull down the North and South Gates and on 24 September 1754 unanimously passed the motion that was to set it up as a developer in its own right on Corporation ground called Cockey's Garden situated to the north and east of the disputed ground in the Milsom affair. The Corporation appointed a management committee of three, including Thomas Palmer, a prosperous glazier who was also a close associate of Thomas Jelly the builder–architect selected for the task. The final decision to proceed was made in May 1755 and in July the Corporation became a developer and entered into building leases according to plans approved by the Corporation. The completed project, Bladud's Buildings, was described by Ison as, 'probably unique among the Bath terraces in that both elevations, facing east and west, were regarded as being equal in importance, and were similarly composed and ornamented.'[8] It was a fine achievement for the Corporation's first venture into speculative building and an unintentional reminder that at this time the Corporation was Janus headed; as its support for the Companies in 1755 shows, it was still facing two ways on competitive economic development.

In 1760, with Bladud's Buildings successfully launched, and in the depths of depression in the building industry the Corporation decided to build a new Town Hall and to propose a building development of mutual benefit to themselves and to Daniel Milsom's successor, Charles Milsom, wine cooper and common councillor. Since local interest and mortgage rates were as low as 4 per cent yet offered a return higher than the current yield on consols, they were sensible decisions. The proposal put to Milsom was for a joint development by him and the Corporation on the ground held by Milsom on lease from the Corporation. The Corporation would grant a new 99-year lease and take half the rents arising from building under-leases. Milsom, apparently contrasting the briefness of his life with the immortality of the Corporation, rejected the proposal. Instead, in September 1762, he agreed with the Corporation for a 99-year lease but that he would receive all the rents for 35 years, this being the remainder of the term of his existing lease. At the end of 35 years all rents would revert to the Corporation. Milsom would prepare the site and construct a common sewer and the Corporation would grant him a right of way through the Burrough Walls. The result of this decision was the building of Edgar's Buildings in 1761 on the Town Acre and the start of Milsom Street in 1763 on this ground, Milsom's Garden and Rack Close. A typical Corporation building lease for the Milsom Street development is that with Thomas and Daniel Brown, carpenters, on 21 December 1763. It was for 99 years absolute from 1765 and required the lessees to pay an annual ground rent of £4 8s. 0d. to Charles Milsom for the two years 1763 to 1765 and for twenty-nine years thereafter. At the end of that period the rent was payable to the Corporation for the remaining years. It was on this site too, that, in consequence of the Corporation's new powers under the Act of 1766, Somersetshire Buildings was begun in 1779. The Corporation added the elegant Paragon Buildings to the line of Bladud's Buildings in 1767.

These Corporation development schemes and Wood's development of Queen Square, the King's Circus and Gay Street effectively shifted the focus of the city northwards and westwards of the old town. This shift was detrimental to other projects already begun and about to start on the southern borders of the city, in Avon Street and the Ambury. In short, during the years 1750 to 1765 the Corporation passed from conservative and cautious economic corporatism to an acceptance of the developmental ethos and joined the ranks of the dynamic entrepreneurs with their ideology of aggressive individualism. Economic corporatism simply took on a new face. The timing of this transformation did much to stimulate economic activity in the city in the building boom of the late 1760s. Further, the location of these Corporation developments, an accident of landownership as well as the result of corporate property rights and powers, also did much to pull fashionable development away from the southern boundaries of the city, and, thereby, to determine the social organisation of space in it.

Once the Corporation had committed itself to development there was no end to the devastation of corporate property it would carry out in order to enrich itself, its members, and the development-minded citizens of Bath. The North and South Gates disappeared in 1754, the site for the new Town Hall and markets was cleared in the 1760s, Corporation land outside the walls was given over to speculative building in 1755 and the early 1760s, and parts of the Burrough Walls were demolished to give access to it. By 1765 corporatism as an ideology from the past was dead. In that year the knell was sounded for social corporatism by the legal decision on Glazby versus the Merchant Taylors and the Corporation's subsequent inaction, and the knell was sounded for conservative economic corporatism by the Corporation's resolution to seek an Act for the improvement of the markets and granting it new powers for the compulsory purchase and transfer of land. At the same time the Corporation also decided to rent the ground on which the Burrough Walls had stood since time immemorial for one shilling per foot. This decision was reached to assist the development of Westgate Buildings whose developers, John Cottle and John Walker, respectively tailor and weaver, claimed they could not proceed unless 369 feet of the Burrough Walls were destroyed.[9]

As a result of this latter decision development in the south-west corner of Bath had come full circle in rather less than thirty years. By the destruction of the Burrough Walls and the building of Westgate Buildings, Chandos Buildings, once the most modern development in the town possessing an open-ness and grand prospect across fields unsurpassed by any other lodgings in the town, and the product of a world of money and aggressive individualism not previously met with within it, now looked out upon a public thoroughfare and a range of new buildings. It was most effectively cut off from its prospect. Since it was also isolated from the more fashionable upper town it declined in attractiveness and status. Even the new Westgate Buildings could not match Queen Square and Milsom Street. Like the Avon Street and Ambury developments the Westgate Buildings project never really stood a chance of rivalling the upper town; Wood and economic corporatism between them were too strong. One reason may well have been that the organisation of space in the upper town possessed a dynamic aesthetic quality which these other buildings, mere products of aggressive individualism and fashionable style never had. To see how this may have been so, the narrative must again be broken to start once more with John Wood even before the start of Queen Square and when the Corporation was still conservative and cautious and the market in Bath was provincial still and bawdy.

III

As an architect–developer Wood had to reconcile two contrasting parts of his being; on the one hand, capitalist, member of civil society and creature of the monied interest, on the other, creative architect and advocate of moral virtue in society rather in the tradition of Lord Shaftesbury. Wood's books suggest that he well understood the dilemma this posed for him; that without success as an entrepreneur he would be unable to create. There was an additional problem. He was a deeply religious man, but, as a struggling capitalist entrepreneur and architect, he catered for the high consumption demands of a self-indulgent clientele 'in a sink of iniquity'. It would seem that he could neither succeed as a capitalist nor create anything unless he continued to produce what satisfied this market in the context of and according to the conditions of agrarian capitalism already described. This was the only market open to him that would enable him to do anything at all and the contradiction it contained left its mark on his work. Consequently, his career was marked by one compromise after another; Queen Square, North Parade, and the Exchange building in Bristol are only three of them. Wood was also fully conscious of the socially disruptive nature of this 'civil society' in which he so actively participated. Writing in and of an age yet to be blessed by Adam Smith's invention of the hidden hand, he expressed his wish to put limits to the exercise of absolute self-interest in it. He wrote:[10]

> Reason as well as Experience sufficiently demonstrates that without Law there can be no Government; and without Government, mankind cannot long subsist in Civil Society with one another.

I shall attempt to argue that the tensions produced by the contradictions of this state of 'disorder' in the milieu of Bath are evident in his work and I shall suggest that they were the source of the prodigious energy he displayed in designing and carrying through his projects in the face of opposition, legal difficulties, capital shortage, labour deficiency, and economic depression. They may also account for the fact that he was a prickly sort of man. In any case, his were certainly atypical responses to the 'disorder' of civil society in early eighteenth-century Bath and to the anomie of a developing market economy. Fortunately for him and for posterity, they brought him recognition as a valued participator in the new society.

A study of his work, which may be seen as both a protest against that society as well as a way of adjusting to it, may take us nearer to both the expressive and documentary meanings of Bath.

In order to understand Wood's buildings at the expressive and documentary levels, as well as to know them objectively as lodging houses, it is necessary to read his books as well as look at his buildings. This injunction to read Wood's writings is not always observed. John Wood, astronomer, antiquarian, and mythologist as well as architect and successful entrepreneur, was what learned men have described as 'self-taught'. As a result he is often regarded as untutored within the rigid boundaries of formal subject learning. His contribution to building apart, he is thought unworthy of serious consideration and his books have been either largely ignored or dismissed as a farrago of nonsense. Yet these books show how Wood, whose work shaped Bath so much in his own image, saw the world and his own place and the place of his buildings in it. They were: *The Origin of Building: or, The Plagiarism of the Heathens Detected* (1741), *An Essay Towards a Description of Bath* (1742 and 1749), and *A Dissertation Upon the Orders of Columns* (1750).

Furthermore, in order to 'read' the early eighteenth century in Bath as Wood read it and as he tried to write it in his buildings and not as we see it now after two and a half centuries of change, destruction, and growth, it is necessary to learn the language of his polemic signs. These are those signs which, in Duvignaud's terminology, are a group of activities with a double function: to generate a recognition that there is an obstacle (either of participation or expression) to be overcome; and to assert the real or imagined attempt to overcome the obstacle. Duvignaud claims that these functions often endow the work of art with a dynamic value of which perhaps the artists himself is unaware.[11] This is, perhaps, the case with Wood's work. But Wood's polemic signs have their origins in his mythical understanding of the ancient world and in order to comprehend them it is essential that we look at the landscape in and around Bath as he saw it and described it, and from that try to understand his perception of nature, towns and buildings. Only then will it be possible to grasp their significance and the documentary meaning of his buildings.

It is often said that Wood wished to build an imitation of a Roman city in Bath and that at the expressive level of meaning Wood's Bath is an imitation Roman city, therefore, an expression of the Augustan mood of the early eighteenth century in all its secular, rational, republican, oligarchic and martial glory – a sort of pale preview of Edinburgh New Town. Yet the paragraph in which Wood came closest to making that claim referred as much to a period of time as to a specifically Roman style of building. Moreover, the sense in which there is truth in the claim depends upon Wood's view of the nature of the Roman world, as we see here.

Wood saw the pre-Roman and the Romano-British world and Bath's place in it through a vision steeped in the Britannic myth of origin. This myth, with its written origin in the twelfth-century work of Geoffrey of Monmouth and its printed roots in an edition of that work printed in Paris in 1508, was very much alive in oral tradition in Bath in the early eighteenth century in the story of Bladud and the origin of Bath.[12] This myth was untainted by ideas about property, the market, credit, or by highly developed notions of economic individualism. It was pre-Lockeian and highly emotionally charged. It is true it was rationalistic but it was also heroic, noble, cultured and harmonious – in some respects it picked up some of the themes of the Augustan world view. But, above all, it was British. And, in Wood's hands, Christian and Greek.

As Wood saw Bath it was but the core of an earlier city the size of Babylon built originally by Bladud, descendant of a Trojan prince, about 480 BC. Bladud, under the name of Abaris, High Priest of Apollo, had spent eleven years in Greece as 'a Disciple, a Colleague, and even the Master of Pythagoras.'[13] Bladud was really a Greek. He was, as might be expected, a devotee of a heliocentric system of the planets from which the Pythagorean system was probably derived. This Bladud/Pythagorean system was the reason for the great size of Wood's antique Bath; for, by enlarging it to a triangle with sides fifteen miles by ten by eight he incorporated Stanton Drew. At Stanton Drew there was an impressive circle of standing stones which Wood carefully measured and showed to be a model of the Pythagorean planetary system built by Bladud for use in the Stanton Drew university for British Druids. Wood drew attention to the use of circles in this work and pointed out that the chief ensign of Druidism was a ring. Moreover, the Temple of the Moon at Stanton Drew was identical with the Temple Cyrus ordered the Jews to build in Jerusalem. According to Wood, Bath was the metropolitan seat of the British Druids.

Nearer to the surviving core of the city Wood noted the existence of five hills with characteristics of small mountains. Their names meant: Mars Hill, the Moon's Hill, the Sun's Hill, the King's Hill, the Holy Hill. Hills the elevation of which was such, 'that their Summits command a Country so exceedingly beautiful, and of such vast Extent, that the Eye that views it, and the Mind that considers it with Attention, can never be enough satisfied.'[14] From the tops of these hills Wood reported no sign of the impact of agrarian capitalism, no glimpse of the Bristol slave trade, no contact with the monied interest and no sound of manufacture from the thickening cluster of woollen towns which had crept like Triffids to the boundaries of the city – Wood was no Defoe. Instead, he set his *Essay towards a Description of Bath*, his account of his own contribution to the building of the city, against a portrayal of a fantastic historic landscape peopled with Druids, Greeks, and cultivated Britons engaged in building temples, altars, castles, palaces and forums, all in the antique style. Their forums had a particular fascination for Wood for they applied them to the most noble purposes and in them 'convened the People, held their solemn Assemblies, sacrificed to their Gods, delivered their Orations and proclaimed their Kings.'[15] The city was also a place where the Britons, 'placed all their other Idols about the hot Fountains, so as to make the City appear as the grand Place of Assembly for the Gods of the Pagan World.'[16] Wood located the site of Bladud's own palace through his belief that the Saxon word Ham signified a King's palace. Therefore, it lay in the Ham just outside the south-eastern wall of the town and then in the possession of Richard Marchant. Bladud's oracle also stood near the north-west end of the Ham, 'in a Piece of privileged Ground, a Place of Sanctuary no doubt, now bearing the Name of Grove'.[17] Nearby was the Ambury. This was the site of a great rocking stone, a mathematical contrivance and a 'Masterpiece of King Bladud's Musick'.[18] Thus Bath was a city dedicated by a Pythagorean to Apollo, a God whose chief quality, 'was Divination; whose Musick was the Harmony of the Spheres; and to whom the Britons ... paid the highest Honours.'[19]

Even as Wood looked at what was really there he saw through the eyes of a Greek. Hippocrates, he said, had said that cities 'that face the East, and are sheltered from the easterly Winds, RESEMBLE the SPRING; ... the Inhabitants have good Complexions; and the Women, beside being very fruitful, have easy Times'. As Wood observed, Bath faced east, was sheltered from the westerlies, and receiving the beams of the rising sun must be, 'in a SITUATION that RESEMBLES the SPRING; ever Youthful, ever Gay'.[20]

In short, Wood looked at the Bath landscape with the eyes of a man steeped in the Britannic myth. Also he saw antiquity in the manner of the Renaissance; for him verisimilitude had little part and the most admirable virtue was harmony. Moreover, in Wood's eyes nature was itself antique. Since Man was part of Nature Man, too, was antique. But antique with a difference. Wood enlarged classical antiquity to include pre-Roman Britain and the pre-Hellenic Holy Land. The point of this was to establish connection and continuity, even harmony between Jewish, Hellenic and British culture in order to anglicise and Christianise antiquity as part of his attempt to overcome his fear of paganism; so that he could feel at one with himself. The problem was that Wood, as a young inexperienced and largely self-taught architect building in a new style for a sensual, albeit puritanically developing, society felt threatened by the pagan origins of the Palladian style. And, whereas the artists and architects of the High Renaissance, influenced by Ficino, had achieved a relaxed synthesis of antique form and Christian content, Wood was an architectural late starter, a provincial and puritanical Briton, who continued to be plagued by Christian doubts about pagan forms similar to those of the proto-Renaissance. It was the observation of attempts to resolve these doubts which led Panofsky to formulate the 'principle of disjunction'. This principle claims that, wherever in the high and later Middle Ages a work of art borrows its form from a classical model, this form is almost invariably invested with a non-classical, normally Christian, significance.[21] The principle seems equally true for Wood in the eighteenth century. It is my belief that in consciously seeking to reconcile paganism and Christianity, Wood opened up to his secular art emotional spheres which had hitherto been the preserve of religious worship and transformed his buildings in a secular 'sink of iniquity' into symbols of religious and social harmony. His building projects adapted from the antique are polemic signs indicating a social and religious utopia; an harmonious society contrasting with the luxurious and competing society in which he lived and worked. Sadly, for Wood it was a utopia unlikely to be achieved because the increasing strength and diversification of the agrarian and commercial capitalism (in which he was such an active and activating agent) was destroying, in its ideal form, what he set out to build.

Evidence for this assertion about the polemic nature of Wood's architecture is set out in his first book published in 1741. It was entitled, *The Origin of Building: or, the Plagiarism of the Heathens Detected*, and contained:[22]

An ACCOUNT of the RISE and PROGRESS, of ARCHITECTURE, *from the Creation of the world to the Death of King Solomon; and of its Advancement in* Asia, Egypt, Greece, Italy, *and* Britain, *'till it arriv'd to its highest Perfection.* WHEREIN *the Principles* of Architecture, *the proper* Orders *of* Columns, *the Forms and Proportions of* Temples, Basilicas, Churches, *and other celebrated* Edificies, *as well Antient as Modern, are Explained, and Demonstrated to have their Rise from the Works of the* Jews, *and not* Grecians, *as suggested by* Pagan Writers, and their Followers.

In the body of the book Wood argued that beauty in building and classical architecture were brought into the world at God's command with the building of the Tabernacle. God *was* the Divine Architect. He worked only with, 'perfect harmony, and the most delightful proportion'. Above all others he preferred and expressed himself in the circular form. Since, in his *Essay on Bath*, Wood also emphasised the importance of circles and circular movement in the Bladud/Pythagorean heliocentric system and in the construction of the Druidical university at Stanton Drew, the threefold and unifying symbolism of the circle should be plain. It was Jewish and, thereby, Christian first, then British and Greek; the polemic sign of God, and, therefore, of absolute beauty; of absolute beauty, and, therefore, of God. In this manner Wood re-synthesized for himself antique form and Christian content and freed himself from threatening pagan associations. I believe that in doing so he released his creative genius to incorporate religious polemic signs in every aspect of his organisation of space.

God as absolute beauty was unknowable except through man as made by God in his own image. But this was sufficient for Wood, who considered Man a good starting point from which to move towards a comprehension of God. He wrote:[23]

> In the works of the Divine Architect of all things, we find nothing but perfect figures, consisting of the utmost *Regularity*, the sweetest *Harmony*, and the most delightful *Proportion*: And as his works universally tend to a circular form, and are as universally constituted of three different principal parts, so those three parts generally carry with them, in the whole, and severally, the properties of *Use, Strength and Beauty*: to illustrate which, the figure of a Man, created in the image of GOD, is the most notable example.
>
> The parts of Man are mostly circular; and of the infinite

number with which he is composed, there is not one superfluous, or that do not answer some particular use, conducive to his existence.

Man consists of three principal parts, namely, the head, the trunk, and the limbs; all the parts, in their utmost extent are comprehended in a square, or in a circle; and so exact is the mechanism of his whole structure, that all the parts mutually assist each other, and contribute to the *Strength* of the whole.

Man is a complete figure, and the perfection of order.

Man so comprehended was God. Seen in this light Wood's architecture, which can be thought of as a re-creative imitation of nature and of Man, was also a re-creative imitation of God. The symbolic representation of this idea of the omniscience, essence, and beauty of God, and of his unity with Man as his most perfect work embodying order, proportion and harmony, is the Vitruvian figure referred to by Wood in the previous extract. This is a naked man, arms and legs diagonally outstretched with the points of his feet and hands touching the circumference of a circle and the perimeter of a square. Palladio's religious architecture derived from this concept and he employed abstracted versions of the Vitruvian figure in their construction. Wood, a disciple of Palladio, also worked with the concept and used versions of the Vitruvian figure as polemic signs in his secular architecture.

Before we explore Wood's use of the circle and of the Vitruvian figure as polemic signs in his building, two other aspects of the Judaeo-Christian content he gave to antique forms must be described. They concern windows and the principal orders of columns. Windows were Tabernacles. For example, Wood described the windows in Belcomb Brook Villa as a model of the Octostyle Monopterick Temple of *Delphos*, and those in Titanbarrow Logia as 'dressed so as to become compleat Tabernacles'.[24] We are already acquainted with the significance of the Jewish Tabernacle in his account of the origin of building. It appears likely that Tabernacle windows acted as polemic signs pointing to God as the Divine Architect and served to remind Wood himself of his denial of the pagan origins of antique forms. Wood's views about the orders of columns are more fully documented. The evidence shows the complexity of their symbolism, while the fact that he published a third book solely on columns indicates the importance he attached to them. The principal orders, Doric, Ionic and Corinthian, had a threefold symbolism. First, they represented Nature in general and trees in particular; all pillars were imitation trees. When describing the Corinthian order at Titanbarrow Logia, Wood wrote:[25]

> And all the mouldings and sofits in the whole front, proper to be carved, are to be fully enriched, that nothing may be wanted to decorate the order, which, as it represents nature in all her bloom, requires the greatest profusion of ornament to embellish it that can be put together with propriety and elegance.

Second, the three orders were, 'the most lively Symbols of the Robust Man, of the Grave Matron, and of the Sprightly young Girl'.[26] Consequently the north side of Queen Square, built in the Corinthian order and symbolising a sprightly young girl as well as Nature in all her springlike glory, is described by Wood as soaring above the other buildings with a sprightliness which gives it the elegance and grandeur of a palace. And this in a city itself likened by Wood to spring, youthfulness and gaiety! So to the third symbolic meaning of the orders of columns which flows only from the fusion of all three orders considered as a total re-creative imitation of Man made in God's image. When the three orders are placed upon one another, Wood wrote, 'a Harmony will, in many Cases attend the Composition beyond any Thing that can be produced by Columns of unequal Altitudes sustaining one another'. Moreover, by making the shafts of the columns of each order of one and the same diameter at bottom:[27]

> the Delicacy and Stateliness of one entire Column above the other becomes still more Conspicuous. For as the Orders advance towards Virginal Beauty and Elegance, the Columns increase in their Altitude, and thereby one Order receives a Majesty above the other, even in Miniature upon Paper, which words can scarcely describe.

One could almost imagine the impossible and believe that Wood had not only seen Botticelli's *The Birth of Venus* and equated Venus with the Corinthian order, but also understood Botticelli's portrayal of divine or transcendent love. Certainly no one who looks at Wood's Bath knowing what Wood tried so desperately to say can ever again look at the orders of columns and see merely pillars – he should at least see Venus or the Three Graces, and pretend he can see God.

So, what are we to make of Wood as, within the context of the

Britannic myth, he worked to assemble his contribution to Bath as a total polemic sign consisting of circles, squares, Vitruvian figures, Tabernacle windows, the orders of columns, all expressed harmoniously according to the idea of unity in diversity, of three in one, and built in and for a market economy? Principally, Wood contrived to put a frame rather like a proscenium arch around the urban environment of civil society with the purpose of enhancing Man's awareness of himself as made in God's image, and, thereby, his awareness of God.

Look first at the plan for Queen Square (Figure 10). This square was a novelty in Bath; it let far more light and air into its surrounding houses than reached those built by Wood himself in Chandos Buildings and by Strahan in Beaufort Square, or those in the courts of early eighteenth-century Edinburgh. But the enlargement of the space enclosed does not alter the fact that what Wood planned was an enclosure and not a street or an isolated block of houses. Further, all the surrounding houses were to face into the central area of this enclosure which was designed as a perfect square and intended to be perfectly level. At the centre of the square was to be a perfect circle radiating four diagonals, each ending in smaller circles. The whole geometric design looks like an abstract Vitruvian figure (Figure 10). This visual impression should be borne in mind when one reads what Wood wrote about the purpose of the enclosure, which he persisted with in spite of the heavy expense involved and the piecemeal nature of his leases. He wrote:[28]

> But yet I preferred an inclosed Square to an open one, to make this as useful as possible: For the Intention of a Square in a City is for People to assemble together; and the Spot whereon they meet, ought to be separated from the Ground common to Men and Beasts, and even to Mankind in General, if Decency and good order are necessary to be observed in such Places of Assembly; of which, I think, there can be no doubt.

Clearly, Wood intended the enclosure as an environmental determinant of good order (Figure 11). It was to be a place in which a chosen few would be able to assemble apart from the bustle of everyday things, the animal kingdom, and the generality of men – apart, that is, from civil society. As these few contemplated the north side of the square their spirits would soar in the manner already described. Nature, except in the shape of a green turf and formal shrubs, was expressly excluded. There were to be no forest

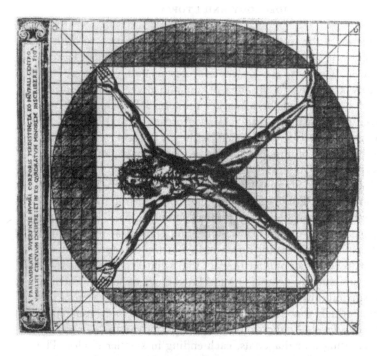
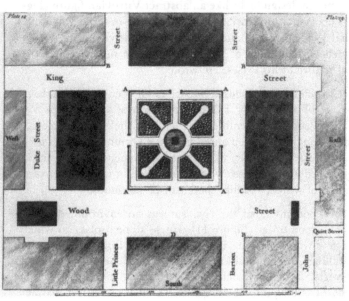

Figure 10 Plan of Queen Square, from John Wood, *Essay towards a Description of Bath* (1765), with Vitruvian Figure from Cesariano's edition of Vitruvius (Como, 1521)

Figure 11 Queen Square, Bath, 1784, Thomas Malton

trees in the square, only low stone walls and espaliers of elm and lime. The fact that the exquisite chapel dedicated to the Virgin Mary and built in the Doric order as part of the whole development scheme attracted a very high demand for building sites in the neighbourhood, suggests that many of his customers, even in the midst of iniquity, fancied the form, if not the substance of his own social and religious beliefs.

When Wood began his next development in 1739 he did so on the north side of the Ham. There, in the Parades, he turned the square inside out; the houses of the Grand Parade and of the South Parade parallel with it became the central square form, while the associated places of assembly were opened up to the surrounding countryside (Figure 12). Nevertheless, his main purpose was to create paved open areas for the practice of public walking and talking, activities which distinguish men from beasts (Figures 13 and 14). He hoped to render these activities more congenial in the South Parade by letting in the winter sunshine and developing the open space as a forum. For St James Triangle, the open space in front of the Grand Parade, he designed a formal garden in the shape of a Vitruvian figure (Figure 12). As in Queen Square this open space was important since, while he thought of the houses on the Grand Parade as outward looking, he also intended that they should be viewed from *across* the formal garden. Perhaps he wanted people to look at what he might have thought of as a re-creation of Bladud's great palace! In this way Nature, except in its antique and formal shape, was still kept at a safe distance and provided only a subdued background to his man-centred buildings. Moreover, whatever aesthetic appeal Nature had was to be derived from its antique and religious associations. The principal natural feature to be seen from the Grand Parade was Solsbury Hill. In Wood's mythology this had been the site of the Temple of Apollo. He wrote, 'If those Works had still existed; their Tremendous Look, from the *Grand Parade*, must have inspired Mankind with a Religious Awe as often they should consider that the Great God of Heaven and Earth was Adored by them.'[29]

It is in the design of his third great work, the King's Circus, that Wood gave fullest expression to the ideas he published in 1741 (Figure 15). He planned the King's Circus as two perfect circles, one inside the other. The outer circle of buildings is 318 feet in diameter, which is virtually identical with the present circumference

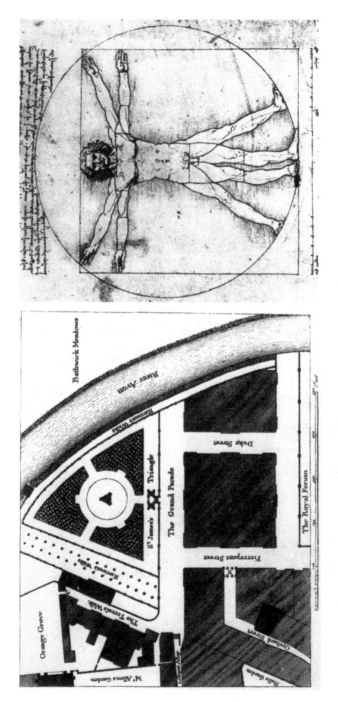

Figure 12 Plan of the Grand Parade, from John Wood *Essay towards a Description of Bath* (1765), with Vitruvian Figure (Leonardo's version)

Figure 13 South Parade, 1775, Thomas Malton
Figure 14 North Parade, 1779, Thomas Malton

of the chalk wall at Stonehenge, which measures 320 feet from crest to crest, and close to the north-south dimension of Queen Square which is 316 feet. Wood's design also incorporated a threefold expression of his idea of the trinity and of unity in diversity; he cut the outer of the two circles into three equal segments, made three approaches to the centre circle, and piled the three principal orders of columns one on top of the other. This piling of the orders had the further symbolic meaning already described. Combining virginal beauty, elegance, and altitude they generated a majesty beyond words. The whole was topped with giant acorns the symbolic seeds, perhaps, of Druidical oaks.

Since a circle of buildings throws the eye more towards the centre and seems to enclose the space within more effectively than a square of buildings so the King's Circus, enclosing a smaller area than Queen Square, was even more inward looking. Moreover, the King's Circus was built without any incline on a level ledge cut into the hillside. It was also designed to be totally devoid of natural vegetation. Only its southernmost entrance let in the sun and a distant view of Beechen Cliff. It was designed as pure space enclosed by three equal segments of a perfect circle. Since, as I have argued, Wood's architecture sprang from tension involving a sense of the awfulness and omniscience of God, which he infused into the antique forms with which he worked, this austerity of the King's Circus and the deliberate exclusion of forest trees and of all nature is an integral part of the King's Circus as a total polemic sign. In designing the King's Circus Wood was not concerned to unite town and country or to plan towns; rather, in the midst of the corruption of civil society and in its interest, he worked to glorify God by writing 'The Whole Duty of Man' in stone (Figure 16).

Other historians have offered different explanations of Wood's Bath. With the aid of a deterministic biographical approach to history, which emphasises simple casual relationships between environment and action, it is possible to explain Wood's achievement in terms of the existence and influence of a style. Such 'stylistic' explanations are generally made with one eye firmly on the linear history of architecture and town planning. In these stylistic explanations it is claimed that Wood was simply working in the Palladian tradition as brought to England by Inigo Jones. In some respects this is true and Wood's debt to Palladio and Vitruvius has already been acknowledged. Nevertheless, it may also be urged that even

Figure 15 Plan of the King's Circus, John Wood. The shaded area indicates building site, the ground rents on which secured Garrard's rent of £163 for the nine acre site.

Figure 16 The King's Circus, J. R. Cozens

in his approach to the Britannic myth and the place of Greeks and Druids in it that Wood could have derived his understanding from Inigo Jones's own essay *Stoneheng. . . .Restored*, first published in 1655 but republished in Wood's own lifetime in 1725. This seems unlikely because Inigo Jones in his essay deliberately set out to refute the claims about Stonehenge contained in the Britannic myth. In doing so he argued that the Britons were a savage and barbarous people who never applied themselves to the study of arts nor practiced any of the sciences. 'Touching of the manner of the building of the ancient Britons', he wrote, 'I find them so far short of the magnificence of the Antiquity, that they were not stately nor sumptuous, neither had they anything of Order, or Symmetry, much less of gracefulness and Decorum in them.'[30] Moreover, the Britons lived in tents and their cities were without walls and the country without towns. On the question of architecture in general Jones wrote, 'Architecture, which among the Greeks was youthfull only, and vigorous, under the Romans, their Empire grown to the full height, became manly and perfect, not in inventions and elegancy of forms alone, but also in exquisiteness of Art, and excellency of materials.'[31] In accordance with this notion Jones considered Stonehenge to have been built in the Tuscan order. In his view Stonehenge was both a Roman and a pagan temple, was not built by the Britons, and was untouched by Christian and Druidical symbolism. On the other hand, even though a ground plan of Stonehenge in the 1725 edition of Inigo Jones's essay is reminiscent of the ground plan of the King's Circus,[32] the symbolism Wood incorporated into this building of the King's Circus was devised by him within the context of his version of the Britannic myth. Thus, although the architectural style was undoubtedly Palladian, the idea that the creative impulse for the building itself was derived by Wood from Inigo Jones's Roman and Palladian mythology is implausible.

Moreover, as I have emphasised, Wood's creative responses to his circumstances were atypical. Atypical responses cannot be explained by general causes. Objective conditions such as the existence and character of agrarian capitalism and its ideology, the demands of a wealthy clientele, the nature of land law and the structure of land ownership, the developing puritanism of society, the existence of a style and the availability of technology, the enduring character of Whig patronage, and the circumstances of personal biography can set the boundaries of objective possibilities and

Figure 17 A Plan of the City of Bath, 1735, John Wood

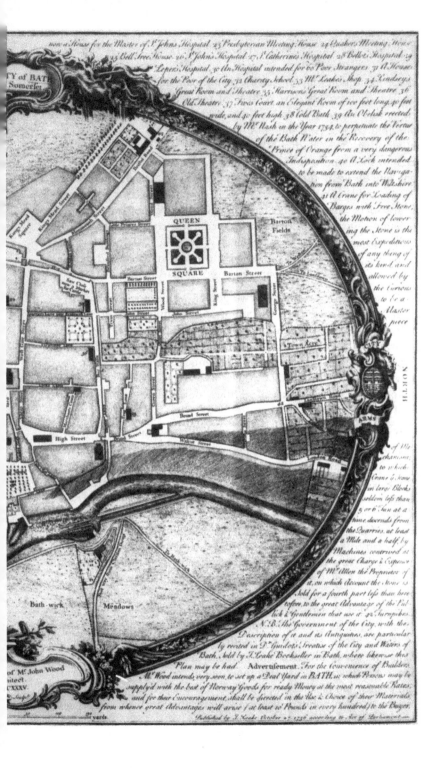

shape conditions for creativity. They can neither determine nor explain its form; there were at least ten architect builders in early eighteenth-century Bath building in the Palladian style, but only one John Wood. And therein lies a deal of the difficulty we have in attempting to see Bath as Wood saw it and, as I believe, meant it. His finished works do not obviously spring, soar, or uplift; indeed, one might well question whether strictly classical architectural forms could ever do so. Furthermore, few of Wood's customers in civil society, then or since, had enough grasp of the language of his polemic signs to enable them to read these appearances into his buildings and to grasp his message. Writing in 1749 Wood seemed to have understood this himself. Following a devoted and detailed description of the three country houses he had built he wrote:[33]

> These modern Instances shewing us in Miniature how happily *Bath* is situated for the execution of beautiful works in Architecture; let the contiguous Building of the City now Demonstrate the Great Regard that hath been lately shewn to display the Free Stone of the Country to as much Advantage as can be well expected in a Place where the Houses, in general, are applied to such Uses as Bring them down almost to the Rank of common Inns.

If this was the view of the author of many of them it is little wonder that while many people could see a generalised beauty in Bath, particularly when the city sparkled white on a clear spring morning, most missed the point of Wood's Bath. Smollett, himself a moralist, nevertheless made his Matthew Bramble dismiss the King's Circus as 'a pretty bauble; contrived for shew' and let his Lydia Melford, a lovesick modern miss, delight in it as a sumptuous palace in an earthly paradise, a view endorsed in the twentieth century by the doyen of English architectural historians, Sir John Summerson, who finds it, 'quaintly beautiful – as if some simple-minded community had taken over an antique monument and neatly adapted it as a residence.'[34]

Perhaps no-one was so impressed with the outward appearance of Bath's architecture nor so satirically blind to Wood's polemic signs and social architectural purpose than the author of *Bath – a Simile*. Writing in 1779 with a more jaundiced, but no less accurate, comprehension of the real purpose of the place than Sir John Summerson, he pin-pointed its social significance with the help of his own set of symbols. According to our author, Bath's architecture reflected its function as a centre of conspicuous consumption. Like the decoration of the saloon at Blenheim Palace it spoke for its occupants. 'Look at us and admire,' says Laguerre's design, 'We are eating.' 'Look at us and admire,' says Architecture in Bath, 'We are drinking tea.' Accordingly the author likened Bath to a monstrous tea-set – 'A huge Tea Equipage' made of yellow ware with the baths themselves as slop basins, 'where many dirty things are washed' and the houses,[35]

> All shapes and sizes jumbled;
> That one on t'other seem to stand,
> Tea things together tumbled

Among all this table-ware the King's Circus was a mere plate,[36]

> The Circus so precisely round,
> With all its pomp and state,
> Will but on scrutiny be found,
> A handsome Wedgewood plate.

Which is what it was; an architectural expression of conspicuous leisurely consumption with something about it that was reassuring about the harmony and organic unity of society.

Many of Wood's contemporaries, both customers and builders, shared his liking for harmoniously designed enclosed spaces, designed to provide some isolation from the economic bustle of civil society and free from the intrusion of the labouring population who built and serviced the city. There are several examples of this preference. Chandos's choice of site for Chandos Buildings in 1726 and the development there of a three-sided space was in part influenced by the prospect it gave across Kingsmead. About the same time Strahan built Beauford Buildings on a smaller scale, and Kingsmead Square was built. In 1749, when William Galloway granted leases for the building of Galloway's Buildings close to the Grand Parade he wrote into them that he would, 'not permit or suffer any horses, coaches, chariots or other wheel carriages whatsoever to come into or upon the said street called Galloway Buildings.'[37] Sixteen years later, Margaret Garrard, Gay's heir, let five acres of the Ambury on a building lease for £100, for the site of Thomas Street (St James

Parade). The stated model for the houses were those in Gay Street and the under-leases gave the builders power to fix gate-posts at each end of the street to keep out all wheeled vehicles and animals and to prevent any unloading by coal-carts and other delivery waggons.[38] For a time, up to the early nineteenth century, the street was a fashionable one at least for members of the learned professions. Subsequently Catherine Place was designed by Wood II in 1780 and St James Square in 1790 by Thomas Palmer. On a smaller scale Southcot Place was built in Lyncombe and Widcombe in 1817. The Corporation even acted to keep noise away from residential areas and prevented coal waggons from passing through the town and directed that they pass around the Burrough Walls.

This is not to say that these builders and developers shared Wood's Utopian vision in the way I have described it. They were more like Matthew Bramble; private developers were more interested in providing a little peace and quiet, the Corporation in protecting its own interests. Developers, in acting in the ways they did were, of course, responding to the demands of the market in a given social and spatial context. And one might suggest that while the company at Bath looked at Wood's Bath without a knowledge of his polemic signs, the dynamic and aesthetic quality those signs imparted to his work gave the buildings and the space they encompassed the strength to speak for themselves. Consequently the company was as eager for the attractions and spatial organisation of the city as earlier in the century gamesters had been for its games, among them England's and Europe's landed aristocracy. In the autumn of 1765 these people were so enamoured of Bath that 148 of them visited it; three princes, four dukes, four duchesses, one marquis, two marchionesses, twenty-four earls, twenty-two countesses, fourteen viscounts, forty-three viscountesses, twelve barons and twelve baronesses. As well there was one archbishop and five bishops.[39] And that in spite of the fact that more discriminating visitors had long since found Bath grown too large (Figure 17). As Jonathan Swift wrote as early as 1736, 'This town is grown to such an enormous size, that above half the day must be spent in the streets in going from one place to another. I like it every year less and less.'[40]

This comment of Swift's should also remind us that with the passing of time the spatial context of Wood's buildings also changed; one building and spatial arrangement affected the location and space of another and so on. More particularly, while Wood's buildings influenced the location and designs of his contemporaries and successors, Palladians all, his son's development of the Royal Crescent, first projected in 1764 and carried out between 1767 and 1774, also made a great impression on their work (Figure 18). The Royal Crescent presents a unified front of thirty houses consisting of a plain basement storey – a vast base, supporting large Ionic columns passing through two storeys capped with a balustrade and roofed with stone tiles – a sort of collective palace for an itinerant and socially mobile agrarian capitalist élite. It was simple and uniform in design, dignified in appearance, and spacious in its outlook across broad landscaped acres; it was consciously outward-looking, across a subdued nature. To ensure that it would continue so, the lease placed restrictions on the use of land belonging to Sir Benet Garrard, the landowner of the site for the Royal Crescent, which was not included in the lease itself. On Kingsmead Furlong and part of Hayes Lower Furlong, on which Garrard had grubbed up the cross-fence in order to throw them together to create an open space, he was prevented from growing any tree more than eight feet high and from erecting any building of any kind. Should he do so Wood was given right of entry to cut trees and destroy buildings. Further, any hedge or wall had to be built parallel to the diameter of the Royal Crescent. In addition Wood was granted power to construct a private walk forty feet wide, bounded by a handsome wall or iron palings, to link the Royal Crescent with Queen Square. The lease also gave him power to grant or refuse access to the walk to occupiers of Brock Street and the west side of the King's Circus and Gay Street according to their willingness to contribute to this undertaking.

Once Queen Square, the King's Circus, the Royal Crescent, and the Corporation's development in Bladud Buildings, Edgar Buildings and Milsom Street had been completed, the demands of the market and the slope of the ground dragged Bath further up the south face of Lansdown. As this happened a new generation of architects, Eveleigh and Palmer paramount among them, who were not tortured like Wood about the pagan origins of their style, and who were wholly in tune with the market for their work, built in lighter vein. They built with exquisite adaptation of style to terrain, existing buildings, and spatial arrangements such that Eveleigh's creation of Somerset Place marks the perfection of domestic building

Figure 18 The Royal Crescent, 1769, Thomas Malton

in Bath. This crescent, secluded from the main tourist routes is composed of a double curve – the curve of its crescent is moulded over the curved brow of the hill on which it is built – rather than built on its levelled top, or, as was the common practice, stepped angularly down its slopes. And the line of stones which marks the break between the ground and first floors follows those curves. The curve of its crescent also matches the curve of a segment of the Royal Crescent which it overlooks across a sloped area of open ground. It is an object lesson in total design. Because architects built in this fasion and although Wood's polemic signs were possibly private things manifesting an intensity and breadth of creativity not matched in Bath, not even by Eveleigh, the over-all result of building in Bath was to produce a social organisation of space in the seventy years after 1727, such that Wood's message of an urban Utopia at odds with the world in which it was produced, and his views about the way in which urban men ought to arrange the space around them in order to make urban living bearable, even today force themselves upon us from almost every perspective. Therefore although the city as a whole was never planned, a social consensus among those with wealth and power produced a social organisation of space such that it seems planned in appearance, an urban Utopia resulting from creative responses antagonistic to the disorder and anomie of the developing market society in which it was built.

IV

The appearance of eighteenth-century Bath in the twentieth century is misleading. Therefore, the description and explanation of it offered above cannot account for, nor yet encompass, even the visible aspects of eighteenth-century Bath. Indeed, it can only hold for that part of eighteenth-century Bath selected by subsequent generations as possessing architectural merit worthy of high esteem. Since most of that not so selected is no longer with us it cannot figure even in appearance. Therefore, present appearance can never be the arbiter of what was. And, since the stones that might once have spoken for themselves no longer stand it is the record that must be squeezed until it speaks.

A necessary corollary of spatial isolation from the economic bustle of civil society for some was the concentration and confining of the many, with all their noxious trades and sweating labour, to restricted areas of the city but within reasonable walking distance of the market for their labour. Just as the reverse side of high consumption by men of property and of a high level of innovation by entrepreneurs was the exploitation of indigeneous and cheap migrant labour, the reverse side of Wood's Utopia was the crowded alleys and courts of the parish of St James and the southern part of the parish of Walcot. For all that men might have wished it, it was not possible to have one without the other.

Yet, in the first few decades of the century, separate and sharply distinguished areas of settlement for different classes would have been difficult to find. Consequently developers and builders, in response to various pressures and the availability of sites, attempted to create areas of quality building throughout the city and on the southern as well as the northern edge of the old town. Indeed, Chandos's own development was located in the southern half of the town and Galloway's Buildings situated to the south-east of the Abbey. Wood, too, built the Grand Parade on the south-eastern edge of the town, on the flood plain of the river Avon and on land previously used as a common jakes. Then, as late as 1762 the Duke of Kingston undertook the redevelopment of his property around the Abbey, and in 1765 Thomas Jelly and his partners began the Ambury development, including Thomas Street just outside the South Gate.

While all of these developments kept much of their social attractiveness for several decades the general rebuilding and building in the city not only changed its physical shape but resulted in a specialisation in the use of its space.

Fortunately the survival of the rate books used in recording the rates levied under the Bath Act of 1766 provide a very clear picture of the social organisation of space at that time. The distribution table in Appendix C and Figure 19 show clearly that while quality building was concentrated in the newly-built part of the city, particularly in the areas of the Parades, Queen Square, King's Circus and Milsom Street developments, there were still pockets of highly rated houses – houses paying more than 15s. – in the city centre. The first of these was around the Market Place and the Abbey extending to Wade's Passage, Abbey Street, Kingston Street and Church Street. The other was around the Cross Bath.

However, the main areas of low quality housing were concentrated at the approaches to the city around the North and South Gates. Thus in Southgate Street, Marchant's Passage and the Quay, 66 per cent of houses paid less than a 2s. rate while in Ladymead, outside the North Gate, the proportion paying less than 2s. was 72 per cent. The effect of these concentrations of low quality housing clustering around the North and South Gates on the distribution of housing in the parishes of the city is summarised in table 6.1 and Figure 19.

The distribution table in Appendix C and Figure 19 also show the existence of another area only marginally above the lowest quality in housing. This is Avon Street, begun during the first building boom in 1726–32 as a medium quality development lying outside the south-western boundary of the town but already, in 1766, on the way to earning the unsavoury reputation it gained in the early nineteenth century. Already 52 per cent of its houses paid less than a 2s. rate and none more than 5s. Moreover, four of its houses were described as poor, others as tenements, and five were empty, there were also a brewery and seven stables. Since the fate of Avon Street was also to be that of Milk Street and Kingsmead Square, and since this area adjoined that part of the Parish of St James lying outside the south-eastern boundary of the town outside the South Gate, including Southgate Street, Marchant's Passage and the Quay already described, they combined to form an arc of low quality housing about 400 yards wide around the whole southern boundary of the old town, at least by the 1790s.

The emergence of Avon Street as the focal point of this low quality housing in Bath in the late eighteenth and early nineteenth centuries was closely connected with transportation as well as with its low-lying location close to the river. It is necessary therefore, to say something about the influence of traditional traffic routes through the city on the social organisation of its space.

Situated as it was within a great loop of the Avon, Bath was approached from London, Oxford and Gloucester from its northern side. Consequently the bulk of traffic, after passing along Walcot Street or Broad Street in the Parish of St Michael, entered it through its North Gate. Then, in High Street, it passed on one side or the other of the Old Guildhall, turned right into Cheap Street, then left down Stall Street and out of the town through its South Gate. From there it passed along Horse Street, past the Quay to cross the river

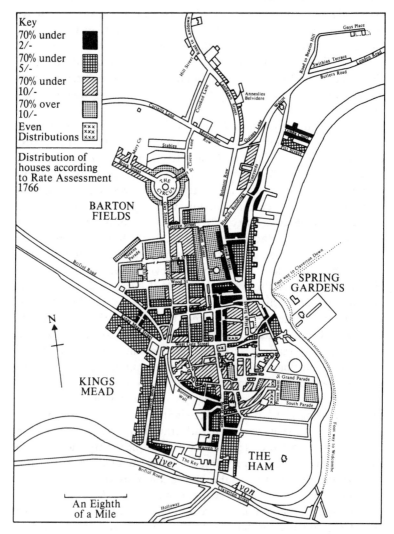

Figure 19 Map, the City of Bath: distribution of houses according to rate assessment 1766
Source: *Bath City Rate Book 1766*, GAB

TABLE 6.1 Distribution of houses in Bath in 1766 by parish, according to contribution to rates under the Bath Act, 1766

Parish	Total	Up to 1s. No	%	Up to 2s. No	%	2s. to 5s. No	%	Up to 10s. No	%	Up to 15s. No	%	Up to 20s. No	%	Over 20s. No	%
St. P & P	319	30	9	72	23	87	27	89	28	26	8	10	3	5	2
St James	418	83	20	75	18	126	30	81	19	30	7	11	3	12	3
St Michael	401	128	32	94	23	93	23	70	17	14	4	2	0	0	0
Walcot	559	36	6	93	17	236	42	120	22	63	11	9	2	2	0
Total	1,697	277	16	334	20	542	31	360	22	133	8	32	2	19	1

Source: *Bath City Rate Book 1766*, GAB.

by the Old Bridge. At the turn from Cheap Street into Stall Street another stream of traffic passed along Westgate Street, out through the West Gate to join the Bristol Road. Although the Corporation tried to keep coal-carts from travelling this route, at least after 10.00 p.m. and although the Grand Parade, Galloway Buildings and Thomas Street were all built as traffic-free areas, problems associated with a continuous flow of wheeled traffic, particularly iron-shod wheeled traffic at night, were great. Furthermore, contrary to the Act of 1707 horses and waggons were frequently left standing and those responsible for pitching and paving were generally reluctant to carry out the required work. Therefore, by the early 1750s the volume and weight of traffic and the costs of repair were such that at Bath Quarter Sessions the Grand Jury spent much of its time presenting local authorities as well as whole streets of citizens for failure to meet their obligations.[41] For example, in 1751, the Corporation itself was presented for failing to cover a ditch in Horse Street and throughout 1755 the Parish of Walcot was repeatedly presented for not keeping the lanes leading towards the North Gate in proper repair while all 'the inhabitants of Horse Street from South Gate to Mr King's Stables'[42] were presented for not mending the pitching before their doors.

Associated with traffic problems were nuisances arising from noxious trades and the accumulation of waste in closely settled and busy streets. Even part of Wood's Utopia, the Parades, was not exempt from abuse as slaughter houses outside the East Gate were a frequent source of public nuisance to its occupants. And what better evidence of public nuisances is there than the Act of 1757? Designed to overcome the problem of pitching, paving and scavenging, the Act recited that, 'Many persons do frequently pick and sift, dirt, dust, ashes in the publick streets within the city and liberties of the City of Bath, and in the triangular piece of ground lying before the South Parade respectively, to the great annoyance and disturbance as well of the inhabitants, as of the persons passing by and through the said streets and places.'[43] Clearly, as early as 1750, the market, left to itself, would have clogged the main traffic routes through the city, destroyed the surface of the roads, deposited waste and noisome odours everywhere, and created unbearable noise, particularly at night. Hence the urgency of the Acts for cleansing, paving and lighting of 1757 and 1766 designed to maintain the amenities of the city and preserve its privileged organisation of space.

It was not only deterioration brought about by the traffic itself which fixed the use of space along these traffic routes and worked against the interests of those who lived close to them and the city centre. Equally important were the uses to which houses and building sites along the traffic routes were put. For example, after the completion of the Avon Navigation, Horse Street and other roads approaching the Quay on the Avon became a focus for a cluster of warehouses, stables and small workshops. Additionally the streets along the route became lined with licensed alehouses. In fact, by 1776 and although there had been some decline in the ratio of alehouses to houses in the city, from 1:10 in 1743 to 1:16 in 1776, half of Bath's 143 alehouses were located along the line of the main traffic routes already described. They were distributed as follows:

Walcot	9	The Quay	1
Broad Street	10	Westgate Street	5
Northgate Street	4	Kingsmead Street	3
High St, Market St		Kingsmead Square	4
and Market Row	5	Monmouth Street	3
Cheap Street	3	Horse Street	14
Stall Street	11		

Total 72

The distribution of alehouses in 1780 was much the same, 78 out of 163 were in these same streets, 12 were in Stall Street and 15 in Horse Street.

With the exception of Avon Street, yet to be discussed more fully, only three other streets, the Burrough Walls, the Grove, and Quiet Street had more than two alehouses and in each there were three alehouses. This concentration of alehouses along the main traffic routes and in the old city centre meant that the noise and scenes associated with continuous drinking – drunkenness was the cause of ten drownings and five other deaths by violence between 1776 and 1799 – was largely confined to the parishes of St Peter and Paul and St James and the southern-most part of Walcot around Avon Street. In these parishes one house in nine or ten was licensed as an alehouse whereas in Walcot generally, which was the parish of the wealthy, only one house in thirty was so licensed. If one removes from the calculation the number of houses licensed in Avon Street, where the ratio was as high as 1:8, the ratio for Walcot parish drops to 1:38. Thirty years later, in 1806, although there had been a further fall in the over-all ratio to 1:32, the parishes of St James and St Peter and Paul were relatively worse off. In these parishes the ratio was then 1:18 and 1:12 respectively, whereas in Walcot it had fallen as low as 1:75. While it may be true that the mere number of alehouses is not in itself a sufficient indicator of sobriety – the wealthy of Walcot may simply have got drunk at home – it is an indication of the way urban space was used and of the way in which almost continuous public drinking with its attendant nuisances was kept away from the Utopian areas of Bath. The location of so high a proportion of alehouses along the traffic routes, which reduced their attraction as quality residential areas, shows clearly the influence of the market in fixing the organisation of space in the city.

Avon Street was no exception. Although it was not on a main traffic route it was itself a route for traffic. It seems to have become so some time before 1755. In that year John Lockyer of Walcot was presented by the Grand Jury for altering the footpath at the bottom of Avon Street, which led from the Quay to Great Kingsmead, 'by making a dangerous slip for watering horses and not making the necessary fence for the safety of passengers. Also the watering place being very dangerous as had been proved by woeful experience there having been several men and horses lost for want of a proper fence.'[44] Thereafter this slip at the bottom of Avon Street was the principal watering place for horses. As a result the street became a regular thoroughfare for great waggons with wheels six inches wide drawn by teams of six and eight horses. While the horses were watered the waggoners drank. And, by 1776 there were eleven alehouses in Avon Street, roughly one in eight of the houses in the street and its connected courts.

Some consequences of this concentration of traffic and alehouses were road accidents, frequent drownings and a general lowering of the social tone of the place such that the Methodists who lived and had their meeting room there in 1757 must have been decidedly uncomfortable twenty years later.

This effect of competition and the life cycle of decay, social neglect and further decay, was already complained of in 1786. Addressing himself to the authorities appointed under the Act of 1766 one Avon Street resident wrote, 'I am sorry that present circumstances makes your attention necessary in Avon Street, which with the large quantities of all kinds of nastiness thrown out by its inhabitants for a whole week together and the interspersion of here and there a group of pigs makes a perfect dung muckson from one end to the other. Because 'tis Avon Street once a week is thought sufficient for the scavenger to cleanse it but from the disorderly practices of most of its inhabitants makes it necessary it should be well swept etc. every day, which I shall leave to your consideration.'[45]

But so little was Avon Street considered that by 1821 it was the home of 1,519 people (5.4 per cent of the population); a place where the parents in one third of families were unmarried and one quarter of children were illegitimate. It was then so unsavoury and poor that even the alehouse keepers had deserted it. As early as 1806 only three alehouses remained in it and only one, the Smith's Arms, was a survivor from 1776. Moreover, flooding, intensified by the narrowing of the river channel caused by building along its banks, was an annual problem. It caused effluent from its sewers and drains and waste from its pigsties and a slaughter house to be periodically washed back into the basements of its houses and into the streets themselves. The problem was so great that in the cholera outbreak of 1831, 27 out of 49 deaths in the city were in this street alone, while the majority of the remaining deaths were either in streets contiguous to Avon Street, such as Corn Street, or in Holloway. Then, in 1838, a little more than 100 years after it was built, Avon Street became the site for the Refuge for the Destitute where, every night, itinerants were relieved with a meal of coarse bread, gruel and cheap soup, and a sack of straw. And the street generally was notorious as a sanctuary for thieves, prostitutes, gamblers, juvenile delinquents, vagrants and the destitute. One might say that this part of the city, more than any other, was then the home of the lumpenproletariat. It was tucked away and out of sight, literally at the bottom of the town; the heartland, at the end of the eighteenth century, of an area of working-class settlement extending along the Upper Bristol Road, Kingsmead Street, St John's Place, Milk Street, Avon Street, and Corn Street, where, for example, in 1800 38 per cent of building workers lived. There were other areas, too, housing the labouring population, built where the ground was low-lying, as in the Dolemeads in the parish of Lyncombe and Widcombe; along traffic routes, as in Walcot Street; or, where the ground had proved itself unsafe for quality building as in Hedgemead and Snow Hill. In this latter area, in Margaret's Hill, James Buildings and Dover Street there were clusters of small back-to-back houses while in Upper Hedgemead there was, until the 1960s, a line of thirty houses built with their backs against a great stone wall built into the hillside. Only in Lampards Buildings, Ballance and Morford Streets, built from the 1770s to the 1790s, did artisans experience something of Wood's Utopia. But even there there were narrow courts with houses almost indistinguishable from back-to-back houses.

The plain fact was that market forces and competitive building in Bath by the last decade of the eighteenth century had created a city that was a hodge-podge of architectural styles and of private and corporate developments. It was also a city marked by separate areas of settlement for its visiting company and its labouring population. Moreover, during its building booms the noise and bustle of its traffic was heightened by the incessant activity of building and its building workers such that as its population went about knocking down and building up, Utopia must sometimes have seemed a distant prospect to most of them.

Socially, too, Bath was a network of contradictions. Just at the time when the Corporation began its break with the older ideology of social and economic corporatism and to merge indistinguishably with all other private developers in an aggressive race to get rich and to crown its achievements with expensive monuments to its own glory and interests, John Wood had built in protest against such self-interested materialism and against the competitive practice and ideology of civil society. Yet Wood and his son were as aggressively enterpreneurial in the race to build as any other developer and more tied to the world of money and credit than many of their peers. There was, therefore, tension between social and economic corporatism and individualism, tension between economic corporatism and Wood's Utopia, and Wood at odds with himself.

Such contradictions and tensions were inherent in absolute property and the doctrine of self-interest from their very beginning. Accordingly vestigial social and economic corporatism was found necessary for the very success of its individualistic developers as well as for the preservation of that utopian appearance so attractive to its company. Therefore, the Corporation, through its Mayor and

Justices meeting as magistrates and in Quarter Sessions, kept householders up to the mark in regard to their responsibilities for pitching and paving, regulated crime and the poor, and controlled prices and the quality of food sold in their markets. As far as development was concerned they built the markets and the Guildhall. Above all, in the Act of 1766, they secured new powers which were to be important in facilitating private building in Bathwick as well as in Milsom Street and in High Street and important, eventually, in the whole redevelopment of the centre of the old town. These powers included powers of compulsory purchase and exchange, and powers of entry and breaking up the soil of any private ground within two miles of the city for the provision and maintenance of an adequate water supply, with the exception of ground belonging to the Duke of Kingston.

Seventy-six years later this Act, 6 Geo III (C70), was praised by Chadwick as the very model of conditions for the public control of water supplies to cities. It was noted that although there were five water companies in Bath at that date (1842), the Corporation supplied three-quarters of the town's water and provided five public pumps. It was with the powers granted to them under this Act of 1766 that the Corporation built the Markets and the Guildhall and entered into agreement with William Pulteney for the development of Bathwick. In these ways the Corporation also significantly influenced the organisation of space in Bath and economic corporatism in its new guise was still an important factor in shaping the organisation of space in the city. Thus, although in general the market ruled, it did so within an existing social and political structure. This conjuncture of the existing distribution of power and market forces led to a further concentration of economic and political power in the hands of the Corporation.

But, in other areas of social activity lying outside the competence of the Corporation, the market and the ideology of self-interest emerged triumphant to add other components to the organisation of space in the city. One of them which focuses attention on the role of ideology and utopia, concerns the Assembly Rooms.

Throughout the first three-quarters of the eighteenth-century the needs and purposes of a class of agrarian capitalists dictated the social mood of the place. Men who mattered, and those who did not, still looked at their world through spectacles coloured by tradition and thought about it in the language of orders and ranks.

Accordingly, those with power and privilege hoped for the preservation of social order and for the maintenance of old, if not of the oldest, ways. According to their lights they wanted a sort of harmony. They had this much in common with Wood, and it is possible that they gained some reassurance in these matters from his buildings. And, whether they did so or not, they had certainly drawn comfort from Beau Nash who was the very symbol of Bath's need to generate social order out of the anomie and aggressive social mobility of civil society; why else would a wit like Lord Hervey and an intelligence like Sarah Scott put up with the flamboyant coarseness and boorishness of the man himself? But, in 1761, he too, was dead. And, in 1765, the year in which the Glazby decision marked the end of social corporatism, the Assembly Rooms in the lower town, through which Beau Nash had strutted in his white suit and cocked hat, to impose a sort of social order, were threatened by that growing characteristic of the times; a new and uncontrolled competition.

In the 1760s there were two sets of Assembly Rooms; Harrison's later Simpson's, built originally in 1708 and remodelled in 1749, and Lindsey's, later Wiltshire's, built in 1728. Both were small, rather old-fashioned, and situated in the lower town on inconvenient routes from the upper town and not far distant from the main traffic routes already described. Both were licensed as alehouses.

The threat to their popularity first appeared in May 1764 when John Wood the younger entered into an agreement with Sir Benet Garrard, a member of the Gay family, for a lease of one and a half acres of ground on the north-west corner of Queen Square: His purpose, to build an Assembly Room.[46] The threat became real in November when a proposal to start building the Rooms with a capital of £12,600 raised by 120 shares on a tontine was made public. When 112 shares were immediately taken up objections began to flow. Some of the prospective shareholders, wishing to preserve their separateness from the socially harmful effects to be expected from an alehouse, objected to the proposal to build a tavern as part of the scheme. It was, they thought, 'an improper appendange to a set of Public Rooms.'[47] Even the proposal to substitute a theatre for the tavern was insufficient to stifle opposition. Fortunately for the opposition, as the building boom from 1762 to 1771 got under way, tenders for the building proved too high and Wood abandoned the project. He built instead a terrace of twelve houses as an unplanned addition to Queen Square. The reprieve was short lived. Robert Adam, probably at the instigation of William Pulteney, a man we have yet to meet as one of Bath's most enterprising and successful entrepreneurs, had also prepared a design for a suite of Assembly Rooms. These were to be built east of the King's Circus. This scheme also proved too expensive for its undertakers. Instead John Wood's more modest plans for the site were accepted.

The foundation stone for this development was laid in May 1768 and the New or Upper Assembly Rooms were opened for business in September 1771. The £20,000 they cost to build made the Assembly Rooms the biggest investment in a single building in Bath. It was, moreover, a corporate enterprise which raised the required capital on a tontine from seventy-two shareholders. These shares were transferable and by 1780 only thirty-one of the original shareholders held shares. Although there was no mention of limited liability in the articles of agreement the shareholders had clearly given considerable thought to the problem of limiting their liability and there can be little doubt that the enterprise, known as the New Assembly Rooms, was an innovation in corporate capitalism such as the city had never seen before. Because the purpose of the investors was capital gain the enterprise had to make a profit. Consequently it was licensed as an alehouse – in 1776 the man who stood surety for its licensee, Robert Hayward, was the distiller Francis Ansty who also had an interest in two other alehouses, The Chequers in Stall Street and the Duke of Cumberland in Orchard Street. Hayward, too, had a complementary interest as surety in Ansty's wine and spirit business in Stall Street.

The threat of competition from the New Assembly Rooms forced the closure of Wiltshire's Rooms and the building was turned into a warehouse. But, Simpson's, lately Gyde's, with William Wade as MC, smartened itself up and an era of lively competition began. By 1774 a committee of users, of the nobility and gentry, headed by three members of the landed aristocracy; Lords Cadogan, Camden and Southwell, moved to eliminate competition and to preserve what they regarded as the proper social order and economic decorum – in memory they looked back to the days of Beau Nash. This committee proposed a scheme to divide the market between the competing Assembly Rooms while Wade began to dissuade visitors from subscribing to either of them without first consulting him.

That is, he began to assert a public authority over the two sets of Rooms which was not his to claim. This was too much for the proprietors of the New Rooms who, incidentally, also included in their ranks three members of the landed aristocracy; Lady Ladd, Lord Northumberland and the Marquis of Carnarvon. The proprietors of the New Rooms replied to the self-appointed committee of social order by simply resting their case on their inalienable right to use their collective property in any way they alone might see fit. They placed the following notice in the *Bath Chronicle*:[48]

> They (the Proprietors) beg leave to declare, that as they cannot think it reasonable that they should submit the management of their property and servants to any set of men, much less can they be willing to submit the control of them to an individual. They always have been, and still are willing to allow, to a Master of the Ceremonies, every power and authority requisite to preserve and promote order, decorum and regularity at the public amusements held at their rooms; but they must ever think it necessary to determine for themselves, what use shall be made of their property, and what servants shall take care of it.

So, they declared, the Rooms would be open every evening except Fridays and alternate Sundays and there would be a ball every Monday and a concert every Thursday.

The committee of social order headed by Lords Cadogan, Camden and Southwell found such an expression of intent and conduct most extraordinary. They resolved to withdraw their subscriptions to the New Rooms and, in high dudgeon, declared, they, 'will not at anytime hereafter subscribe or resort to the New Rooms.' They also granted Mr Gyde, the proprietor of the Old Rooms, full liberty to open his Rooms, 'when and in what manner he shall see fitting, under the control of the Master of Ceremonies.'[49] In reply to this gesture the shareholders in the £20,000 investment stated their rights to trade as they alone thought fit. Although they conceded that consumers had an equal right to purchase their product at the price offered, or not, as the consumer might wish, they also denied that consumers had any right to determine the nature of the product or the times at which it would be on offer. In short, they rested their case on their right to absolute property and the determination of the market. That they did so two years before Adam Smith made their case theoretically clear and explicit in *The Wealth of Nations* is evidence enough that experience of the operation of the market was a sufficient forcing ground for an ideology of absolute self-interest. And in Bath at that!

The significance of this event was recognised at the time. Just as, in 1779, the author of *Bath – a Simile* had recognised architecture in Bath as a monstrous tea-set, symbolic of the latest fashion in consumption, matching the trivial round of the tea drinkers it housed, another of Bath's poets grasped the social and economic significance of the Assembly Rooms.

A storm in a tea-cup, perhaps, but a pointer to things to come for those who had yet to realise that they had happened already. The piece of doggerel in question, *The Coblers of Bath: An Allegorical Story* appeared in the *Bath Chronicle* on 8 December 1774 under the authorship of Clarissa.

In order to understand the thrust of its social comment it helps to know that of all the classes needed in the construction and servicing of Bath and who lived in places like Avon Street, that cobblers, cordwainers and shoemakers were the lowest. Their work with leather in the making of shoes and boots was dirty and marked them with an unmistakably unpleasant smell. Even at their weddings they were described as, 'uniformly more dirty and ill-dressed, than any other class of persons.' Worse still they were frequently ostracised even by their fellow workers. Since they commonly employed their wives and women to work alongside them the designation 'shoemaker's wife' was a term of the greatest approbrium. Perhaps the measure of their condition is that, when, in the 1830s, the average age at death of labourers and their families was 25, that for shoemakers and their families was 14 years. Moreover, there were so many of them; in the early nineteenth century they were the biggest single occupational group and some of them had grown into capitalists and into positions of wealth without status. The Cobblers referred to in the following verses were a successful group of entrepreneurs, the proprietors of the Assembly Rooms![50]

THE COBLERS OF BATH: AN ALLEGORICAL STORY

> A Cobler there was, and he built him a stall,
> Sweet region of pleasure and taste,
> Receptacle meet for the great and the small
> Sad soles that are running to waste.

Of possession grown proud, now the coblers decree
The neighbourhood long to disclose,
Men and Maidens run slipshod to hear and to see,
And stood on the tip of his toes.

That Mondays were pump days he deign'd to reveal,
And importantly dealt out the news;
That Wednesdays were fix'd for nice work for the heel,
And Thursdays for old shoes.

The rest of the week to his neighbour John Trot,
In the regions below one and all
They might go, or decline it, he valu'd them not,
For a Cobler is King of his Stall.

The old Cobler grumbled his rival to see
Assume such a resolute face,
And begg'd that both ladies and gents would agree
To humble his pride in disgrace.

The Lords and the Ladies agreed one and all
His arrogant schemes to undo,
But alas! they repair'd but the more to his Stall,
For the world still is fond of what's new.

Then prithee my friends, about the trifles agree,
Full of sweetness is Concord's fine flower,
This world fosters weeds, its distinctions are three,
Independence, Advantage, and Power.

Clarissa

And, there it stands, the New Assembly Rooms, its existence an affront to Utopia and good order, and its location the very negation of planning – it squats behind the King's Circus, with no planned spatial relationship to the Circus itself. It is the product and symbol of the struggle between ideology and utopia. Like Avon Street, it too marks the victory of absolute property and absolute self-interest, which were there in the beginning, even in the Corporation's corporatism and in John Wood's utopia. As Clarissa wrote, 'This world fosters weeds, it distinctions are three, Independence, Advantage, and Power'.

But the Rooms, once its proprietors had successfully eliminated their competitors, carried out the same social task. For a price it provided a social forum for the preservation and promotion of order, decorum, and regularity in society; at least at the upper levels. It was, therefore, not only an expression of competition but also a secular symbol of the moral order felt necessary for the efficient functioning of a market society. Without such a moral order, the market economy of civil society is ever in danger of degeneration, of collapsing into licence, even within the ranks of the propertied – absolute property breeds absolute self-interest. Worse still, absolute property and absolute self-interest produced places like Avon Street and the labouring population who inhabited them. It was no mere accident, therefore, and no figment of historical imagination, that as social corporatism died and as economic corporatism put on a new developmental face and as individualism emerged triumphant to produce an organisation of space which emphasised the separation of the classes that, in 1763, the journeymen tailors of Bath took their first faltering steps to protect themselves, organised their first recorded strike in 1775, and, in 1784, resorted to force to protect their interests against those of their employers. Here, indeed, were the stirrings of a search for a different utopia. In the ensuing uneven contest between the social classes the utopian imagery of Wood's contribution to the organisation of space in Bath had no part to play. And, although social conflict was to be physically structured by the organisation of space he had helped to produce, it was the social structure of society which underpinned that organisation of space that was to matter most. We take up the theme of ideology and utopia in the consciousness of the people in the final two chapters.

CHAPTER SEVEN

PROPERTY AND ABSOLUTE SELF-INTEREST

The Manor contains by a late survey about 600 acres. When it was purchased by Lord Bath from the Earl of Essex 40 years ago, the whole except a trifle was out upon lives, but during that Period about 440 acres have come into Hand some part of which has been let out for terms of years, and there remain still about 160 acres held by the surviving lives Lord Bath having granted no renewals . . .
 If a Bridge is built over the Avon somewhere near the City Prison, it is expected that a good deal of the Ground near the Bridge will be taken by Builders for erecting Houses and that they will agree to pay considerable Ground Rents . . .
MS. 1809 Pulteney Estate Papers, 1768

The two waves of building before 1760, during which the work of all the persons and classes who have appeared so far in this book transformed the city and much of the parish of Walcot, left almost no mark on Bathwick. Apart from the development of Spring Gardens as a pleasure resort around 1735, the 600 acres in the manor of Bathwick remained in agricultural use and the most notable building in the parish was a woollen mill. Its appearance was misleading. As in Walcot and Bath significant change was taking place. This change began in 1726 when the property passed into the hands of William Pulteney, a man committed to belief in the rights of absolute property and to the doctrine of self-interest; it was said of him, in 1737, that he opposed a reduction in the interest on the national debt because his wife's fortune, some £60,000, was invested in it! His own fortune, too, was immense. Worth at least £50,000 per annum he was, like Chandos, a millionaire. And it was as part of his drive to amass wealth that he determined to eliminate the lifehold tenancies on the Bathwick Estate. By 1768 he had succeeded in that task on 440 acres of it and raised its gross rental to £735 per annum. This much has already been described in chapter 3. The rental of £735 represented a return of 25$s.$ per acre and a gross return on its capital value, in 1726, of rather less than 6 per cent. Compared with the rate per acre paid by builders in Walcot it was, of course, a very meagre return. Even so it represented a substantial hidden achievement by the *'Patriot'* champion of the small landowner.

Pulteney's ability to exploit the estate still further was prevented by the lack of a bridge between Bathwick and Walcot where the main development was taking place. An attempt to bridge the Avon to the Walcot side, recorded in an agreement with Samuel Bishop Esq. in 1757, had come to nothing and Pulteney died in 1764 having made no progress on another scheme to build a bridge in the vicinity of the South Parade.[1] Yet his death, plus the fact that his own children were also dead, virtually ensured that the estate would pass to a man even more in tune with the developmental ethos of the second half of the eighteenth century than Pulteney himself. Pulteney's immediate heir was his brother General Pulteney. He, too, was childless. The next in line was Frances, granddaughter of Pulteney's uncle. Frances however, had been married off in 1764 to the younger son of a small Scots landowner, William Johnstone who, on marriage, took the name Pulteney. He was to inherit the Johnstone Baronetcy and the family estate at Westerhall in Scotland when his brother died in 1797.

At the time of his marriage and his wife's inheritance of the Pulteney estates in 1767, William Johnstone Pulteney or, Mr Pulteney, as he was known in Bath, was an Edinburgh lawyer and a partner in a Dumfries bank. Reputedly he was 'a quiet man of plain, unadorned language and strong personality'.[2] As a member of Parliament he was always received in the House with respectful attention. He also had an eye for talent, and in 1787 was the patron of Telford, the road and canal builder, in the matter of his first important appointment as a Surveyor of Public Works for the County of Salop. From 1787 to 1793 Pulteney also employed Telford to work on the Pulteney estates and Telford came to know him well.

Telford thought Pulteney remarkably engaging, 'a man who does not court popularity; he is distant, courteous, and reserved to mankind in general, but I believe to the few in whom he can confide there is no man more open.'[3] He had a reputation for parsimony in private affairs and is said to have lived for many years on a diet of bread and milk. On the occasion of his marriage to Frances Pulteney his friend George Dempster wrote to him, 'The contents of your last letter afford me most sensible pleasure. I long to see you at the head of £20,000 per annum. Few things are more pleasing to a disinterested man than to see an old friend in a new character and a higher station. I already anticipate every patriot spirited and generous purpose to which it will be applied.'[4]

Pulteney, however, had to wait on the side-lines for another three years, until General Pulteney died in 1767. Even then he was never 'owner' of the Bathwick estate. It was entailed. Accordingly, Frances, Pulteney's wife, was only tenant for life and on her death the estate would pass to their daughter Henrietta Laura. Consequently there were other trustees to consider and there were other claims on the estate. Pulteney's position was, therefore, more akin to the senior, although most important, administrator of a large corporate enterprise, one of the largest in England. It was in this capacity that in 1769, he drew up a proposal for building a bridge across the Avon and circulated it among the other trustees of the estate. The proposal was an attractive one. Its principal argument was as follows:[5]

> If a Bridge is built over the Avon somewhere near the City Prison, it is expected that a good deal of the Ground near the Bridge will be taken by Builders for erecting Houses and that they will agree to pay considerable Ground Rents. The ground where the Circus is built was let to Builders at £5 per acre and it is expected the Ground in Question will let for a good deal more, and even as to the Fields which may not be built upon, the Rent will be much increased by means of the Bridge because at present it is necessary to go near two Miles round to the present Bridge in order to carry Horses or Cattle from Bath to this Manor and all Carts with Dung from Bath or with the produce of the Estate to Bath must make the same Circuit and must also pay at a Turnpike but after the Bridge is built, these Fields which are chiefly in Grass, will be found very convenient

for pasturing Horses and Cows belonging to the Inhabitants and the Carriage of Dung and of the produce of the Estate will be attended with less than half the Expense.

It is supposed too that many of the Inhabitants will choose to build Villas along the face of the Hill as the situation and prospect are remarkably fine.

The Village too of Bathwick which is upon this Manor and where there is a considerable Woollen Manufactory will be brought in effect a Mile and a half nearer to Bath by means of this Bridge and there is great Reason to expect that the buildings in that Village will be greatly encreased.

The prospect was good. The third wave of building was already well under way in Bath and it looked as if nobody could lose from the development of Bathwick. At the same time it was felt that the cost to the estate of building the bridge would be slight. First, a concession of water rights to Bath Corporation. In return the Corporation would be expected to co-operate with Pulteney in an exchange of land and in the purchase of property in Bath; these were necessary to build an access road to the bridge from the Bath side. On the matter of water rights Pulteney was reassuring. There was enough water in Bathwick not only for the city, 'but also to supply 5,000 houses, if so great a number should be built on this manor.'[6] Equally encouraging was the knowledge that, early in January 1769, the Corporation, by a vote of 14:6 had agreed to Pulteney's proposal and approved the design of the bridge. Secondly, there was the question of the capital cost. Privately Pulteney anticipated no difficulties on that score either. He had consulted Thomas Lightoler, the architect of the Octagon Chapel in Milsom Street, who had provided him with an estimate of £1,000. Bearing in mind the probable cost of providing land for access on the Bath side and of getting an Act of Parliament granting power to the trustees to carry out the project, Pulteney guessed that a mortgage on the Bathwick estate of £3,000 would more than cover all the necessary costs.[7] It was on this basis and with the consent of the trustees of the Pulteney estate and Bath Corporation that Pulteney rapidly pushed the Bill through Parliament in 1769.[8]

Under the Act for building the bridge the trustees of the estate were given new powers to do collectively that which otherwise would have been impossible. They were given powers to grant building leases, to grant water rights to Bath Corporation, to allow the Corporation to build a reservoir in Bathwick, to extend the powers of Bath's magistrates to Bathwick, to sell and exchange land and to raise £3,000 on mortgage. The bridge itself was to be free of tolls. Armed with these new powers Pulteney continued to act expediently believing that, 'The great rapidity with which the new buildings are going on in other parts of the town, makes every delay hurtful to this scheme.'[9]

Pulteney's decision to build the bridge on its present site was influenced by an earlier decision of the Corporation to redevelop its own property on the eastern side of the town. In order to do so the Corporation had also sought and gained additions to its own powers. And under powers granted to it by its own Act of 1766 the Corporation had already begun to build a new Guildhall and improve the markets. As part of this project it also intended to widen the High Street and open up a parade along the river from the Orange Grove to the site of the proposed bridge. All of this development was intended to improve access to the Baths, Assembly Rooms, and Pump Room. Pulteney hoped to benefit from it too. He also depended upon the Corporation for an exchange of land for the site of the city gaol, which stood on ground needed for access to the bridge on the city side of the river and he needed the help of the Corporation in the acquisition of the rest of the ground for this approach road; most of this ground was held by private individuals on leases from the Corporation.

In the middle of 1769 Pulteney was kept busy in Bath negotiating for these sites and seeking tenders for building. It was at this stage that cost as well as speed began to appear vital. As a result, it was not long before he began to have doubts about the viability of the whole enterprise. The Corporation's tenants of the ground he needed demanded £6,950 to relinquish their titles. Almost half of this was demanded by one man, Edward Collibee, who well knew what Pulteney had in mind, he was a member of the Corporation. Collibee demanded £3,150 for the title to his ground. Of course such sums were far beyond the powers of the trustees as granted to them by the Act of 1769. Pulteney, too, was reluctant to venture his own funds in buying the titles even though he might have been able to resell the ground not needed for the roadway.

Even more disquieting was the proven unreliability of Lightholer's estimate, which at £1,000 could have been no more than a guess. It was a very low one and probably arose out of Pulteney's original plan which was for a very simple bridge, one that would merely link Bathwick with Bath. Even so it was a very low estimate indeed; less than £7 per foot compared with an actual cost of £14 per foot for the North Bridge in Edinburgh, which was already being built. One suspects that, while the estimate of £1,000 may have served its purpose in influencing the other trustees, Pulteney himself ought to have known better. As a result of trying to extricate himself from a difficult position Pulteney has left an account of his proceedings which throws much light on the planning and building of the bridge as it now exists. The full story will show that the bridge, frequently regarded as another fragment of purposeful planning in Bath, was also a happy although expensive accident influenced by economically motivated attempts to undo the worst effects of Lightholder's mistake. Pulteney wrote:[10]

> With regard to the Bridge itself I at first proposed to build it with one arch, but upon considering that the ground is low on the Bathwick side, and that so large an arch must rise very high and thereby occasion too great an ascent, I have thought it best to have three arches, and I find by estimates made of both, that three arches will be cheaper than one owing to the great expense of timber for supporting one large arch and the greater strength of abutements. I propose the Bridge to be 30 feet wide the same as the street viz. two footways of 5 feet each and 20 feet for the coachway. It is of importance to the success of the whole plan that the communication be made not only easy but pleasant. I have got a plan of the bridge with three arches, made by Mr Paty an architect of good character, who was entrusted with the direction of the New Bridge built at Bristol by Act of Parliament which cost above £15,000. I send your Lordship a copy of that plan which though made in a hurry, I believe is tolerably exact. I also send you an estimate made out by Mr Paty by which he reckons the expense at £4,569. But I have found out people of character here who are willing to find security to build the bridge according to Mr Paty's plan and to support it for 7 years or rebuild it if it should fall, for a much less sum that he has reckoned and I send your Lordship a copy of their estimate amounting to £2,389.11.0d.

Paty's design, which was the one accepted and according to which work was started, was for a 150-foot bridge with three arches, a thirty-foot carriageway with two footways of five feet each. It was to be a bridge without shops. With its approaches it could be expected to cost at least £9,340. So, it was with some bitterness that Pulteney wrote, 'I find Mr Lightholer's estimate is utterly erroneous and I have reason to repent my having given the least credit to it.'[11]

Faced with a minimum outlay of £9,340 Pulteney had only the £3,000 mortgage authorised by the Act of Parliament and raised from a consortium of three: John Burton Esq., from Devon, Leonard Burton Esq., from Northampton and James Fisher, merchant from Norwich.[12] Therefore he was forced to use his own resources, and it was £6,950 of his own money that was used to finance the purchase of the titles to the land needed for the western approach road. Since some of this land was later resold for £4,450 the net cost to Pulteney was eventually only £1,500. Unfortunately the place of his Scottish banking connections in this operation is hidden from us. Even so, the funds available were insufficient. By March 1773 the cost of building, first estimated at £1,000, then at £2,389 had risen to £8,183 and the total cost had risen from an estimated £3,000 to an actual cost of £10,998. In anticipation of this cost rise Pulteney had secured a second Act of Parliament in 1772. This Act authorised a further mortgage of £3,500 which was raised from Isabella Pitt of Middlesex.[13]

A major reason for the rise in costs was that by mid-1770 Pulteney had literally changed architects in midstream. The original building contract, given to Messrs Lowther and Ried, had been for a simple and economical three-arched bridge according to Paty's design.[14] For about a year work on Paty's design had been carried out to the value of £2,651.[15] However, by July 1770, Pulteney seems to have agreed with the Adam brothers to make the bridge much wider and to build houses or shops on either side of it,[16] 'It being apprehended that the design now carrying on of building a Bridge over the river Avon will not only be improved but a benefit will arise to the owner of the Manor of Bathwick for the time being if the said Bridge be so constructed that a row of shops of the width of 10 feet be built on each side thereof with a space of 30 feet between the rows of such shops.'[17] It was also said that the redesigned bridge would add considerably to the annual value of the estate.[18] Although this agreement to extend the bridge in this way was not referred to the other trustees until 17 May 1771 a new start on the bridge according to Adam's design seems to have been made by mid-1770[19] without the approval of the other trustees and without prior consultation with Bath Corporation whose co-operation on the original proposal and bridge had been essential. Understandably the Corporation was much concerned about the change of plan. Indeed, it was so upset about the change and what it heard about the new-fangled old-style bridge that it wrote at length objecting to it. There can be little doubt that if the Corporation had had their way Mr Pulteney's bridge would have been the plain and simple affair he had originally planned for and begun building.[20]

To William Pulteney Esq.

We the Mayor, Aldermen and Common Council of the City of Bath beg leave to represent

That when we entered into treaty with him relative to the intended Bridge from Bath to Bathwick, the advantages arising therefrom appeared to us to be reciprocal. We therefore confined Mr Pulteney neither to dimensions nor Plan depending on him to make the Avenues not only commodious but as compleat as the nature and circumstances of the affair would admit of.

Tho' we would wish to intermeddle as little as possible where the expense of the undertaking does not immediately fall on ourselves we must nevertheless consider that the welfare of the City of Bath is entrusted to our care; that we have given up a valuable part of the City Estate to compleat this Design and that consequently we may be allowed at least to hope that it will be carried into Execution conformable to our expectations.

We have learnt from the Surveyor that a Row of Houses is intended on each side of the Bridge, a scheme which if pursued we conceive must be disadvantageous to Both Parties; and the general Dissatisfaction of the Town convinces us that we are not singular in our opinion.

We presume that Mr Pulteney himself on re-considering the matter will see the Impropriety of it, that the circulation of Air will be prevented, that the Smoak will greatly incommode the neighbourhood on each side the River, that if a concourse of people constantly pass over it, which must be the case before the shops can be of any value, the dimensions of the Bridge will then be too narrow to make the Passage convenient. That a street on a Bridge of no greater breadth than thirty feet will never be thought, according to the modern Ideas of Buildings, to have an elegant Appearance and that it has been for some years past an uniform practice throughout the Kingdom to avoid and condemn incumbrances of this kind.

As we never expected this plan to be adopted so we conceive that we never concurred in granting Ground for the purpose. Half the river is the property of the Corporation. In our treaty as well as contract with Mr Pulteney no Houses ever were mentioned. What we granted was for the Conveniency of a spacious and Commodious Communication only therefore no more can be implied to be granted than what is necessary for such a communication.

We therefore hope from this Representation of the case that Mr Pulteney will lay aside his scheme of Building any Shops on the said Bridge and leave it open and unconfined like those of London and Bristol.

In spite of such a strong expression of hostility to his new design and having failed to consult the other trustees Pulteney persisted with his project, underwriting it with his own resources until such time as the trustees agreed to further Acts of Parliament extending their powers of borrowing. Subsequently he appears to have laid to rest the worst fears of the Corporation, particularly in respect to the width of the bridge.[21] It was to be 50 feet rather than 30 feet wide. This widening of the bridge and the necessary strengthening of the piers and abutments was an important factor in increasing the cost of the structure. Another, was the cost of building the shops. They added £2,549 to the bill. These improvements plus increased administrative charges pushed the total cost of the bridge and its approaches to almost £11,000. The bridge itself cost £59 per foot, which was four times the cost of the Edinburgh North Bridge and rather more than twice the cost of the Tay Bridge; both bridges being built at the time of the building of Mr Pulteney's bridge. In consequence of the increased cost and in order to reimburse Pulteney for his expenses involved in acquiring the ground for Bridge Street, a third Act of Parliament was passed empowering the trustees to raise an additional £4,239 on mortgage. The total mortgage charge was, therefore, £10,739. By 1777 the accumulated interest charge on this debt meant that the bridge-building scheme had cost the trustees a sum equal to the capital value of the Bathwick estate in 1726. It was indeed, a most risky undertaking.

If the views of the Corporation are to be trusted, the bridge was not even in the best of taste (Figure 20). Also, according to the Bath Grand Jury, its building had created something of a nuisance. In order to raise the approach road to the bridge above flood level on the Bathwick side and to keep the road as level as possible it had been necessary to raise a great embanked causeway leading to the bridge. Until houses were built on either side of the causeway it remained unfenced and a hazard to pedestrians. By 1777 it was felt to be so dangerous that the Grand Jury presented Pulteney because, 'the way from the New Bridge to Spring Gardens (was) very dangerous, having no walls to prevent passengers from falling from such a precipice as may endanger their lives, or kill them on the spot.'[22]

More damaging for the estate was the fact that the bridge had not begun to pay for itself. Some nine months after the bridge had been finished early in 1774 its shops as well as stables and warehouses on the Bathwick side were still without tenants,[23] the reason being that Pulteney had missed the peak of the building boom in Bath. Building activity, which had added an average of fifty-six houses a year between 1766 and 1773, was reduced to a level adding only thirteen houses annually in the years 1773–6. In fact the peak had been reached in 1771. Thereafter demand was depressed and was not to recover until after the end of the war with America. The result was that no building leases were taken up on the Bathwick estate until December 1787 and June 1788 when a revival of demand produced a fourth wave of building. Therefore, the return on Pulteney's speculation was long delayed; rents on the Bathwick estate rose only slowly from £735 in 1768 to £1,179 in 1777.

Perhaps another reason for the sluggishness of demand for building sites on the Bathwick side, at least during the early 1770s and before the effects of the war made themselves felt, was the collective opposition by locally powerful interest groups to another aspect of Pulteney's grand design which only slowly became clear to local people. Early in 1771, when the bridge was still a long way from completion, Pulteney proposed to seek a further Act of Parliament granting him powers to build a bridge across the Avon at Bathford and put in a new turnpike road linking that bridge with the as yet uncompleted Pulteney bridge. The effect of such a design would

Figure 20 Pulteney Bridge

have been to divert the main London traffic away from the turnpike through the Parish of Walcot with its northern approach to the town and to draw it towards and across the Bathwick estate to enter the city across Pulteney Bridge. Clearly Pulteney's hope was for a consequential rapid rise in land values and, perhaps, the building of the 5,000 houses he had mentioned in his proposal of 1769. Before proceeding with the scheme Pulteney sought the co-operation of Bath Corporation. This time, however, no doubt with some of its members remembering the sudden unannounced change of plans about the shops on the bridge, the Corporation was hostile to Pulteney's proposal. By a decision of a large majority, 16:4, a counter petition opposing the scheme was drawn up to present to Parliament stating: 'There is no foundation for such Pretensions (of public advantage) that it is a scheme intended only for Private Emolument and if carried into Execution will by laying additional Duties on the Public be highly injurious to the City in general and to your Petitioners and their respective lessees holding estates under them in particular.'[24]

Pulteney's proposal was also opposed by the trustees of the Bath turnpike. This was done at a large meeting packed with representatives from Bath including Ralph Allen, John Wood, John Jeffreys as well as Messrs Ditcher, Attwood, Coward and Hanford.[25] In the face of such collective opposition Pulteney abandoned the idea – for the time being.

With the bridge completed in 1774 and in anticipation of support from the Corporation Pulteney tried again to advance his scheme for a bridge at Bathford and a new turnpike. But the Corporation was still solidly opposed to the proposal and again decided to support a counter petition against it. The trustees of the turnpike also took prompt action to oppose the scheme and, once again, it came to nothing.[26] Nevertheless, Pulteney continued to have high hopes for the Bathwick estate and in 1777 and 1782 Robert Adam drew up several sketch plans for its development. They, too, came to nothing. Consequently the only substantial building built in Bathwick between 1774 and 1788 was the new gaol. It sat incongruously on the north side of the bridge only a few hundred yards away from the pleasure resort of Spring Gardens, an organisation of space intended by no one!

As the American War came to an end demand for Bath recovered and costs of building began to fall. With the bridge already built

Pulteney was in good position to benefit from the boom and he was one of the first to exploit the new more favourable conditions in Bath. Consequently, from 1787 building leases on the Bathwick estate were rapidly taken up. The sequence of the building boom as reflected in building in Bathwick is shown in table 7.1.

TABLE 7.1 Building leases granted on the Bathwick estate, 1784–93

1784	1785	1786	1787	1788	1789	1790	1791	1792	1793
1	1	0	6	32	12	32	11	18*	0

*plus 16 for rebuilding shops on the bridge.
Source: *Bathwick Estate Collection*, GAB.

Although the market was a necessary condition for the development of Bathwick, Pulteney seemed determined to leave little to chance. Rather he acted positively as entrepreneur and financier to try to ensure the success of builders' responses to the market. It is probably true to say that, in the boom of the late 1780s and early 1790s, Pulteney was to Bath what Chandos and Wood had been in the first building boom sixty years earlier.

Like Wood, Pulteney exercised firm control over his builders. Indeed, a comparison of the results in Queen Square and Laura Place suggest that he was rather more successful than Wood in imposing a planned uniformity in building at his first attempt. When the first leases were granted Pulteney was already prepared with plans and elevations drawn by Thomas Baldwin. A typical building lease is one for a house in Great Pulteney Street granted in March 1788 in the name of Henrietta Laura Pulteney to William Phillips, a carpenter of Bath.[27] It was for ninety-nine years and it specified that Phillips had to build according to plans drawn and according to specification. The six houses contracted for had to be roofed with Welsh or Cornish blue slate, and pipes and guttering had to be provided at the rate of six pounds of lead per square foot. The lowest floor level had to be built two feet above the highest flood point as shown on John Warren's mill, and the whole had to be built and roofed before 5 March 1790. Three months after that the paving and roadway in front of the house had to be completed. As part of the development, drains measuring ten inches by eight inches had to be built into a common sewer constructed by the estate but charged to the accounts of the builders. This common sewer was to measure three feet by five feet. Lamps, too, had to be installed outside each house and kept burning from sunset to sunrise, and the street had to be kept clean by the builder for the first eight years. Further, each house had to be insured for two-thirds its value. In the event of fire, insurance money had to be spent on rebuilding. As an encouragement to building no rent was payable for the first two years of the lease while building was in progress. Thereafter the rent was to be £5 15s. 6d. for sites on the north side of Great Pulteney Street and £5 2s. 6d. for those on the south side. Some building leases also specified the minimum outlay on the buildings to be erected and all provided for free use of the estate's wharf on the River Avon.

The difficulty in enforcing these covenants is shown by the case of one builder who is known to have broken them in a most outrageous manner. Instead of building just one house on each of three sites contracted for he also built ten small tenements and a wash house on the same sites![28]

Pulteney also seemed to favour builders who would build on a large scale. As a result a distinctive feature of the Bathwick development was the high proportion of sites taken up by a handful of big builders. Of 128 leases taken up between 1788 and 1792, 27 were taken up by William Phillips and 16 by William Matthews. Between them they took up 34 per cent of the leases. One other builder contracted for nine houses, one for six and three for five. This left only 21 per cent of sites to be taken up by builders who built one or two houses. Further, Pulteney encouraged these big builders, Matthews, Clark and Phillips by granting them special licences to quarry stone on Bathwick Down for a fee of 5s. per annum rent and 2s. 6d. per foot of the frontage of the houses concerned. The sum of money raised in this way was to be paid to the banking house of Sherlock and Mortimer for the purpose of keeping the road to the quarry in good repair.[29]

As a further encouragement to building, Pulteney also provided mortgage money. While it is not possible to estimate the amount of funds supplied or the sources from which it came (did he, for example, use his Scottish banking connections?) there is enough evidence to suggest that Pulteney's advances were very substantial. William Matthews, one of Pulteney's big builders, who was also the proprietor of Bathwick cornmill, received mortgage funds from Pulteney for eleven of the sixteen houses he contracted for, including five houses in Laura Place, which was to be the show piece of the new town. Some of these houses were among the most costly in Bath. As additional security for these mortgages Matthews agreed to pay an extra ground rent of 3*s*. 6*d*. per foot.[30] Two other mortgage agreements involving Pulteney survive. One is for a mortgage of £750 to John Ricketts in 1790, the other for £2,590 on three houses to Joseph Smith by 1795.[31]

As this account shows, from the time William Pulteney came into the management of the Pulteney estates as the husband of Frances, herself only tenant for life, he was the central figure in the development of Bathwick. It is almost as if he were adopted into the family for this very purpose. Certainly he was a most dedicated entrepreneur. He was also a lawyer and member of parliament able to use the full power of the law to enable him to achieve for the family and its estates an economic success not open to other men. As part of this project he continued the policy of the Earl of Bath in extinguishing lifehold tenancies and succeeded in eliminating the remnants of the peasantry in Bathwick. He, too, vigorously pursued the task of building Pulteney Bridge. Together these two policies created conditions for the rise in land values and for the planned layout of high quality houses in Bathwick. Thereafter it was he who negotiated for and pushed through the three Acts of Parliament which alone gave the trustees the powers to create building leases and raise funds on mortgage. He also provided, out of his own resources, short-term funds to speed the building of the bridge and rode roughshod over the objections of the Corporation to building shops on it. Also he supplied mortgage money, particularly at the outset and to big builders who he also favoured by granting special quarrying licences.

Unfortunately for Pulteney and the estate the return on these initiatives was a long time in coming. Over twenty years elapsed between Pulteney's first proposal in 1769 and the first payment of ground rents in 1790 and 1791. Thereafter, the urban development in the years up to 1792 added over £1,000 to the annual income of the estate. Then, ground rents in Great Pulteney Street alone brought in £485 and the annual rent of houses built on sites in the street came to £5,569. This represents a capital investment of £83,535. By 1817 total house rent at £18,932 in Bathwick indicated an investment in building of almost £300,000. Consequently, Pulteney, acknowledged as Telford's patron and as a major influence in the developmental work of the British Fishery Company, must also be recognised as a developer of an urban estate equal in the range if not in the scale of his activities, to the Duke of Bedford in London. He was certainly one of the most successful of Bath's property developers. Even so, when set against his own planned expectation, which was for a much more extensive development focussing upon a turnpike running from Pulteney Bridge to Bathford, his work and its lasting contribution to the townscape has to be seen to be as much the result of opposition to his planning as it is of the planning itself.

What exists today in Bathwick, to be often admired as the planned result of the intentions of men in the past, is in fact the unintended result of the workings of the market place and more especially of conflicts between interest groups. It reflects both Pulteney's planning and the opposition of the Corporation and the Bath Turnpike Commissioners to that planning. It is the product, on the one hand, of absolute property and absolute self-interest and on the other of conflicts between different interest groups based on the control of property rights. In fact, the survival of Mr Pulteney's bridge depended more upon the defeat than on the success of Pulteney's planning. This is so because the bridge, in spite of the expense of its building, was not strong enough to bear the weight of traffic upon it. As a result, on several occasions, extensive rebuilding had to be carried out. The shops, for example, were rebuilt as early as 1792, and by 1798 repairs were so urgent, 'otherwise the whole of the said Bridge must fall down which would prove a great loss and detriment to the said trust Estates as well as injury to the Builders who have erected expensive houses thereon upon long leases.'[32] Then, in 1800, flooding so weakened the piers of the arches in the River Avon that it became necessary to take down and repair the shops above them. To carry out this work another Act of Parliament was passed authorising the estate's trustees to raise a further mortgage of £3,230. The work carried out under this Act was so long delayed that in July 1802 it was reported to Sir James Pulteney that the parish offices of Bathwick and St Peter and Paul were threatening an indictment stating that both Pulteney Bridge and the temporary Bridge built to ease the weight of traffic were nuisances.[33] It seems certain, therefore, had Pulteney's plans for the development of Bathwick come to fruition and the London traffic had been siphoned off the London Road at Bathford to enter Bath through Bathwick, that the structural weakness and narrowness of Pulteney Bridge would have become a major problem long ago. Some measure of this traffic is given by the turnpike records. They show that by 1823 the weekly traffic entering Bath along the London Road totalled 1,225 wheeled vehicles. They included 19 nine-inch waggons, 118 six-inch waggons, and 144 stage coaches. Also there were over 800 horses and 400 cattle and sheep. Over the years the addition of such traffic to the actual flow across Pulteney Bridge would surely have destroyed the bridge entirely. In fact a successful implementation of Pulteney's 'plan' would have generated an even greater volume of traffic as Bathwick grew in size. Further, the character of the place would have changed as Great Pulteney Street became, like Walcot Street and the London Road, a main traffic route. The result of Pulteney's plan might well have been, therefore, the loss of the bridge and the disappearance of the attractiveness of Sydney Place as a more desirable address than the Royal Crescent in the early nineteenth century. The fact that neither happened was brought about by the opposition to Pulteney's turnpike by the Corporation and the Trustees of Bath turnpike. Their opposition stemmed from self-interest. They were concerned only with protecting their own property rights, not the amenities of Bathwick. As a result we have in Bathwick an outstanding example of how space in Bath was socially organised rather than planned.

No other developer in Bath in these years had financial resources and legal power equal to those of Pulteney, not even the Corporation. Nevertheless, the emergence of new financial institutions did much to overcome the sort of financial stringencies which had faced John Wood in 1727. And, with the revival of demand for the pleasures of Bath in the late 1780s, and with absolute property and absolute self-interest in the ascendant, the conditions were ripe for a sustained summer of building.

One of the most successful architects attracted to Bath by these circumstances was John Eveleigh. Eveleigh is a shadowy although rather baroque figure; his chief buildings, Camden Crescent, Somerset Place and Grosvenor Place seem to catch the speculative mood of Bath in these years much more than Baldwin's strictly Palladian design for Bathwick. In Camden Crescent and in Grosvenor Place he broke a strict rule of classical design by using five and seven pillars respectively to hold up the central pediment, much to the dislike of some architectural historians. Additionally, in Somerset Place, he designed the most plastic of Bath's buildings, a crescent moulded over the brow of a hill. His actvities as a developer were also closely bound up with the growth of new financial institutions and his story highlights the part played by these institutions in the last great building boom in Bath and shows that he was as adventurous in his attitude to the rules of sound finance as he was flexible in his approach to building.

Eveleigh began working in Bath in 1788. He seems to have done so by working and drawing plans for others and on other occasions he worked for Baldwin as his assistant. In 1789 he set up as an entrepreneur in his own right with very little capital of his own. According to an entry in his ledger he started building with £312 5s. 6d. made up from the following:

Had when begun building	£115
Sold Tools and Books	£56 8s. 0d.
Sold horses	£140 17s. 6d.[34]

His subsequent accounts show that from November 1789 to 1793 he paid out at least £15,850 to numerous subcontractors and in 1793 had assets valued at £26,150.

Eveleigh's first major project was for Dr Denham Skeet. This involved Eveleigh in laying out £12,450 in the building of Bailbrook Lodge for which he was paid £11,950. Payment was made by a series of bills drawn by Eveleigh on Skeet which he discounted with various banking houses. The outstanding balance of £630 was still owing, according to Eveleigh, in 1793.[35] While this work was in progress Eveleigh, in partnership with Richard Hewlett, a builder and William and John Townsend, silversmiths, began Grosvenor Place in June 1791. The centre house of this terrace was to be developed as an hotel and private pleasure gardens to be exploited as a commercial enterprise. The gardens were to include a large and elegant banqueting room, greenhouses, hot house, gravel walks, archery, open orchestra area, swimming pool and changing rooms (Figure 21).[36] Up to November 1792 Eveleigh had spent £13,498 on the project most of which had been raised on mortgage; Hewlett and the Townsends had advanced £7,345 and Clements and Company, a Bath bank founded in 1773, had advanced £2,384, also on mortgage. A further £900 on mortgage had come from another of Bath's banks, Attwood and Company, sometimes known as the Bladud Bank founded in 1790.[37] While this project was going ahead,

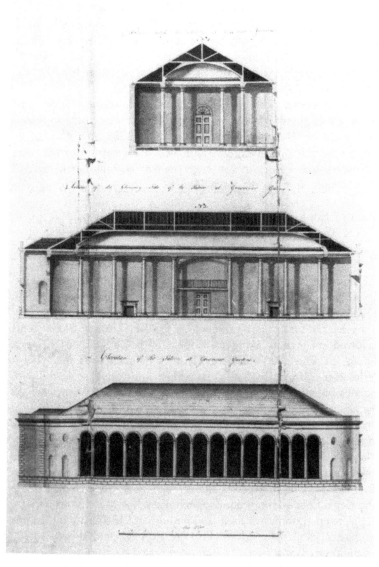

Figure 21 a and b, John Eveleigh's drawings of proposed buildings at Grosvenor Gardens to be financed by an Equitable Trust in 1794

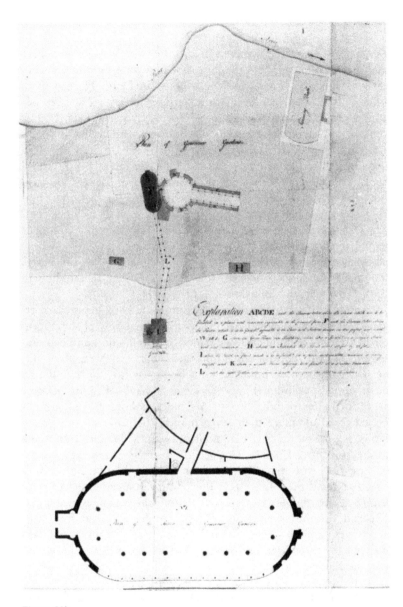

Figure 21b

Eveleigh also became involved in the Bathwick development. He built his first houses there in Cheapside and Johnson Street. Then, early in 1792, he began work on a house in Laura Place, which, when finished in December, was advertised for letting at £120 per annum. It had the special attraction of two water closets. In this venture, too, he became heavily dependent upon loans from bankers. He borrowed £700 from Bayly, Gutch and Cross of the Bath City Bank, established in 1789, £1,300 from Barry and Death, bankers of Chippenham, and, probably to repay the £1,300 loan from Barry and Death, £700 from Thomas Davis of Lyncombe and Widcombe. All these mortgages were for six months at 5 per cent. The fact that Eveleigh was able to borrow £1,300 from a Chippenham Bank as well as £700 from Bayly, Gutch and Cross, whose partners came respectively from Bath, Wells and Bristol indicates the superabundance of funds now seeking outlets in building in Bath.[38] But that was not the end of it.

In addition to these long- and medium-term bank loans on mortgage Eveleigh was greatly assisted by a ready supply of short-term credit. His financial agent was James Cogswell who had been employed in John Jeffrey's office from 1787 to 1792 where, no doubt, he had gained some financial knowledge. In July 1792 with the boom already well under way, he seems to have set up in business as a discounter of bills. From then until February 1793, over a period of a little more than seven months, he provided short-term funds, mainly on notes at two months, to many builders and others to the amount of £10,873. Cogswell frequently shared the expense of these bills with one or other of three banks; Bladud Bank, Bath City Bank and the High Street Bank whose respective shares were £2,113, £894 and £896. Cogswell's principal customer was John Eveleigh. In the seven months indicated he provided him with short-term funds to the extent of £3,102 of which £1,813 was supplied by the three banks referred to earlier. Apart from Cogswell it was the Bladud Bank that was most deeply involved in furnishing short-term funds to Eveleigh – to the extent of £988.[39]

As the building boom in Bathwick and north Walcot got rapidly under way with the help of such abundant supplies of credit, labourers, too, were attracted to the city in unprecedented numbers. Consequently other developers and builders thought it worthwhile to build lower-priced houses more suited to their needs. It was probably the attraction of this market that had led William Hulance, one of the builders on the Bathwick estate to build ten tenements and a wash house contrary to the covenants in his leases. This market for working-class housing was also met by builders building in Chelsea Buildings, Half Moon Street and Snow Hill in north-east Walcot. The story of this development also shows the importance of abundant credit and the national network of financial institutions for quite modest building schemes.

This development began in 1789 when two carpenters, Isaac Bennet and Robert Moxham, paid £105 in cash and £42 per annum for ground in the Lower Tyning belonging to the Rev. Thomas Robin of Hull in Gloucestershire.[40] The two developers undertook to lay out £2,000 within five years and to pay the first rent in 1792. Before work got under way, early in 1792, Moxham sold his half share to John Giles, variously described as carver, dealer, chapman and gentleman, and himself became a builder taking up underleases on the site for the building of eight houses in Chelsea Buildings. Most of these houses were mortgaged to Giles for sums of £350 to £400 each. Also Giles granted mortgages to five other builders to build twenty-four houses in Half Moon Street, Dover Street and Snow Hill. The average mortgage for these houses was £66. (A later assignment stated that these houses were insufficient security for the sum advanced on them.) By 1794 Giles's advances to his builders totalled at least £1,600. But Giles was himself indebted to the London banking firm of Elizabeth and Moses Staples which had advanced him £1,500 on the security of these properties. Subsequent dealings between the Staples and Giles, when Giles came to them asking for more money, show that by the 1790s the procedure whereby mortgage money was transferred by the use of the bill of exchange was well established. The 1795 agreement between Giles and his bankers stated:[41]

> The said John Giles hath agreed to constantly keep in his account in the Banking House of the said Elizabeth Staples and Moses William Staples the sum of one thousand pounds in cash at least and the said Elizabeth Staples and Moses William Staples have therefore in order to accommodate the said John Giles agreed to accept such Bills of Exchange (drawn by Giles) so long as they shall find it convenient to them or until they shall give notice to the contrary to the said John Giles so as such Bills of Exchange do not at any one time

amount together to more than the sum of £6,000 . . . including the said sum of £1,500 or such other sum as to them shall seem proper and so the said John Giles do supply them with cash from time to time for payment of such Bills of Exchange in manner here in after mentioned and constantly keep cash in their Banking House to the amount aforesaid.

The Staples also agreed to advance money at 5 per cent to Giles to cover bills for which he had insufficient cash and to charge him a commission of 5s. per £100 for accepting his bills. Security for this arrangement were the twenty-four building sites, houses and rent charges already referred to. In this way it was probably London Money that financed the building of some at least of the 'two up' and 'two down' houses of the courts and streets of the Snow Hill area. A commission of bankruptcy made against Giles in December 1797, shows that for some time during 1796 or 1797 he was also a partner in the short lived Union Bank in Bath.

The accounts of Eveleigh and Cogswell, and of Giles's speculation in the Snow Hill area, show the extent to which the boom of 1788–92 was helped on its buoyant way by abundant and easy credit obtained from newly-created banks and other financial intermediaries in Bath as well as from London banks. By this time there were six banks in Bath all but one of which had been founded between 1775 and 1790. (Bath's first bank, the Bath Bank of Cam and Co. had been founded in 1768.)[42] They were, therefore, a very new force in Bath's economy. With their countrywide connections they brought new money into the city and mobilised local resources more effectively. What we know of their activities in financing building, plus the evidence of Pulteney's energetic financial and entrepreneurial role in Bathwick, support the view that the boom was characterised as much by a financial as by a building mania and that it was generated more from the supply than the demand side. A very good example of this is the role played by John Lowder, one of the partners in the Bath Bank, in financing Charles Spackman's speculation in building Lansdown Crescent. Although Spackman was the entrepreneur and John Palmer the architect it was Lowder's money that was crucial for the actual building of the crescent. By the end of 1792 Lowder had advanced £14,317 on mortgage to Spackman.[43] It was this range of buildings, in conjunction with Eveleigh's Somerset Place and Fielder and Company's St James Square, that continued to pull the city up the southern slope of Lansdown as a counter to the growth of Bathwick.

Earlier it was mentioned that Pulteney's development of Bathwick was connected with the Corporation's own plans for the redevelopment of the city centre. Here I tell the story of that redevelopment. It is a long and tortuous story culminating in the boom years 1789–92. It also had several consequences for the organisation of space in Bath.

The first plans for the redevelopment of the city centre originated in 1760 with a decision to build a new town hall. But, the economic depression of the early 1760s and conflict within the Corporation had effectively prevented any further developments until 1765. Then it was decided to seek comprehensive powers, including powers of compulsory purchase, in order to carry out substantial improvements, not only to the markets but also to the Pump Room, and to widen roads and create new ways to the upper town. The importance of the Act of 1766 embodying these powers in several areas has already been commented upon. It was also followed by a revival of interest in the building of a new Guildhall. One of the men who figured prominently in the ensuing conflict over the gains to be won from this enterprise was Thomas Warr Atwood, a member of the Common Council serving on the building Committee. Atwood was a wealthy plumber, developer and, in 1775, partner in the Bladud Bank. He also obtained for himself the position of architect to the city estate and water works. In this capacity he had an advantage over other builders and architects and obtained the contract for building the Guildhall. As was to be expected there was much criticism of him from other builders and from other members of the Corporation who favoured a design by John Palmer which was undoubtedly much cheaper. When Atwood died in 1775, after a fall on a demolition site, the plans were redrawn by his successor Thomas Baldwin, a speculating builder and the architect of the Bathwick development.

Building on the new Guildhall did not begin until 1776. By this time, however, the upper town had been considerably enlarged and the battle of the Assembly Rooms fought and won with victory going to the Upper Town. Consequently the redevelopment of the city centre by the Corporation lagged behind the development brought about by speculating builders elsewhere. Moreover, although Mr Pulteney's bridge and Bridge Street had been completed and opened with the blessing of the Corporation, the bridge brought little new traffic into the heart of the city. Indeed, fearful of the effects of Pulteney's grand design the Corporation had opposed any further development of Bathwick to protect what it believed to be its own interests. Then in 1780 there had been the affair of the anti-Catholic riots. This had frightened people away from Bath and added to the effect of the general decline in consumption connected with the American War. As a result Bath was generally depressed and the improvement of the city centre languished. In these circumstances, in 1783, John Symons, a leading surgeon and Common Council man, declared that the more the Corporation dragged its feet the more would the Baths, the very life blood of Bath, be ruined by private interests. Adding another damper to the prospect for the city centre, he wrote:[44]

> whilst private property remains in the neighbourhood of the Baths, the virtues of the hot water will always be in danger of being impaired, by the mixture of cold springs with them, as long as the proprietors of the houses have a right to dig cellars, wells, or other they may stand in need of . . . There are still greater dangers attending the springs than those I have mentioned; namely from drains which are not discoverable: The Cross Bath formerly was emptied every day; fourteen years ago it was emptied three times a week, and now it is only once a week; The loss of that spring Mr Wood foretold thirty years ago.
>
> I could mention several other instances of hazarding the loss of the hot springs, by people raising the water in their own houses for private use, digging foundations for building, and removing blocks of stone of several ton weight, laid on purpose to secure the springs.

Therefore Symons indicated his intention to approach the king to get him interested in Bath. 'Our Royal Sovereign,' he wrote, 'has always been a great encourager of the arts and sciences, and surely the health of his subjects is not a less important object.'[45] Then, too, he said, he would approach every member of the Houses of Lords and Commons to support a Bill in Parliament in order to get something done about the Baths. 'But,' he added, 'the endeavours of an individual will be very ineffectual, if the Corporation does not heartily concur in the measure.'

Much to Symon's dissatisfaction the Corporation was in no hurry to enter on any improvement scheme. It could not afford to be. From 1765 to 1783 the corporate debt, resulting from the acquisition of sites and building associated with the Guildhall, had risen from £3,110 to £26,400 and the interest charge on it had risen from £158 to £1,249, which then represented some 30 per cent of its annual expenditure. There seemed no way, as a Corporate body, that it could finance any major improvement. Nevertheless, the improvers persisted in their demands until in 1784 a committee was appointed to inquire 'into thirteen clauses drawn up by some members of the Corporation for an Act of Parliament for the better government of the City.'[46] Yet another year elapsed before the Corporation agreed to build a colonnade in front of the Pump Room according to a plan of Thomas Baldwin provided that, 'the Committee also report that the expense thereof will not exceed one hundred and thirty guineas.' At the same time Dr Harrington moved in Council to enlarge the powers of the city, 'in particular in taking down houses near the Baths and other near or adjacent parts and throwing the same open for the convenience of Health, Air and Public Utility.'[47] The Committee of six, appointed to look into this matter included John Symons; it reported three days later, 'that the most eligible method of doing it is by making very convenient thoroughfares through the City; which can only be done by widening some of the old streets, making an open communication between the Upper and Lower Town, and laying the Baths as open as possible, to complete which, Mr Baldwin is desired to draw an accurate plan of the city, describing where such improvements are most necessary to be made.'[48]

After this efficient start things again moved very slowly. Over a period of two and a half years the Committee met twenty-nine times – Symons attended nineteen meetings – and five Public Halls were called to consider the improvements. Finally, in March 1788, Baldwin's plan and estimate for £47,163 17s. 5d. was accepted and the Corporation decided to get an Act of Parliament giving them the necessary powers to redevelop the city centre.

The Corporation's estimates were detailed and optimistic.[49] The cost of acquiring property in the development area was estimated at £82,373. Since it was hoped to recoup £42,203 by the resale of improved houses, the net cost was estimated at £40,170. It was proposed to meet this in three ways. First £34,714 of the Corporation property was to be vested in newly-appointed Improvement Commissioners in order to use £7,006 of income generated from it. Second, the Corporation would make a direct contribution of £7,163 at the rate of £700 per year. Third, £25,000 would be borrowed on the security of the tolls on the Bath Turnpike. The Corporation would also repay this loan at the rate of £700 per year after ten years. The whole was to be administered by a number of Improvement Commissioners consisting of the Mayor, Recorder, Aldermen, Common Council men and Town Clerk together with the two MPs and twenty others, including William Pulteney, Lord Webb Seymour, George Allen and William Gore-Langton. A quorum of this body was to be five and to have full powers of decision in regard to compulsory purchase and the amount of compensation. A jury of twelve would act as a court of appeal on matters of compensation and the decision of the jury would be final.

The whole improvement scheme showed that the lesson of the battle of the Assembly Rooms had finally been learned. It was an ingenious and optimistic one designed to refurbish the city centre, improve the Baths and Pump Room, and create improved access between these Corporation-owned facilities and the rapidly expanding upper town. At bottom the plan was a defensive one made with all the legal power and advantage of property the Corporation could muster. It was designed to ensure the Corporation's control over the development while limiting its financial obligation, but allowing it to milk another public body in order to underwrite its own borrowings. But, its timing shows too that the Corporation was also caught up in the speculative fever of the late 1780s; the decision to proceed was made in March 1788, the same month in which the first stone was laid in Laura Place on the Bathwick estate.

As soon as the details of the application to Parliament for an Act of Parliament leaked out, particularly as they included a proposal to raise half a toll on the Bath Turnpikes, there was an outburst of opposition to it. The trustees of the Turnpike called a public meeting to consider petitioning against it and a committee was appointed. Other groups also felt threatened. Consequently, in May there was report of a joint petition against the Bill by the Turnpike Trustees, local landowners, colliery owners, coal haulers, and the citizens of Bath. They claimed that the extra half-toll proposed would raise prices, decrease custom and lower rents, and that local people would pay the toll even though not going to the city. The plan, they said, 'has for its object the immediate interest of estates held under and belonging to the Corporation, whereas plans may be formed which will be of equal benefit to the town in general.'[50]

A majority of Freemen particularly felt badly treated. They thought the time was ripe for the development of the town commons rather than the city centre and petitioned the Corporation to that effect. They said that an acre of ground on the commons let on building leases would produce £400 a year, more than the current total value of the commons which was let for £230 per annum. And they also brought a suit in Chancery against the Corporation claiming the rights of Freemen to control of the town commons and alleging misappropriation of £700 of the income earned from it. To this the Corporation replied that they were only trustees for the commons and, therefore, had no powers to grant building leases. Moreover, since every Freeman had only a life interest in the revenue from the ground even the Freemen collectively could not make leases binding on future generations, particularly as some Freemen were against leasing for building. Therefore, the Corporation claimed, the commons, 'should be ordered, governed, hayned, fritted, stocked, stinted, and husbanded, according to Orders and Constitutions to be made by the Mayor and Common Council of the said City, for the time being.'[51] The judge in Chancery agreed with the Corporation with the result that the town commons remained undeveloped until part of them was used to create Victoria Park in 1830. As a result of this decision the Corporation was free to pursue its own objectives in the city centre.

The Improvement Act was finally passed in June 1789. It included the financial provisions as set out in the Corporation's proposal, the core of which was the power to borrow £25,000 on the security of an additional half-toll on the Bath Turnpike. This toll was to be levied once a day only at existing gates or, if preferred, at new gates and effectively only on visitors to the town travelling in carriages or on horseback. The Act expressly exempted from the toll all working horses going out to plough, pasture or water, and all wagons carrying corn, meal, coal, cloth, wool, provisions and raw materials, mail coaches, and horses carrying vagrants or electors going to elections. It also exempted the carriages of residents in Walcot and Lyncombe and Widcome passing to and from the city. Therefore the toll charges used to underwrite the redevelopment of the city centre to make it attractive to visitors and increase the value of Corporate property were clearly expected to be borne by the visitors themselves.

The Improvement Commissioners were also granted the powers of compulsory purchase they required and compulsory powers of entry in order to make surveys and valuations prior to purchase. So, in July 1789 began another phase in the social organisation of space in Bath. It was backed by the force that statute law gave to the Improvement Commissioners and by the powers that law gave them to compel sales of other peoples' property and to levy a tax on visitors to the city.

Initially the Improvement Commissioners had some difficulty in raising the £25,000 they were authorised to borrow. Having resolved to build five new strees – Union Street, Cross Bath Street, Nash Street, Hot Bath Street, and Beau Street – they authorised a loan at 4 per cent. But, well before the year was out, on 6 November 1789, they rescinded this authorisation 'It being found that the money cannot be raised at that rate of interest.'[52] Instead they authorised a loan of £18,000 at 4½ per cent. £17,900 was actually subscribed. Of this £4,600 was taken up by seven women, described as spinsters or widows – no doubt in search of a safe and regular 4½ per cent return on their investments. A further £6,800 was

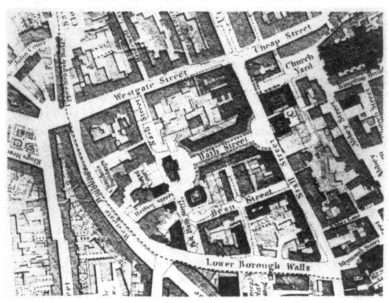

Figure 22 Improvement Proposals for the City Centre, 1789. The light dotted lines indicate proposed widening of streets

taken up by five members of the Corporation, one of whom was Dr Harrington, who had first moved for increasing the powers of the Corporation for purposes of development in 1785. Two others were apothecaries. No doubt all five, as Improvement Commissioners, had an interest in the success of the project. Certainly, as investors, they were guaranteed their 4½ per cent on the security of the tolls. Most of the rest was taken up by men, mainly from the leisured and professional classes, including two men with a major interest in the Bath Fire Insurance Company who invested £3,000. £1,100 was invested by men described as yeomen. All except four of the twenty investors were local men and women. These four exceptions lived at Box in Wiltshire and invested £1,000. The rest of the loan, £7,000, was not raised until April and May 1791. Of this, £700 was taken up by a Bath spinster, £600 by a maltster from Stratton-on-Fosse, and the remainder by six local men from the professional and leisured classes, including a wine merchant and a bookseller.

Raising the loan was, perhaps, the easiest task facing the Commissioners; at 4½ per cent there was plenty of money about. Far more difficult was the business of acquiring the sites of the 119 houses and redeveloping them. The first problem was that the administrative structure established by the Act was both too simple and too cumbersome – there were fifty-four Commissioners with a quorum of five! This was clearly designed to facilitate business but it ended by generating confusion. For example, having decided at the outset to proceed in opening up the five intended streets and to rebuild the Pump Room, and having ordered Baldwin to produce plans and elevations for Union Street in 1791, work on Union Street progressed only very slowly. Henry Phillot, proprietor of the Bear Inn, on the site of which Union Street was to be built, believed, in 1791, that he had contracted for the sale of the inn for £13,500. In 1797, according to his sons and executors, Charles and Joseph Phillot (Joseph was a member of the Corporation and twice mayor, in 1797 and 1805), Henry Phillot had agreed to take £2,000 in cash and the Commissioners' security for £11,500 at 4½ per cent until they could pay the balance. According to the Commissioners this was not so. After a delay of six years they said there was no contract with Henry Phillot, only an agreement. Furthermore, the actual agreement, they said, was only between five of the Commissioners (the size of the quorum) and not the Commissioners as a whole! In any case it was only for an exchange of property and a payment to

Phillot of £4,406. Therefore the Commissioners rejected the idea of a valuation by jury and elected to proceed to a suit in Chancery brought by Phillot's trustees, one of whom, Joseph Phillot, was mayor at the time. Then, in 1798 the Commissioners reaffirmed their intention to open up Union Street. Subsequently there were various proposals and valuations until, in 1802, the Commissioners finally settled with Joseph and Charles Phillot for the building of Union Street as a private development involving only a transfer of corporation property to the Phillots and the purchase by them of some other properties. In return the Phillots agreed to build the street with a 22ft 6in. carriageway at no further cost to the Commissioners.[53]

Indeed, it was cost and poor financial administration, as well as bad forecasting, which, more than anything else, held up work on the planned redevelopment of the city centre and led to the ten-year delay in the building of Union Street. As a result two other streets were never even started and the only completed work was Hot Bath Street, the Pump Room, and some widening of Cheap Street (Figure 22). This problem of inflating cost also arose from defective administration. At the outset the Commissioners failed to establish any formal organisation for supervising the accounts or directing the work of Thomas Baldwin their surveyor. And it was not until May 1791, after nearly eighteen months of business, that they appointed a committee to examine the accounts. Then, in the following January various tradesmen and the treasurer were ordered to be examined by a committee of five, and Baldwin as well as the treasurer was ordered to produce his accounts. There was also much discussion about the use of costly materials, whether lead or copper with which to cover the roof of the Pump Room. More significantly there was a bitter dispute about the propriety of proceeding with the acquisition of the sites of the fifty-four houses in the second schedule of the Act and raising another loan of £7,000.

The initial decision to proceed with the second schedule was made in January by a meeting attended by six Commissioners: Sir John Riggs Miller, William Watson, Dr Harrington, Morgan Nichols, Zachariah Bayly and John Jeffereys. Jeffereys was Town Clerk, Dr Harrington a committed developer, Watson and Nichols were members of the Corporation, and Bayly a partner in the Bath City Bank heavily committed to development in Bathwick. A month later there was a move to rescind this decision. This time Joseph

Phillot voted for proceeding but three other members of the Corporation, two of whom had banking connections, voted against; Richard Atwood, Edward Anderdon, and Charles Crook. But, the decision to proceed was reaffirmed by a vote of 8:4. Not to be outdone, the same minority joined by two other members of the Corporation, Randell and Coward, moved to block the authorisation of the £7,000 loan at a meeting in March. They also lost this vote by a vote of 12:8.[54] It is noticeable that while on this vote Corporation Commissioners were evenly divided 5:5, the non-Corporation Commissioners were in favour 7:3. Thus, although the Act in principle gave majority control to the Corporation Commissioners, practice meant that non-members of the Corporation could take decisions with financial implications for the Corporation. Moreover, this £7,000 was not authorised by the Act. Although it is difficult to trace this loan in the accounts, it does appear to have been taken up as a mortgage at 4½ per cent by a client of William Percival, a solicitor, on the security of ground rents in Bath Street and the Yard of the Bear Inn. It seems likely that this client was Walter Wiltshire, who was mayor in 1772, 1780 and 1791, and creditor of the Corporation to the extent of £7,700. This appears to be so because in January 1793 these ground rents, worth £260 per annum were sold to Wiltshire for £6,780 16s. 0d. It is probably this item which appears under the title donations and legacies in subsequent accounts.

Even this infusion of money was not enough to get the Commissioners out of their financial difficulties. In June 1792, as part of their economy drive, the Commissioners reduced the rate of interest on the £25,000 loan from 4½ to 4 per cent. Then, in September, all work was stopped because Baldwin had still failed to produce his accounts. When he finally produced them in October work was restarted but only at a rate to keep expenses down to a weekly sum of £10. In April 1793 work was again stopped and in May a further subcommittee, packed with Corporation Commissioners, including the Corporation's two most committed developers, John Symons and Dr Harrington, was set up to investigate the accounts. In June, Baldwin, who was by now bankrupt, was suspended and John Palmer was appointed in his place. Still things did not go right. The Commissioners had trouble with their clerk, Mr George. Although he resigned in 1795 they were still considering taking action against him in 1804 for not producing all the necessary papers. The Pump

Room, the centre piece of the whole improvement scheme, was not finished until 1806!

Table 7.2 indicates more clearly than any catalogue of instances the sporadic and long drawn out nature of the work of the Improvement Commissioners.

TABLE 7.2 Expenditure by improvement commission and net produce of the tolls, 1790–1815

	Expenditure £	Net produce of tolls £		Expenditure £	Net produce of tolls £
1790	19,333	1,106	1803	3,189	1,247
1791	11,547	1,095	1804	3,897	1,204
1792	2,534	1,202	1805	7,007	1,218
1793	1,867	1,261	1806	4,080	1,187
1794	1,391	1,185	1807	5,728	1,211
1795	1,539	1,058	1808	5,712	1,324
1796	9,113	1,110	1809	3,201	1,262
1797	2,185	1,148	1810	3,547	
1798	5,511	1,161	1811	5,614	
1799	1,900	1,234	1812	2,568	
1800	1,976	1,236	1813	2,202	
1801	3,477	1,148	1814	1,951	
1802	3,189	1,129	1815	2,247	

Source: *Improvement Commissioners Box*, GAB.

A balance sheet drawn up in 1821 shows that only a little more than half the amount intended to be expended on the acquisition of property was actually spent and that the resale value of property so acquired provided only a third instead of a half of that amount. It also records an item not estimated for in the original accounts, since it was intended to be paid out of the tolls, this was £32,577 interest on the £25,000 debt. Thus, the real cost including the interest charge of completing about half the work originally planned was close to £116,000. The main sources of finance for this were:

Borrowing	£25,000
Corporation	£20,000
Resale of property	£16,000
Tolls	£42,000
Other	£13,000

The importance of the tolls in this venture are clearly beyond dispute. They show, in a very real sense, that the improvements were in part paid for by the visitors to Bath who alone paid the half-toll due to the Improvement Commissioners.

Nevertheless, the Corporation did have a substantial financial responsibility. By 1821 it had already paid out £20,000 and was committed to repaying the outstanding debt which in 1821 stood at £12,450. In fact, the Corporation's total debt, which was £27,100 before the improvements were started had risen to £51,000 (£64,000 with the residue of the Improvement debt) by 1821. Clearly the Corporation had simply met its obligation to repay the improvement debt by new borrowing. The total cost to the Corporation, exclusive of interest charge on its own debt, was in the region of £45,000.

A consequence of the increased debt and interest charge which, in the years 1820–24, accounted for 20 per cent of the Corporation's annual expenditure, was the reluctance of the Corporation to spend large sums on any further improvements to the city. Therefore, nothing was done about the worsening floods. These particularly affected the poorer parts of the parishes of Walcot, St James and Lyncombe and Widcombe. Although in the early 1820s both Thomas Telford and James Montague recommended the building of a new bridge to improve the flow of water and reduce flooding[55] the Corporation was adamant; it could not and would not meet the cost of a new bridge, even by borrowing. All it was willing to do was widen the existing bridge in order to improve the flow of wheeled traffic brought about by the expansion of the new suburb of Lyncombe and Widcombe. Flooding continued. Consequently the social cost of the Corporation's improvement of the city centre in its own interest was borne by the inhabitants of Avon Street, the Holloway, and of the new working-class area in the Dolemeads.

This story of the improvement of the city centre from 1760 to the 1820s reveals the many interlocking dimensions of the organisation of space in Bath. It connects with Pulteney's development of Bathwick and with the Corporation's opposition to Pulteney's grander purposes; it connects with the Freemen's interest in the town commons and with the expansion of the city northwards. While some of the consequences for the organisation of space of conflicting interests and property rights involved in these connections may be thought of as happy accidents, and while the new public buildings and improved streets added to the attractions of the central area of

Bath, other connections with the plight of the lower town also served to emphasise differences between the depressed conditions of that part of the city lived in by the labouring population, and the elegance and refinement of the crescents of Lansdown and the grandeur of Great Pulteney Street. Therefore, just as one might look at Wood's pillars and see Venus or the Three Graces and pretend to see God one might well look at the Pump Room and walk the length of Bath Street troubled by an inward glimpse of floods in the Dolemeads and cholera in the Holloway but calmed, perhaps, by a memory of Victoria Park!

The Corporation's financial plight brought on by the improvement scheme was not entirely of its own making. Like other developers in Bath it, too, was caught up in a sequence of boom and slump – the dynamic of capitalist expansion. Therefore, the consequences of the Corporation's actions for the organisation of space in Bath were also consequences of the conjuncture of the economic, political and ideological aspects of that capitalist dynamic. One might say that the Corporation's financial plight and its social consequences were contained in the very growth of the city itself, in the uneven nature of that growth, and in the inherent instability of its financial institutions.

The boom from 1789 to 1792 had produced the most extensive and rapid period of expansion in the city. Thus, between 1780 and 1793, the number of houses increased by 45 per cent, coach services from London increased by 70 per cent and traffic on the Avon Navigation more than doubled. The Corporation's Improvement scheme had been only a small part of this expansion and the local boom but a fragment of a nation-wide boom in house- and canal-building and in foreign trade. As we have seen, at the peak of the boom in Bath five banks and a variety of other financial intermediaries added the fuel of easy money to an already buoyant economy. Indeed, the mania for building was such that speculating builders taking part in the development of Norfolk Crescent initiated by the attorney Richard Bowsher were willing to build with only the verbal promise of money made at a Tavern Dinner.[56] And, even as the boom broke, in the third quarter of 1792, Nathaniel Bayly, partner in the Bath City Bank was still offering loans of up to £40,000 at 4 per cent on the security of freehold land.[57] In fact, this selfsame bank had so increased it liabilities during the boom that early in the financial collapse in March 1793 it was forced to close its doors. The bank's records show something of the financial problems involved.

The Bath City Bank had been established in 1776. Through its individual partners it seems to have had connections with other banks in Bristol, Bridgwater and Warminster. In 1789 a new agreement between James Cross of Bath, Zachary Bayly of Lyncombe and Widcombe, Nathaniel Bayly of Bath, Robert Gutch of Wells, Thomas Wells of Bristol, and James Cross the younger of Bath virtually re-formed the bank but maintained its connections with Bristol and Somerset. By mid-1791 it had liabilities of £197,446. These consisted of £65,034 in promissory notes in circulation, some of which were for twenty days at 3½ per cent, and deposits to the value of £133,412. To meet these liabilities it held the following assets:

Cash in hand	£30,187
Bills	£83,073
Debts	£88,623
Dubious and bad debts	£1,705
	£203,588

Clearly the bank's cash ratio, the ratio of cash in hand to notes in circulation and deposits, was low. But, at 15 per cent, it was higher than that of many other banks and does not suggest that the partners were especially incompetent according to the banking standards of the time. Where they were probably at fault was in tying up too much of their investment in mortgages on real estate and in holding bills drawn on developers and builders like Eveleigh.[58]

Since the stability of the building industry and, therefore, of a large part of the economy of Bath, depended upon the continued and efficient functioning of these financial institutions, any hint of a cessation in the ready supply of credit to developers and builders could bring economic disaster. The precariousness of the situation was undoubtedly enhanced by the fact that by 1792 much of the mobile wealth of the city and the local region was held in the form of mortgages on land and buildings and that many claims on banks and other financial intermediaries were held in the form of bills drawn on the security of buildings. As trade slackened at the end of 1792 and as the supply of houses increased, those in need of liquid funds to complete projects started late in the boom, such as Grosvenor Gardens and Norfolk Crescent, began to find it difficult to obtain them. As this happened confidence in the financial system faltered. The break came in July 1792 when George Davis, attorney and banker of Bridge Street failed.[59] Then, in September, following the peak in the tolls on the Avon Navigation, the Corporation called its first halt on work on the Pump Room. As the war with France, which had started in January 1793, added to the strain on the financial system, confidence collapsed. A public meeting called on 11 March to affirm public confidence in all local banks agreed, 'not only to give full credit to the notes of ALL THE BATH BANKS, but also to abstain from unnecessarily withdrawing deposits at interest.'[60] But, on 21 March the Bath City Bank closed its doors to join the Bath and Somersetshire Bank in bankruptcy. As they collapsed they dragged bill brokers like Cogswell with them.

As the banks broke public and private building came to an abrupt end. Builders toppled like nine pins. Bowsher never did produce the money he promised, he was himself in debt to a firm of London Bankers for £1,700, and Pulteney and the Corporation brought their fine schemes to an end. In place of advertisements in newspapers offering sums up to £40,000 at 4 per cent there were, throughout 1793, notices asking for money on mortgage at 5 per cent.[61] In 1794, as part of a rescue operation, there was an ingenious attempt to add the form of the equitable trust to the other ways of raising money for speculative ventures. This was done to raise £10,000 to complete work on Eveleigh's Grosvenor Gardens. The fact that nearly £5,000 was raised from numerous investors in £50 shares indicates the continuing optimism of Bath's small tradesmen. It was of no avail. Eveleigh's successors were also bankrupted.[62]

The effect of the crash of 1793 was to plunge Bath in deep depression. Thus, there were more persons examined for settlement in 1793 than in any year since 1790, four times as many removals as in 1791, and a great recruitment for the army as 253 men were attested soldiers and taken out of the work force and away from depending on poor relief. Even the number of bastardy examinations shows a considerable increase over the boom year in 1791. In 1793 real wages were lower than in 1780 and 18 per cent lower than in 1792.

The crash of 1793 was more than a short-term crisis for Bath. Rather it marked the onset of a secular stagnation in its attraction as a place of resort. The outline of the story is most sharply revealed in the amount of the Bath tolls received by the Improvement Commissioners. Since these were tolls on visitors they may serve as a good indication of the demand for Bath. These figures show a 15 per cent increase in takings between 1789 and the year ending in July 1793. Thereafter they show a fall off in earnings until mid-1795 caused by the post-1792 depression. They show, too, over a longer period of time, the failure of Bath to fulfil the expectations of its developers; the tolls show no rise above the level reached at the height of the boom in 1792 until 1807–8. Even then the rise was only a slight one and the level of tolls for the early 1820s was only 3 per cent higher than at the height of the boom.[63]

In 1841 A. B. Granville put forward an explanation of this stagnation in the demand for Bath and of its decline as a place of resort which is probably reliable.[64] First, there was the rising cost of treatment by Bath's doctors. Second, the growing preference for private as distinct from public entertainments, which had been Bath's speciality. But, above all, after the boom of 1788–92, Bath was just too big and bustling to attract the exclusive company who had made it popular seventy years earlier. Its size was particularly damaging because of competition from newer, more exclusive and fashionable resorts like Cheltenham and Brighton and, when the war was over, places in Europe.

Thus, absolute property and absolute self-interest and the conjuncture of elements in the capitalist dynamic, which had made it possible to build Bath as an attraction to men of property and wealth, worked also to destroy that attraction and undermined its prospects as a planned organisation of space for a privileged few. As a further consequence of the crisis of 1792–3, unfinished buildings, like so many eighteenth-century follies, added their ruined skeletons to the appearance of the place. Indeed, Camden Crescent, built in a hurry on untested ground, never was finished as planned and the unstable ground below it was given over to rows of cheap housing. And, in that juxtaposition as in the starkly truncated form of the Bathwick development, it stands as a memorial to the demise of the eighteenth-century dream of an ordered and gracious society.

CHAPTER 8

SOCIAL STRUCTURE AND ECONOMIC WELFARE

AVERAGE AGE AT DEATH IN BATH, 1841

Number of Deaths	Category	Average Age of Deceased
149	Gentlemen, Professional persons and their families	55
242	Tradesmen and their families	37
894	Mechanics, Labourers and their families	25
?	Shoemakers and their families	14

General Report on the Sanitary Condition of the Labouring Population of Great Britain, 1842

The merely physical growth of urban regions cannot be easily distinguished from the relationship of such growth to changes in social structure. Yet, Granville's explanation for the relative decline of Bath only hints at the fact that the physical growth of the place was not Bath's sole problem as a resort. The growth of Bath brought with it not only more visitors and the problems of the decay of its central areas and of the distance of the upper town from existing public places – problems which inspired the Corporation's improvement policies and Wood's building of the New Assembly Rooms – but, also those problems of the social use of space some of which we have already mentioned. We have seen how the development of the city in response to the demands of its visiting company conjured up a labouring population that was necessary to, yet alien from, the world in which it worked. And this growth of the labouring population and its impact on the townscape of the city is evidenced by both the decay of the southern parts of the parishes of St James and Walcot, which began almost as soon as they were built, and the new development of Snow Hill in the 1790s. It is in this sense that the social organisation of space in Bath ought not to be thought of only in terms of its architecture nor yet in terms of its total arrangement of space.

Bath may also be defined in terms of its job market and by the function and unity of its daily life; the provision of goods and services for its wealthy residents and visiting company. As the demands of the latter increased in volume and diversity the labouring population necessarily increased and diversified. In chapter 2 we have already looked at some aspects of the origins and experience of labouring people, at least up until the 1790s. We have seen, too, how in the course of development one social structure and set of relationships was replaced by another. In the rural parishes of Walcot and Bathwick, even in the parish of St James, landowners and changes in landownership destroyed a peasant society based on lifehold tenancies, and developers and builders replaced them with physical structures housing the wealthy and powerful. In the city itself the activities and interests of migrants and entrepreneurially minded citizens successfully challenged the traditional relationships of social and economic corporatism. All the while the numbers of the labouring population increased and in the matter of the decline of Bath it was this press of numbers that mattered most.

Outwardly, however, it was by no means clear in 1800 that the boom and crises of 1788–92 marked a watershed in the history of Bath. In 1800 Bath was still a prosperous and expanding city. Its population, over 33,000 in 1801, grew by 16 per cent from 1801 to 1811 and by 21 per cent from 1811 to 1821; rates of growth which roughly matched the rate of population growth of the country generally as well as of the neighbouring city of Bristol. The wealth brought into the city by the visiting company was sufficient still to encourage much building of architectural merit. The eastern end of Great Pulteney Street, Cavendish Crescent, Sion Hill Place, The Corridor, The Bazaar Rooms, the west side of Queen Square, the United Hospital, Cleveland Place, Cleveland Bridge and North Parade Bridge were all built in the first thirty years of the nineteenth century. Further the mood of optimism shown by these undertakings was periodically enlivened by the floating of large scale ventures; in 1804–5 the theatre was rebuilt at a cost of over £15,000, the Kennet and Avon Canal, begun in 1796, was finally opened for the whole of its length in 1810, and in 1817 the Gas Light and Coke Company was started with a capital of £25,000. There was successful coal-mining at Batheaston in the first decade of the century, and throughout the 1820s constant speculation about the opening of a railroad from Bath to Bristol. According to local observers Bath in the early nineteenth century was still a social success and the measure of its standing was Milsom Street. Then, having become the great shopping centre of the city, it was:

> The very centre of attraction, and till the hour of dinner time it is the peculiar resort of the Beau Mond. . . The street is elegant and imposing. . . all is bustle and gaiety: numerous dashing equipages passing and re-passing and then gracing the doors of the tradesmen. The shops are tastefully laid out; capacious and elegant; . . . in short Milsom Street and Broad Streets afford to the utmost extent everything towards supplying the real or imaginary wants of the visitors.[1]

Even in the 1830s it was being reported that its, 'Baths were crowded, the concerts were unrivalled, the Theatre second only to London.'[2]

Yet the writing was on the wall. The intercensal rates of growth of 16 per cent and 21 per cent were as nothing compared with the tenfold increase in population in the previous seventy or eighty years and were already well below the rates of growth of seventy-two principal towns in England. In fact only two parishes matched the growth rate of these seventy-two towns; the parish of St James with 33 per cent from 1801 to 1811 and the parish of Lyncombe and Widcombe, just south of the river from St James, with 34 per cent from 1801 to 1811 and 57 per cent from 1811 to 1821. By 1831 Lyncombe and Widcombe was a small township of its own. With a population of nearly 9,000 it was three times its size in 1801. Compared with this phenomenal growth two other parishes in the city centre, St Michael and St Peter and St Paul were together only fractionally bigger in 1821 than in 1801 and smaller in 1831 than in 1821. Bathwick had maintained some of its momentum and had almost 50 per cent more people in 1821 than at the beginning of the century. Walcot had only 37 per cent more. Consequently, within the area of eighteenth-century Bath, that is, excluding Lyncombe and Widcombe, the intercensal rates of population change from 1801 to 1821 were less than those for Bristol, much less than those for the seventy-two towns, and equivalent only to the rate for England and Wales. The different population histories of the parishes of Bath reflect above all the changing social structure of the city.[3] The intercensal rates of change are shown in table 8.1.

TABLE 8.1 Intercensal rates of population change, 1801–51

Decade	Area of 18th century Bath %	Bristol administrative area %	England and Wales %	Principal towns in the UK %	Lyncombe and Widcombe %
1801–11	14	16	14	23	34
1811–21	18	20	18	30	57
1821–31	3	22	16	32	48
1831–41	3	19	14	26	14
1841–51	2	10	13	25	0.5

Source: *Census of Population*, 1801–51 and B. W. E. Alford, 'The Economic Development of Bristol in the Nineteenth Century: an enigma?' in P. McGrath and J. Cannon (eds), *Essays in Bristol and Gloucestershire History*, Bristol, 1976. See also Appendix I.

The census returns may also be used to draw a picture of the social structure of Bath and its constituent parishes. In 1831, when the population totalled 50,800 and the population of males was 21,035, the occupations of 8,556 males over twenty years of age were recorded. Of these, 1,196 (14 per cent) were designated 'Capitalists, Bankers and other Educated men'. The rest were found to be engaged in the occupations listed in table 8.2. Men in the over-20 age group were mainly artisans, masters in a small way of business, or retailers either in business on their own account or working as shop assistants. Yet 20 per cent were unskilled labourers and 7 per cent were employed in boot-making and shoe-making, a trade generally held in low esteem by other members of the labouring population. Almost eight per cent were in the cloth trade.

A comparison of the figures for Bath with occupational figures for the whole of the county of Somerset shows that a century of

TABLE 8.2 Occupations in Bath, 1831

Occupation	Number of males over 20 years of age	Percentage of males
Building trades	1,074	14.6
Furniture and coach making	351	4.8
Shoemaking	529	7.2
Tailoring	349	4.7
Domestic service	670	9.0
Cloth-working	565	7.7
Labouring (non-agricultural)	1,480	20.0
Labouring	110	1.5
Other (mostly retail trades but including some craftsmen)	2,232	30.3
Total	7,360	99.8

Source: *Census of Population*, 1831.

urbanisation had made of Bath a place very different in terms of its social structure from the countryside as a whole. Bath's population of males over 20 was one-twelfth of the county total. Proportionately the numbers in this age group employed in Bath in various occupations was much higher than in the county. Bath was the home of one in ten of the county's population of coachmakers and printers, one in eight of masons and carpenters, one in six of shoemakers and glaziers, one in five of tailors, one in four of hatters, one in three of pastrycooks and one half of its painters. These figures also show that the differentiation of occupations, already apparent in the 1760s, was even more a feature of Bath in the 1830s.

Clearly Bath was not a homogeneous entity and it is a central yet simple thesis of this book that while spatial arrangements in the city were not planned the use of city space was socially organised and that it was a social product brought about by competing interests and claims. Accordingly, different parts of the city were used by different groups for different purposes; alehouses lined the main traffic routes, the town commons remained an undeveloped open space, Bathwick and North Walcot were quiet residential areas, Avon Street was a slum, Snow Hill an area of low priced working-class housing and so on. As part of this social organisation of space the parish of St James was the main focus of manufacturing and the home of a high proportion of the city's artisans and tradesmen (Figures 23 and 24). Thus, while 12 per cent of the male population of Bath, including Lyncombe and Widcombe, lived in it, the proportion of artisans housed in the parish was far higher; the overseers list of occupations in 1831 shows that it was the home of 28 per cent of tailors, 24 per cent of shoemakers, and 19 per cent of carpenters.[4] In fact the proportion of the parish's adult males employed in building, furniture making, coachmaking, shoemaking, and tailoring was twice that for the city as a whole. On the other hand the parish housed only its due proportion of labourers and a mere 5 per cent of male and 7 per cent of female servants.

There is reason to believe that while many of the artisans of St James worked on their own account many more were employed as wage earners in workshops or as outworkers attached to them, particularly in tailoring and shoemaking. This should be clear from the discussion of tailors and tailoring in chapter 2 which suggested that a workshop organisation already existed in that trade by the 1760s. Further evidence of industrial militancy on the part of journeymen tailors in the 1770s and again in 1802 also suggests that there was considerable differentiation between poor and prosperous tailors at that time. By 1813 the extent of differentiation was such that when the journeymen tailors negotiated successfully for double wages during the general mourning, they did so with nine master tailors who publicly acknowledged their agreement.[5] Of course, it would be difficult to argue that these nine were then the only employers in the tailoring trade, but it is reasonable to suppose that they were a majority of influential master tailors. Given that they were, then it is likely that they or their successors in the 1830s employed most of the 350 tailors in Bath and that most tailors were, therefore, wage earners. Twenty-eight per cent of tailors lived in the parish of St James.

The situation in bootmaking and shoemaking was much the same. In 1831 there were 529 shoemakers in Bath, a quarter of them in the parish of St James. Twenty years later there were 747 male shoemakers, 133 female shoemakers, and 308 'shoemakers wives.' In all 1,225 persons engaged in shoemaking at mid-century. In 1831 a majority worked for some ten or a dozen master shoemakers with establishments employing between thirty and sixty workers. As a result of the division between capital and labour a Union of Cordwainers existed as early as 1803 and there were strikes, some of which were well organised in 1804, 1805, 1808, 1813, 1824, and 1847. In 1803 and 1804 the local society worked in conjunction with a national body with headquarters in London. In 1808 thirteen journeymen shoemakers were prosecuted under the combination laws and sentenced to three months imprisonment. The union's particularly 'black' employer was J. Cooper of the Shoe Manufactory who employed large numbers of apprentices as cheap labour contrary to law. The scale of operation of some of Bath's master shoemakers is indicated by the fact that in 1834 S. Rogers of the Boot and Shoe Warehouse in Abbey Churchyard had a chain of retail outlets in Bristol, Coventry, Birmingham, Chester, Liverpool, York, Hull and Edinburgh. There can be little doubt, therefore, that most shoemakers, like tailors, were journeymen wage earners employed by, and negotiating with, relatively few employers in a workshop situation.[6]

Other enterprises with a workshop or factory organisation in the parish of St James included the following: George Cox's hatting and undertaking business in Stall Street, Brough and Deverall's steam-engine manufactory on the Quay in 1802, and a brewery with malthouse, stock and engine house worth £10,000. These enterprises plus a brewery in Northgate Street with a 3-horsepower Boulton and Watt engine in 1800, a brass foundry in 1812, a pin factory in 1814, a flax factory in 1819, a steam-operated cut-glass factory in Westage Buildings after 1828, and two soap factories in the 1830s, point to incipient industrialisation in the city, particularly in the 1820s and 1830s, much of it concentrated in the parish of St James. By 1839 almost all the premises in Dorchester Street, Newark Street, Broad Quay and Little Corn Street, all in the parish of St James, were occupied by warehouses, yards and workshops.[7]

The firm whose story most clearly illustrates the theme of incipient industrialisation in Bath brought about by the growth of the city in general, and by the last great boom of the eighteenth century in particular, is that of George Stothert. George Stothert was born in 1755 in Shaftesbury in Dorset. In 1779 he was already in Bath employed as superintendent of one of Bath's four firms of ironmongers; a firm employing smiths, braziers, tinmen, and planemakers and situated in Horse Street in the parish of St James. By 1785, on the eve of Bath's most rapid growth, George Stothert was in charge of his own ironmonger's business on the same premises. No doubt the boom was good for business – in 1792 George Stothert was a shareholder in the Sydney Gardens enterprise – because by 1796 Stothert's firm had established itself as a major outlet in Bath for the products of the Coalbrookdale Works, and between 1799 and 1807 supplied much of the ironwork used by the Kennet and Avon Canal Company. When George Stothert died in 1818 his net worth was £17,000. In the meantime, in 1815, his son George had gone into business as an ironfounder at 17 Horse Street. By 1823 this branch of the firm had supplied tread mills to workhouses at Taunton and Shepton Mallet and was using steam-driven machinery at the Newark foundry by 1827 if not earlier. A few years later the firm was sole agent for Finlayson's Harrow and tendered for the iron work in the Victoria Bridge in Bath. At mid-century the firm was producing in Bath the cranes for which it established a world-wide reputation. However, the firm's expansion to Bristol in 1836 to build railway locomotives is not a part of Bath's own history.[8] As a result of the growth of the metals and engineering industries generally, in which the growth of Stothert's ironfoundry in the parish of St James played a central part, there were 540 men employed in them in 1851.

In addition to the concentration of industry and artisans in the parish of St James there was a contiguous area in the southern part of the parish of Walcot centred on Avon Street already described as the home of the lumpen proletariat (Figure 25). By 1839 the place had deteriorated further and four out of five houses in 182 houses in the streets, courts and alleys connected with Avon Street and Milk Street were worth less than £15 per annum. (In the King's Circus three out of five houses were worth more than £150 per annum and none less than £110). In north Walcot there was a further area of low-quality housing in Walcot Street, close to the Hat and Feather Yard and Ladymead, and in the Snow Hill, Dover Street area. In Morford and Ballance Streets, also in north Walcot, there was an area of more substantial working-class housing.[9] Some of the details of the distribution of houses according to their annual values is shown in Appendix C and in Figure 24.

The growth of manufacturing and of factory industry in the southern half of the city, which underpinned the concentration of artisans in St James, also influenced the phenomenal growth of

Figure 23 Bath in 1900, the Parish of St James in the foreground. Compare with the groundplan of the Parish of St James in figure 24. The figures may be aligned by identifying either St James Parade or the Broad Quay

Figure 24 Street plan of the Lower Town, the Parish of St James. Source: Ordnance Survey Map (1888). See also figure 23

In the 1830s in the streets and courts shown on this map (excluding the Parades development) 83 per cent of houses had an estimated rental of less than £30 per annum (about 10s. per week), 34 per cent had a rental of less than £10 per annum (about 4s. per week). They compare with houses in the Royal Crescent and the King's Circus where 80 per cent of houses had an estimated rental of over £150 per annum and 33 per cent had a rental of over £200 per annum. The Courts associated with Avon Street and Milk Street where half the 198 houses had an estimated rental of less than £10 per annum were: Phoenix Court, Lockyers Court, New Quay, Lambs Yard, Bakers Court, Dills Court, New Court, Avon Street New Court, Seville's Court and Avon Court. Other Courts in St James parish in which almost all houses had an estimated rental of less than £10 per annum were: Harris Court, Taylor's Court, Marchant's Passage, Howell's Court, Selden's Court, St James Court, Brimble's Court, Bolwell's Court, Margaret Passage, Hucklebridge's Court, The Quay, Little Corn Street and Back Street. That part of the parish not characterised by low rental housing was occupied by workshops, warehouses and yards. Source: *Rate Book for Cleansing and Lighting*, St James Parish (1839); *Highway Rate Book*, Walcot Parish (1830), GAB.

population in Lyncombe and Widcombe. Very early in Bath's development Lyncombe and Widcombe had been the site of Ralph Allen's tramway from his quarries to his wharf on the Avon. But it was the expansion of the manufacture of fine woollen cloth that distinguished the parish occupationally from the rest of Bath. It was there that all the 565 males engaged in the manufacture of fine woollen cloth lived. If this figure from the 1831 census is correct it shows that this new township, a suburb of Bath, was second only to Frome in numbers of males employed in woollen cloth manufacture in the county, and more important than Twerton with 284 males employed in the industry; except that Twerton was undoubtedly a factory area where several hundred women and children were employed, even at the beginning of the century. As well as housing this large number of textile workers, catering for a market much larger than Bath, Lyncombe and Widcombe was the home of railway labourers and coal carriers and, according to some, 'the residence of most of the thieves and prostitutes who spread themselves over the several parishes of Bath.'[10] Whatever the truth of this statement it is certain that a class of unskilled and semi-skilled workers lived in two areas in the parish; the Holloway on the road to Wells, and the Dolemeads, a wedge-shaped low-lying area between the river and the canal. Both areas were subject to repeated flooding.

Outside these main areas, the poor crowded into tenements and houses in Galloway Buildings, which had not fulfilled its developers expectations, Chapel Street, Trymme Street and a variety of odd courts and alleys throughout the city.

The story so far in this chapter is as follows. From 1800 to 1820 Bath's population continued to grow, much more slowly than in the eighteenth century, but at a rate equal to that of the country as a whole. This superficially high growth rate masked significant differences between parishes and obscured significant social structural changes taking place in them. Bath's adult male population consisted overwhelmingly of skilled artisans, tradesmen and unskilled labourers. The wealthy were a mere 14 per cent of the male population. Different parishes and parts of parishes were occupied by markedly different groups; St James was conspicuously the home of artisans many of whom were employed in small workshops and in factories, and Lyncombe and Widcombe was the home of workers in the woollen textile industry. These were the parishes in which population growth was most evident. Other areas, particularly in the low-lying parts of the city such as Avon Street, were occupied by the very poor and the destitute.

Figure 25 Avon Street, nineteenth century

As this discussion suggests, there were four clearly identifiable social strata in Bath's male population: (1) leisured and professional, 14 per cent, (2) tradesmen, 26 per cent, (3) artisans, ranging from printers and coachmakers to shoemakers, 33 per cent (4) unskilled labourers, 19 per cent. There was also a stratum of the very poor concealed within the last three categories; perhaps as much as 10 per cent of the total male population. To this group must be added the mass of itinerant poor who periodically swelled the ranks of the lumpenproletariat, numbering about 20,000 every year.

However, adult males over 20 were less than one-sixth of the population and only a little more than one-third of the total adult population of men and women. Which is to say that for every 100 males over 20 there were 167 women in 1821 and 197 women in 1851. In the residential areas of Bathwick and Walcot in 1851 the ratios of men to women were 100:248 and 100:250 respectively. Table 8.3 contains the basic information.

This feature of Bath's demographic history reflects the fact that, as the city declined as a pleasure resort and became instead a place of

SOCIAL STRUCTURE AND ECONOMIC WELFARE

TABLE 8.3 Number of females per 100 males, Bath 1821–51*

Age group	1821	1841	1851
Under 10	105	102	106
10–20	130	124	138
20–30	150	178	203
30–40	168	151	173
40–50	165	146	120
50–60	166	165	148
Over 60	180	197	205

*Figures exclude Bathwick and Lyncombe and Widcome.
Source: *Census of Population*, 1821–51.

permanent residence and retirement for an affluent upper-middle class, young women could still find attractive employment there. The high ratios of women in the over-50 age group also reflects the fact that a high proportion of the city's affluent residents were women. Thus, in 1851 there were 10,767 spinsters in the city, but only 4,057 bachelors; 3,980 widows, but only 1,086 widowers. The residential part of Bath was, therefore, largely populated by retired elderly widows and spinsters – no wonder everyone could claim to have an aunt in Bath – and their servants, most of whom were young, single and female.

Table 8.4 summarises the main occupations in which women worked in Bath in 1851.

TABLE 8.4 Employment of women in Bath, 1851

Domestic servant	7,751
Washerwoman	1,436
Seamstress	509
Staymaker	171
Tailor	129
Milliner	1,829
Shoemaker and shoemaker's wife	441
Total	12,266

Source: *Census of Population*, 1851.

Because of the preponderance of females in the population of

Bath – 32,517 compared with 21,737 males in 1851 – and because of the employment opportunities for women in Bath, more women than men were in employment. The number of employed women was 12,266, the number of employed men was 10,603. This plenitude of women gives them first place in the next part of this chapter. It begins with an account of their conditions of employment and then attempts to look at the general condition of life as experienced by them, and by other members of the workforce who occupied and defined its space.

Some 3,000 women worked in skilled trades. In the linen, silk, hosiery, haberdashery and clothing trades generally they worked as seamstresses, tailors, milliners and shoemakers. Because of the ready supply of women into these occupations their conditions of work and wages were probably worse than those of their male counterparts in tailoring and shoemaking. The organisation of their work was similar to that in the men's trades, a mixture of workshop production with associated outworkers. For example, in 1817 Mesdames Smith and Jones kept a shop in New Bond Street and supplied it with merchandise from their own 'Establishment' at 1, Ainslies Belvedere. This was a large house with extensive outbuildings, a sort of manufactory, where, 'the friendless, the infirm, the unfortunate; and many who having seen better days turn to a source of pecuniary emolument those talents once cultivated as an elegant accomplishment'.[11] Smith and Jones produced and sold a wide range of hand-done embroidery and needlework and claimed to employ about 150 women. A high proportion of these were probably outworkers. The drudgery and degradation of such skilled employments is shown most clearly in a letter written by a man to the *Bath and Cheltenham Gazette* in 1825. The letter also indicates that a workshop organisation was characteristic of the clothing trades in Bath.[12]

> During our most fashionable seasons of the year, when plays, balls, masquerades, and riots, are the order of day, it is by no means unusual for delicate females to be following an unhealthy sedentary employment to the destruction of their sight and constitution, for 16 and even 18 hours out of the 24; and this is not in solitary or occasional instances, but day by day and week by week during the greater part of the season.
>
> Imagine, Sir, a number of unprotected females from the humbler walks of life (I allude to the outdoor assistants) leaving their employment at 11 and 12 o'clock at night, and sometimes

at 1 and 2 in the morning, to return to the abodes of their parents or to their lodgings . . . and calculate upon the chances of temptation thrown in their way by the licentious of our sex.

The inmates, to my certain knowledge, are doomed during the dreary time of winter, and even extending in many instances to midsummer, to drag a life of servitude far more oppressive than the Indian Slaves, by being compelled to work 20 hours a day from Sunday night 12 o'clock, until Saturday 12; and that too without intermission for months; and their employers, not considering they have reaped a sufficient harvest from their labours during these unwarrantable hours, go further, and modestly and feelingly require their services, 'a little on the Sabbath.'

In this city, I should consider the first rate houses employ, on salary and apprentices, 200 females, inmates; and I have no hesitation in stating that three fourths of that number are so impaired in health, that the foundation of disease is laid, and a premature grave the inevitable end.

In shoemaking conditions were worse. Women shoemakers and 'shoemakers' wives' shared the squalor and smell of a shoemaker's shop with their men. According to Francis Place they were totally degraded by the manner of their work. His account of conditions in London also describes their plight in Bath:[13]

> The nominal wages of boot and shoemakers, except for the very commonest kinds of work, are high, particularly those at the west end of the town. But the wages earned are not higher than those earned by other tradesmen. It is all piece work, almost all the men work at their own lodgings, and have generally to wait between job and job. When a boot is cut out, it is sent to the closer, and when partly closed is returned to the maker, and is then sent again to the closer to be completed. Many of the wives of the snobs (shoemakers not belonging to a trade club) are closers, and it is quite common for two or three men and a woman to work in the same room. The work is dirty, and as it generally happens that one or more of the parties is waiting for a job, he, being idle, gets to drinking, and the others drink too; By the time he gets a job, he is not in a state to begin it, and by that time another is perhaps without a job, and thus it is that the snobs are less respectable than

most other tradesmen. It is a singularly great evil for a man to have to work in the room he lives in with his wife, and if she works with him, too, the evil is greatly increased.

Without doubt most of the employed women, successors of Martha Abraham and Mary Banks in the eighteenth century, were domestic servants. There were 7,751 of them by 1851, over 14 per cent of the total population and nearly one-quarter of all females in Bath. The nature of their employment makes it very difficult to generalise about the conditions under which they worked and lived their lives. For example, in 1806 Sarah Hancock, a young girl employed as a servant by a baker was paid one shilling a week plus meat, drink, washing and lodging.[14] Another girl, employed by a laundress to help with the washing, seems to have shared in the family income made up out of earnings from the laundry and poor relief.[15] These girls were little more than skivvies. On the other hand, in 1816, an upper housemaid in charge of two other housemaids could earn twelve guineas a year plus tea and sugar.[16] About the same time another girl, Elizabeth Pain, earned £7 per year. A cook could earn £10 a year.[17] One thing that servants did get that was often not available to other workers was medical attention, particularly if their masters and mistresses were subscribers to one or other of the dispensaries or hospitals. Accordingly in 1865, eighty-nine servants attended Bath's United Hospital. Their average wage was £11 5s. 9d. But they ranged in income from one servant earning 6d. a week with board to three whose earnings were £40 a year! Altogether 52 earned less than £8, 9 between £8 and £10, and only 28 more than £11, a figure very close to the average.[18] Compared with the scatter of figures available for the mid eighteenth century these figures suggest that only the well paid upper servants were any better off than their predecessors.

Throughout Bath's history, first as a resort and then as a place of residence, all the women in the labouring population worked long hours either in sweated trades or in domestic service. Yet, however diligent they were, it seems unlikely that many wives and daughters in labouring families could have contributed more than four or five shillings a week to the maintenance of the household to which they belonged. Thus the most a woman could earn was her own subsistence. This would have been the case whether she lived at home or in the house in which she worked as domestic servant or needlewoman. Consequently, if, as was common, a woman through death or desertion should find herself the sole support of a family the impoverishment of the family was virtually certain. Hence the high proportion of women among applicants for poor relief in the eighteenth century. In the nineteenth century the situation was no different and the plight of such a family in 1837 is sharply drawn in a statement put out by the Bath Guardians to justify stopping the payment of poor relief to the family. The Guardians wrote:[19]

> Mary Price aged 47, a laundress in good employ, and living in a house at the annual rent of £7. For the washing of one family she receives 6/6d per week. She washes for others at her own house and occasionally goes out to work; and in addition to this she has a valuable mangle, from which she must derive considerable emolument. The pauper keeps a servant, who resides with her to assist her in her occupation as a laundress. Mary Price has a family of four children: viz, Mary aged 19, in service at £8 per annum wages, William aged 10 at school, James aged 8 ditto, Sarah aged 7 ditto. On this evidence the board determined that her weekly relief should be taken off, against which decision no appeal has been made.

Mary Price's case became something of a *cause célèbre*. It was taken up enthusiastically by those who opposed the New Poor Law on the grounds of its lack of humanity. They pointed out that half of the income from washing went on the expenses of washing and that the payment of the servant's wages would also reduce the profits of washing. In any case, they said, Mary Price had only received 2s. per week. Accordingly they started a fund to help Ma·y and her family; they were the lucky ones. No one took up the cases of the other 1,435 washerwomen employed in Bath. And no one took up the problem of widows or deserted wives, except, perhaps Edwin Chadwick, who, in his *Report on the Sanitary Condition of the Labouring Population of Great Britain*, 1842, used the example of Bath to illustrate his thesis that a large part of the burden of Poor Relief was caused by the early age of death of husbands. Such early deaths and consequent early widowhood brought with it a great body of dependent orphans who constituted a main part of the dependent poor. Any reduction in mortality through improved sanitation and housing, he argued, would produce a great social saving. The figures he produced for Bath are shown in table 8.5.

TABLE 8.5 Widows in Bath Union, 1842

Age of death of husband	Number of widows	Number of dependent children	Causes of death of husband	Number of husbands
25–30	9	28	Respiratory organs	40
30–5	13	52	epidemic, endemic, contagious	4
35–40	12	52	digestive organs	3
40–5	18	84	nervous disorder	5
45–50	9	37	violent death	5
50–5	4	15	old age	–
55–60	1	6	other diseases	8
60–5	1	4	undescribed	2
Total	67	278		67

Source: *Report on the Sanitary Condition of the labouring Population of Great Britain*, 1842.

As well as the 278 dependent children of these widows in 1842 there were many illegitimate children maintained by the parishes – 186 in the parish of Walcot alone in 1820, and the children of pauper families with both father and mother. By 1846 there were, therefore, nearly 1,000 pauper children and over 2,000 pauper adults in Bath.

Overall there can be little doubt that working-class women, whether in work, widowed, married or as the mothers of illegitimate children, were in a worse position than any other group of workers and it is unlikely that they fared any better during the early nineteenth century than that group of workers only marginally superior to them, the unskilled labourers. Indeed, for those who were wives of unskilled labourers and the mothers of their children their welfare was inextricably bound up with that of their husbands. And, while it may not be possible to say much about changes over time in the welfare of working-class women in Bath, it is possible to describe in some detail the changes in the economic welfare of unskilled labourers in Bath. Thereby, one may infer that the mass of working-class women who were not servants but who were wives of workers, or workers themselves in other occupations, experienced changes in their economic welfare no better than those of unskilled labourers.

Unskilled labourers, about 24 per cent of Bath's workforce, were among the lowest paid male workers in the city. We have already seen how their real standard of living fell during the last twenty years of the eighteenth century and fluctuated at a level 25 or 30 per cent lower than in 1780 during the first fifteen years of the nineteenth century. How they fared during the next twenty years is not easy to say. The only continuous indicator for the whole period, 1800 to 1846, is an index of retail prices (Appendix D). Nevertheless, it is possible to show that, by 1832, the real wages of labourers were at a level comparable to that in 1780 and that, during the boom of 1835, they reached a level 22 per cent higher. This recovery was short-lived. The years 1837 to 1840 were generally bad ones for unskilled labourers and it was not until 1841 that real wages showed a definite and sustained improvement. By the mid-1840s their real standard of living when in full work was about 50 per cent higher than it had been seventy years earlier.[20]

To say this, however, gives little impression of the reality of life itself. Even with full employment all the year round a labourer's wage in the 1840s could not have kept the man, his wife and a family of two children at the level of pauper dietary established by the Bath Union in 1836. In order to live at even that modest standard of living, which might be taken as a minimum necessary to sustain working life, it was estimated that such a family would have to spend as shown in table 8.6.[21]

TABLE 8.6 The charge per week for keeping a poor man, wife and two children with nothing superior to gaol allowance

	s. d.	Percentage
Subsistence for man, wife and two children	7. 9	64.5
Beer	8	5.5
Clothing and shoes	1. 4	11.1
Washing, soap, candles	3	6.2
Fuel	6	
Rent	1. 6	12.5
	12.0	99.8

Source: *Bath Journal*, 17 January 1831.

The 7s. 9d. allocated to subsistence in this budget, which was set out in 1831, would not have bought the amounts of food set out in the pauper dietary of 1836. These were: 33½ lb bread, 1 lb 11oz. meat, 1 lb 1 oz. bacon, 4½ lb cheese, 6 lb potatoes. At the lowest cost in Bath market in 1837 this basket of goods would have cost 8*s*. 10¾*d*. Thus, even if all the other items remained unchanged in price then the weekly budget for this family of four, in 1837, would have required a weekly wage of 13*s*. 1¾*d*. Since weekly wages for unskilled labourers in Bath were never more than 11*s*. 10*d*., and then only in 1851, even the increase in wages after 1840, by which time they were 50 per cent higher than in 1780, was inadequate for the maintenance of a minimum standard of living as understood by men in the 1840s. Consequently, even with the man in full work at least one other income brought in by a wife or child was essential to sustain life. Without such family earnings an unskilled labourer, like a widow with children, would have to seek and win help from the poor law authorities or from private charities. In the hard winter of 1840–1 such assistance would have been especially urgent – there was then six feet of snow on the Mendips and 22 degrees of frost in the city. One result of this, coupled with the cessation of railway building, was the case of John Edwards. Edwards was an unemployed railway labourer – he had been out of work for five weeks during this winter – and both he and his wife had fallen ill. According to the coroner's report he died of, 'cold and want of nourishment.'[22]

In times of high unemployment conditions for such families must have been intolerable. Therefore, in spite of the rise in real wages, the mid-1840s in Bath were disastrous and unhappy years for at least a third of the population. Accordingly, in 1845, the Bath Union relieved 3,000 paupers and 175 tramps and the Monmouth Street Society aided 509 poor families and 5,097 travellers. In St James Parish it was reported, 'not fewer than 700 or 800 families (about half the population) are either in absolute poverty, or so little raised above want, that judicious assistance, on the most moderate scale, would be felt as a real and substantial benefit; while there are resident within the Parish but very few individuals who possess to any large extent, the means of relieving the poor.'[23] And, according to the Chairman of the Bath Union, Walcot, with about 1,000 paupers, was a pauperised district in which unemployed men lived on the earnings of their wives and a place where most of the registered poor were, 'widows, or mothers of illegitimate children who were exceedingly depraved or resentful.'[24]

In these circumstances many families in Bath must have lived in absolute poverty. Take the case of Joseph West.[25] His body:

> was reduced by emaciation to a very skeleton (and) lay on the bare floor, its only covering being a thread bare blanket. There was not an article of furniture in the apartment, which was occupied by the deceased, his wife and four children; a heap of shavings in the corner of the room seeming to point out the sleeping place of the family, save which there were neither goods nor chattels in the place. The wife of the unfortunate wretch . . . deposed that her husband was formerly a porter to Mr Tulley, but had been out of service since January last (it was now October). From that time he had been unable to work, through sickness and had depended for subsistence on the earnings of his wife and eldest girl. Witness occasionally earned one or two shillings a week as a charwoman, but had done nothing for the last three weeks; the daughter earned two shillings per week in the market, and they had been supplied with one shilling a week and a quartern loaf by Mr Douglas, the relieving officer, for the past three weeks. This was all the family of six persons had to live upon: though it was admitted that neither witness nor deceased had ever applied for more assistance. Day after day their only food was two meals of dry bread, and tea; a halfpenny worth of tea and a twopenny loaf being bought each day, and taken about twelve o'clock at noon and at six in the evening. The children shared these meals. The quartern loaf got from the Union lasted Friday evening and the whole of Saturday.

This family had not tasted meat in three weeks, since the eldest girl brought home 1½d. worth of bacon. There was no bedding in the room measuring ten feet by eight which they rented for 9d. per week, and there was rarely a fire since they bought coal in 1d. worths. Water was boiled on a neighbour's fire and the family drank their tea sitting on borrowed chairs.

Even so only those who experienced absolute poverty could fully comprehend its awfulness. It was with them day after day of their lives. Contemporary observers, like modern historians, could only come to an understanding of it through virtually impenetrable barriers of class and time. Nothing, I think, shows the nature of this problem and, therefore, reveals the unknown depths and spread of poverty in Bath than the story told by William Napier against himself. Napier, historian of the Napoleonic Wars, was a humane radical, more perceptive and caring than most of his class. At his home near Bath he wrote:[26]

> I have lost my poor old man who worked in my garden. He has been killed by the cold, and I have some uneasy feelings on the subject. He was so clean, and brisk, and good tempered, that I did not know he was ill-clothed – he made everything look well. I had given him a blanket and a pair of woollen socks, but one day I was told he complained of cold; I saw him that moment and gave him a flannel jacket and drawers, and made him put them on, I also gave him ten shillings to buy a warm coat. He was then, he said, quite well, but in a few hours he fell ill not withstanding all our medical care he died. I certainly could not help it; I did not lose five minutes in giving him the flannels after I heard of his being so cold from the children; but I ought to have thought more about him in the frost.

In 1848 economic conditions were worse than in 1845. The mass of unemployed and paupers in Bath was increased by the vast numbers of unemployed travellers passing through the city. In that year the Monmouth Street Society relieved 7,553 of them, 50 per cent more than in 1845,[27] and the cost of poor relief was in the region of £10,000 annually. Young men, faced with the facts of such widespread unemployment and partially relieved poverty began to leave Bath in their hundreds; joining the travellers in search of work. Faced with these facts a writer in *The Bathonian* in a masterpiece of understatement wrote, 'The most painful reflection which can occupy the contemplative mind of the visitor to our beautiful city (is) the strong contrast presented by wealth and poverty ... which threatens 'ere long to be of serious import to the well being of its inhabitants.'[28]

Bearing in mind what has just been said, it is possible to see from table 8.7 that the improvement of living standards shown by the rise in the index of real wages from 1840 to 1844 was a rise from an intolerably low level of living, one scarcely removed from absolute poverty. Even this improvement owed little to conditions peculiar to Bath. Thus, money wages of labourers only began to rise significantly in 1839 as a result of the start of work on the construction

TABLE 8.7 Earnings and real wages, non-agricultural labourers in the city of Bath, 1812–44 (1838=100)

Year	Average weekly earnings (1780=100=Sept.1838)	Bath retail prices	Price of quartern loaf	Real wage
1812	117	182	192	64
1816	112	129	133	87
1832	96	90	94	106
1833	97	85	84	114
1834	86	82	84	105
1835	95	78	73	122
1836	95	90	84	109
1837	95	102	94	93
1838	98	100	100	98
1839	103	101	105	102
1840	128	105	105	92
1841	127	103	100	123
1842	134	97	94	138
1843	134	83	78	161
1844	137	84	84	163

Source: Highway Accounts Walcot (for 1816, Widcombe District Accounts vol. 143) and *Bath and Cheltenham Gazette* 1812–44.

in the neighbourhood of the GWR. By the middle of that year work was under way on a viaduct, alterations to the road from Wells, and on the permanent way. By the end of the year the Kennet and Avon canal had been turned from its course and construction started on tunnels, the skew bridge and the railway station. The result was, 'The contractors appeared to put an embargo upon all the disposable labour of the city and its suburbs.'[29] The lift given to wages was, therefore, the consequence of decisions taken elsewhere and not the result of developments of or within the city itself. This external intrusion, which placed the station and railway yard in the southern half of the parish of St James, also served to give added emphasis to the growing industrial appearance of this part of the city.

The contribution of falling prices to the improvement in the standard of living was also the consequence of factors outside Bath such as the fall in the price of bread caused by the general rise in wheat yields in the 1840s and by the modification of the corn laws and then their repeal in 1846. Import prices also fell. As a result of this conjuncture of events unskilled labourers in full work in Bath began belatedly to enjoy some of the material fruits of England's economic development. Their wives and children possibly benefited also.

People in Bath in the 1840s were certainly able to claim that living in Bath was better than living anywhere else – even for the labouring population. The 'Utopian' organisation of its urban space like the neat appearance of Napier's old man still 'made everything look well.' Moreover, they had an impeccable authority to which to refer. This was Chadwick's *Report on the Sanitary Condition of the Labouring Population of Great Britain* published in 1842. This showed that Bath was an exceptionally healthy place in which to live – table 8.8 summarises the main comparative evidence used by Chadwick in his report.

TABLE 8.8 Average age of death in families in three classes in selected towns, 1841

Families of	Bath *	Bethnal Green	Bolton	Kennington	Leeds	Liverpool	Strand	Whitechapel
1. Gentlemen and Professional persons	55	45	34	44	44	35	43	45
2. Tradesmen and farmers	37	26	23	29	27	22	33	27
3. Mechanics, labourers, agricultural labourers	25	16	18	26	19	15	24	22

* Figures for Bath exclude all visitors and occasional residents.
Source: Chadwick, *Report on the Sanitary Condition of the Labouring Population of Great Britain*, 1842.

The comments of the man who collected the Bath figures for Chadwick, the Rev. Elwin, were also quoted at length by Chadwick to support his argument that improved housing, sanitation, and water supply could result in significant material improvement in the quality of life and that public expenditure on these things could result in over-all social saving. In this way, through the labours of the

Rev. Elwin, Bath's social organisation of space was made to look especially well and found a place in the history of nineteenth-century social reform. Elwin's argument is worth reading. It is a contemporary comment upon some of the themes in this book.

Couched in terms of a class analysis Elwin's case was that the organisation of space in Bath matched the class organisation of its social structure. Nevertheless, he argued, the organisation of space in Bath, designed and produced for the wealthy and powerful, produced some spin-off in terms of welfare for other social classes. This spin-off was greater for tradesmen than for the lower classes of society. For example, one very early by-product had been the Act of 1766 giving the Corporation substantial powers over water supply. This as well as improvements in housing had benefited all social classes. Although he was himself surprised at how small the benefits had been for the lower classes Elwin was persuaded that their material environment was better than elsewhere. He wrote:[30]

> The difference in the ages at death of these several classes (in Bath) presents to my mind a tolerably exact scale of the difference of their abodes. The large houses, the broad streets, looking almost invariably on one side or other upon parks or gardens or open country, the spacious squares, the crescents built upon the brows of the hills without a single obstruction to the pure air of heaven, give the gentry of Bath that superiority over other grades and other cities which their longevity indicates. And herein, it appears to me, consists the value of the return. It shows that the congregation of men is not necessarily unhealthy; nay, that towns, possessing as they do superior medical skill and readier access to advice, may, under favourable circumstances, have an advantage over the country. The situation of the tradesmen of Bath, inferior as it is to that of the gentry, is better than that of their own station in other places. The streets they chiefly inhabit, though with many exceptions, are wide and swept by free currents of air, with houses large and well ventilated. The condition of the poor is worse than would be anticipated from the other portion of the town. They are chiefly located in low districts at the bottom of the valley, and narrow alleys and confined courts are very numerous. Yet even here we have an unquestionable advantage over most large towns. It was only yesterday that I was ex-

pressing my horror to a medical gentleman at some portions of the habitations of the poor, when he replied, that it excited little attention, because they were so much better than what was to be seen in other parts of the kingdom.

In fact, wrote Elwin, the average age of death in gentlemen's families would have been as high as 60 but for 'a small but damp district, in which numerous cases of fever brought down the average to 54.'[31] So it was, he said, with shopkeepers and labourers. Indeed, for a comparative study of the effects of housing and spatial organisation on mortality Bath was a perfect laboratory. He wrote:[32]

> Bath is a favourable town to institute the comparison, from presenting such marked contrasts in its houses, and the inquiry being little complicated by the presence of noxious trades, which in some towns would necessarily disturb every calculation of the kind. Even here a colony of shoemakers would bring down the average of its healthiest spot to the age of childhood. My attention was called to this circumstance by the clerk incidentally remarking that more shoemakers were married at his office, and were uniformly more dirty and ill-dressed, than any other class of persons. The proneness to marriage or concubinage in proportion to the degradation of the parties is notorious, and I anticipated from the fact an abundant offspring, afterwards to be carried off by premature disease. Accordingly I went with this view through several of the registers, and the result was, that while the average age of death among the families of labourers and artisans in general was 24 and 25, that of shoemakers was only 14. Had the shoemakers been excluded from the former average, as for the purpose of comparison they should have been, the disproportion would be some years greater.

As was to be expected the worst area of all was Avon Street. Some of its history has already been told. Built with pride in 1730, it was a traffic route for watering horses in the Avon in the 1770s and in 1830 the home of the lumpenproletariat. In the cholera epidemic of 1831 it was the site of more than half the deaths in Bath from the disease. Seven years later it was also the main area swept by the smallpox epidemic which affected about 300 persons in Bath but touched no member of a gentleman's family and only one or two in tradesmen's families. Elwin commented:[33]

> I went through the registers from the commencement, and observed that, whatever contagious or epidemic disease prevailed, – fever, smallpox, influenza – this (Avon Street) was the scene of its principal ravages; and it is the very place of which every person acquainted with Bath would have predicted the result. Everything vile and offensive is congregated there. All the scum of Bath – its low prostitutes, its thieves, its beggars – are piled up in the dens rather than houses of which the street consists.

Indeed, had Elwin read the First Annual Report of the Registrar General, which covered the last two quarters of 1837, he would have seen that the Bath registration district had a very bad record in the smallpox epidemic. With a population of 69,083 and 151 deaths from smallpox Bath was second only to Liverpool with a population of 218,233 and 634 deaths; the ratios per 1000 living were, Bath, 2.2:1000 (Abbey District 3:1000), Liverpool, 2.9:1000. Moreover, mortality in Bath might well have been higher still because by July 1837, when registration began, the worst of the epidemic in Bath was already past. Thus, of the 151 who died of smallpox, 71 died in July, 60 in August, 20 in September. The figures also show that mortality in the central and working-class areas of Bath was two-and-a-half to three times as high as in the Bathwick registration subdistrict. In 1848–9 things were no better. Indeed, the second cholera epidemic in Bath was worse than the first; there were 90 deaths from cholera and 101 from diarrhoea. In this outbreak Avon Street and its contiguous streets and courts, with 20 out of 90 deaths from cholera, was still the focal point of the epidemic although now it was joined by the low-lying areas of Widcombe. The relationship between spatial organisation and this epidemic is shown in table 8.9. Unfortunately the figures are recorded according to Registration Districts and not according to parish. Nevertheless, if it is noted that the Abbey District includes the old parish of St James and that Lansdown District includes the whole of the southern part of the parish of Walcot, including Avon Street, the distribution can be roughly matched to the parish areas previously mentioned. The figures show that in the most working-class districts the level of mortality from cholera and diarrhoea

SOCIAL STRUCTURE AND ECONOMIC WELFARE

combined was four to five times as high as in the most favoured district of Bathwick.

TABLE 8.9 Deaths from cholera and diarrhoea in Bath, 1848–9 and from smallpox in 1837

Registration District	Population	Deaths from cholera	Deaths from diarrhoea	Deaths from Cholera and Diarrhoea per 1000 living	Deaths from smallpox	Deaths from smallpox per 1,000 living
Bathwick	6,610	4	1	0.8	7	1.1
Walcot	12,089	0	18	1.5	27	2.2
Abbey	12,104	10	19	2.4	36	3.0
Lansdown	14,111	21	21	3.0	36	2.6
Lyncombe	9,920	21	11	3.2	25	2.5
Twerton	7,037	17	13	4.3	9	1.3
Batheaston	7,212	17	18	4.8	11	1.5
Total	69,083	90	101	2.9	151	2.0

Source: Registrar General, *Report on Cholera in England, 1848–1849*, p. 257, and *First Annual Report of the Registrar General* (two quarters only).

The Rev. Elwin's comments on the smallpox epidemic of 1837, and the location of the main incidence of that epidemic and the cholera epidemics of 1831 and 1848 suggest that, try as they might, it was difficult for contemporaries to make everything in Bath look well. Avon Street and its contiguous area stuck out like a sore thumb, the home of one in twenty-five of the population. Other areas of low quality housing, in Snow Hill, the Dolemeads and Widcombe were equally conspicuous. As for the shoemakers, about one in twenty of its workforce, they were undoubtedly more difficult to meet with. Yet their mortality figures, reported by Elwin, suggest that the rise in real wages for unskilled labourers in the early 1840s was not shared by all other groups of workers and that the whole life experience of some of them was little removed from absolute poverty.

Accordingly, although there were many places in England where more people were little removed from absolute poverty than in

Bath, there could have been few other places in England where the contrast between the life styles of the rich and the poor was as sharply drawn as in Bath. For example, even the differences between the ages of death for the different classes was not as favourable as the report made out, particularly since Bath had experienced only incipient industrialisation and was not, like London, a great city. In Bath the average age of death in the families of mechanics and labourers was as low as 45 per cent of that for the families of gentlemen. In four other places listed in the report: Bolton, Kennington, Strand and Whitechapel the gap between the two social classes was less. Only in Bethnal Green where the figure was 36 per cent was it much higher. Of course the figure for the families of gentlemen in Bath, at 55, was also considerably higher than for comparable figures in other towns. Yet, I suspect that the average figure for Bath was much inflated by the very high proportion of women, particularly domestic servants, in the city. Female mortality was lower at all ages. Further, the average age at death of women members of the families of mechanics and labourers was no doubt higher than it might otherwise have been since so many girls and women lived and worked in high quality residential areas as unmarried servants. Indeed, the higher expectation of life for all women coupled with the highly selected group of gentry – men and women – who in the 1840s had settled in Bath, must also have played an important part in keeping up the average age of death to 55. In a very real sense many of the gentry in Bath were survivors, their children grown to adulthood or already dead, even before they retired to Bath. This probably explains why, in the families of gentlemen, only one out of every eleven deaths occurred in the under-5 age group whereas, in the families of mechanics and labourers who married and reared children in Bath, half the deaths were of children under 5.

In fact only infant mortality rates for different classes and areas in Bath for the first half of the nineteenth century would resolve this puzzle. Only then might we be able to be as certain as the Rev. Elwin about the effects of the organisation of space and its spin-off in terms of welfare for the labouring population. Unfortunately it is not easy to reconstruct these figures. Nevertheless, the prospect is not quite so gloomy as it appears at first sight. *The First Annual Report of the Registrar General, 1838* and *The Registrar General's Report* on *Cholera in England, 1848–49*, include some useful tables comparing mortality in Bath with mortality elsewhere in the country.

According to the first of these reports the smallpox epidemic in Bath in 1837 was second only in severity to the outbreak in Liverpool. In this epidemic the mortality rate in the five registration districts in the heart of the city (nearly 3:1000) was only marginally lower than that for Liverpool while the proportion of deaths under 2 years of age was far higher. Other general tables in the *Report on Cholera* classify Bath as one of thirty-three Unhealthy Statistical Districts compared with twenty-one Healthy Statistical Districts in the period 1838–1844. They show that Bath was less healthy than Morpeth, Lewisham, Ipswich and Salisbury and on a par with Colchester, Stoke-on-Trent, Gateshead and Northampton. These tables are reproduced in full in Appendix F. Here I record only mortality rates for the 0–5 year age group in selected towns for the years 1838–44. They help to place the effects of the social organisation of space in Bath in perspective. It was not an especially healthy place in which to be born or in which to live (see table 8.10).

Table 8.10 Mortality rates per 1,000 living 0–5 years 1838–44

	Male	Female
Merthyr Tydfil	108	102
Bristol	107	92
Birmingham	96	84
Leeds	96	84
Exeter	96	82
Salisbury	79	76
Ipswich	76	74
Northampton	85	74
Bath	86	73
Clifton	81	70
Gateshead	81	70
Cheltenham	80	68
Canterbury	76	58
Bedford	68	54

Source: The Registrar General, *Report on Cholera in England in 1848 – 49*, pp. cxviii –cxix.

If we recognise, however, that Elwin's purpose, like that of Chadwick and the Report itself, was social engineering aimed at preserving the structure of society it should be apparent that doubts such as those raised here could not be allowed to colour the argument. In fact it was only the hope of social engineering that could justify the work at all. Elwin wrote:[34]

> Whether we compare one part of Bath with another or Bath with other towns, we find health rising in proportion to the improvement of the residences; we find morality in at least a great measure, following the same law, and both these inestimable blessings within the reach of the legislature to secure. When viewed in this light, these investigations so often distressing and disgusting, acquire dignity and importance.

As a result of his researches conducted in the context of social engineering Elwin became far more perceptive and intellectually honest than other writers on Bath such as the Rev. Richard Warner who wrote: 'Bath has little trade, and no manufactures, the higher classes of people and their dependants constitute the chief part of the population; and the number of the lower classes is small.'[35] Unfortunately it was Warner's rather than Elwin's view of the social composition of Bath which for long entered into modern historiography and coloured interpretations of Bath's history. It is unfortunate because Elwin was almost certainly right about one group in Bath, the tradesmen. It is to that class that I now turn.

The figures in the Report show that the average age of death in the families of tradesmen who, like the mechanics and labourers married and reared families in the city, was as high as 67 per cent of that for the families of gentlemen. Only in the Strand, where the average age for gentlemen was as low as 43, was the comparative figure for tradesmen at 77 per cent any higher. In Bath the average age of death in tradesmen's families was 37 and only a quarter of deaths in those families were in the under five age group – in the country generally it was nearly one in two. By the 1830s about a quarter of Bath's adult males were in this category. They were employed in the multifarious activities that made Bath a focus of highly skilled tradesmen and Milsom Street the measure of its standing – if England was a nation of shopkeepers Bath was its shopwindow. Its shopkeepers were the intermediaries between its retired and visiting company and its resident workers. They were, perhaps, the most crucial element in its workforce. Without them men and women of wealth and luxury, whether seeking pleasure or health in Bath, would have been disturbed by too close contact with the direct producers in its workforce. It was far more comfortable for them to shop at Mesdames Smith and Jones in New Bond Street than to call at their 'Establishment' in Belvedere, far less disturbing to the senses to buy shoes from Rogers's warehouse in Abbey Churchyard than to seek out a journeyman shoemaker in Corn Street. Accordingly, there can be little doubt that the portion of the structure of space occupied by tradesmen and shopkeepers, mainly in the parishes of St Michael and St Peter and St Paul, was essential to the ensemble of activities that was Bath. The quality of the space they occupied was, therefore, a necessary consequence of the social structure as a whole.

As might be expected in a competitive age stamped with absolute self-interest, tradesmen were an unstable group. They were also distributed over a wide spectrum of incomes. The first point is shown by the high turnover in the licencees of alehouses and the second by the distribution of licences which ranged from the New Assembly Rooms in the upper town to Tumble Down Dick's in the Orange Court. At one extreme members of this tradesmen group touched, even if they did not merge with the clientele they served. The City Corporation for example, had always consisted of men of this kind; in 1700 its members were almost all successful tradesmen and thirteen of its twenty-six members were owners of lodging houses or inns. Eighty years later its membership included two linen drapers, a hosier, a laceman, a silk weaver, a bookseller, and a coach contractor.[36] These men rubbed shoulders at meetings with physicians, surgeons, bankers and attorneys. Occasionally one or other of them, more successful than the rest, like Ralph Allen, was befriended by generals, bishops, leading politicians, and poets and sometimes invited them into his house. Others, who had yet to achieve success, like Thomas Gainsborough and many a master tailor, were admitted into the houses of the rich to perform some necessary service. At the other extreme they merged with the journeymen they employed, and their journeymen, sometimes through diligence and generally through marriage, merged with them. At this level they were scarcely distinguishable from journeymen artisans working and selling on their own account and living at a level of real income perhaps twice as high as that of the unskilled labourers. Some, too, rose from positions as shop assistants, and would have known what it was like to work from 6 a.m. to 7 p.m.

Figure 26 Coat of Arms of Bath Fire Office. A unique depiction of two of Bath's labouring population in 1769

in winter and from 6 a.m. to 9 p.m. in the summer, six days a week, and up to 3 p.m. on Sundays. At this level, therefore, there was a constant circular flow of personnel – some rising, more falling as the simple and extended reproduction of labour power maintained a sufficient supply of tradesmen, self-employed artisans, and journeymen.

But at the heart of this social stratum was always a core of substantial tradesmen separate from both the rich and powerful as well as from the journeymen whose products they sold or whose services they organised. These men were neither rich nor poor, neither great employers nor employees, neither powerful and great, nor deferential and patronised. They were the heart of the middling-class. These men were the pushing entrepreneurs of their day. As a class they both helped to produce Bath and were produced by it. Like the landowners, developers, financiers, and builders of eighteenth-century Bath they were committed to a belief in absolute property and absolute self-interest. In terms of social class they were the heirs of the men, and sometimes the women, who had built and serviced Bath and who, at the height of its prosperity in the late 1760s and even after the crash of 1793, joined with each other to pool their resources and use the legal system to achieve collectively what they could not do as private persons, or what members of the Corporation could achieve collectively. Two examples of their economic activity and the diversity of their trades must suffice. Both are in the form of lists of subscribers, one for the Bath Fire Office in 1767 (see table 8.11), the other for an Equitable Trust in 1794. Both lists indicate the existence of a body of small wealth holders amongst the tradesmen in Bath willing to venture their funds in collective entrepreneurial ways. The first list of sixty partners in the £30,000 Bath Fire Office also shows these men in Bath leading the country in the field of fire insurance. The Bath Fire Office was the first in the country since the Bubble Act of 1720 (Figure 26).[37]

The second list (table 8.12) is for the Equitable Trust formed for building Grosvenor Gardens in 1794.[38] This trust was also a notable innovation in its day and an example of how the limitations on capital raising imposed by the Bubble Act was circumvented by enterprising men. The list omits the two silversmiths and the builder who initiated the scheme and invested £5,500 in it. The subscribers listed invested only in £50 shares.

TABLE 8.11 Distribution of subscribers to the Bath Fire Office, 1767
(Total capital £30,000)

Leisured and professional men		Building trades		Service trades		Other	
Esquire	15	Carpenter	4	Draper/Mercer	7	Blacksmith	1
Gentlemen	7	Mason	4	Baker/Pastry Cook	2	Carrier	1
Apothecary	4	Brazier	2	Grocer	1	Clerk	1
Doctor	2	Plumber	1	Confectioner	1	Cabinet-Maker	1
Surgeon	1			Brewer	1	Coachmaker	1
				Vintner	1		
				Barber	1		
				Tailor	1		
Totals	29		11		15		5
					20		

Source: *Articles of Agreement*, 1767, BRL.

For as long as wealth flowed into Bath from its visiting company, say up until the 1820s, and then continued to flow into it from its new class of residents and its expanding population until the early 1840s, Bath continued to provide opportunities for men like these, men prepared to venture and innovate.

By the early nineteenth century, of course, there were no fortunes to be made in building and quarrying – there were no John Woods, Ralph Allens or William Pulteneys in Bath in these days; conditions had changed. Although wealth could still be accumulated through incomes arising from earlier property developments, the glittering prizes of new wealth based on property development had been seriously damaged by the crash of 1793 and by the transformation of Bath's economy after 1820. Now the prizes went more to men in commerce and trade who produced for the immediate rather than for the longer term needs of consumers; men like William Kemp, banker, dealer and chapman who sold all but his banking business in 1844 for £9,000, Caleb Hornby whose drapery founded in Union Street in 1829 grew into James Colmer, a firm with a capital of £100,000 sixty years later, George Cox, the hatter who grew from apprentice hatter in 1805 to master hatter and undertaker in the

TABLE 8.12 Distribution of Bath subscribers to the Equitable Trust for Grosvenor Gardens and Hotel, 1794
(Total capital £10,500)

Leisured, and professional men		Building trades		Service trades	
Esquire	1	Carpenter	3	Brewer	7
Gentlemen	11	Statuary Mason	2	Wine Merchant	3
Widow	2	Mason	1	Cornfactor	2
Spinster	2	Painter	1	Music Seller	2
Banker	2	Plasterer	1	Coal Merchant	2
Apothecary	3			Auctioneer	2
	—		8	Innholder	1
	21		—	Bookseller	1
	—			Ironmonger	1
				Dealer in china	1
				Tea Dealer	1
				Linen Draper	1
				Hairdresser	1
				Measurer	2
				Brushmaker	2
				Printer	2
				Coachmaker	1
				Tailor	1
				Cordwainer	1
					34

Source: R. S. Neale, 'An Equitable Trust in the Building Industry 1794', *Business History*, vol. VII, no. 2, July 1965.

1830s, Joseph Pearson an enterprising draper, A. Moore the shoemaker, employer of many journeymen shoemakers, Henry Stothert, ironmonger turned ironfounder and so on. At any one time there were many hundreds of them, inheritors of the world built for them by the Allens, the Woods, the Palmers, the Eveleighs, the Pulteneys, the Attwoods and all the speculating builders, tradesmen and artisans of the eighteenth century. How one might visualise this middling class in the context of other classes is shown in Figure 27. How their class consciousness developed in the early nineteenth century and interacted with the needs and consciousness of other social classes in Bath, to make it as politically volatile in the 1830s as it had been economically and architecturally alive in the 1730s, is the subject of the final chapter. In that chapter we will see, too, how spatial organisation, itself structured by class relations and competing interests, contributed to defining new class relations and to the development of a working-class consciousness. Such a consequence of spatial organisation in Bath was, of course, never intended, least of all by John Wood; instead of glorifying God, and as well as appealing to the wealthy and powerful in their desire for separation and status, the organisation of space in Bath created conditions for glorifying even the lowliest of men.

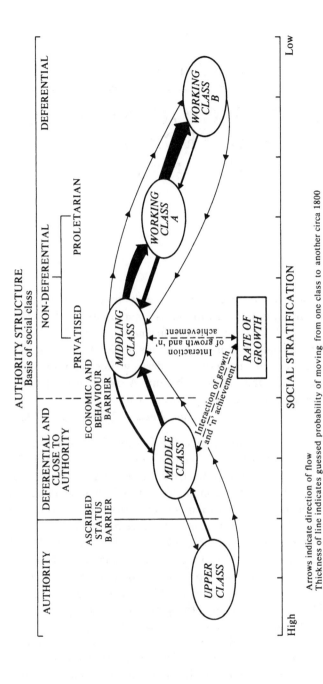

Figure 27 The middling class in relation to other classes

CHAPTER NINE

THE CONSCIOUSNESS OF THE PEOPLE: 1680–1815

> That the wild doctrine of equality newly propagated is unknown to the English Constitution, is incompatible with Civil Society, and only held forth as a Delusion to mislead the lower ranks of the people, to poison the minds of his Majesty's subjects, to subvert all distinctions, to destroy subordination between Man and Man, and to substitute Anarchy in the place of our present mild and happy Government.
>
> *Bath Journal*, 12 December 1792

The Charter of 1590, which gave the Corporation its powers to govern the city, excluded the Freemen from any direct say in its affairs and they could only indirectly influence its government and administration through the Companies to which they belonged. In the election of the city's two Members of Parliament the Freemen had no say at all. Despite petitions by the Freemen claiming a share in parliamentary elections in 1661, 1675, 1705, 1715, and 1728, and despite their repeated claims to a share in the management of the town commons the Corporation maintained its exclusive powers until the Reform Act of 1832 and the Municipal Corporations Act of 1835. Therefore, throughout the period of Bath's growth and during its ascendancy as the premier resort in England, political power locally was held by only a small élite. Underpinning and strengthening the Corporation's political and administrative powers within the city was its economically dominant position as the major landowner within the city walls. The significance of these powers

THE CONSCIOUSNESS OF THE PEOPLE 1680–1815

for the development of the city and the social organisation of its space has been one of the themes of this book.

The theme of this chapter is the evolution of political consciousness within the social groups produced by that development who possessed little or no property or political rights. Although it is not about class consciousness in a strictly Marxist sense, it is about the development of forms of consciousness, hereafter referred to as class consciousness, within the ranks of Bath's labouring population.

Because Bath was not an isolated city republic this story can only be told within the context of national political relationships. Accordingly while the Corporation was both economically and politically powerful within the city walls there were many others outside its boundaries with property rights. Some of these people, who also had rights of access to and a share in the national centres of power, such as the Earl of Bath, were also politically powerful. Moreover, Corporate power in Bath was subordinate to greater powers above it as well as in competition with other powers alongside it. Hence national law and the national framework of legal institutions alone set the conditions within which economic development could occur, social structural change take place, and new political consciousness emerge. Therefore, there could be no development of political consciousness in Bath nor attempts made to challenge or usurp the status of the Corporation that were not structured by these national considerations and relationships. Indeed, as the city expanded outside the city walls into the parishes of Walcot and Bathwick, each with its own local administration, and on to lands belonging to big landowners other than the Corporation, and as the problems generated by the consequent social organisation of space and transformation of social structure grew in number and complexity these wider political and legal relationships became more important than merely local affairs. The fact that men began to perceive this to be the case is itself an aspect of the development of that political consciousness with which we are concerned.

Of course, at the start of this history, political men, such as members of the Corporation, were already conscious of the importance of national affairs for their own well being. In 1678, at the outset of what is now known as the 'Exclusion Crisis', which was a concerted and almost successful movement under the leadership of the Earl of Shaftesbury to exclude the Duke of York (later James II) from the succession to the English Crown, one of Bath's aldermen, Walter Hickes, expressed sentiments hostile to the Duke of York.¹ The problem was that the Duke of York was a known Catholic. As every Anglican Englishman knew, Catholic kings and Catholic regimes, such as that in France, were inclined to favour absolutist policies hostile to the rights and interests of the holders of private property rights such as big landowners and city corporations. So, when Hickes, frequenting one of Bath's coffee houses and reputedly rather the worse for drink uttered, 'dangerous words concerning the Duke of York', he probably voiced opinions shared by others of Bath's citizens. Nevertheless, the rest of the Corporation, conscious, perhaps, that the Crown had twice preserved its rights against the claims of the Freemen, were overtly loyal to the Crown. Hickes was deprived of his aldermanship and forced into hiding. Then, in 1680, the citizens of Bath delivered a loyal address to the king, enough it has been said to earn them the title 'papist'. Yet the turn out of 200 citizens on horseback with bells ringing to welcome the Duke of Monmouth when he came to Bath at the outset of his western progress shows how divided loyalties were. Consequently, by 1683 Hickes was back in the Corporation, not only as alderman but as mayor! But, two years later, when the Duke of Monmouth's army in rebellion against King James II came within hailing distance of the walls of the city, it closed its gates to the rebels and one of the Duke's men was shot dead by one of its defending band of Somerset Militia.²

After Monmouth's defeat and after Judge Jeffreys had done his worst six of Monmouth's men were ordered to be executed at Bath as a deterrent to others. They were ordered to be hung and cut down alive. Their privy members were to be cut off and they were to be disembowelled and their bodies burnt before their eyes. Then they were to be quartered and their heads cut off. The six were: Walter Baker, Henry Body, Gerard Bryant, John Carter, Thomas Clatworthy and Thomas Collens. According to one of them, Henry Body, a seaman from Lyme Regis, speaking before his execution in Bath, the central issue was the legitimacy of power in society. The Duke, he said, was his 'Sovereign's Son and Heir'.³ He and the others paid dearly for that belief in what must have been one of the bloodiest sights in Bath's history, so bloody indeed, that the story and its telling entered into Radical consciousness in Bath more than 100 years later.⁴

Only four of the sentenced men survived to be mentioned in the warrant of the Sheriff of Somerset to the constables of Bath. This warrant shows the orderly and prosaic manner in which the whole brutal weight of the coercive power of the state was brought to bear against these four men and how, through the mediation of officers of the Corporation and the public spectacle they provided, the state used them as a warning to others. The warrant read:[5]

> These are therefore to will and require you immediately on sight hereof to erect a gallows in the most public place of yor said cittie to hang the said traytors on, and that you provide halters to hang them with, a sufficient number of faggots to burne the bowels of fower traytors and a furnace or caldron to boyle their heads and quarters, and salt to boyle therewith, half a bushell to each traytor, and tarr to tarr them with a sufficient number of spears and poles to fix and place their heads and quarters, and that you warne the owners of fower oxen to bee ready with a dray or wayne and the said fower oxen at the time hereafter mentioned for execution and yourselves togeather with a guard of fortie able men att the least, to be present on Wednesday morning by eight of the clock, to be aiding and assisting to me, or my deputie, to see the said rebells executed.

In a postscript the Sheriff added, 'You are also to provide an axe and cleaver for the quartering of the said rebells.'

Throughout these events the Corporation remained loyal to King James but whether this was in consequence of this ferocious example or the benefits bestowed upon them by the Crown is difficult to say. In 1687, when James was about to call a managed election to confirm himself in power by public acclamation, the Corporation declared their allegiance and Bath was reported safe for the Crown. Then, in June 1688, several loyal addresses from Bath rejoiced at the birth of a Prince as legitimate heir for James. Since some of Bath's citizens claimed that conception had taken place in the city as a result of the beneficial effect on the Queen of its waters, Bath claimed a special interest in the birth. Yet, at the end of the year, in November 1688, the citizens of Bath were as politically circumspect as ever – these were difficult times in which to make political choices.

When William of Orange landed in the West Country the burghers and prosperous innkeepers of Bath and its Corporation, like the bourgeoisie throughout England, sat in the sidelines simply waiting for the outcome of the Dutch invasion and the final revolt of the Generals. No doubt, when they heard news of the battle of Wincanton some of them trembled a little, remembering the fate of Monmouth's supporters a few years earlier. The Carnes, for example, were lodging-house keepers and Catholic to boot. They could have much to lose from a Dutch Protestant victory. One of their sons was Master of King Edward's Grammar School – an office conferred on him by James II in 1687.[6] Nevertheless, when William was victorious and King James left the throne vacant, making room for William and Mary, there were no acts of personal violence or offences against property in the local anti-Catholic reaction, certainly nothing comparable to the execution of Monmouth's men two years earlier. Carne was peacefully replaced as Master of King Edward's School by William Baker, the man he had displaced, and the Corporation, desperate for a demonstration of its Anglican orthodoxy, resolved to remove, 'The Crowne of Thornes in the Cross Bath and the cross thereon and all superstitious things belonging thereunto.'[7] At the coronation of William and Mary in 1689, the Corporation included a song in the local celebrations:[8]

> In praise of him who came with Heaven's high hand
> To drive Rome's priests (these vipers) from our land,
> Those locusts who to Lucifer bespoke us,
> Whose mock religion is a hocus pocus.

The ultimate balance of loyalties in the city is best judged, perhaps, by the fact that the number of known Catholics in Bath, 176 adult Papists in the whole of the diocese of Bath and Wells in 1676, was very small. Nevertheless in the early years of the Protestant succession Bath was never wholly for the Dutchman. What with the war in Ireland, recurring bouts of militant Jacobitism and political divisions within the Corporation itself, too strong a commitment was to be avoided. So, while some of Bath's citizens and card sharpers drank the health of James II and hailed any of William's military set backs with jubilation, the Corporation hedged its political bets. Until 1741 it always returned one Tory and one Whig to Parliament, preferably men with strong local connections such as William Blathwayt of Dyrham, Robert Gay of the Barton Estate, and Colonel John Codrington of Sodbury.[9]

As the revolutionary settlement of 1688 endured and as the protection it gave to private property rights began to produce benefits, at least for those with property, as a result of which Bath was built as I have described it, Jacobitism waned and Corporate support for the Protestant succession increased. Even so, one might note that the Catholicism of Francis Carne did not prevent him from re-establishing his social position by becoming the proprietor of Bath's first theatre, nor did Marchant's Quaker faith prevent him becoming a substantial man of property. On the other hand, discreet political service in the Hanoverian cause could benefit a man enormously. It is said that Ralph Allen laid the political foundations of his material fortune through services to the government at the time of the Jacobite rising in 1715.

While many men adapted to the new political world by going about their lawful business and while some may have sought preferment by political service all were duly impressed by another manifestation of the coercive military power of the state; the second in Richard Marchant's lifetime. In 1715, in anticipation of a Jacobite uprising in the West Country, Bath was occupied by a regiment of horse, a cavalry unit under Colonel Pocock, and a regiment of dragoons. The whole force was under the command of Major-General Wade. This occupation led to the discovery of a cache of arms and, in 1722, to the Corporation's election of General Wade as Member of Parliament for the city. It was in 1722 also that Ralph Allen was first elected by the Corporation to a place on its Common Council. By 1734 Wade's brand of Whiggism and his donations to the City's finances were so popular that he was re-elected as MP without opposition. He continued to represent the city until 1747. By that time he had also made his mark as the road-builder whose military roads contributed so much to the suppression of Scottish Jacobitism after 1745. It was in 1745, too, that Allen publicly demonstrated his loyalty to the Hanoverian Cause. At a personal cost of £2,000 he raised a company of men clothed in blue and red. With guns, drums, halberds, pikes, belts and swords they exercised in the Market Place at Bath before some thousands of spectators, 'and gave great satisfaction.'[10] Subsequently the Whiggish Allen, by now a substantial man of property, became a man with considerable political pull in Bath, probably responsible for persuading the Corporation to elect William Pitt as one of its MPs in 1757 and 1761.

This outline of the political history of Bath is a story of adaptation to, rather than cause of, change. It shows above all how local élites, prosperous citizens as well as the Corporation, deferred to those in power at the centre and how those in power, whatever their religous or political persuasion, did not hesitate to use the full coercive power of the state against recalcitrant groups nor to use local agencies in enforcing their control. On the other hand the various administrations following the revolutionary settlement demonstrated very clearly their intention to protect and enlarge existing property rights. Accordingly the Corporation was strengthened rather than weakened by the Revolution of 1688; three times Parliament rejected petitions from the Freemen asking for voting rights and three times confirmed the Corporation in its exclusive authority; in 1705, 1715 and 1728.

Then there were other developments in property law advantageous to property owners and favourable to local élites, including the Corporation and those others who became the leading developers and builders in Bath. The Bill of Exchange, so important to men like Marchant and the Duke of Chandos and all subsequent developers, was granted legal status. The equitable courts, free from the exercise of royal influence, developed the legal conditions for an increase in the number of settled estates. The legal form of the 'Use' in the form of the equitable trust was further developed, later to be applied to the system of turnpikes, insurance companies and building enterprises. The equitable courts also evolved the principle of equity of redemption and so guaranteed the right of mortgagees to the interest on loans secured on settled estates.[11] In addition Parliament through statute law generally granted Corporate bodies the collective powers they requested, including those powers of compulsory purchase already mentioned. There can be no doubt that the Revolutionary settlement had been good to men of property. The Corporation certainly had no cause to complain.

On the other hand those who might have wished to act in politically oppositional or disruptive ways found it increasingly difficult to do so. And those with only customary legal rights and no political weight found the whole force of law and legal institutions used against them. In a space of thirty years the people of Bath were twice confronted by the coercive power of the state and three times its Freemen were excluded from the franchise. In the country generally the Septennial Act and the Property Qualification Act also narrowed political choices. As a result England and Bath with it was in some ways less affected by popular political activity after 1832 than in 1688.[12] Some might say that it was less democratic. Then, in 1725, the Black Act, by adding fifty capital crimes to the list of offences against property, set out to coerce those who sought to maintain customary communal property rights against those of private property. This Act was twice used by the proprietors of the Avon Navigation as a threat against men breaking open locks on the waterway, in 1731 and 1738, yet the Navigation Company's own powers to compulsorily enter and acquire property had been granted to them by an Act of Parliament in 1711 and the Bath Turnpike and Bath Corporation had acquired similar powers, also by Act of Parliament, in 1707 and 1766 respectively. It was in such ways that economic power was firmly vested in those with property rights secured by law. It is not surprising, therefore, that while Bath's citizens and labouring population were allowed to compete freely in the market place, at least after 1765, most of its citizens and all of its labouring population were firmly excluded from the political community.

To most of Bath's population such exclusion was of little importance. Only the Freemen were outwardly concerned about it but their collective influence on affairs was greatly weakened by the Glazby decision which highlighted their legal and, therefore, their political powerlessness. For the majority of the population exclusion from the local political community was but one aspect of their total exclusion from social and political life. They were a largely immigrant population lacking any developed sense of community in their new urban environment and they lived their lives according to the precepts of the prevailing deferential ethos. This was an amalgam of ideas about orders and ranks derived from earlier forms of society and those ideas about the matching of property and moral virtue characteristic of the protestant ethic and the early stages of capitalism. According to these views those with authority and power were expected to act paternally and benevolently towards those in subordinate positions, those in subordinate positions were expected to act deferentially. That the matching of expectation and action was more to be expected from those in subordinate positions was also an accepted part of the prevailing value system. Earlier I referred to this local conjuncture of structure and attitudes as social corporatism. Further, although I have described the way in which the building of Bath fostered attitudes of self-interest and generated a developmental ethos, I have also emphasised that its social organisation of space was constructed so as to preserve and perpetuate the structures and values of just such an ordered and deferential society. These structures and values were also particularly emphasised in Bath through its dependence upon a visiting company attended by a subordinate servant class. One might suppose, therefore, that Bath was an especially deferential society wholly inimical to the generation of new forms of consciousness among its labouring population.

Nevertheless we have already glimpsed some signs of non-deferential behaviour in and around Bath; the atavistic Luddite behaviour of men with blackened faces who attempted to destroy locks on the Avon Navigation in 1731 and 1738, and the actions of those involved in bread riots in the 1740s, 1765, and 1799. Although the latter, taking place within the framework of the 'Moral Economy' of the eighteenth century, may also be regarded as structured by the relations of a deferential society. There were also manifestations of newer forms of consciousness; Quakerism from the 1650s, although not very challenging in Bath, Methodism from the 1730s, trade unionism from the 1760s. In 1780 there were the Gordon Riots.

These riots pose problems of interpretation. While they may be regarded as manifestations of loyalty to the Revolutionary Settlement of 1689 and of hostility to the Roman Catholic religion they have also been interpreted as a popular movement directed against property. The London riots, in which 285 rioters were killed, 173 wounded and 25 executed, have been described as, 'Perhaps the most violent and the most savagely repressed of all the riots in London's history.'[13] Compared with this London experience the riot in Bath, in which one rioter was killed, one wounded and one executed, shades into insignificance. Yet, in its local context, it too, points to the existence of class hostility. According to the Catholic priest who had been hunted by the mob, most Catholics in Bath were 'gentlemen of family and property.'[14] Moreover, the chapel and five houses either in or adjoining St James Parade, which had been destroyed in the riot, were a Catholic property development particularly conspicuous for being carried out in the most econ-

THE CONSCIOUSNESS OF THE PEOPLE 1680–1815

omically depressed year in Bath since 1748; they were either newly-built or recently renovated. In one of them a suite had been 'very elegantly furnished for the occasional residence of Lord Arundel.'[15] This group of buildings was later valued for purposes of compensation at nearly £4,000.[16] The funds for the original development had come from leading Catholic families outside Bath, including the Duke of Norfolk and Lords Arundel and Stourton.[17]

The riot was also more than a one day affair. It had started on the afternoon of 9 June yet, on the night of 10–11 June, seventeen rioters, including several colliers from surrounding villages, were arrested, some of them in the Lower Bristol Road on their way to assemble in Bath.[18] And, as late as 18 June the town clerk of Bath felt it unsafe to remove eight prisoners to the county gaol at Ilchester or to the bridewell at Shepton Mallet since he feared a planned general assault on prisons in the county.[19] In this fearful atmosphere many of the visiting company left Bath and Francis Bennett, a linen draper and a substantial creditor of the Corporation who was also one of Bath's Justices of the Peace and Mayor in 1773 and 1781, wrote to the Mayor of Bath. His letter expresses his reactions, as a man of property, to the riots. It probably reflects the mood of many other property owners in Bath, a mood which, no doubt, accounted for the speedy despatch of John Butler, the only one of the eight rioters against whom sufficient evidence could be produced to win a conviction. Butler was charged and convicted at Wells Assizes. He was tried on Friday, sentenced on Saturday, brought to Bath on Sunday and on Monday 28 August was publicly executed in Bath at the intersection of St James Parade and Peter Street.[20] His execution like that of Monmouth's men, was a warning to others. Bennet's letter was as follows:[21]

Most worthy Sir,

It is with horror and grief I inform your worship that Gordan's mob, who lately destroyed the Romish chappel and building adjoining thereto in this once famous and most beautiful city, threatens likewise to destroy many more before it be long, if Providence don't interfere; therefore, kind sir, let me earnestly beg the favour of your worship to put your self and this almost ruined city in a proper posture of defence before it is too late, as your worship and the everworthy Mr Phillott at the Bear are in imminent danger, likewise the new prison and the Town Hall. It is true I spent many thousands in this city, and that with a deal of pleasure and satisfaction, and would be heartily sorry to leave it on account of a destructive and rebellious set of ruffians, as it is the only part of England I like best. Therefore, if I thought that I could live in peace and safety, I should, with many more worthy and respectable gentlemen of my acquaintance, rest contented and fear no danger. Those ungrateful, and wicked miscreants, I am credibly informed, intends, as soon as the town is a little quiet and evacuated of its present trifling force, and the militia encamped, to assume their former destruction, with double force, and are certain to gain their most abominable point if not timely repelled by force and justice. O, what an unparrell'd scandal it has brought on all faithful protestant subjects and our holy religion, and that all over Europe. Yet I hope that the judicious and ever worthy mayor and corporation of this city will do all that lies in their power to re-establish its former lustre and secure its noble benefactors from the fury of the irreligious and plundering vagabonds who glory in their neibours' downfall and utter distress.

I am most worthy sir,
your worship's most humble servant.

P.S. Slight not this, I beseech you, as it comes from your sincerest friend.
The worshipful Francis Bennett Esq., Belmont.

Yet, while the Gordon Riots seem to point to a widening discontent among the labouring population, their protest was still without form or clear direction, hence the patently obvious anti-Catholic objectives of its leaders. It is not surprising, therefore, that the mob was never more numerous than when demonstrating in favour of a church and a king both of whom were welcomed as wholly protestant and distinctively English! Thus, in 1792, on the eve of war with France, the mass of the adult male population in Bath, including the whole of John Eveleigh's workforce, turned out to sign a document expressing their allegiance to the Crown. This document declared:[22]

> That the wild doctrine of equality newly propagated is unknown to the English Constitution, is incompatible with Civil

Society, and only held forth as a Delusion to mislead the lower ranks of the people, to poison the minds of his Majesty's subjects, to subvert all distinctions, to destroy subordination between Man and Man, and to substitute Anarchy in the place of our present mild and happy Government.

This declaration was to be the basis for the formation of an Association for preserving Liberty, Property and the Constitution of Great Britain against Republicans and Levellers. And only just in time for it was not long before such republicans and levellers actually made their appearance in Bath.

The first of these seems to have been Thomas Wylde, a labourer of Walcot who, in November 1793, was tried for inciting to subvert the government. He was said to have expressed a wish that all the British troops should be taken prisoner by the French and that the Duke of York's troops, 'may be cut to atoms in the next campaign'. 'We live,' he said, 'under a damned arbitrary government and I hope it will soon be abolished.'[23] The sentence passed on him, six months in prison and a 40s. fine and an obligation to enter into a recognisance for good behaviour for twelve months on a surety of £50 before his release, seemed designed to keep him in prison for ever. Six months later he was joined by Benjamin Bull, a tailor of the parish of St James, charged with being, 'A malicious, seditious and ill-disposed person and being greatly disaffected to the constitution and Government of this Kingdom'.[24] Bull's offence was that he had published and distributed Tom Paine's *'The Rights of Man'* as a malicious and seditious libel containing a passage stating, 'It requires some talents to be a common Mechanic But to be a King requires only the animal figure of a man.'[25]

But, the cases of Wylde and Bull were straws in the wind and, like the Gordon Riots, pointers only to an underground movement of social protest. More widespread and widely-held views were those published in the *Bath Journal* in 1792 on the occasion of the formation of The Association for preserving Liberty, Property, and the Constitution. In typical Bath fashion they were offered as a poem:[26]

Liberty, Property, Old England For Ever. 1792

Rise up Hearts of Oak, honest Britons free born,
The Arts of designing Seducers we scorn,
United and steady in Liberty's cause
We'll ever defend both out King and our laws.

THE CONSCIOUSNESS OF THE PEOPLE 1680–1815

> Great George, may God bless him and long may he reign,
> Our Freedom and Property still to maintain,
> Without Rule and Order we ne'er can be free,
> And where without laws would Property be?
>
> While industrious in bus'ness ourselves we employ.
> The fruits of our labor we now can enjoy;
> For our children and wives we may lay up in store,
> Be cheerful and happy; and what would we more.
>
> Old England for ever, her Trade is our Boast,
> Our ships fill'd with Merchandise cover her coast,
> While our neighbours are ruined! their trade at a stand,
> And Rapine and Bloodshed dishonour their land.
>
> These sons of Sedition can never be quiet,
> We know what they wish is to stir up a Riot,
> But if they molest us, we'll lead them a Dance,
> And send them to join the disturbers of France.

Such an expression of loyalty to a dynasty a mere hundred years after it had been placed in power by invasion and revolution does indicate a certain deficiency in the historical perception of a people. And, while the assent of the mass of the labouring population to such sentiments simply mirrored the accommodation of local and national élites to the revolutionary settlement of 1689 within the general value system of a deferential society, it also points to the problem of harnessing the discontent there was to clearly defined alternative social and political objectives. This, in its turn, leads to the question of the available stock of ideas and myths around which movements of social protest could form. This is an important question because men always enter a world, including a world of ideas and myths, not of their own making. Therefore, their ability to express felt discontents and degrading social experience is circumscribed, at least initially, by the ideas and myths available to them. What they do with or make of those ideas and myths in their own situation is, of course, something of their own making. It is important, therefore, to display the range of ideas even if we cannot display the range of myths available to the labouring population in Bath as they began feebly to struggle against their own social predicament – a struggle in the 1780s and 1790s still mainly distinguished by a diffused rage directed against themselves and socially approved targets. This is not easy. As the case of Benjamin Bull shows, some men in Bath knew and approved of the works of Tom Paine, which were firmly grounded in the rationalistic tradition of the early eighteenth century. Others may have known something of the Saxon myth of the legitimate origins of power and society in England. Certainly, outside Bath, many eighteenth-century Radicals and critics of society seemed to have drawn cultural and emotional support for their anti-government and critical social stance from the idea that Saxon kingship and society were organically related parts of a political libertarian whole and from the notion that the Saxon kings, including Alfred, were the only legitimate source of English liberties which had been usurped by conquest and the aristocratic descendants of conquerors.[27] Yet, while Wood's belief in the Britannic myth of origin is commemorated in his books and in his architecture and, therefore, in great expanses of Bath's townscape, and while Philip Thicknesse used the Bladud myth to conclude, 'Had there been no swine, there had been no Bath waters,'[28] there is no written record of the Saxon myth in eighteenth-century Bath and it is recorded in stone only in one place, the bust of Alfred set in the portico of the door of 14 Alfred Street built in 1772. There is also little evidence to show that other critical ideas were widely canvassed, especially among the labourers, servants, and artisans who made up the majority of the city's population.

Yet there were new social movements significantly associated with Bath in the eighteenth century. Perhaps the most well known was Methodism. Something of that and of Wesley's connection with Bath has been mentioned in the chapter on the Company. In this chapter I wish to emphasise that aspect of Methodism in which Bath might be regarded as a forcing ground.

Under the influence of Whitfield the Countess of Huntingdon sought to evangelise the upper classes of society with her version of a rigorist Christian doctrine. Some of them responded enthusiastically to her message. Some did not. One of those who did not was the Duchess of Buckingham. She thought the Countess was giving a lead to the poor, encouraging them to overthrow the values of the deferential society. She wrote to the Countess:[29]

> I thank your ladyship for the information concerning the Methodist preaching; their doctrines are most repulsive, and strongly tinctured with impertinence and disrespect towards their superiors, in perpetually endeavouring to level all ranks and to do away with all distinctions; It is monstrous to be told that you have a heart as sinful as the common wretches that crawl on the earth. This is highly offensive and insulting, and I cannot but wonder that your ladyship should relish any sentiments so much at variance with high rank and good breeding.

But, the Duchess had nothing to fear from the Countess who had no wish to separate from the Anglican church nor from the idea of hierarchy. On the contrary her great desire was to reform the church not democratise it, and the hard core of her doctrine was predestination, and her enthusiasm was for hierarchy. Consequently her rigid brand of Calvinism and Wesley's more relaxed Arminianism could not stay under the same roof together, in 1770 she broke with Wesley. Thereafter she pursued a completely independent course and her chapel, Lady Huntingdon's Chapel, built in the vineyards in 1765, served as the focal point for her own sect, by now, also separated from the Anglican church. Freed of such latitudinarian connections the Countess of Huntingdon's persuasion, with its physical roots firmly in Bath, became a particularly autocratic sect, and the Countess, as a peeress of the realm, claimed a right to employ her chaplains at any time and place she thought fit. In fact it was the Countess' intolerance that led to the building of the Argyle Chapel in Pulteney Street; the story is that when, in opposition to her rigid Calvinism, a few members of the original congregation broke away to form their own church at 'The Tabernacle' in Morford Street, the parent body purchased the Tabernacle over their heads and turned them adrift. Later this dissident congregation eventually found a home in Argyle Chapel built especially for them. The point is that while Methodism might be thought of as throwing out a challenge to the power and privileges of the upper classes, the Countess of Huntingdon's Persuasion sought to place them more firmly under the control of a doctrinaire church. Furthermore, Methodism generally, particularly its Primitive Methodist branch, taught people to bear with things as much as to protest against them and it is difficult to assess the contribution made by Methodism to movements of social protest. In the eighteenth century in Bath it seems to have become integrated into the scheme of things although in the early nineteenth century, dissent, particularly in the form of the Baptist sect, which from its foundation in 1726 had grown rapidly in Bath in the second half of the eighteenth century, was to have an important part to play in the growth of radical consciousness.

There is another area of social practice in which Bath might be regarded as a forcing ground. Like the Countess of Huntingdon's Persuasion this other instance also had its genesis in a concern about the self-indulgence of upper class life. Its outcome was not a dissenting sect but a work hailed as a feminine Utopia two hundred years ahead of its time. Its author was Sarah Scott, one of the two sisters whose correspondence sets much of the scene for the description of the Company in chapter 1.

By the early 1750s Sarah and her friend Lady Barbara Montague lived close together at Batheaston where they ran a charitable school for poor children. Since Sarah's description of her Utopia, published in 1763, centred upon a similar school one might suppose that the book, *Millenium Hall*[30], was a fictionalised account of her work with poor people in the neighbourhood of Bath and of her aspirations for them. Since it was an original work and the most advanced of its kind it may be taken as an account of the best social practice available locally in written form to Bath's labouring population. Had any of them read it it might have conveyed to them a vision of a Utopia different from Wood's and from the world in which they lived. Had none of them read it then the values and attitudes it embraced should have been carried to them in practice by their contact with concerned people like Sarah Scott and Lady Barbara.

The nucleus of the community at Millenium Hall was a group of some thirty gentlewomen and their children. Their leaders all had unhappy experiences in marriage and society and had renounced the kind of social life epitomised by that at Bath. Like the ladies of Llangollen who had read *Millenium Hall*, they had gone into retirement. One said:[31]

> Do you mistake a crowd for society? I know not two things more opposite. How little society is there to be found in what you call the world? It might more properly be compared to

that state of war, which Hobbes supposes the first condition of mankind. The same vanities, the same passions, the same ambition, reign in almost every breast; a constant desire to supplant, and a continual fear of being supplanted, keeps the minds of those who have any views at all in a state of unremitted tumult and envy

whereas a true society was, 'a state of mutual confidence, reciprocal services, and correspondent affections.'[32] This world, however, torn as it was by Hobbesian conflict, was a world of trials: the poverty of the lower orders tested their industry and patience, the riches of those with property tested their temperance, humility and humanity. Theirs was the more difficult lot. But if they acquitted themselves well, their rewards would be greater. In the next world there would be no inequality.

The community, having renounced society, declared there were to be no card parties, no assemblies, no plays, and no masquerades. 'We wish not for large assemblies, because we do not desire to drown conversation in noise – and we have no occasion to conceal our persons in order to obtain either liberty of speech or action.'[33] Instead the community devoted its resources and energies to the care of the poor, the sick, the old, the orphaned, and the outcasts of society. They ran a school for girls and boys, a carpet factory employing several hundred people from 6 to 80 years of age, and almshouses for the old. The community was a good employer, it paid good wages and paid the very young and the old more than the value of the product of their labour, 'as a proper encouragement and reward for industry in those seasons of life in which it is so uncommon.' The community also paid those who were off work through sickness at rates equal to their weekly wages and provided them with a free nursing service. They also provided marriage benefits in the shape of a house for every couple marrying plus a dowry of £20 to £100 for every bride. In addition they stocked her dairy and supplied her with poultry. As children were born to these families, beyond four in number, they were helped by some of the old women who cared for them up to the age of 4 or 5, after which they went to school. The community also took special care of the physically deformed, such as giants and dwarfs, and employed about the house a housekeeper with a claw hand, a kitchen maid with one eye, a cook with crutches, a deaf dairy maid, a housemaid with one hand, one musician with asthma and another with 'a violent fit of the stones'.

Above all these 'retired' gentlewomen ran their school for girls with the purpose of turning them into good housekeepers, children's nurses or governesses. They measured their achievement by drawing attention to the fact that they had succeeded in apprenticing thirty girls to good trades and had placed sixty in excellent domestic situations. Another thirty had married. Their girls were so well trained, socially as well as vocationally, that they were in high demand in the neighbourhood. As one of their spokeswomen said, 'Lest their being always in our company should make them think their situation above a menial state they attend us while we are dressing, and we endeavour that the time they are thus employed shall not pass without improvement. They are clad sparse and plain for the same reason, as nothing has a stronger influence on vanity than dress.'[34]

Millenium Hall, for all that it was humane, was benevolent still and deferential, shaped in the image of an ordered society based on property. Its consciousness for women was withdrawal or retirement from society for gentlewomen, and passive docility for the servant class. Said one of their leaders, 'We do not set up for reformers, we wish to regulate ourselves by the laws laid down to us, and as far as our influence can extend, endeavour to enforce them; beyond that small circle all is foreign to us; we have sufficient employment in improving ourselves; to mend the world requires much abler hands.'[35] So, Sarah Scott's object was not to create conditions for the development of *self*-help and *self*-improvement for all women but to stimulate upper class women to, 'Sentiments of Humanity' and to 'lead their minds to a Love of Virtue.'[36] And to stamp more firmly into woman's consciousness Sarah's own perception of herself as a nurse in a hospital and her image of woman's role; a young woman giving an old man suck through a grate.

It is not surprising, therefore, that unlike some other utopias *Millenium Hall* did not mark the beginning of any kind of social movement for women other than the fad for 'retirement', nor that the book has no place in a history of utopias. The fundamental reason for this was the framework of religious belief within which it was written and Sarah's consequent failure to challenge any of the institutions of property. As its title suggests, *Millenium Hall* was an illusion. Like Wood's Utopia it, too, was in the Shaftesburian tradition, its vision foreshortened, bounded by the present and dependent upon the past. Its place in the history of class consciousness in Bath is that it shows how little the best available social practice touched or could touch the lives of its labouring population other than to bind them more firmly to their 'superiors' by bonds of humility and deference. In fact one may doubt whether any of the Utopias which were gaining currency in the second half of the eighteenth century were likely to offer real or even possible solutions to the problems of new capitalistic urban centres such as Bath. This is so because of the influence of the dominant ideology arising from and emphasising the importance of property in land which pervaded all the critiques of society, including *Millenium Hall*.

Even in the writings of more radical critics like William Ogilvie, William Godwin, Thomas Spence and Charles Hall property in land was still regarded as a natural right. According to Ogilvie it was, 'a birthright which every citizen retains.'[37] It was argued, therefore, that the propertyless were oppressed through their lack of property which deprived them of the means to a full and independent life. And the solutions put forward by these critics always involved some redistribution of the land and the creation of some form of idyllic rural community. In this latter respect *Millenium Hall* is in the same tradition.

While a book on Bath is no place to dissect the writings of all the eighteenth-century social critics whose ideas and remedies may have been available to its labouring population, the work of one of them does warrant a special consideration. This is *The Effects of Civilization* published in 1805 by Charles Hall, a Devonshire doctor.[38] The reason for this is twofold. Hall's general analysis of the social and economic situation in England is particularly apposite as a contemporary critical analysis of the undesirable social consequences of the production of Bath, while his solution to those undesirable consequences illustrates further the deficiencies in the range of social critical thought available to the city's labouring population forty years after *Millenium Hall*. The latter is an important consideration, for without access to relevant critical thought, it was unlikely that the natural ignorance, social deprivation and deferential attitudes of the mass of the labouring population would give to their developing consciousness strength to resist the blandishments of religious groups and the benign influence of religious social engineering such as that aimed at in *Millenium Hall* and by all proponents of mass education.

According to Hall wealth was that which gave power over and commanded the labour of the poor. In the late eighteenth century this power was based on landed wealth. Since landed property was unequally divided society consisted of two orders, those with and those without property. Those without property were deprived of the means to life itself, to mental and spiritual improvement, and to happiness. In a more detailed way he described the constituent parts of the superior of the two orders of society:[39]

> I have often imagined that the first state of things (monarchy) might be aptly represented by a cylinder of a great length, but whose thickness or base was too small for it, when placed perpendicularly, to continue in that position. Around this towering royal cylinder, other cylinders, about two thirds of its height, are placed: These may represent the late princes of the blood in France; to these another row is put, somewhat shorter, composed we may say, of dukes, archbishops etc.: next follows a circle of cylinders, which we call counts, barons, bishops: after this another of knights, and other men of great landed estates: then a row of cylinders representing merchants, master manufacturers, wholesale dealers, lastly, one of lesser landlords, etc. etc.: each succeeding row lessening in height. The individuals in each row standing close to each other, and every inferior one closely encircling the next above it: and having now acquired a broad basis, it stands firm and immovable against the utmost efforts of all the rest of the people, how superior so ever they may be in numbers. This conical figure would equally resemble a republic if the first cylinder was a little shortened.

The economic and social consequences of this land based and order dominated structure of wealth and power arose from the distortion of production brought about by the power of demand for luxuries exercised by the rich and powerful. Whereas Bernard Mandeville had praised the luxury demands of the rich as the fount of production and national greatness, Hall denounced them as the cause of the degradation of the poor.

Hall began the economic analysis underpinning his views with a discussion of the causes of the great scarcity and high price of corn in the years 1799–1800, that scarcity which generated so much unrest in Bath and revealed its administrators and wealthy classes as incapable of effective action. Hall argued that the reason for the scarcity was an insufficient supply of labour in agriculture brought about by a cause of a moral nature. His description of that moral cause is especially apposite to Bath. It was a diversion of labour from agricultural industry into manufacturing brought about by a luxury demand emanating from the wealthy, idle, non-productive and powerful orders of society. This diversion of resources into manufacturing was also further stimulated by the growth of an import trade in luxuries demanded by this same powerful group. In order to pay for imported luxuries the labour of English working men was diverted from production for the domestic market to production for export. Consequently production, especially agricultural production, was lost to domestic consumers. Then there was war. War was an additional burden. The brunt of it was borne by the poor as consumers, taxpayers, and soldiers and sailors.

The essence of Hall's argument was that the pattern of production and the allocation of resources was determined by income distribution and income distribution in eighteenth-century England was the product of the unequal distribution of land and power in a society structured as described in his conical image of it. Therefore, there was a general deficiency in agricultural production and the resulting suffering of the poor. The question was, said Hall, almost as if he had Bath in mind as his model of luxury, whether '500,000 souls shall perish annually, and that eight tenths of all the others should be pinched, distressed, and diseased, in order to furnish this small number with the superfluities?'[40]

Hall's own answer to this question was an unequivocal, no! His solution was twofold. In the short term he would abolish the laws of inheritance, ban the import of luxuries other than necessary medical supplies, and put more labour to work in agriculture. In the long term he would nationalise the land and redivide it into equal unalienable freeholds of three-and-a-half acres and one cow for each family. After this redistribution no horses were to be kept, 'till we can get rid of the prejudice that prevails against eating them.'[41] Then, with the land equally divided and the rich destroyed, 'the inhabitants of a parish would seldom be led out of their parish for anything wanted; every place would produce everything that there was real occasion for'.[42]

Although it might be possible to isolate Hall's analysis from his conclusions and thus to comprehend his work as an expression of class feeling in an increasingly industrial capitalist world, and, therefore appropriate as a rallying cry for at least some of Bath's labouring population, both his analysis and his conclusion were inseparably connected in his own estimation. There can be no doubt that both Hall's analysis and his prescription were predicated on a society characterised by property in land; great landed property in his analysis, small landed property in his prescription. As such it could never have been a rallying cry for any except the gardeners of Bath. Hall made this plain when he attacked Thomas Spence for preserving too much of the existing commercial relationships in his new Spensorian world. To Thomas Spence, Hall wrote, 'I think what we should each aim at would be to go back a good way towards our natural state, to that point from which we strayed, retaining but little of that only (to wit of the coarser arts) which civilization has produced, together with certain sciences, ... To this state we should return as being the most natural and simple, ... your plan seems to be too complicated.'[43]

Bath provides no record of any movement or group expressing support for Hall's programme. Understandably so because by 1800 peasant agriculture in and around Bath was a thing of the past. Moreover, its tradesmen and artisans were an integral part of the commercial world denigrated by Hall, and the City's labouring population in general was too well acclimatised to the urban, commercial, and manufacturing world which gave it birth to seek solutions to the problems of that world in peasant agriculture. But, look as they might during the next forty years they would have found the same deficiencies in the solutions and utopias put to them by popular writers. Almost all of the schemes available to the labouring population of Bath were framed within a milieu of ideas favouring the avoidance of direct confrontation with the established landed authority and advocating withdrawal from the existing economic system. There were many different utopias put to them: peasant self-sufficiency, agrarian co-operative production, agrarian and manufacturing co-operative production, small-scale capitalist production, Tory welfareism. Moreover, most of the solutions the critics offered were based on the creation of small units located in particular places rather than on national class relationships as the context for merely local relationships. Thus, in these critical writings, labouring men were to find life, purpose and redemption in small communities: the working family, the parish, the voluntary community, the joint stock company, the small enterprise. But, never in association with all other labouring men organised for collective industrial and political opposition to a class of capitalists.

What is remarkable in these circumstances: a politically inert and deferential labouring population, ill fed, badly housed and unhealthy, coupled with a dearth of economically and socially relevant ideas in a society increasingly dedicated to the rights of property and self-interest, is that many members of the merely labouring population moved boldly and sometimes successfully to organise themselves for purposes of self-help and self-protection.

First, they formed benefit societies. The first of these, The Loyal Bathonian United Society was formed as early as 1749. By the end of the century there were fourteen others including: The Lyncombe and Widcombe Society of Tradesmen, 1777, The Union Society of Carpenters and Joiners Only, 1790, The Union Society of Plasterers and Tilers, 1791, and The New Bath Loyal Society of Chairmen, 1794. In 1803 The First Bath Friendly Female Society, the first of four female societies, was formed. By 1814 there were twenty-nine benefit Societies in Bath with a membership of 2,265 or nearly 6 per cent of the population.[44] Of course these societies posed no threat to the established centres of power and were frequently established with the consent and co-operation of those in authority.

More important as indications of the developing consciousness of Bath's labouring population were the many attempts at combination and strikes they made. It was shown in chapter 2 that the first recorded combination among Bath's workers was that of the journeymen tailors in 1763. They also struck in 1775 and met with some success. Apparently some customers were forced to send orders to London for their new clothes and at least one master tailor agreed to pay the 2s. 6d. a day demanded.[45] Another resisted the wage demand and claimed to be able to employ any number of tailors and, 'to make a suit of clothes for any gentleman in nine hours.'[46] The journeymen tailors struck again in 1784, when they used force and the threat of firearms to support their claims, and again in 1802 when they won a weekly wage of 21s. or its equivalent in piece-work.[47] Piece-work, arising from the bespoke nature of the trade and its organisation, was a special problem for tailors and, in 1809, the journeymen tailors endeavoured to organise a piece-work House of Call in Kingsmead Street.⁴⁸ It seems that the idea was to establish something like a labour exchange where both masters and men could meet to grant and receive work.

There were many other trades allied to tailoring such as staymaking and retailing in which there were signs of militant union activity. There was a strike by staymakers in 1792 which was broken by bringing in workers from London,⁴⁹ and there was concern about hours and conditions of work for shop assistants in the linen, drapery, millinery, hosiery, silk and haberdashery trades from the 1820s.⁵⁰ It was shown in the last chapter that in these trades making was intermixed with retailing and that most of the employees were women and girls. The fact that these were women's trades carried on in a multitude of establishments, big and small, made worker organisation particularly difficult. Nevertheless, in 1825 shop assistants in these trades organised themselves to reduce the hours of work from eighteen hours a day. They sought the following hours: November to February, 6 a.m. to 7 p.m. March, April, September and October 6 a.m. to 8 p.m., May to August 6 a.m. to 9 p.m.⁵¹ In spite of appeals to the public and reports that these hours had been accepted by employers in London, Bristol, Lewes and Portsmouth nothing was achieved. In 1838 the case of the shop assistants was taken up by William Shenstone, a liberal Alderman active in the Mechanics Institute. Once again in spite of numerous public meetings and temporary reductions achieved by the assistant drapers, their situation was no better in 1845 than twenty years earlier. In 1845 a committee on short hours claimed to have negotiated the following hours:⁵²

> Drapers, Hatters and Hosiers close at 7 p.m. except Saturday in summer. Tea Dealers, Grocers, Provision Dealers close at 8 p.m. except Saturday in summer. Pork Butchers close at 9 p.m. except Saturday in summer.

Yet, the Drapers Assistants were having to organise once again in order to make a fresh start to deal with an apparently intractable problem.

When one considers that after 1765 entry into all these trades in Bath was relatively easy and that in their search for better wages and shorter hours workers in them needed the goodwill of customers as well as the acquiescence of many small employers, their slender achievement appears more substantial than at first sight. What is most noteworthy, particularly in face of laws against combination before 1825, is their recurrent determination to organise and protect themselves with negligible influence from outside their own ranks and contrary to the prevailing deferential ethos.

Perhaps the most sustained organisational effort was that made by the most lowly and despised of Bath's labouring population, the shoemakers. There is a tantalising entry in the Record of Convictions and Acquittals 1724–1812 held in the Guildhall Archives which shows four cordwainers charged with riot and assault against John Ellington in 1735.[53] Unfortunately the reasons for the offence are not recorded and the first well-documented attempt at organisation among shoemakers was noted early in 1792. This was a boom year in which the city's staymakers and 2,000 local colliers also came out on strike for higher wages. In this year the claims made by journeymen shoemakers were modest and modestly couched. They wrote:[54]

> The masters having refused to give them such moderate wages as the present prices of every article of life absolutely claim. The men, though oppressed, wish not at present to disclose the profits of the masters, but only declare they are such as would justify them in demand for much higher wages than they have asked, which is only two pence on each pair of shoes, and sixpence on each pair of boots; and when it is considered that the price at present paid to the men is no more than was paid twenty years ago, any person must be convinced of the necessity of the proposed advance.

The shoemakers also expressed the earnest hope, 'that others of their trade in different places will not attempt coming to Bath at present, nor assist in the oppression of those already too much oppressed.'[55] Unfortunately, there is no other record of this strike. In 1798, eight men who may have been shoemakers, were charged with conspiracy and combination.[56] They were all acquitted.

By 1803 the journeymen shoemakers were better organised and much more militant. In November of that year the secretary of the local society, Thomas St John, wrote to the national organisation of shoemakers with headquarters in London to tell them of the formation of shops' meetings in Bath and to indicate their readiness to participate in a nation-wide system of clearances aimed at preventing strike breaking but also at relieving local societies from paying strike pay by facilitating the movement of approved strikers. Believing themselves strengthened by their affiliation with the national society Bath shoemakers decided to strike. Their claim was for a 11 per cent increase in piece rates: coming at a time of falling food prices and economic prosperity it promised a substantial increase in real income. Support for the strike was widespread, so much so that they divided the Union branch into one for 'Men's Men' and one for 'Women's Men' and ordered the printing of 500 clearances. The number of clearances suggests that the Union anticipated withdrawing the labour of all shoemakers in Bath and sending them on 'tramp' equipped with written permission to join any other branch of the national society in order to get work at the going price. This was necessary, they said, 'We having no fund prepared to give a little relief to those whose situations will not admit of their leaving town.'[57] The shoemakers came out on strike on 6 February 1804. Within a week six master shoemakers had agreed to their terms. Certainly they appeared to be successful. Then they struck again early in 1805, although this time the dispute seems only to have concerned one employer. That strike, too, was settled to the satisfaction of the men. Then the employers counter-attacked. In 1808 thirteen journeymen were prosecuted under the Combination Laws and all were sentenced to three months imprisonment. The prosecution was immediately followed by an advertisement addressed to parents and signed by four master shoemakers stating that they would take a number of boys as apprentices without premium. One of these employers was Cooper of Bath Street who repeatedly fell foul of the Union for keeping, 'A large number of apprentices contrary to the law and to the great injury of the mechanic.' In 1813, the Union struck and won against Cooper. But, in 1824 another employer, Phipps of Margaret's Buildings, announced his intention of employing forty non-union men and precipitated union action. The outcome on this occasion is unknown but, in the next year, the men won a general wage increase after a strike lasting two weeks. There are no further recorded cases of militant trade unionism among shoemakers until 1845 when high demand provided the opportunity for them to win further increases in rates for piece-work.[58]

Although this evidence is fragmentary and spread out over half a century, it does seem clear that at the time when Bath reached its peak as a resort, its shoemakers were a militant and well organised group of workers. They were employed as indoor and outdoor workers by a handful of employers with whom they were in continuous competition for the rewards of the general flow of production in which they participated. That is to say that, while they did not work as detail workers in big factories, they were close to forming the nucleus of a working-class at the level of a fully-developed trade union consciousness. Nevertheless, they and the militant tailors, staymakers and carpenters, who were also involved in trade union activity in the early years of the nineteenth century, particularly after the repeal of the Combination Laws in 1825, fell far short of developing a consciousness of themselves as members of one whole body of workers whose interests were opposed to those of their employers as a class. Their interests and energies were circumscribed by a merely trade interest. Thus, although the shoemakers were nationally organised by 1803 and 1804 and the tailors were on strike in 1802, there was never any suggestion that the labouring population of Bath was in any way involved when, in 1802, the Wiltshire shearmen rose in open revolt against gig mills, shearing frames and factoryisation, and threatened open warfare against clothiers in a manifesto plastered on the New Inn at Freshford. Nor did Bath workers show any open support for the Bradford Weavers in 1816, for the 'Bread and Blood! Hunt for ever' riots in the mining areas of east Somerset in 1817, for the Gloucester, Wiltshire and Somerset Weavers in 1822, nor for the agricultural labourers' desperate struggle in the 'Swing' rebellion in 1830. Nor did any of these groups show interest in the plight of the tailors and shoemakers of Bath. In fact it was not until the 1830s that some among the labouring population of Bath actually began to see themselves as belonging to a class with loyalties transcending local and trade loyalties and cutting across the vertical and deferential loyalties that led earlier mobs to demonstrate in favour of Church, King and Constitution in the 1780s and 1790s.

Before that happened, however, other more purely political and constitutional movements in the country and in Bath acted as catalysts of political awareness among other strata of Bath's population, more particularly among its tradesmen and artisans some of whom were Freemen and some of whom, no doubt were also militant tailors and shoemakers. It is to that story that we must now turn our attention.

CHAPTER TEN

A RADICAL UTOPIA: 1812–1847

Bath is a dark blot on the present general election. At a time when other places are, to their high honour, throwing off the trammels of modern Liberalism, Bath has put them on in their worst shape. It has returned not merely radicals or ultra-radicals, but persons who are 'something more'. We are taunted throughout the country with having sent to Parliament two disciples of revolution . . . 'Hotbed of all that is wild, reckless, and revolutionary in politics' is the phrase which is abundantly used in speaking or writing of Bath.

Bath Chronicle, 8 July 1841

I

The aspiring political community in Bath, Freemen, tradesmen, and artisans, like the trade unionists, seemed to have found little to engage their attentions in the Utopias of the eighteenth century. They, too, looked elsewhere for their inspiration. The political claims they eventually made show that most of them found it in the programme of political reform advocated by John Cartwright as early as 1776. Accordingly they were to seek only to share in existing political institutions, not to supplant them, nor yet to escape from the commercial and industrial world in which alone they achieved some status; except that the political share they were to demand would have replaced all existing forms of privileged political authority with their own. It was this political authority that they were to regard as their birthright, not land. The local context for their attempts to realise this birthright was the increasing control by the landowning aristocracy over the political choices of the Corporation.

At the end of the eighteenth century, the independence that had been a feature of the Corporation's electoral record, had begun to change. It is true that after 1801 one seat was always held for the Whigs by John Palmer and then by his son, Major, later Major-General, Palmer, in traditional eighteenth-century fashion, and that Palmer, a successful mail-coach operator, was a local man. On the other hand from 1790 to 1832, the second seat was permanently occupied by a member of the family of the Marquis of Bath who was also Recorder for the city. This hardening and extension of aristocratic influence, coming as it did, at a time when Bath had developed as a large urban centre producing the transformation in social structure described in chapter 8, and at a time of growing national concern about the inequities and waywardness of forms of representation based on interests rather than persons, was calculated to provoke popular opposition whenever the time was opportune. That time came in 1812.

The lead was given by John Allen. Allen was a Freeman, not of the Common Council, and a considerable property-owner in the city with a rent roll reputed to be in the region of £5,000 per annum. He claimed to have experienced considerable losses as a result of the Corporation's improvement project of 1789. The occasion was the election of 1812. At the outset of the election Allen issued a challenge and an appeal:[1]

> You have again heard the mock call to assemble for the purpose of electing your representatives for this city. Will you obey the call like men? . . . or will you once more neglect it like slaves? If you will come forward on the day of the election, and depute me by your voices, I will spare no pains in my endeavour to recover for you, your almost forgotten rights, and to rescue from the pilfering grasp of your OPPRESSORS those privileges of which they have so long deprived you.

Bearing in mind that it was not long since the Freemen had filed a plaint in Chancery charging the Common Council with neglectful misconduct in relation to the development of the town commons and with the unlawful retention of £700 of the Freemen's money, the phrase 'pilfering grasp' had a double connotation. It referred both to the Freemen's exclusion from the franchise and to their exclusion from the management of the town commons. With these things at stake John Allen and Colleton Groves, accompanied by a group of Freemen, entered the Guildhall on the day appointed for the election to have the names of the Freemen entered as voters on behalf of Allen and Groves. This was refused. But, amid a popular clamour for a poll, both men were nominated and seconded. Then, when the Council proceeded to the election of Lord John Thynne and General Palmer, Allen remained in the Guildhall while his poll clerk collected twenty-eight names in his favour. The next day he declared himself and Groves elected and the 'iron chain of corruption broken'. When he went again to the Guildhall the doors were shut against him. Undeterred he addressed the assembled crowd from a carpenter's bench. But, while his speech 'held them mute' a large body of armed constables came out from the Guildhall, attacked Allen, dragged him from the bench, and ripped his clothes. The crowd, in coming to his assistance, compelled the constables to withdraw. Spurred on to further expressions of rage by this retreat the crowd attacked the Guildhall itself, breaking windows and tearing open the doors until at 1 p.m. the riot act was read and the Oxfordship Militia, called in from Trowbridge, arrested six men. Allen escaped to become:[2]

> The Man of Pledges,
> The Child of Promise.
> The Disturber of the Corporation,
> The Citizen's memento.

During the next three months three of the arrested men were maltreated in Ilchester gaol. Subjected to solitary confinement in chains and a weekly diet of a 2*d.* loaf with straw for a bed and no stove, although it was winter, they became heroes in the radical cause. Then, in December, Cox, a local chairman for twenty years, lost his licence, so the story went, for helping Allen to escape. Incensed by all this the Freemen purged their committee of those who had, 'tendered their tribute of time serving adulation to that odious self constituted Junta the Corporation'.[3] They also gave a dinner to Allen and Groves at the York Hotel where the toasts were, *'The People, the source of all Power,' 'The Constitution, King, Lords and*

Commons freely chosen by the People,' and '*Peace, Freedom, and Religious Liberty all over the World*'. When the words of the last toast spread to the crowd outside, the cry was taken up 'by thousands' for 'a reform of parliament'.[4]

It was a heady moment and the first of many over the next twenty years during which the tradesmen and artisans of Bath grew confident of their new found political consciousness. The essence of this consciousness was stated in a manifesto distributed to the Gentlemen of Bath and its vicinity by the Freemen's Committee. It read:[5]

> The late occurences which have so greatly disgraced the City of Bath, when those who possess the important right of electing members of Parliament were debarred the exercise of it, call loudly for the consideration of every thinking man: that Right may sleep, and from disuse be forgotten; but let it be deeply impressed on the mind of every man, that it can never die. Too long already a few individuals in this City, by a system of encroachment, have been enabled to exercise exclusive power, and to claim exclusive privileges, not given them by the Charter, not delegated by the Constitution. Shall they be suffered to maintain those assumed Rights? Forbid it Justice, and forbid it Reason. Too long have these individuals usurped and exercised the exclusive right of electing Members of Parliament; too long have they been suffered to supply vacancies among themselves, without any reference to the body of the Freemen. These individuals are now estranged from the Freemen ...
> The preservation and government of the City, the interest of the Freemen, church preferment and the appropriation of £18,000 a year should no longer be confided to men of ordinary capacity, of no particular respectability, and of inconsiderable property and consequence. . . . The Freemen are roused; they will resume the exercise of their long forgotten Rights.

The Freemen's arguments, couched in terms of a demand for the resumption of traditional but lost rights and later published in a context including reference to an earlier dispute about the town commons in 1619 and the bloody events of 1685, were very similar to the land reformer's arguments about the usurpation of the birthright in land, and reminiscent of claims about the sources of legitimate power in the Saxon myth. As such, they point to the existence of something like a collective, almost popular memory. In spite of much of the rhetoric of violence surrounding them, they point too, to the underlying uncertainty and weakness of the radical position. Oddly enough, unlike the shoemakers and tailors, the political radicals were reluctant to admit that they were in fact making new demands. Even Allen, their leader and inspiration, was slow to face up to the fact that a political reform affecting only Bath was impossible. As he finally told his supporters, 'your disputed right to elect Members of Parliament is in some degree interwoven with the general system of domestic politics'.[6] And it was not until this was realised that local Radicals came out into the open in increasing numbers.

The election of 1812 seemed to have acted as a catalyst in this respect and almost before the furore over the election was over a petition asking for the reform of Parliament was prepared. It lay at the offices of the *Bath and Cheltenham Gazette*, at a perfumer's shop in Union Street, at John Allen's house in Phillip Street, in St James Parish, and at the home of Cottle, a carpenter at Widcombe Turnpike. The petition alleged that the administration of Lord Liverpool had produced war, taxation, the decay of trade, depravity in morals, pauperism, and a shortage of bread. To remedy this its signatories demanded three things:

1 Representation co-extensive with direct taxation.
2 That such representation, as a common right, be throughout the community, fairly distributed.
3 That Parliament henceforth have only a constitutional continuance, that is, not exceeding one year.[7]

This radical awakening in Bath was also part of a nationwide movement. Indeed it is more than likely that it was the example of Henry Hunt in standing as a Radical in the Bristol election in July 1812 that inspired Allen to stand in Bath in October. At the Bristol election Hunt received 235 votes including the votes of four Bath men who, as Freemen of Bristol, were entitled to vote. All four were artisans; a tailor, a cork-cutter, a saddler and a wheelwright.

Four years later a series of meetings took place at the Spa Fields in London at which Hunt declared for universal suffrage, the ballot, and annual parliaments – a far more radical programme than that so far supported in Bath. (Subsequently Watson, Thistlewood and other Spenceans were charged with high treason.) The London meetings were followed in December 1816 and January 1817 by meetings in Bristol and Bath, organised by Hunt, to petition for the same three points. The response was overwhelming, 25,000 signatures in Bristol, 20,000 in Bath. Hunt, representing Bristol and Bath accompanied by John Allen, also as representative for Bath, took these petitions to the third Spa Fields Meeting on 24 January 1817. They had specific instructions to support demands for universal suffrage as set out in the petitions. At the venue, the Crown and Anchor, leading Radicals, including Cobbett and the ageing Cartwright, took the view that Sir Francis Burdett would not go so far as to present a petition including universal suffrage. Therefore, they moved to substitute household and direct tax-payer suffrage and John Allen, without consulting Hunt, supported their motion. Hunt, however, stuck to his brief as set out in the petitions from Bath and Bristol. His own motion in support of universal suffrage was carried. Subsequently both petitions were presented with the result that Lord Camden, attacked in the Bath petition as a holder of sinecures worth £37,500 per annum, resigned from one of them, Teller of the Exchequer worth £35,500 per annum.[8]

Hunt's assessment of these meetings points to the significance and strength of radical feeling in Bath at that time:[9]

> I wish I had a copy of the resolutions and petitions by me, that I might insert them here, as I conceive this (the Bath petition) to have been the most momentous petition that was ever presented to the House of Commons; and the effect which it produced was more important than that of any other petition that was ever passed at any public meeting, not excepting that which was passed at Spa Fields.

It might well have been as a consequence of this massive public demonstration of support in Bath for a radical reform of Parliament that at the next suitable occasion, the election of 1820, a move was started by the Marquis of Camden, Lord Lieutenant of the County, to manoeuvre General Palmer out of his seat as member for Bath and to get a firm Tory grip of its representation. It was to be done by getting the seat for Sir William Scott, an eminent lawyer in the Ecclesiastical Court. Scott would then act as a sort of 'locum tenens' until Camden's son became a man and could take the seat in his own right. To suggest such a blatant jerrymander in a city so recently conscious of itself as in the forefront of the radical movement was bound to cause a reaction. As soon as it was mooted

A RADICAL UTOPIA 1812–1847

abroad local feeling boiled over at the thought, 'that Bath will have the honour of being represented by two relatives of two Marquisses, and thus draw closer the bonds of union betwixt our Body Corporate, our Noble Recorder, and our Noble Lord Lieutenant.'[10] Palmer declared his intention to contest such an election as illegal on the grounds of interference by a Peer in an election to the lower House and, in the end, not even the self-appointed and partly absentee Common Council was prepared to be quite so politically cynical. The idea was dropped.

When the election did take place the Guildhall was reported filled beyond all precedent and every sentence of Palmer's speech was received with acclamation. He said:[11]

> The question of this contest has been neither more nor less, than whether the Representation in Parliament of this great and populous City should have been handed over, and made subservient to the will of the Crown and the Administration, or that the members of the Body Corporate, acting on behalf of their fellow citizens, should be left to the free exercise of their own discretion in the choice of their Representative.

Indeed, that was the question and more besides, for the 1820s were also the years of the Six Acts, the suspension of Habeas Corpus and memories of Peterloo.

When the poll was declared twenty-three had voted for Lord John Thynne and twenty-one for Colonel Palmer and both men were elected. But, Palmer's victory was short-lived. In 1826 the move to tighten the grip of the Tory aristocracy on political representation in Bath was successfully concluded. Lord Brecknock, son of the Marquis of Camden, was elected with Lord John Thynne, brother of the Marquis of Bath. Brecknock gained sixteen votes, Thynne seventeen. But the apparently snug unanimity of earlier years was gone. The contest showed that twelve members of the Common Council, nine of whom were plumpers, voted for Palmer. They seemed opposed to further extensions of aristocratic political influence in Bath. Nevertheless, Brecknock was re-elected twice more, in 1828 and again in 1829. On the last occasion he was elected with a majority of one after a first vote which showed him drawn with Palmer. By then the Radicals were incensed. 'Never', declared the *Bath Journal*, more radical now than the *Bath and Cheltenham Gazette*, 'Never were the citizens of Bath made more sensible of their degraded condition, for never were members returned more completely in opposition to the well known wish and judgement of the people in county, city or borough – why exhibit their puppets in the way of a triumphal show to the insulted citizens, in order to prove how completely they hold their opinion on the subject in contempt!'[12]

As a result of this election Palmer became the Radical's hero, a figure representing reform and liberty. He was lauded to the skies. 'He is one of us – he is a sojourner in our land – he is connected with the city, both by birth and affectionate attachment – he is no plunderer of the people.' As for Thynne and Brecknock, 'They are aristocrats – they are sprigs of nobility – they are tories, and, as a matter of course, have an influence with ministers – Lord John Thynne has represented the Corporation, it appears, thirty years – what has he done? Why he has procured the court place of Groom of the Bed Chamber for which, he pockets £1200 per annum of the people's money'.[13] After the declaration of the poll the two noble lords were chaired but not cheered.

The growth of radical consciousness: faint stirrings in the 1790s, outwardly active in 1812, ebullient in 1817, and suffering the slings and arrows of aristocratic reaction in the 1820s, was not restricted to national politics and matters of the franchise, although in the end everything did come back to it for the issue was clearly one of national political power. Local Radicals were also active in vestries. They used them as places of public meeting and as a vehicle for public protest, particularly in connection with appeals against the Assessed Taxes; taxes on houses, windows and male servants. Other avenues for radical intervention were offered by the problems of unemployment and education. In 1816 the Radical, John Hawksey Ackersley, put forward a ten-part plan for dealing with poverty and for the employment of the poor. It required the co-operation of all the parishes under a 'Supreme Committee of Manufacturers and Gentlemen of intellect and Active Minds.'[14]

Under this scheme the parishes were to form subcommittees, skilled men were to be appointed as overlookers, subscriptions raised, premises rented, stocks of work provided, apprentices trained and profits ploughed back. But this radical initiative was aborted; not only was it in advance of its time, it was also impossible to administer; in matters of the poor law there was no local centralised administration and no attempt was made by the Corporation to

A RADICAL UTOPIA 1812–1847

acquire or develop such needed authority. Consequently provision for unemployment remained a parish responsibility and unemployment remained a matter for the poor law and private charity.

In education the most successful development, illustrating the spread of radical consciousness among artisans, was the formation of the Mechanics Institute in 1825. This was done despite considerable opposition. At the outset it had about 100 members and a management committee consisting only of master tradesmen and mechanics. Within four years enthusiasm had waned and the Institute came increasingly under middle-class control and religious influences.[15]

It seems that in the absence of stirring themes consciousness-raising was a tedious and time-consuming business, more honoured in the initial act than in its subsequent application. Yet political Radicalism was on the march and its most stirring struggle, for the Reform Bill of 1832, was not far off.

In Bath the immediate preliminaries to the Reform Bill focused on the election of 1830. There were three candidates, Lord John Thynne, Lord Brecknock and Major-General Palmer. Brecknock secured thirteen votes and Thynne and Palmer fifteen each. With this success Palmer became the focus of enthusiasm for the reform movement. Although he had been a Member of Parliament from 1808 to 1826 without ever revealing himself to be anything more than a reliable Whig he did his best to respond positively. When the rejection of the Reform Bill precipitated a new election, enthusiasm for Palmer knew no bounds. When he was re-elected – by an electorate voting for its own extinction – the crowd went wild, Palmer was greeted with cries of 'The Bill, The Whole Bill and Nothing but the Bill.' Thynne who was also elected, was met with brickbats. When the Reform Bill was again rejected by a vote in the House of Lords a mood of mourning settled over the town, the shops closed and a muffled peal of bells rang out from the parish church of St James. The set-back was only momentary. Permission to stage a massive demonstration was sought from the Mayor and the County Justices, and a meeting was arranged for Monday 13 October.

The day of the demonstration began like a day of general mourning. All the shops in the town were closed as the mass of the people, in earnest political mood like never before, made their separate ways to the places of assembly for the start of the intended procession. Most citizens assembled at Queen Square, putting it to its first use as a grand place of assembly since it was built. The parishioners of St James assembled on their own ground. As the main procession moved off it was headed by representatives from each of the trades carrying a succession of banners inscribed, 'The United Trades' – 'We Are All Agreed' – 'The Bill or nothing Else'. Then came a band followed by members of the printers' union, some of whom were using a printing press to print broadsheets to distribute to the crowds lining the streets:[16]

> Hall to the Press! to thee we Britons owe
> All we believe, and almost all we know;
> Resistless pleader of the People's Cause,
> Strong Guardian of our liberty and laws!
> Knowledge and truth by thee the Million gain,
> And Lords shall strive to make thee slaves in vain.

Then came the unions representing the organised descendants of those who had made the first moves to unionisation in 1763; coachsmiths, tailors, shoemakers, carpenters, cabinet-makers, masons and plasterers, painters and sawyers – each contingent carrying banners. The whole procession was liberally interspersed with bands.

The procession moved slowly along George Street, down Milsom Street, through Cheap Street and High Street, across Mr Pulteney's Bridge into Great Pulteney Street. From there the men in the procession could see the spacious hustings in front of Sydney Hotel, built for 250 people – 'gentlemen of the first respectability in Bath and its neighbourhood.' From the hustings these men could see the whole length of Great Pulteney Street, and watch the procession and a vast concourse of people advance slowly down the street with banners flying and music playing. 'At this time, the whole length of the street, with those also near the Hotel, and their windows, walls, copings and every place affording standing room, appeared occupied by one mass of animation, estimated by a military gentleman present as amounting to above 22,000 persons.'[17] There, too, the main procession of the trades would meet with the men of St James separately assembled – a symbolic union of the respectable and political classes with organised workers and with men from the most industrial and artisan-populated parish in the city.

In the chair for the occasion was Captain Mainwaring, chairman of Bath's *ad hoc* committee set up to deal with the cholera outbreak and a recent convert to reform. Alongside him were E. A. Sandford MP for the county and Major-General Palmer. Then the lectures began. The talk was about the 'wonderful and unparalleled unanimity,' that existed between the, 'lowest classes and those immediately above them,' about the support there was for reform, and about the dangers of violence, for, 'if any symptoms of violence occur, you will have the invincibility of the law in front of you.'[18] And so they listened, the tradesmen, artisans and labouring population of Bath for on that day only the journeymen hatters of Oldland Common, who had travelled seven miles, were allowed to contribute their working class 'mite in support of our loyal and patriotic King and his Ministers, in their endeavours to obtain for us a just and equal representation.'[19] For the rest of the united trades, they were to listen and obey.

Yet more was done for the labouring population that day than the men on the hustings could possibly have imagined. As the *Bath and Cheltenham Gazette* observed:[20]

'The Reform Measure has already elicited a new character in the citizens of Bath. Shut out from all share in the election of Representatives in Parliament for a long series of years, Bathonians have been universally regarded as mere drones in the political hive. But the rejection of the Bill which was expected to enfranchise a large portion of the inhabitants, has drawn them out in a manner altogether novel and respectable, and far beyond expectation.

As a catalyst in raising the class consciousness of the labouring population, particularly that of the tradesmen and artisans, the meeting was impressive. It had brought together the separate trades, cut across social stratification, and had fused, even if only momentarily, the great majority of the adult male population in Bath into one political whole – The People. And they had used the space their forefathers had built in a manner never before contemplated. They had appropriated the streets as a politically disciplined force as unlike the mass of 1780 and 1812 as chalk was from cheese.

What happened seventeen days later, on the afternoon of Sunday 30 October, was also far beyond expectation and without precedent in Bath. On this occasion the Bath troop of the North Somerset Yeomanry had been called out to go to the assistance of the authorities in Bristol who were overwhelmed by the outbreak of three days of riot, arson and slaughter brought about by the rejection of the Reform Bill. The commander of the Bath troop, Captain Wilkins, on his way to muster his troop, was set upon by an organised party of men estimated to be a thousand strong. He was forced to take refuge in the White Hart Hotel while his troop remained unmustered and the riots in Bristol raged unrestrained. In spite of Wilkins's protestation that he, too, was a reformer – he was also well known as the owner of two woollen mills at Twerton employing a thousand hands – his attackers helped themselves to bludgeons from a faggot pile in the Bristol Road in order to break open the shuttered windows of the hotel. By the time they had broken into its coach office and from there into the coffee room Wilkins had escaped in civilian clothes through a rear window. When that was discovered, a group of the attackers was detached to invest the Guildhall to prevent any interference from the police force. But 300 special constables were called out and by 2 a.m. all was quiet and six men had been arrested. Fear of further rioting kept Wilkins and his troop in Bath until Monday morning and led to Wilkins's workmen turning out to protect the mills at Twerton. By the time Wilkins arrived in Bristol, the worst was already over.[21]

The details of this event are worth dwelling on for they raise important unanswered questions about the development of class consciousness among sections of Bath's labouring population. They certainly indicate an ability on their part to identify their interests with others living and acting politically at some distance from Bath. They also suggest the existence of an organisation with knowledge of Wilkins's objective, capacity to raise a substantial force to intervene at a convenient point on his route, and the wisdom to invest the Guildhall to prevent police action. That is, they point to the existence in Bath of a political community among the labouring population prepared to act outside the framework of legitimate union activity and of subordination to political initiatives by the liberal and radical middle classes. Certainly many of these latter classes in Bath feared this to be the case. Consequently, several hundred of them speedily enrolled in the special constabulary and volunteered to keep a regular daily watch on the lower part of the city, including the parish of St James. Then, as soon as possible, examples were made of the six arrested men. Two were sentenced to six months, one to four and one to three months imprisonment.

The other two were remanded to appear before the next assizes where they were indicted for riotous assembly and feloniously beginning to destroy the White Hart Hotel. Both men, Richards a 40-year-old sawyer and Smith a fish and oyster seller, were found guilty and sentenced to death although later reprieved and transported for life. Of the other four, three were young men under 21, one was a labourer, one a watchmaker, and one a shoemaker. The sixth man was a 30-year-old labourer.[22] If they were representative of the composition of the force involved in the attack on Wilkins then it must have included many other artisans and small dealers and only few of the poorest inhabitants of the courts and alleys of Bath.

While this outbreak of controlled violence was fresh in memory, a meeting of some 3,000 people, mostly from the labouring population, met at the Tennis Court in Morford Street on 7 November to form a Political Union. The inspiration for this was the Birmingham Political Union formed in 1830 but the immediate influence came from the Bristol Political Union, which was an outgrowth of the Union of Trades started in Bristol during the May election in 1831.[23] As we shall see the difference was an important one.

The meeting was chaired by Mr Keene, editor of *The Bath Journal*. Other leading Radicals and reformers who had been invited to attend were not present. General Palmer sent to say that he had arrived home too late to attend, Captain Wilkins that he was prevented by force of circumstance, and W. Metford, the convenor of the Sydney Hotel demonstration, that he had toothache. Only J. Hawksey Ackersley wrote expressing approval of the meeting and the idea of the Political Union, but only if formed on the pattern of the Birmingham Union with middle-class control of its organisation. The absence of leading middle-class reformers, noted in the press, was apparent to the mass of artisans and tradesmen. One of them addressed his fellows:[24]

> They leave us to do as well as we can without them, we can do without them. The time may come when they will want us, and our presence will be valuable to them; should that time arrive, we will not leave them as they now leave us, to do as well as they can, we will not retaliate. No! we will protect them and their property too, at the hazard of our lives, we will do our duty, and then see if they will do theirs.

The abdication of the middle-class reformers in the face of initiatives coming from artisans and tradesmen meant that the strongest influence at the Tennis Court meeting came from delegates of the Bristol Political Union who had come to encourage the Bath people. The Bristol Union was working-class and militant. Their spokesman, a Mr Powell, began his address by placing the blame for the Bristol Riots, still fresh in the mind of all those present, squarely on the Tories. It was, he said, an act of Tory madness. He had come to place the scenes of that outrage before the people of Bath, 'while they were yet warm upon his feelings – the blood as it were, streaming before his eyes, the cries of the widows ringing in his ears, and the uplifted hands of orphans spread open before him.'[25] He did so to persuade them of the urgent need to unite as one man and protect their own city against the possibility of further acts of madness. And so it went on. The result was the formation of the Bath Political Union with a majority of artisans on its council and James Crisp, Baptist and long time Radical and master hatter, as its first president. Within six months it reported a membership of 1,500.

The reaction of the Liberal and Tory press was predictable. The Liberal *Bath and Cheltenham Gazette* could not 'see the advantage of insisting on a majority of mechanics in the council of a Political Union, of which the Gentry, Tradesmen, and men of wealth and leisure in such a city as Bath are invited to become members and one of the leading features of which was announced to be the Union of All Classes. . . . The interest is ONE, and there should be no jealousies, nor any signs of them'.[26] The Tory *Bath Chronicle* was totally hostile. It found no threat to Englishmen's political rights – after all they could still draw up petitions – and no grounds for setting up permanent political combinations, particularly any that would destroy existing good relations between masters and workmen and lead to the sober and industrious mechanic learning, 'that he is as good as his master and that universal equality is the proper state of man'.[27]

The artisan-controlled Bath Political Union was a great success. Even so it did not have a monopoly of political initiatives in the crowded month of May 1832. In that epicentre of artisanal and tradesman radicalism, the parish of St James, a committee of seven, including John Allen and George Cox, a Baptist who had begun his working life in 1804 as an apprentice working until two or three o-clock on the Sabbath Day, produced a petition against the House of Lords, against voting supplies and in favour of Reform. They got the support of the parishioners assembled in vestry. This initiative was followed by all the other parishes in the city, and, in the parish of St Michael James Crisp, president of the Bath Political Union, spoke at length, and the parish called upon the Commons,[28]

> to make a decided and uncompromising stand against the inroads of that flagitious Borough Oligarchy which has so long swayed the destinies of this distracted country and battened on the toils of an impoverished people.

When the English aristocracy, under the fear and threat of violence in the country collapsed and allowed the truncated Reform Bill to become law, the exhilarating political climate of the previous two years in Bath turned into the most glorious of Indian Summers. In Bath, as in all closed corporations, the Act worked a political revolution. At one stroke the new £10 franchise increased the electorate from 30 to 2,835 – one-third of the total adult male population of the city. While some saw this as the consummation of radical politics others saw it as only the first step to a total reform of political institutions. In any case there was something for everyone to celebrate, unless a Tory. The Bath Political Union took the initiative and organised a massive demonstration in honour of the Reform Act to take place on 28 May, suitably enough, on the town commons.

To demonstrate that the event was intended to mark the beginning and not the end of reform the procession was headed on this occasion by the sons of 800 members of the various Political Unions. They carried banners emblazoned with the words: 'Liberty shall grow with our growth', 'From Acorns rise the sturdy oak', 'If God be with us, who shall be against us?'. Then came the Bath Political Union. Its banners declared, 'Unity, Trade and Commerce', 'Order is Heaven's First Law', 'Britons never more will be Slaves', 'Liberty or Death'.[29] Interspersed with the banners of the Political Union were those of the various trades. Then there were bands and contingents from other Political Unions; 2,000 from Frome, 1,000 from Holt, hundreds from Trowbridge and Bristol, the hatters from Bitton and Oldland, and men from Twerton, the latter with Cobbett-like philosophy, carrying a large blue flag displaying a quartern loaf mounted on a pole with the words 'The Old Times: a sixpenny loaf in 1790'. (In 1832 the quartern loaf cost 9*d*.) Finally, there was a white banner emblazoned with the words:[30]

A RADICAL UTOPIA 1812–1847

> Britains Sons have sternly sworn
> With one United breath,
> Their streaming standard shall be born,
> To win Reform or Death.

Fortunately the weather was kind. It was reported that 55,000 people, 12,000, of whom were members of Political Unions, turned out to celebrate. The platform honours were shared by Allen, Crisp and Cox. Under their ministrations the audience was regaled with pro-reform speeches of great length and little import and several resolutions were passed with acclamation. Only Colonel Jones seemed to introduce a note of discord. 'Hear me', he said, 'as I make this my solemn declaration – that I am resolved should the Duke of Wellington by any act of baseness – by any intrigue, again come into office, and then attempt to impose on us the hateful fetters of his oppression, if he should conspire against the liberties of this country – this arm then, and only then, shall be raised against him – then I say this arm shall be raised to strike the tyrant to death.'[31] He was received with rapt attention and rapturous applause. It was a great and glorious moment.

When the time came to select candidates for the election of 1832 the differences between Liberals and Radicals, submerged in the euphoria of the May demonstrations, surfaced once more. While the anti-Tory and anti-aristocratic mood in the city was such as to preclude any Tory from nominating, the merely liberal Whigs hoped to ensure that both members elected would be cautious and moderate men no more prone to press for more reform than John Wood would have been to build in the vernacular style. Accordingly, Major-General Palmer was assured of one seat and Palmerston was rumoured to be a candidate for the other. But the question was raised whether he was 'one at whose feet we should with such breathless haste, throw our virgin franchise, as if it were a bauble to be sported with?'[32] Crisp, on behalf of the Political Union and with a guarantee of 1,500 votes and an election free of all expense, gave his answer by offering the seat to Colonel William Napier. Napier, a humane, almost radical Liberal of many years standing, had lived at Freshford, near Bath since the end of 1831 and was held in high esteem by most Radicals. Although he was attracted by the offer and the Radical programme, the abolition of tithes, shorter parliaments, reduction of the armed forces, and an overhaul of crown lands and corporate property, Napier declined. His family commitments were too great and his history of the Peninsular Wars too big an undertaking.

The initiative then passed to the liberal Whigs and W. H. Hobhouse. Hobhouse was a local Whig banker of the Burdett School, he regarded the Reform Act as the consummation of reform politics. When he announced his intention of standing his move was countered by John Allen who wrote from Middlesex offering himself as candidate pledged to abolish tithes, repeal the assessed taxes, revise the corn laws, repeal the Septennial Act, and abolish sinecures.

There the matter stood until Hobhouse addressed the parishioners of St James on 2 July. He told them he would support a transfer of taxation from consumption to capital and wanted a reform of the currency. He thought there should be some relief from the assessed taxes, a partial abolition of slavery, the commutation of tithes and a reform of the Septennial Act, 'the moment its continuance shall be felt as a grievance to the country'.[33] Long time Radicals like Cox and Crisp were critical, Crisp especially so. He listed the omissions from Hobhouse's programme: reduction in the standing army, abolition of assessed taxes and pluralities, abolition of £30 million pounds spent on sinecures, justice for Ireland, triennial parliaments, the ballot and abolition of slavery. Then he asked Hobhouse whether he would support a motion in favour of the ballot and triennial parliaments. Hobhouse replied, 'No'. Asked about support for a speedy and total abolition of tithes, Hobhouse refused to answer. With that, Crisp and Cox recommended the men of St James not to commit themselves to Hobhouse and offered to bring forward, 'a good old reformer of forty years standing'.[34] With that the meeting closed.

It was clear by now that the Radicals in Bath, particularly those in St James Parish and the Bath Political Union, wanted a candidate who would incorporate three main elements in his programme. First, he must agree to relieve dissenters of their grievances about tithes and support their wish for a total abolition of slavery. Second, he must agree to relieve tradesmen and small producers of the burden of the assessed taxes and of the burdens of excessive and privileged expenditures. Third, he must support a programme of constitutional reform, one in which short parliaments and the ballot would have pride of place. Neither Palmer nor Hobhouse was such a man.

The rumour also grew that Hobhouse was a government nominee put up by his brother John Cam Hobhouse and protected by Stanley, an influential member of the administration. Palmer apparently believed this and it was hinted at by James Crisp. As the suspicion grew that a coalition, 'was going on in this City between the Ultra Tories and the Whigs, or pretended reformers',[35] the need for a committed radical candidate grew even more urgent. The result was that a fraction of the professional classes and liberal tradesmen broke with the Whigs and formed an Independent Association.

The aim of the Independent Association was to prevent the election of men of ultra Tory principles and to find an acceptable Radical/Liberal candidate. The Chairman of the Independent Association, who was also Vice-Chairman of General Palmer's election committee, was Thomas Falconer. Falconer was the son of Dr Thomas Falconer of the King's Circus and a member of a group of radical lawyers and law students who met regularly each week at the Freemason's Tavern in London. There the talk was on political and economic matters. He was, therefore, familiar with radical politics in London. Through him the Independent Association approached Joseph Hume and asked him to suggest the names of suitable candidates. Although a similar approach to Hume had already been made by leading members of the Bath Political Union acting in their private capacities, the subsequent negotiations were conducted through Falconer and the Independent Association. Hume's reply to the Independent Association was considered at a meeting on 16 August 1832. Hume suggested three names, including that of J. A. Roebuck (Figure 29). Roebuck was a young lawyer of 25. He had spent much of his early life in Canada and was a friend of J. S. Mill and known to Thomas Falconer through his part in meetings at the Freemason's Tavern. He was a Philosophic Radical. At the August meeting Moline, a leading Radical and self declared republican, moved that Roebuck he objected to, 'in consequence of his Republican principles'. The motion was carried unanimously. Immediately, on 17 August, Falconer posted to London, wrote to Hume from his lodgings, and arranged to see Roebuck to examine him about his alleged republicanism. He came away convinced that he was not a doctrinaire republican and could not, therefore, be objected to on that score. Falconer returned to Bath, immediately to be followed on 20 August by Roebuck and Joseph Hume.[36]

Roebuck always maintained that he didn't know why he was the chosen candidate and his biographer glosses over the event by focusing attention on the words of Roebuck's future wife, Falconer's sister, Henrietta. She is reported to have said to her brother, 'This is the one candidate to choose; the letter is well written, and in the hand of a Gentleman'.[37] It is a pleasant story but I feel that it would be more instructive to know what happened in the drawing-room of 29 The King's Circus on 20 August and what hard political bargaining went on from then until 28 August when the Independent Association met for the last time. What is clear is that, just as the Independent Association had split from the merely liberal Whigs, the Association was itself divided over Roebuck. Consequently those at the meeting on 28 August agreed on joint support of Palmer but that individuals should go their own ways and support whom they wished for the second seat. The Independent Association then dissolved itself.

A letter to the London *Times* signed by fifty of Roebuck's supporters,[38] committed to returning him free of all expense, shows that all the leading and long standing Radicals in Bath were behind Roebuck. They included: John Allen, James Crisp, George Cox and William Hunt as Chairman of Roebuck's election committee. In addition there was Thomas Falconer's brother, Alexander, Henry Stothert, ironfounder, Robert Uphill, the County Coroner and Henry Smith, land surveyor, as chairman of the Bath Political Union, all men in the upper strata of the middling class.

By the end of August the battle lines had been drawn. All that remained was for the 2,800 electors to determine their loyalties, and vote (Figure 30). Even General Palmer had to choose. In the contest between Hobhouse and Roebuck he reluctantly aligned himself with Roebuck mainly, it seems, because he suspected some attempt at ministerial intervention on Hobhouse's behalf. Apart from that he was a lacklustre candidate. His speeches and opinions contribute little to understanding the issues involved. The real contest was between Roebuck, the joint nominee of the Radical/artisan-dominated Political Union and of the radical middling-class fraction of the Independent Association, on the one hand, and Hobhouse, the candidate favoured by the merely liberal Whigs and moderate reformers angling for the Tory vote on the other.

Hobhouse's programme was much as he announced it in the Parish of St James early in July except that he added a proposal to remodel the corn laws, and strengthened his views about the abolition of the assessed taxes and slavery. On the question of further measures of constitutional reform he was vague. He mentioned only the continuation of peace, the practice of retrenchment, and the reformation of all existing abuses.

Roebuck's programme was much more clear cut. It included the repeal of the Septennial Act, demand for the ballot and a taxpayer suffrage, the destruction of monopolies, the break up of closed corporations, abolition of the monopoly of the Bank of England and the China trade, abolition of the corn laws, the assessed taxes, and slavery, reduction in expenditure on the armed forces, cheap justice, national education, repeal of the Six Acts, and the extension of civil and religious liberty.[39]

More important than the list of items in election programmes was the symbolism of the programmes listed and the political style of their proponents. Hobhouse was a wealthy, well-connected, outwardly staid and conservative figure. But, as he trimmed his programme to capture votes, he laid himself open to charges of electoral opportunism and as the campaign degenerated to the level of personal abuse he attracted charges of business sharp practice. It was said that as a partner in a Calcutta Bank he had retired from partnership with £25,000 knowing the bank was already insolvent. With his connections in the government and his still successful banking business in Bath he presented the image of a wealthy bourgeois, acceptable to Tories as well as to Whigs. His programme, couched in general terms and replete with calls to see, 'the principles of the Reform Bill instilled into the policy and institutions of the country',[40] matched that image.

Roebuck, on the other hand, was without property, except for that needed to qualify as a parliamentary candidate and even that had to be arranged for him. His only resources were personal ones, his intellect and his ambition. He was a slightly built man, dynamic, impetuous, intolerant, waspish. A political democrat certainly, a republican probably, and an atheist. A man of principle, he refused to treat or canvas in order to buy votes. Like all the 'Ultra' Philosophic Radicals he hung his hat on the demand for the ballot and never wavered. He was a charismatic figure with whom many artisans and tradesmen in Bath could identify. A popular jingle said it for them:[41]

SAYS STRAIT FORWARD ROEBUCK TO HOBHOUSE THE SHUFFLER

Says Hobhouse to Roebuck, 'I've friends in high places,
The Corporate Body and Wealth of the Town;
Your supporters are rabble with unshaven faces,
Asham'd to appear when Sir Francis came down.
We heard
His eloquent speech about Westminster Town.'

Says Roebuck, 'I care not for "Westminster Glory"
Naked truth I avow without fear of a frown;
I'm not tied to Radical, Whig or to Tory,
I'm a friend to the People, so long trodden down.
Come, see,
The People stand up who were long trodden down.'

Roebuck's programme certainly seemed to have something for every man who knew or felt himself to be outside the established ruling class and on the fringes of its attendant bourgeoisie. Such men as possessed some measure of economic independence or special skills and abilities from which they derived a sense of their own esteem and integrity as producers but who also felt their identities as men denied by the social and political exclusiveness of Bath. To the Political Union, the artisans, the liberal press, and the Independent Association, Roebuck offered short parliaments, an extended suffrage, and the ballot. To Dissenters he held out the promise of religious liberty, the abolition of tithes and the abolition of slavery. To the newly-enfranchised parishioners he offered the repeal of the assessed taxes and to all tax payers a reduction in government expenditure. To the small trader he promised to restrict the power of monopolies. To frustrated Freemen he offered a share in the offices and spoils of local government. Everything Roebuck proposed was designed to further the cause of the individual against the authority of the state and the presumptuous power of persons, and to remove all vestiges of privilege and corruption. An extended suffrage and the ballot would emphasise the political worth of individuals and protect them from intimidation. Cheap justice would ensure equality before the law. A system of national and secular education would produce a discerning and sceptical public, eliminate privilege and reduce the power of established religion. All his other proposals were attacks on existing positions and interests.

Presented as this programme was within an urban society socially structured and transformed as previously described – containing that is, large and permanent strata of artisans and tradesmen vitally important for the functioning of its economy, yet economically exploited and denied social and political equality by their aristocratic and wealthy patrons – it gained a ready acceptance. The content, style and person of Roebuck is the measure of the development of class consciousness among the tradesmen and artisans of Bath as they threw in their lot with middling-class radicalism.

The election campaign got under way in September. There had never been anything like it before in the constituency; four local newspapers argued about it, processions thundered in support of it, dinners were given in honour of it and jingles were sung about it. Everywhere election posters implied a parallel between Paris in 1788 and Bath in 1832 (Figure 28). For people to whom the bloody Bristol riots were only one year and twelve miles away it was a parallel not without meaning. These same posters frightened the citizens by demanding: Did they wish to be dominated by a political caucus in London? Did they wish to be represented by a Republican and a Democrat? Did they wish to see their churches turned into barracks? Did they wish to see the barricades go up? If they did then they were advised to vote for Roebuck, who was not only a Democrat and a Republican but an atheist to boot. He was also born in America![42]

When the results of the poll were declared Palmer and Roebuck were elected. It was a triumph for the Radical cause.

The overall result was as follows:[43]

	no. of votes	% of total votes
Major-General Palmer	1,534	41.0
J. A. Roebuck	1,136	30.9
W. H. Hobhouse	1,040	26.7

These figures for the constituency as a whole mask differences in voting behaviour between the city's six parishes. Therefore they mask the importance of the part played by class structure and by the different social composition of the parishes in shaping voting behaviour. That is to say, they do not show how the social construction of space, itself a product of the class structure, was also a factor

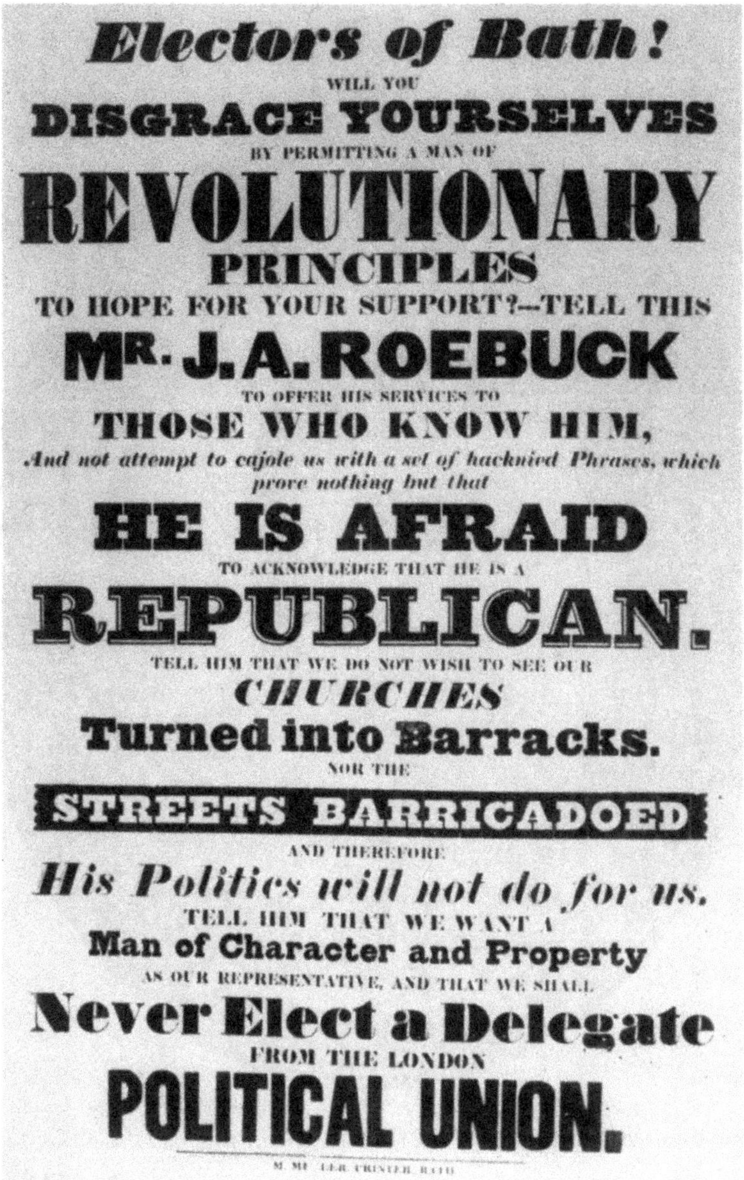

Electors of Bath!

WILL YOU

DISGRACE YOURSELVES

BY PERMITTING A MAN OF

REVOLUTIONARY
PRINCIPLES

TO HOPE FOR YOUR SUPPORT?—TELL THIS

MR. J. A. ROEBUCK

TO OFFER HIS SERVICES TO

THOSE WHO KNOW HIM,

And not attempt to cajole us with a set of hacknied Phrases, which prove nothing but that

HE IS AFRAID

TO ACKNOWLEDGE THAT HE IS A

REPUBLICAN.

TELL HIM THAT WE DO NOT WISH TO SEE OUR

CHURCHES
Turned into Barracks.

NOR THE

STREETS BARRICADOED

AND THEREFORE

His Politics will not do for us.

TELL HIM THAT WE WANT A

Man of Character and Property

AS OUR REPRESENTATIVE, AND THAT WE SHALL

Never Elect a Delegate

FROM THE LONDON

POLITICAL UNION.

Figure 28 Anti-Roebuck election poster, 1832

Figure 29 John Arthur Roebuck (1801–79), MP for Bath 1832–7 and 1841–7

BATH ELECTION.

The Committee for conducting the Election

OF

Mr. ROEBUCK,

AND

Major-General PALMER,

Solicit the honour of your Vote & Interest.

Committee Room for Walcot Ward,
King William Inn, Thomas-street.

[KEENES, PRINTERS.

Figure 30 Roebuck's voting card, 1832

in shaping the political consciousness of the people who occupied it. Table 10.1 represents an attempt to meet that objective.

Evidence from the Poll Books shows that while Roebuck received 1,136 votes, nearly half of his votes were cast by voters voting for him alone. About one-fifth of the electorate voted only for Roebuck. The other half of his votes came from voters who also voted for Palmer. They show, too, that he had least support in the wealthy and suburban parishes of Walcot and Bathwick and in the central parish of St Michael, the location of most of the better class shop and traders. In these three parishes alone the proportions voting for Roebuck and Hobhouse were in reverse order to the proportions in the electorate as a whole; 33 per cent voted for Hobhouse and only 26 per cent for Roebuck. Their clear choice was for Hobhouse. In Bathwick alone Hobhouse got 39 per cent of the votes. The order of voting in the other three parishes, two in the southernmost commercial and industrial part of the town, and the other its most rapidly expanding industrial suburb, was of an entirely different order. In these three parishes Roebuck got the support of over half the voters and topped the poll with 42 per cent of the votes cast compared with 19 per cent recorded for Hobhouse. Above all Roebuck was supported by the voters in the parish of St James; 67 per cent of them voted for him and he topped the poll with 45 per cent of the vote. Hobhouse got 14 per cent. This parish, with 11 per cent of the population and of the voting population in Bath gave Roebuck 18 per cent of his vote.

Since these voters, on several occasions, also took independent and locally important political initiatives there can be no doubt that the parish of St James was the stronghold of Radicals in Bath. It

TABLE 10.1 Percentage of voters on the roll, according to parish, voting for J. A. Roebuck, 1832

Parish	Bathwick	St Michael	Walcot	St Peter St Paul	Lyncombe and Widcombe	St James
%	30	31	37	51	51	67

Source: *Poll Books*, 1832.

was the level of class consciousness to which its parishioners had risen which laid the foundation of Roebuck's political career. Since this was so, some measure of the component parts of that class consciousness would appear to be suggested by Roebuck's own position on various issues. Thus, in the earliest years of his career Roebuck had been the chief advocate of the revolutionaries of lower Canada and the author of a democratic alternative to the Durham proposals. Then, for a time, in his *Pamphlets For the People*, he had led the fight against the Newspaper Stamp and, until he lost his seat in the Drunken Election of 1837, appeared the man most likely to draft the Charter and present it to Parliament. Moreover, it was in *The Pamphlets For the People* in 1835, that H. S. Chapman, a close colleague of Roebuck's, set out the *minimum* requirements for good government as advocated in the *Pamphlets*. The programme was a seven-point Radical charter demanding:

(1) an extension of the suffrage to all occupants;
(2) an abolition of property qualification;
(3) secrecy of suffrage, by means of the ballot;
(4) the abolition of the present complicated system of registration, and the reduction of the expenses of elections;
(5) a more equal distribution of members, according to population and territory;
(6) the duration of Parliaments to be shortened; and
(7) the tax on knowledge to be abolished.[44]

These seven points, with one exception, summarised the irreducible minimum of Roebuck's political programme. The exception was Roebuck's own commitment to universal suffrage. They may also be taken as the basic demands of his supporters in the parish of St James. It was on the basis of these seven points and his personal abilities that Roebuck, at one time, seemed a likely leader of the Radicals in Parliament. In short, he was undoubtedly a very active and sometimes an influential critic of many aspects of government, he was a Philosophic Radical of the first rank. Since he received continued and massive support in Bath, particularly in the parish of St James, it would be interesting to find out a little more about the class origins of those supporters.

One way to do this is to allocate voters to designated categories such as middle-class, artisans, tradesmen, publicans and lodging house keepers, and so on according to their manner of designation in trade directories. Another, greatly favoured by some historians, is to identify voters according to occupations as listed in poll books. Although I mention below some results of attempting such an allocation for Bath I find such methods too subjective. These methods only result in an occupational analysis of voting behaviour, and unless one assumes that men listed under a particular occupation are members of an economically and socially homogeneous group, they provide a very unreliable guide to the class composition of voters in the early nineteenth century. Nevertheless, both methods show that in Bath artisans and tradesmen were more likely to vote for Roebuck than for his liberal Whig or Tory opponents. Thus, in the election of 1841, in which the contest was more clearly between Radical and Tory than in 1832, men listed in the building trades, with the exception of builders and plumbers, showed a high preference for Roebuck and the Radical cause. The proportion in each occupation voting Radical was as follows:

Percentage voting Radical
(number in category in brackets)

Plasterers	75	(24)
Carpenters	69	(62)
Labourers	67	(37)
Masons	66	(37)
Architects	66	(6)
Painters	64	(31)
Plumbers	46	(13)
Builders	41	(12)

One occupational group sometimes singled out to show the usefulness of an occupational analysis of voting behaviour is that of shoemakers. They are held to be an economically homogeneous group of self-employed workers and it is said that since their votes were generally evenly distributed between candidates that there was no class basis for their electoral behaviour. Yet this was not the case in Bath. As we know, shoemakers in Bath ranged from employers of thirty or forty journeymen, through the self-employed, to the majority of journeymen shoemakers organised in militant unions at least from the 1790s. Their voting figures in the 1847 election in Bath, when the contest was between Roebuck and Lord Ashley, a leading exponent of Tory welfareism brought in to break Roebuck's hold on the constituency, do not support the general case. In that election shoemakers in Bath cast their votes by a ratio of 2:1 in favour of Roebuck; of the 108 shoemakers who recorded a vote 68 voted for Roebuck and 38 for Ashley. In the parish of St James the ratio was 5:2. But the analysis need not stop there. In order to find out how social class division within occupations, as well as occupation and parish, influenced voting behaviour it is necessary to use something other than lists of occupations.

Perhaps the best way to get some measure of the social class distribution of voters is to relate men identified in poll books to the same men identified in rate books according to estimates of the gross rental of the houses they occupied and on the basis of which they qualified for the suffrage. Unfortunately this can only be done for Bath for elections in the 1840s. Table 10.2 presents an analysis along these lines for shoemakers in 1847 in two parishes.

Table 10.2 shows that in these two parishes more than half of Roebuck's shoemaker supporters, 19 out of 37, occupied houses with a gross rental of less than £19 per annum and were barely qualified to vote, whereas less than one-fifth of Ashley's shoemaker supporters were in this low category and nearly one-half were occupiers of houses with a gross rental of over £30 per annum. Indeed, Ashley's shoemaker supporters included two men with property valued at £91 and £141 per annum respectively. The table also shows that shoemakers' support for Roebuck was greater in the poorer artisan populated parish of St James than in the much larger,

TABLE 10.2 Votes of shoemakers in the parishes of Walcot and St James in 1847 according to estimated gross rental of houses and property

Estimated gross rental £	Roebuck		Ashley	
	Walcot	St James	Walcot	St James
10–19	18	1	3	1
20–9	7	5	8	
30–9	1	4	3	1
40–9			2	2
50–9	1		1	
Over 60			2	
	27	10	19	4

wealthier and generally conservative parish of Walcot. In the latter parish 59 per cent of shoemakers voted for Roebuck. In the parish of St James the figure was 71 per cent.

Evidence in the table, which shows shoemakers occupying low rental houses and voting for the Tory Ashley, does show that property distribution and location were not the only determinants of voting behaviour in 1847. Nevertheless, when one considers that Roebuck had lost votes for a number of reasons; those of Dissenters because of his support for a grant to the Roman Catholic College at Maynooth and for an Irish Poor Law, and because of his opposition to Sabbatarianism and sectarian control of education; and those of other erstwhile supporters because of his support for the New Poor Law and because of the success of Ashley's advocacy of the ten-hour day, the strength of the underlying factors of property distribution and location in determining voting behaviour is remarkable. In the parish of St James, among those who barely qualified to vote, the support for Roebuck was in the ratio of 6:1.

One may infer from this that among shoemakers with the franchise far more of them shared and endorsed Roebuck's view of the world and how its abuses should be remedied than shared that advocated by both Whigs and Tories. In a generally Radical environment, as in the parish of St James, their willingness to be seen supporting Roebuck's views was especially high. This might then be explained by attempting to comprehend the totality of social and economic pressures to which men such as shoemakers were subjected. Take the case of a young journeyman shoemaker with ambitions to set up on his own account. Such a journeyman who might also have been a Baptist or a Primitive Methodist, living in a low rental house in a parish administered by a vestry controlled by members of the Church of England, in a city ruled by a close corporation, in conflict via his trade union with his employer over piece rates, legislated against by the Combination Laws and other public decrees, looked down upon by his neighbours as well as by his employer's customers, and watching his family die at the average age of 14, was likely to be seething with barely suppressed resentment against all forms and manifestations of authority. In familiar surroundings, in the company of like-minded men, he was more likely to be non-deferential than deferential. Whether this resentment could be harnessed for industrial and/or political action aimed at changing the economic and social order would then depend on other influences, such as the similarity of his experience with that of his immediate associates, his level of achievement motivation – his ambition, his exposure to articulate spokesmen of protest movements giving voice to his own frustration and resentment, the degree to which he sensed the possibility of changing conditions and so on. Whether his class consciousness would then be stamped with the imprint of individualism or the more collectivist attitudes of a true proletarian would also depend on a variety of factors; his work situation and his relationship to the means of production, ideologies and levels of consciousness prevailing in his neighbourhood, and the availability of groups and movements he could join. The net result of all these forces in Bath was that two-thirds of shoemakers with the franchise supported Roebuck as he translated Philosophic Radicalism into a middling-class programme of political action at constituency level.

Since only 16 per cent of shoemakers were listed in the poll books it is impossible to say even this much about the level and nature of the class consciousness of those barred from legitimate participation in the political community.

An extension of this kind of statistical analysis and interpretative framework to the voting behaviour of more than a 1,000 plumpers in the parishes of Walcot and St James in the election of 1841 illustrates further the relationships between the distribution of property, the urban ecology, and class consciousness and political behaviour. The results of this analysis are summarised in tables 10.3 and 10.4.

In the compact central parish of St James, largely populated by independent artisans and tradesmen, nearly four voters out of five were Radicals – as was the case from 1832 to 1847. Of those who plumped for the Radical cause nine out of ten were occupiers of property with gross rentals of less than £60 per annum – three out of four were occupiers of houses with gross rentals of less than £40 per annum – and only one in five voters occupying property so valued was prepared to plump for the Tory candidates. The Tory minority on the other hand drew nearly one-fifth of its vote from men occupying property with gross rentals of more than £60 per annum, in which strata Tory plumpers almost matched the number of Radical plumpers. Even so the pressures to conform to the prevailing Radical ethos in the parish of St James must have been great, and committed Tories were not easy to find.

A RADICAL UTOPIA 1812–1847

The parish of Walcot was a much larger, richer, dispersed and consequently a much less homogeneous parish than St James. Its inhabitants also showed a very different pattern of voting. First, there were slightly more Tory than Radical plumpers. Of those voting Tory 37 per cent, compared with 21 per cent in St James,

TABLE 10.3 Estimated gross rental of houses occupied by plumpers in the parish of Walcot in the Bath election, 1841

£ p.a.	Radical		Tory	
	No.	%	No.	%
10–19	162	35.5	81	18.1
20–9	90	19.7	45	10.0
30–9	96	21.0	71	15.9
40–9	45	9.9	47	10.5
50–9	16	3.5	35	7.9
60–9	11	2.5	20	4.4
70–9	4	0.9	36	8.0
80–9	6	1.3	25	5.6
90–9	4	0.9	20	4.4
Over 100	21	4.6	67	14.6
Total	455		447	
Total plumpers	488		490	

Source: *Poll Book*, 1841 and *Highway Rate Book*, Walcot 1841.

Notes: 1. Plumpers are those voters who gave both votes to either the two Tory or the two Radical candidates. Radical plumpers also include four voters who voted only for Roebuck.
2. Voters not allocated to any category of gross rental are those rated on business premises only, i.e. stables, shops, public houses, warehouses, and those untraceable in the rate books.
3. When a voter was recorded as rated on two or more properties only the highest rated property was recorded.
4. When two or more voters were rated on the same property each was recorded at the full estimated gross rental.
5. An estimated gross rental of £10–19 placed the property in streets like Avon Street or Lower Camden Place. An estimated gross rental of over £100 placed the property in areas like St James Square, the King's Circus or the Royal Crescent.

occupied houses with rentals of more than £60 per annum. Indeed, in every stratum occupying houses with rentals of more than £40 per annum there were more Tory than Radical voters; in all, 250 Tories as against 107 Radicals. In strata below £40 per annum there were 207 Tories but 348 Radicals. Thus three-quarters of Radical plumpers but only two out of five Tory plumpers occupied houses with rentals of less than £40 per annum.

Perhaps the most striking thing about both sets of figures – those for Walcot and St James – is that whereas the Tory vote was widely distributed over all strata the Radical vote was concentrated. In both parishes Radical support scarcely extended above the three lowest strata, that is, above the £40 limit and almost one out of three Radical plumpers barely qualified for the franchise. In Walcot, however, Radicals were more likely to be found among those who barely qualified for the franchise while in St James Radicals were more likely to occupy houses with slightly higher rentals. Among the very rich, that is, those occupying houses with gross rentals of £100 per annum or more, houses in St James Square, the King's

TABLE 10.4 Estimated gross rental of houses occupied by plumpers in the parish of St James in the Bath election, 1841

£ p.a.	Radical		Tory	
	No.	%	No.	%
10–19	43	23.5	9	17.0
20–9	50	27.3	9	17.0
30–9	44	24.0	9	17.0
40–9	13	7.1	10	18.9
50–9	18	9.9	5	9.4
60–9	4	2.2	4	7.5
70–9	5	2.7	1	1.9
80–9	3	1.6	1	1.9
90–9				
Over 100	3	1.6	5	9.4
Total	183		53	
Total plumpers	189		55	

Source: *Poll Book*, 1841 and *Poor Rate Book*, St James 1839.

Circus and the Royal Crescent, only one in five was a Radical plumper.

It is clear, therefore, that property distribution and its location were important in influencing class consciousness and voting behaviour. Regarded as indicators of income and social stratification these rental calculations show that stratification along a spectrum rich to poorer did help to shape voting preferences. They are an objective factor distinguishing Radicals from Tories. Therefore, to regard all those who gained the franchise under the Reform Act, as 'middle class' or as members of 'the gentry' is either to misread the record or to use the terms so broadly as to strip them of meaning.

To understand the gulf separating the life styles of voters living in Bath, who lived in houses with an annual value of £150 to £200 who voted overwhelmingly for Ashley, from those who lived in houses with an annual value of £10 to £19 who voted overwhelmingly for Roebuck, one must look at and in houses in the Royal Crescent and compare them with those in Lower Camden Place. These latter houses must then be transported in imagination to the parish of St James, now a glossy shopping precinct productive only of a consumer consciousness. Then the gulf between the worlds of their respective occupants will be seen to have been unbridgeable. Voters in the upper town were protected by a portcullis of property, privilege and prejudice. And it was the living experience of leading Radicals in the Bath Political Union and of Radical Professional men in the Independent Association that led them to understand this about Bath. It enabled them to match Roebuck's political genius to the constituency. Then, for fifteen years, through his advocacy there of Philosophic Radicalism, Roebuck helped raise the class and political consciousness of its tradesmen and artisans, shoemakers and others still further; to a level no anti-Catholic rioter in the 1780s and no shoemaker in the 1790s, when shoemakers first fumbled apologetically to organise themselves in opposition to their employers could have dreamt of. And for these fifteen years Roebuck was the very mirror of his supporters keeping the support of the majority of them as he published the *Pamphlets for the People*, fought vigorously against the Newspaper Stamp, pressed for the whole of the Radical Charter published in 1835, demanded a reform of the House of Lords to make it, 'not an enclave of oppression, not an asylum where half witted and fractious men may congregate in safety to plot the overthrow of English Liberty,'[45] supported revolution in Canada, and worked almost single-handed in England to bring about responsible Government in Lower Canada and to obstruct the dominion of the mother country throughout the Empire.

It was in recognition of this achievement, apparently cemented for ever at the election of 1841 when the Tories, Lord Powerscourt and Ludlow Bruges, were decisively beaten by Roebuck, who received his highest ever vote, and the Radical Lord Duncan, that the *Bath Chronicle* declared:[46]

> Bath is a dark blot on the present general election. At a time when other places are, to their high honour, throwing off the trammels of modern Liberalism, Bath has put them on in their worst shape. It has returned not merely radicals or ultra-radicals, but persons who are 'something more.' We are taunted throughout the country with having sent to Parliament two disciples of revolution . . . 'Hotbed of all that is wild, reckless, and revolutionary in politics' is the phrase which is abundantly used in speaking or writing of Bath.

That the rewards of this raising of class consciousness were slow in arriving is explicable only in a national context and by reference to the fact that the militant Radical mood in Bath, and in the parish of St James in particular, and in Movement Radicalism generally, was not matched throughout the country. Instead of there being, 'fifty cities and boroughs in the Empire (exhibiting) the same wholesome state of opinion as the City of Bath',[47] there were only a handful. Moreover, successive elections in 1835 and 1837, reduced the Radical faction in Parliament. Soon the Radicals were so weakened that Charles Buller once wrote to Grote saying, 'I can see what we are coming to; in no very long time from this you and I shall be left to tell Molesworth.'[48] Indeed, the measure of the gap between the expectations in the years 1830–2 and subsequent achievement is the failure of the Radicals to get a Commons' majority for Grote's annual motion on the introduction of the ballot. Thus, in 1837, Grote, who had topped the poll in his constituency in 1832, had fallen to fourth place, only six votes ahead of a Tory and the ballot motion of 1838 resulted in a majority of 315 noes to 198 ayes. The judgment of H. S. Chapman, a close colleague of Roebuck familiar with Bath politics, was that the Whigs, 'have betrayed the People; they desire not Reform; their sole object is to hold power against a rival section of the Aristocracy.'[49]

There was more to the decline of the Radicals than this, particularly in regard to their ability to capture a working-class vote. Not all of the political measures advocated by Radicals were calculated to endear them for ever to the mass of their supporters, not even in Bath. Roebuck, for example, gave his full support to the Poor Law of 1834. Defending himself against attacks from his supporters such as George Cox, he declared, 'Every man should maintain himself by his own industry and the talents which God has given him. I carry this principle to the pension list – I carry this principle into the Poor Law.'[50] And nothing would shift him. This crack in his mirror image, soon to be one of the causes of his downfall in the election in 1837, was also to be the symbol of a new shift in the development of class consciousness in the city.

Before this came about, however, one other legislative act did seem to capture the enthusiasm and aspirations of Radicals of all social classes. This was the Municipal Corporations Act of 1835. Passed with great speed and efficiency under the influence of Radicals like Joseph Parkes of Birmingham, it did for local government much more than the Reform Act had done for national politics. In Bath it destroyed the old Corporation and opened the flood gates to the fulfilment of Radical aspirations.

But, first, there was a re-drawing of parish into ward boundaries. One of the Radical parishes, St Peter and St Paul, was split in two. Part of it was incorporated into St James and the other with some addition from the southern part of Walcot became Kingsmead Ward. The remainder of Walcot Parish was also split in two, the eastern, more artisan-populated part, became Walcot Ward, the wealthier part became Lansdown Ward. The political allegiance of the first elected councillors in December 1835, set out in a roughly north-south sequence, is shown in table 10.5.

This distribution of councillors illustrates what we already know. There was a solid tradesman and artisan Radical vote in St James, Lyncombe and Widcombe, and Walcot. And a concentration of the Tory and Liberal vote in Lansdown, St Michael and Bathwick. Only in the new Kingsmead Ward was support significantly divided between Liberals and Radicals. After the election of fourteen aldermen the political composition of the council was:[51]

Tory 11   Liberal 13   Radical 24   Doubtful 2

Two Radicals, Crisp and Allen, were defeated in elections in St Michael's and Walcot wards and seven members of the old closed

TABLE 10.5 Political allegiance of councillors, 1835

Ward	Tory	Liberal	Radical	Doubtful
Lansdown	5	1	–	–
St Michael	4	1	1	–
Walcot	–	1	4	1
Bathwick	1	5	–	–
Kingsmead	–	3	2	1
St James	–	–	6	–
Lyncombe and Widcombe	–	–	6	–
	10	11	19	2

Source: *Bath and Cheltenham Gazette*, 29 December 1835 and *Poll Books*, 1832, 1834, 1837.

Corporation were elected as councillors! Crisp and Allen were subsequently appointed aldermen.

The electoral victory of the Radicals was not as convincing as the Radical leaders might have anticipated. But did it matter? As far as the relief of the social and economic problems of the labouring population of Bath was concerned the answer is 'No.' It is true that an exploratory committee on education was appointed early in 1836 but no action resulted. Then, when the New Poor Law came into operation in the district, it was administered by another body, A Board of Guardians, not responsible to the Council. As economic conditions deteriorated in the mid-1830s and mid-1840s the reformed Council did no more to relieve poverty than the old closed Corporation. In fact the city's sagging economy added point to the Radicals traditional claim for reductions in taxation and cuts in expenditure. What had been a stick with which to beat self-appointed governors and arbitrary governments became a rod for their own backs. The Radicals, as much the victims of the hegemonic belief in absolute property and absolute self-interest as those they had ousted, were more concerned to cut expenditures and reduce rates than to provide services. Consequently they never did do anything about flooding, and in regard to water supply and sanitation they lived on the capital of the old Corporation. It was not until 1846 and 1851 that the Council used the powers available to it to seek to improve its administration and provision of public services and by that time it was Radical no longer. But for as long as it was Radical the Council's main concern was to try to meet the voters demands for economy. For example, in 1838 George Cox appealed against a poor rate and W. P. Roberts, a recent convert to Radicalism, refused to pay at all. Then, a deputation led by these two men, representing six out of the seven wards, appealed against a Borough Rate and demanded as economy measures a reduction of almost half in the police force and a cut in the Mayor's salary. In Council these demands were accompanied by allegations of attempted bribery of the police. In the end an investigating committee recommended a cut in the police force of twenty-three men at a saving of £1,000 per annum.

In parish vestries the mood was the same. The demands of Radical parishioners, particularly in St James, St Peter and St Paul, and Lyncombe and Widcombe, was for a reduction in the assessed taxes, one of which, the Window Tax, was held to be especially burdensome in Bath – 6*s*. 8*d*. per head of population in Bath compared with 1*s*. in Birmingham. As well Radical Dissenters, George Cox in the vanguard, fought and manoeuvred against church rates. These examples show what the Radicals in power were really after. They had demanded and fought for electoral and administrative reform in order to eliminate government even when it was in their own hands. Their objectives were to oppose all government and to cut to the bone the financial exactions of any government. The choice of the police force as the Radical's prime target shows, too, how deeply rooted were their fears of the coercive power of the state. In this respect the Paineite tradition had triumphed. The words with which Tom Paine had welcomed the American Revolution might well have been a slogan for the Radicals in Bath:[52]

> Society is in every state a blessing, but government, even in its best state is but a necessary evil; in its worse state an intolerable one . . . Government like dress, is the badge of lost innocence; the palaces of kings are built on the ruins of the bowers of paradise.

Consequently the idea that the state or, in this particular case, the local authority, even when under their own democractic control might act benevolently in the interests of electors was foreign to them. They were a community of anarchists dedicated to voluntarism. Nothing illustrates this better than the manner of the opposition of Radical Dissenters and churchmen to Church Rates in the parish of St James. The majority vote in vestry was against levying a Church Rate. Consequently the curate received no salary and had to be paid by the rector and various other debts remained unpaid. Then, the Radical parishioners once again assembled in vestry, having demonstrated their strength and made their point, voted to liquidate the accumulating church debt by a voluntary subscription. It was reported that several Dissenters voluntarily subscribed rather more than they would have contributed to a compulsory Church Rate!

This Radical utopia in the 1830s had much in common with the competitive ideology of civil society in Wood's Bath a hundred years earlier. To counter it, Wood had then built Queen Square and the King's Circus as environmental determinants of good order, at least for a select few. And to be fair to the Radicals, the self-interest they raised up as their fiery beacon was also to be hedged around to make it safe for people. This they intended to do, not with buildings or other spatial arrangements, but through education. And the Dissenters among them would have set that education within a rigorist moral setting. Only constrained and thus enlightened would self-interest hold sway. Even then it would have been circumscribed by equal and easy access to the law so that no one would have been permitted to exercise rights contrary to the rights of others and no one could have grown 'more equal' than another. Since the physical and social manifestations of the arbitrary power of élites in an unequal society were all around them as permanent reminders of the merely tentative nature of their political gains, who would say that Radical doubts about government and their suspicions about the coercive power of the state were misplaced?

The Radical's stand on the question of power and on the overriding importance of individual and voluntarist rights which won them massive electoral support in 1832, 1835 and 1841, was to prove their electoral undoing in 1847. Moreover, this shift in their electoral fortunes also had much to do with the spread of Chartism in Bath and with the growth of new working-class initiatives symptomatic of an emerging working-class consciousness. And it is to these events from 1837 that we must now turn.

II

Political initiatives by members of Bath's labouring population had occurred from the time of the involvement of some hundreds of them in the attack on Wilkins in 1831 and in the formation of Bath Political Union in 1832. But, thereafter, during the excitement of the agitation for the Reform Bill and in the first few years of Roebuck's term as MP, organised labour in Bath had generally given its support to the Radical movement. However, while the electoral interests of a large minority of the labouring population had been partly catered for by the Reform Act, the majority of them were still excluded from the political community. It was their interest which was taken up again in March 1837 when the Radicals met to set up a new organisation to patch up differences that threatened to tear them apart and lead to an electoral defeat.

On this occasion the working-class cause was taken up by W. P. Roberts, later known as the Miners' Advocate, who had made his first political appearance in Bath as a Tory attacking Roebuck but who was now a staunch supporter of the working classes. Following an objection to the composition of the committee of the proposed organisation on the grounds of the under-representation of the working class, and sensing the mood of the predominantly artisan attendance at the meeting, Roberts proposed that one-third of the provisional committee should automatically be nominated from that class and that eleven of the management committee of twenty-one should be working class. This should be the case, he said, because he considered that society in general, 'should be a Democracy in which the productive classes should have a preponderating influence.'[53] Old Radicals, Crisp and Shenstone, disagreed but the motion was carried and a new predominantly working-class political organisation was founded.

This disunity within Radicalism could not have come at a worse time. The local economy was depressed and four months later there was a general election. The Radicals came to this election in disarray. Roebuck had upset many erstwhile supporters by his waspish and doctrinaire approach, by his religious toleration, and by his support for the New Poor Law only recently implemented in Bath. At the same time working-class Radicals were feeling politically restless.

On the other hand the Tories had improved their organisation and recovered their confidence. They put up a united front with two candidates, Lord Powerscourt and Ludlow Bruges. The ensuing 'Drunken Election' was fought with all the weapons at hand: the revising barrister, bribery, treating, and organised intimidation of tradesmen. 'The Tories, especially the women, are making a run against all the radical shops,'[54] wrote Charles Napier. And the idea was spread that five years of Radicalism in Bath was the cause of the decay of business in the city. The result of the campaign was a sweeping Tory victory. Compared with 1832 Palmer's vote fell by a third and Roebuck's by a fifth. Both Powerscourt and Bruges were elected. As a result of the election generally the Radical party in Parliament was almost annihilated.

A further consequence of class divisions and disagreement over social policies within the Liberal/Radical alliance was the formation of the Bath Working Men's Association. But, whether this was an outgrowth of the organisation formed in March 1837 with a majority of artisans on its committee is not clear. The WMA, whose president was Thomas Bolwell, a shoemaker, held its first public meeting on 16 October 1837. Apart from James Crisp who took the chair, no other leading long-standing Radicals were present. Instead the guest of honour was Henry Vincent, a fiery young 24-year-old compositor from the East London Democratic Association. Vincent was a man to cheer the heart. According to Gammage he:[55]

> Appeared on the platform to considerable advantage. With a fine mellow flexible voice, a florid complexion, and excepting in intervals of passion, a merit winning expression, he had only to present himself in order to win all hearts over to his side. His attitude was perhaps the most easy and graceful of any popular orator of the time. For fluency of speech he rivalled all his contemporaries, few of whom were anxious to stand beside him on the platform. His rare powers of imitation irresistibly drew peals of laughter from the gravest audience. His versatility, which enabled him to change from the grave to gay and vice versa, and to assume a dozen various characters in almost as many minutes, was one of the secrets of his success. With the fair sex his slight handsome figure, the merry twinkle of his eye, his incomparable mimicing, his passionate bursts of enthusiasm, the rich music of his voice, and above all, his appeals

for the elevation of women, rendered him a universal favourite, and the Democrats of both sexes regarded him as the young Demosthenes of English Democracy.

Roebuck's response to this man and the new initiative he represented was very clear. Although Roebuck had been closely involved with the London Working Men's Association and the preparation of the Charter, and would have presented a petition to Parliament embodying the points first mooted at the Crown and Anchor meeting in February 1837, but for his defeat in the July election, he was very apprehensive about the future of Radicalism under the control of working men. He was particularly concerned by the fear that they would graft new social policies, such as opposition to the New Poor Law, on to traditional Radical demands. He wrote, therefore, to the organisers of the meeting:[56]

> The working men do wisely in their associating together for they have hitherto been excluded from all participation of Municipal Rights, because disunion has rendered them weak and reduced their enemies to condemn their demands. I would say to you, be united, be firm, learn distinctly what rights you ought to have, and steadily and earnestly demand them. While you do this, however, I would entreat you not to mix up social with political reform. Social reforms can come only as the consequence of political ones; and on the one set the great body of the people are agreed, on the other they are at variance. A good government, if attained, would conduce to all good social reforms, and it is not for us to decide before hand what these last should be. I give you this warning, because I have been so long in the habit of advising the people of Bath; and also because I know that the weakness and disunion of the working classes have arisen mainly from their unwisely confounding these two essentially different classes of reform.

In spite of this warning the meeting went ahead and the audience listened attentively to some half-a-dozen other speakers as well as to Henry Vincent who spoke of his pride 'in seeing before him so large a number of citizens of the place that had been foremost in returning one of the most zealous advocates of popular rights.'[57] He spoke of the need for the ballot, the iniquities of the Whig government and of the nature of democracy. The programme finally and unanimously adopted at this meeting: universal suffrage, no property qualification, annual parliaments and the ballot was no different from that frequently advocated at Radical meetings. Indeed, it was a less thorough demand for constitutional reform than that prepared as the Radical programme by H. S. Chapman two years earlier. The novelty was its public announcement at a meeting of Bath's labouring population organised by working men and addressed by a working man as acceptable and presentable as Henry Vincent.

Middling-class Radicals also met at the end of 1837. Their object was to press on with demands for measures that would bring about a total transfer of power unconnected with demands for social reforms. Their political demands were like those of the WMA: universal suffrage, the ballot, shorter Parliaments. But, for them, the central most urgent issue was the ballot. Middling-class Radicals who were also tradesmen in Whig or Tory dominated wards were especially concerned about the ballot. Open voting set up conflicts of interest. So, said, Jolly, an up-and-coming draper, 'Get the Ballot. If possible with an extension of the Suffrage, but if we can obtain no more, by all means let us get the Ballot.'[58] Indeed, the policy issue most clearly distinguishing the ultra-Radicalism of the middling-class from working-class Radicalism was the priority each respectively gave to the ballot and universal suffrage. In Bath it distinguished Radicals from Chartists.

One footnote to the consequence of the Ultra-Radical emphasis on the ballot and of Movement Radicalism in Bath is that the first efficient ballot legislation in the British Empire and in the world, the Victorian ballot of 1856, was drafted by Roebuck's colleague, H. S. Chapman. Chapman, who had drafted the Radical Charter of 1835 – and had two Tory aunts in Bath – was one of the few Philosophical Radicals anywhere to achieve power. He became Attorney-General in the State of Victoria and pushed through legislation giving the state something close to equal electoral districts. Earlier still, in 1835 and 1836, as rapporteur to the French in lower Canada, he had reassured them of the certain success of Movement Radicalism in England and that no English government would use force against them if they chose to take things into their own hands. His advice, mainly based on his friendship with Roebuck and his acquaintance with Radicalism in Bath, was one element in the brew of revolution in Canada in 1837.[59]

When the complete Charter was introduced to Bath in June 1838 Thomas Bolwell was in the chair and Vincent and other local working men were the main speakers. The only old Radicals present were Crisp and W. P. Roberts. This time Napier wrote to give them much the same advice as Roebuck. The meeting noted that advice and heard and adopted the Charter. Subsequently, through the inspiration of Vincent there was much local enthusiasm for the Charter. 'The people,' declared Vincent, 'had been kept down by a phantom; they had bowed down before empty idols; before those who instead of being their superiors, were their inferiors in morals and intelligence. They had been kept down by those who were knaves, Lord John Russell was a knave, Harry Brougham was a knave, Peel was a knave, the Duke of Wellington was a knave,' the only solution, he said, was to overthrow the phantom and for, 'Every village to send forth its Wat Tyler, every city its William Tell.'[60]

Beguiled by the Radical political mood in Bath and by his own rhetoric Vincent made Bath his headquarters. He brought the local Chartist newspaper, The *Western Vindicator*, from Bristol to Bath, publishing it first at 5 Galloway Buildings and then at 4 Northumberland Buildings, not so very far from Queen Square. There was a spate of meetings in support of the Charter, some proselytising of the surrounding towns and rural areas by working-class Chartists, and some outbreaks of violence, most notably when an armed body of men prevented the recapture of women escaped from Avoncliffe workhouse. In April and May armed Chartists from Twerton and Bath paraded through Weston village until dispersed by the military. But all this was a mere overture to the overwhelming demonstration of popular support for the Charter expected to take place on Whit Monday 1839. On that day it was said, 'The whole country for 20 miles round the place will teem with myriads of ardent souls determined to strike a last blow for home, for freedom and for happiness.'[61]

In preparation for this massive demonstration, the new, largely Radical Town Council, the Magistrates, and the Home Office combined forces. And, on the morning of Monday 20 May the forces of order were drawn up under cover in strategic positions: 200 Chelsea Pensioners in the New Market, 600 special constables in the Banqueting Hall of the Guildhall, six troops of the North Somerset Yeomanry in St James Square, 130 police armed with cutlasses at the Police Office, and two troops of Hussars called in from Frome. It was a most impressive demonstration of the coercive power of the state. Nothing was to be left to chance.

Throughout the morning the shuttered and silent city was calm and deserted. The Troops and police remained under arms. About midday a straggle of 200 people set out from Stall Street. They moved slowly and warily along the Wells road to Midford. As the military remained at their posts the crowd took heart. By the time all had assembled in the appointed field, there were about 3,000 of them, men, women and children. Many were in holiday mood and all heeded the slogans on their banners advising them to 'Peace, Law and Order'. There were no William Tells in Bath, not even Henry Vincent or W. P. Roberts, both had been arrested and the Chartists under their second rank leaders made a very poor showing. Yet it is doubtful if things would have happened differently with Vincent in the vanguard. Not even his charisma could have turned away the police and the military and it needed more than his oratory to turn the many political groups in Bath and its neighbourhood into a united political force. Probably there never was any real political danger in Bath from the Chartists – its Radical tradition was essentially a constitutional one, its leadership vested in men of property howsoever small it might be, who were hostile to any hint of collectivism. And its shoemakers, for all their deprivation, were not the stuff from which revolutions were made, they had too little to lose. Consequently the support given by Mealing, Bath's delegate to the London Convention, to an appeal for an immediate general strike put him out of step with the non-militant mood of Vincent, by then a licensed Dissenting Minister and soon to be a Temperance Lecturer and out of step with the *Western Vindicator* and the Bath Trade Unionists.

Vincent's own reaction to the fiasco of Whit Monday was tinged with bitterness.

'Has the spirit of Radicalism departed from the middle classes (of Bath)?' he demanded in the *Western Vindicator*, 'Where are those reformers among them, that at one time agitated this city with Mr Roebuck? Have they abandoned their long cherished principles and gone over to the enemy? Or are they ashamed to mingle with those who are now local agitators?'[62] Yet, had Vincent really been in touch with events in Bath he would have seen that the reply had already been given. In November 1838, Kissock, an active Chartist, had been decisively beaten in a contest for an aldermanic seat in the parish of St James – the vote was 248:196. And, after Whit Monday 1839, there was no doubt at all that Chartist working men could only hope to maintain an effective political presence in Bath in association with the Radicals and the middling-class and on their terms.

The opportunity and enthusiasm for such an association between Chartists and Radicals was provided by the successful re-election of Roebuck in 1841 and the emergence of the Anti-Corn Law movement. After Roebuck's election there was a series of meetings which culminated in the joint Chartist – Anti-Corn Law League demonstration of December 1841 at which Old Radicals, New Repealers and Chartists appealed for the repeal of the Corn Laws and a full and fair representation of the people. But, when the Sturge Declaration in favour of a merger between the Chartists and the Anti-Corn Law League came to Bath, the Chartists split into a Sturgeite majority and an O'Connorite, oppositional minority.

The writing was now on the wall for both Radicals and Chartists. This alliance between Anti-Corn Law Leaguers and Chartists implied for the future that political reform would have to be associated with demands for social reform. For only then would demands for political reform excite substantial popular support. The problem was to choose the right social reforms. In associating with the Anti-Corn Law movement, some Chartists had chosen well. In the first place the Anti-Corn Law movement did attempt to deal with one important aspect of the problem of the standard of living – the price of bread – and seemed relevant to the immediate needs of Bath's labouring population. Second, it was an issue on which all urban classes could agree; it was certainly more popular than the Anti-Poor Law stance of the majority of Chartists. To the extent that the Anti-Corn Law movement was relevant to the immediate economic problems of the labouring population, and there seems reason to suppose that it was, then the consciousness of workers' leaders in Bath might be thought of as developing in response to the real material needs of the working class that had at last emerged in Bath after 140 years of economic development, but that consciousness was in no sense a Marxian class consciousness.

Moreover, there were other reactions to the failure of politically militant Chartism. Henry Vincent became a Temperance lecturer. In this way he seemed to say, first, change the consciousness of men, then, and only then, might their political consciousness change or be changed. Another, similar reaction, was that of the Chartist shoemaker, George Bartlett. Bartlett was a member of the O'Connorite minority. He was an able man acquainted with the ideas of Sheridan, Fox and Owen. In fact he was an admitted Owenite inasmuch as he believed that character was determined by circumstance. And, on the occasion of his trial for advocating the violent overthrow of the political system, he said he felt no ill will towards the magistrates because they were equally the victims of circumstance. They were bound to act in certain ways. He was, he said, opposed to physical force. He was also opposed to mixing social with political reforms. Like Marx ten years later Bartlett had decided that political action must wait on an extensive programme of education. He said, 'We intend in future to have nothing to do with local questions, such as concerns poor houses or Town Councils. We should adopt one prudent course of action – we should endeavour to spread our principles as widely as possible, knowing that upon the progress of information among the people depends the success of our cause.'[63] He was found guilty of sedition and sentenced to nine months imprisonment.

The final break between the two local Chartist factions came in June 1842. Vincent and Philip with the Rev. Thomas Spencer, remodelled themselves as the Bath Complete Suffrage Association with their headquarters at 2 Church Street. The O'Connorite group established a 'Benefit Cricket Club' to attract the youth of Bath and inaugurated a series of lectures. They met regularly every week at Bolwell's house in Galloway Buildings. Thus Henry Vincent, Dissenting minister, Temperance lecturer, moving speaker but unwilling organiser, found his spiritual home with Thomas Spencer, perpetual curate of Hinton Charterhouse, rigid utilitarian and advocate of the New Poor Law. Bartlett and the Bolwells were left with the rump of O'Connorite Chartists, a faction without a home, class basis, or, seemingly, a policy relevant to the immediate material or political needs of the working class in Bath.

By the time Bartlett died in September 1842, the simple clarity of Roebuck's message not to mix social with political reform had long been ignored by both Chartists and Radicals as well as by Roebuck himself as over the years he had supported the New Poor Law, the Maynooth Grant and an Irish Poor Law and opposed sectarian control of education. And it is difficult to see how it could have been otherwise since quests for power are quests for control over social policy, even if that policy is that there should be no social policy, only the free play of enlightened self-interest as in the Radical's Utopia.

As Whigs and Tories realised that these continuing conflicts over social policies had begun to weaken the electoral basis of middling-class Radicalism in Bath they were inspired to form a united front to turn out the Radicals from both local government and national representation. The first move in this direction was taken in 1844. In that year the Tories, acting alone, revised and strengthened their party organisation. What is more they created a local sensation when they decided to put up a Tory candidate to contest the Council election in St James Ward. The resulting campaign, 'was perhaps the most sharply contested which has occurred in this city and ended like an old fashioned Parliamentary Election, by a few of the most zealous and unruly of the candidates friends receiving black eyes if not broken heads'.[64] The Tory candidate was elected by a majority of 203:199. Inspired by this result in the most Radical ward in the city and by other successes in parochial affairs in Walcot the Tories formed the 'Bath Tradesmen and Operatives Conservative Association' to assist in, 'overcoming the prejudices and delusions engrafted on the minds of the lower classes by the specious doctrines of interested and factious demagogues.'[65] A Tory revival was already under way. By 1847, when the local economy was so badly affected that young men had begun to migrate in considerable numbers and the feeling was rife that the decline in business was all the result of Bath's too Radical image, the Whigs and Tories finally agreed to bury their differences.

At the election in 1847 the Whigs and Tories jointly chose Lord Ashley to put up against Roebuck. Their object was to present Ashley, later Lord Shaftesbury, as a social reformer dedicated, as his work in the Ten Hour Movement testified, to the social welfare of working men. To make good their claim they also persuaded an erstwhile Radical and member of the Sturgeite Complete Suffrage Association to ask Thomas Bolwell, as a leading O'Connorite Chartist, to chair a meeting at which several artisans from the north would testify to Ashley's sterling worth and integrity.

Bolwell, Chartist and shoemaker, rejected Ashleyism. He said that Roebuck had gone beyond Ashley in what he had done for, 'he had laid the foundation of a system which would give the franchise to all mankind; and placed in comparison with Mr. Roebuck, Lord Ashley sank into comparative nothingness.'[66] Bolwell refused to be used by the Whigs and Tories.

The task was then given to an old Liberal, William Blair. His speech at the meeting introducing the men from the north began apologetically:[67]

> I beg to say that I come forward as a member of what, for distinction sake, I must call the Liberal or Whig Party, and that, without the consciousness of having abandoned any one principle or opinion that I can remember to have entertained. The old lines of demarcation that separated Whig and Tory are hardly to be traced, so that it would no longer be safe, and scarcely possible, to act upon theoretical and bygone distinctions, or to adhere rigidly to the former badges and watchwords of party.

He got no further. He was interrupted from all parts of the hall and as James Crisp almost came to blows with one of the men on the platform, the police dispersed the meeting. The ritual introduction of the Ten Hour Movement and Shaftesbury was postponed to a second meeting a few days later at which the formalities were able to be concluded. At this second meeting the three men from the north were introduced as practical men seeking support for a practical man. One of them announced his view that Lord Ashley was a practical man who had introduced practical measures 'as will work well for the whole community'. And another said:[68]

> I put it to the people here, whether those who struggle night and day, in season and out of season, with view of propounding measures which may enable the large masses of the population to acquire such education (wise, moral, and religious) – I put it to you whether they are not more worthy of your support than those who have everlastingly the expressions of political liberty on their lips.

And it was argued that the Ten Hour Movement with Ashley at its head would do more for working men than merely Radical rhetoric ever would.

The dangers of such a policy – concessionary social reforms unaccompanied by a transfer of political power, the dangers of Ashleyism, were well understood by Bolwell. Almost immediately he called the Chartists together, both Sturgeites and O'Connorites, to form a committee of active working men to secure Roebuck's election. A last attempt, perhaps, to seek a transfer of political power untainted by social issues. In the event the ensuing election was close run. In spite of desertions from the Radical cause by Dissenters and liberal Radicals, and in spite of his opposition to the Ten Hour Movement, Roebuck retained the votes of 1,093 of the electrorate – only 58 less than in 1841 and a swing against him of a little over 5 per cent. Nevertheless, it was enough to give Ashley a vote of 1,278 and a majority of 185.

At the declaration of the poll Roebuck was in a bitter and despondent mood. He prophesied, 'As sure as the sun will rise tomorrow, you will see a Tory majority in that Town Hall, and two Tory members to represent you.'[69] And so it was. In the next few years there was a glimmer of life in the Chartists on the occasion of the revolution in France in 1848, and brave laughs from them when Bolwell quipped that the authorities, fearing a riot, had, 'called out every old lady in trousers living in the upper part of the town who was willing to place herself at the disposal of the magistrates.'[70] But that was all. In the year of European revolutions and The Communist Manifesto the hitherto Radical electorate of Bath, described in 1841 as the 'Hotbed of all that is wild, reckless, and revolutionary in politics,' returned a majority of Tories to the Town Council thus ending a 'dynasty of Radical Mayors'! This success was followed up in the next year by an arrangement between the Conservative and Liberal Associations not to contest the local election, an arrangement only to be broken in the Kingsmead Ward. It was also agreed that no electoral contest would take place in 1850, but that in each Ward retiring Councillors would be replaced by Councillors of the same political opinions, and the Conservative (Tory) Mayor was re-elected. Finally, in national politics, Radicals offered themselves as parliamentary candidates on two occasions only in the next fifty years, in 1873. Their highest vote was 57. In the same fifty-year period a Tory was elected on eight separate occasions. In 1886, with a Liberal Unionist as well as a Tory Member of Parliament, Bath almost achieved the double forecast by Roebuck in 1847.

So they closed ranks, the wealthy and respectable Victorian occupiers of the upper town. Protected against the taint of trade and manual labour by the skirts of 10,000 domestic servants and against the sight and touch of those who laboured in the lower town by the space around them and their basement railings, they closed ranks to block the political aspirations of the tradesmen and artisans, shoemakers and others of the labouring population. They were able to do so because, after fifteen years, a sufficient number of respectable and middling-class Radicals could be turned against Roebuck and because middling-class Radicalism had spawned a working-class politics that threatened middling-class interests as well as upper class hegemony. And they were able to achieve their ends cloaked as advocates of paternalistic welfareism because Radicalism was too much tainted with those ideas about property and self-interest, characteristic of the society which gave it birth, and too much opposed to the powers of the state to see the state as benevolent even when under its own control. Thus, in Bath, as in England generally, the transfer of political power needed to eradicate the presumptuous power of persons and to prepare the ground for Radical Democracy or, Movement Radicalism, as it was better known to its supporters, never was achieved.

For a time, the consciousness of Radical tradesmen and artisans in Bath, mirrored in Roebuck, gave a glimpse of what might have been: political democracy based on universal suffrage and the Radical Charter of 1835, equal access to the law, no sectarian control of education, no taxes on knowledge, no coercion or religious discrimination in Ireland, responsible and democratic government in Canada and elsewhere in the Empire. But this brief and heroic period, from 1832 to 1847, was a sort of cultural revolution, a raising of political consciousness to undreamt of heights and too disturbing for those already established as men of property, whether Whigs or Tories, Liberals or Conservatives. These demands never were realised except slowly. So slowly, in fact, that time muted their effect; the Radicals of Bath never did come into their birthright. Instead of an immediate impact of new ideas there was adaptation to existing institutions. Instead of a quick transfer of power there was manipulation and political rearrangement. Then, in Bath, there was a further transformation of social structure such that the development of Radical consciousness in the city was overtaken by events. The fact was that the lag between the transformation of social structure in Bath in the eighteenth century, brought about by the building and expansion of the city, and the transformation of consciousness from corporatism and deference and from the Church and King riots and loyalties of the 1780s and 90s, to the Radical anti-establishment demonstrations of the 1830s was too long; even as Radical consciousness blossomed the economic and social structure which fostered it changed. In the end welfareism came close to being a substitute for political consciousness.

Finally, in 1850 the editor of the *Bath Chronicle* hymned the demise of Radicalism and the unity of Whigs and Tories. 'Bath', he said, 'is now at peace within itself.'[71] Although this claim must have had a hollow mocking ring in the ears of shoemakers and others for whom social deprivation and discrimination still remained at the very core of their lives, it was true enough. Compared with itself a hundred years earlier when the city was transformed by incessant entrepreneurial response to a buoyant and expanding market, when old ways were dying and new ones emerging, when skill and labour were in high demand; and compared with itself in the 1830s when it was the paradigm for Movement Radicalism, Bath *was* at peace within itself. As it settled into the sidelines of history it continued so for another hundred years, a place where the wealthy residents had it both ways; they enjoyed the economic fruits of absolute property and self-interest but within a social organisation of space creatively produced from perceptions about urban living at odds with the economic and ideological basis of their wealth and of the production of the city itself. And as time passed the city became a place where neither the occupants of Bath chairs, nor the labourers who felt themselves privileged to pull and push them, challenged the economic and political structures which determined their social relationships (Figure 31). Bath was a valley of pleasure still and, for the poor, a sink of iniquity.

Figure 31 Old Bath Chairs, 1907

APPENDIX A

ECONOMIC ACTIVITY IN BATH, 1700–1832

APPENDIX A

Economic Activity in Bath, 1700–1832

Year	Avon tolls	Avon dividend	Corporation expenditure	Interest	Corporation debt	Bath tolls	Corp. bldg and improv. expend. July to July	Total houses	Bath turnpike	Kingston's Bath rents
	£	£	£	£	£	£	£	NUMBERS	£	£
1700–1			558	33	670					
01–2			759	33	720					
02–3			534	33	720					
03–4			435	33	720					
04–5			1,154	41	1,520					
05–6			367	46	1,920					
06–7			786	70	1,920					
07–8			747	102	1,920					
08–9			—		—					
09–10			652	113	2,270					
10–11			672	113	2,270					
11–12			675	109	2,170					
12–13			914	113	2,270					
13–14			893	108	2,270					
14–15			966	139	2,890					
15–16			1,526	141	3,140					
16–17			651	97	3,440					
17–18			922	167	3,690					
18–19			816	167	3,690					
19–20			737	167	3,690					
20–1			827	177	3,690					
21–2			1,371	161	3,050					

APPENDIX A

22–3				—	—	
23–4				—	113	2,720
24–5				1,250	120	2,920
25–6				—	—	—
26–7				1,120	—	—
27–8				—	164	4,550
28–9				2,260	185	4,550
29–30				1,161	207	4,500
30–1	605			2,933	—	—
31–2	805	20		—	275	4,000
32–3	769	24		1,021	161	4,000
33–4	803	11		1,181	161	4,000
34–5	676	Nil		1,221	161	4,000
35–6	730	10		1,140	101	4,000
36–7	738	19		943	141	4,000
37–8	700	16		951	132	3,400
38–9	693	16		998	138	3,200
39–40	641	Nil		1,312	134	2,700
40–1	560	Nil		791	134	2,200
41–2	585	15		791	144	2,200
42–3	679	24		1,476	188	2,200
43–4	881	21	1,339	1,973	64	1,700
44–5	740	12	1,362	1,032	93	1,700
45–6	655	14.5		2,291	84	2,200
46–7	521	16		1,853	104	2,200
47–8	611	14		1,466	124	2,700
48–9	578	19		1,337	129	2,700
49–50	622	19		1,221	104	2,700
50–1	689	?		1,520	104	2,700
	654			2,250		2,700

APPENDIX A

Year	Avon tolls £	Avon dividend £	Corporation expenditure £	Interest £	Corporation debt £	Bath tolls £	Corp. bldg and improv. expend. July to July £	Total houses	Bath turnpike £	Kingston's Bath rents £
								NUMBERS		
51–2	723	20.4	3,768	76	1,100					
52–3	682	19	2,657	39	1,100					
53–4	846	24	4,335	40	1,500					
54–5	768	17	3,006	56	3,000					
55–6	727	7	1,873	120	3,000					
56–7	713	16	3,272	—	3,900		1,672			
57–8	827	18	1,185	—	3,900					
58–9	866	17	2,272	—	3,400					
59–60	700	18	1,824	122	3,400					
60–1	825	21.6	2,720	116	3,400					
61–2	770	22	1,956	196	2,700					
62–3	864	13.5	3,044	237	4,200					
63–4	939	26.6	3,760	215	4,200					
64–5	1,152	31	2,034	152	3,110					
65–6	1,210	25	3,214	158	4,610			1,712		
66–7	1,191	33	8,874	262	9,510					
67–8	1,099	38	3,327	451	9,910					
68–9	1,271	35	3,524	438	9,910			1,739		
69–70	1,227	31	3,706	437	9,490				4,451	
70–1	1,012	25.5	3,535	473	9,490			1,930	4,524*	
71–2	904	22.5	3,326	445	10,490				4,470	
72–3	854	19.75	5,853	526	10,490			2,015	4,269	
73–4	807	10	2,793	480	10,490			2,030	4,365	

APPENDIX A

Year							
74–5	814	4,999	294	10,990			
75–6	775	8,351	570	13,990			
76–7	767	8,320	755	18,790			
77–8	759	5,734	1,074	25,308			
78–9	680	9,315	819	26,908		2,335	2,088
79–80	610	6,649	1,179	24,758			
80–1	755	3,356	1,092	24,200			
81–2	518	3,491	841	26,100			1,882
82–3	704	4,167	1,249	26,400			1,910
83–4	723	5,173	1,030	26,700		2,576	2,112
84–5	796	4,363	1,184	26,400			2,175
85–6	Nil	4,666	1,184	27,100			2,185
86–7	1,051	4,580	1,206	27,100			2,209
87–8	1,118	4,580	1,206	27,100			2,213
88–9	1,134	5,609	1,210	27,100		2,897	2,214
89–90	1,325	5,609	1,290	45,100	21,345		2,187
90–1	1,425	4,420	1,100	52,100	13,247		2,358
91–2	1,825	4,697	1,212	50,100	4,374		2,276
92–3	1,293	5,032	1,167	50,000	3,504	3,749	2,313
93–4	700	5,607	1,131	48,800	2,605		2,202
94–5	611	**11,511	1,270	54,800	2,289		2,183
95–6	727	6,531	1,246	54,800	10,451		2,173
96–7	721	6,660	1,522	54,800	3,755		2,155
97–8	847	10,340	1,679	58,900	7,176		2,098
98–9	8	6,998	1,664	58,400	3,349		2,101
99–		6,728		57,500	2,731		2,221
1800							
1800–1		7,118	1,615	57,500	5,760	3,946	
01–2		7,467	1,638	56,300	5,231		2,398

4,520 (79–80 column 6), 4,872 (80–1 column 6), 5,859 (88–9 column 6), 6,889 (89–90 column 6)

APPENDIX A

Year	Avon tolls £	Avon dividend £	Corporation expenditure £	Interest £	Corporation debt £	Bath tolls £	Corp. bldg and improv. expend. July to July £	Total houses	Bath turnpike £	Kingston's Bath rents £
								NUMBERS		
02-3			9,381	1,606	53,200	1,366	4,954			2,300
03-4			10,283	1,489	55,000	1,323	4,741		7,935	2,295
04-5			6,952	1,568	54,300	1,337	8,241		7,794	2,508
05-6			7,919	1,582	53,700	1,306	5,964		7,850	2,312
06-7			7,335	1,494	53,600	1,368 Let	7,384			2,332
07-8			8,076	1,421	53,400	1,387 Let	7,532			2,239
08-9			12,652	1,623	56,552	1,333 Let	6,132			2,190
09-10			17,327	1,666	61,500	1,199	11,670			2,136
10-11			10,596	1,969	62,577	1,330	8,841			2,226
11-12			12,211	2,034	64,427	1,416	5,757			2,306
12-13			11,124	2,132	65,527	1,279	4,373			2,541
13-14			11,908	2,230	65,987	1,242	3,962			2,546
14-15			10,910	2,340	66,007	1,365	3,857			2,467
							Corporation only			
15-16			11,658	2,220	64,513	1,358	1,784			2,481
16-17			10,746	2,366	64,213	1,341 Let	2,940			2,507
17-18			17,017	2,529	63,213	1,368	2,436			2,481
18-19			9,886	2,382	61,913	1,392 Let	1,105			2,589
19-20			9,608	2,366	60,813	1,408 Let	1,344			
20-1			13,148	2,145	63,613	1,407	4,060			
21-2			11,365	2,791	63,113	1,409	2,506			

APPENDIX A

22–3	10,496	2,517	62,713	1,172
23–4	10,997	2,179	60,563	1,724
24–5	12,139	2,375	59,463	2,250
25–6	13,047	2,033	58,713	4,020
26–7	11,442	2,265	58,713	2,099
27–8	8,994	2,274	58,713	694
28–9	11,985	2,212	58,713	1,268
29–30	18,453	2,301	64,713	5,978
30–1	18,676	2,287	64,713	6,957
31–2	14,554	2,195	64,713	3,395

* Report in *Bath Chronicle*, 5 September 1771 of increase in tolls arising from extension of the turnpike through Warminster to Salisbury.
** £6,000 paid to Improvement Commissioners.

Sources:

Avon tolls: *The Avon Navigation Accounts*, British Transport Historical Records, London.
Avon dividend:
Corporation expenditure, interest, debt, building and improvement expenditure:
Bath tolls: *Chamberlain's Accounts*, Guildhall Archives, Bath.

Improvement Commissioner's Records, Guildhall Archives, Bath.

Houses: *Rate Books*, Guildhall Archives, Bath.
Bath turnpike: *Bath Turnpike Records*, Somerset County Record Office, Taunton.

Kingston's Bath rents: *Egerton MS.3648*, British Museum.
For notes to the table see over.

APPENDIX A

Notes:

1 *Avon Tolls*: Tolls on tonnage, therefore a volume index except that in 1770–71 the rate of tolls varied, see *Bath Chronicle*, 20 September 1770.
2 *Corporation Accounts*:

Problems of Interpretation of Chamberlain's Accounts

a Although each year was expected to balance and to be complete in itself there were periods when accounts ran over two or three years when under control of the same Chamberlain, e.g. 1777–80, 1784–6, 1786–8, 1788–9.

b Different Chamberlains used different methods of recording income and expenditure. For example, in 1756–7 Purlewent did not distinguish interest payments as interest payments. Not until Anderdon, 1784–5, were accounts regularly recorded under separate heads. Thus, rents were not always distinguished from water rents.

c On several occasions the Chamberlain died in office and the keeping of accounts was interrupted as in 1752–3 and 1758–9. On one occasion there was embezzlement, probably by Baldwin, and the accounts were deficient by £2,824.

d The estimate of Corporate debt is generally accurate. For example, it can be checked against some years in which Chamberlain's figures are clear as in 1777–8 and 1780–81. Moreover, the cumulative figure in 1790–91, £31,500 (excluding the Improvement Commissioner's Debt) is substantiated by the fact that interest was paid on £31,300. Therefore the error is of the order of 0.6 per cent. For 1795–6 the error calculated on the same basis is 8.0 per cent. For 1821–2 a comparison of the cumulative figure with the actual recorded debt shows an error of 9.6 per cent.

e After 1789 Corporate Debt excludes borrowings by the Improvement Commissioners. However, the accounts do include some interest payments on their borrowings and in 1795 on the £6,000 borrowed from Wiltshire at 4 per cent and apparently made over to the Improvement Commissioners.

f Nevertheless the broad outlines of Corporate economic activity may be discerned in the Chamberlain's accounts.

g Expenditure is actual expenditure less loan repayments. This gives a better indication of the Corporation's contribution to stimulating economic activity.

APPENDIX A

Indices of Avon Navigation tolls and Corporation debt
Bath 1726–1832 (1730=100)

	Avon navigation tolls	Corporation debt
1726		66
27		–
28		101
29		101
30	100	100
31	133	--
32	127	89
33	133	89
34	112	89
35	121	89
36	122	89
37	116	76
38	115	71
39	106	60
40	93	49
41	97	49
42	112	49
43	146	38
44	122	38
45	108	49
46	86	49
47	101	60
48	95	60
49	103	60
50	114	60
51	108	60
52	120	24
53	113	24
54	140	33
55	127	67
56	120	67
57	118	87
58	137	87
59	143	76
60	116	76
61	136	76
62	127	60
63	143	93
64	155	93
65	190	69
66	200	102
67	197	211

APPENDIX A

	Avon navigation tolls	Corporation debt
68	182	220
69	210	220
70	203	211
71	149	211
72	141	233
73	133	233
74	135	233
75	128	244
76	127	311
77	127	418
78	125	562
79	112	598
80	101	550
81	125	538
82	86	580
83	116	587
84	120	593
85	132	587
86	–	602
87	174	602
88	185	602
89	187	602
90	219	1002
91	236	1158
92	302	1113
93	214	1111
94	116	1084
95	101	1218
96	120	1218
97	119	1218
98	140	1309
99	116	1298
1800	–	1278
01	–	1278
02	–	1251
03	–	1182
04	–	1222
05	–	1207
06	–	1193
07	–	1191
08	–	1187
09	–	1257
1810	–	1367
11	–	1391
12	–	1432

APPENDIX A

	Avon navigation tolls	Corporation debt
13	–	1456
14	–	1466
15	–	1467
16	–	1434
17	–	1427
18	–	1405
19	–	1376
1820	–	1351
21	–	1414
22	–	1403
23	–	1394
24	–	1346
25	–	1321
26	–	1305
27	–	1305
28	–	1305
29	–	1305
30	–	1438
31	–	1438
32	–	1438

APPENDIX B

PEAKS IN BUILDING ACTIVITY, 1700 – 1800, AND RATES OF INTEREST AND CORPORATE DEBT IN BATH, 1700 – 1800

APPENDIX B

Peaks in building activity 1700 – 1800

Ashton	Parry Lewis	Bath
1701		
1707	1705	1707
1716–18		1718
	1724	
1730		
	1736	1732
1739		1743–4
1753	1753	1755–6 [or 1759]
1760		
1775	1776	1771
1793	1792	1792

Sources: T. S. Ashton, *Economic Fluctuations in England 1700–1800,* Oxford, 1957.
J. Parry Lewis, *Building Cycle and Britain's Growth,* London, 1965.
R. S. Neale, 'Society Belief and the Building of Bath, 1700–1793' in C. W. Chalklin and M. R. Havinden, *Rural Change and Urban Growth 1500–1800,* London, 1975.

APPENDIX B

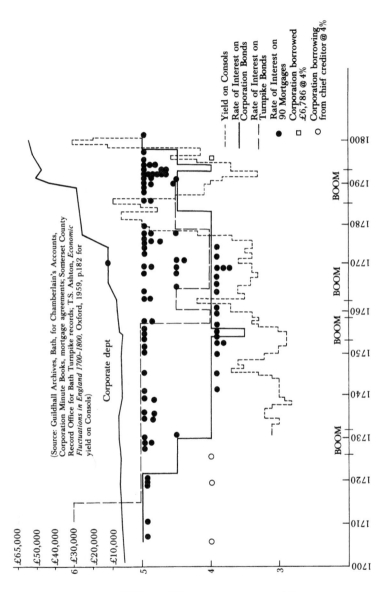

Graph B.1 Rates of Interest and corporate debt in Bath 1700–1800

APPENDIX C

NUMBER OF HOUSES IN BATH ACCORDING TO CONTRIBUTION TO RATE IN SHILLINGS AS LEVIED BY THE ACT, 1766

APPENDIX C

Number of houses by parish according to contribution to rate in shillings in 1766

St Michael	1	2	3	4	5	6	7	8	9	10	11	12	13	14	15	16	17	18	19	20	Over 20	Total
Trym Street			5	3	5	2	1	1	3	1		1										22
Burrough Walls		1	7	1	1		1		1													12
Milsom Street				1				1	1	24	1	5	2	4			2					41
Bladuds Buildings								1	14													15
Broad Street	29	28	4	4	5	5		2	1					1								79
Gracious Street	18																					18
Ladymead	42	41	18	6	4	1	1		2													115
Northgate Street		8	3	6	3	3	1		1													25
Green Street			6	5	2	1	1															15
Burton Street		10	2																			12
Frog Lane	27		1	1																		29
Barton Lane	2	6																				8
Boatstall Lane	10																					10
TOTAL	128	94	46	27	20	12	5	5	23	25	1	6	2	5	--	--	2	--	--	--	--	401

400

APPENDIX C

Number of houses by parish according to contribution to rate in shillings in 1766

St Peter and St Paul	1	2	3	4	5	6	7	8	9	10	11	12	13	14	15	16	17	18	19	20	Over 20	Total
Burrough Walls	1	3	2	2	2		1															11
Market Place		21	2	5	9	4	7	4	3	1		2	1	1			1			1		62
Wades Passage		4	1		4		1	1	1	1	2											15
Orange Grove		1	1	2	4	2	2	2		2	2	1		3	1	2	1					26
Waterside	1	6	1	2						1												11
Cheap Street		2	2	2	1		2	1	1	2	1			2		2			1			19
Cock Lane	16	1	2																			19
Westgate Street		8	7	5	7	2	5	2	1	4	1	1			1						1	45
Parsonage Lane	7	5			2		1															15
Bridewell Lane	5	10		1																		16
Sawclose		5				1																6
Westgate Buildings		1					8	1					1									11
Cross Bath		5	2	3	2	4	4		3	3				2		1				1	1	30
Stall Street			1	4	6	1	4		1		1	1	1			1					1	22
Churchyard			2		1	4			1					1							2	11
TOTAL	30	72	23	26	38	18	27	10	19	15	7	5	1	10	3	5	3	--	--	2	5	319

APPENDIX C

Number of houses by parish according to contribution to rate in shillings in 1766

St James	1	2	3	4	5	6	7	8	9	10	11	12	13	14	15	16	17	18	19	20	Over 20	Total
Stall Street		2	3		2		1				1										1	10
St James Lane			3		1																	4
Abbey Green					3					1				1								5
Abbey Street							1		1	1		3					2			1	2	11
Kingston Street							1		1	1				1			2					6
Church Street			1	2	2		2	2	1	6							1			1		18
Galloway Street							2			5				2						1		10
Lower Walks						1			1	1				2	1	1					1	7
North Parade									1	1	1	1		2	2						5	13
Dule Street							1		1	5		3						1				11
South Parade							1			5	3	1		1						1	2	13
Pierrepoint Street						2	4			4		4									1	16
Orchard Street			3		4	5	1			2				1	1							17
St James Street		2	13	2	2	5			1	1												26
Stall Street	10	6	6	5	6		1		1	1					1							37
Cross Bath and Bell Tree Lane		3	7	1	4		1			2					1							19
Burrough Walls	5	5		1																		11

APPENDIX C

																					Total
Southgate Street	33	20	18	13	12	4	2														102
Marchants Passage	10																				10
The Quay and Ambury	21*	31	3			1															56
Gerrard Street	4	5	7																		16
TOTAL	83	75	62	27	37	17	18	2	9	35	4	12	—	9	5	1	5	1	—	4	12	418

* Includes 7 Poor (+ Void 6)

403

APPENDIX C

Number of houses by parish according to contribution to rate in shillings in 1766

Walcot	1	2	3	4	5	6	7	8	9	10	11	12	13	14	15	16	17	18	19	20	Over 20	Total
Lansdown Road	1	2	2	1	3		2	1		2		1										15
Vineyards		1	7	1	3	3	8															23
Walcot Street	1	3	2	3	5		1															15
Gibbs Court		9																				9
Pitt Street					8																	8
Kings Circus					1									22	1		5				2	31
Brock Street						1	3	3	1	5		2*										15
Gay Street							7	5	1	13	1	3										30
George Street			3	1	1																	5
Miles Court			1		7	2				1												11
Edgar Buildings										5		6		3								14
Barton Street				1	1	1	6	1		1												11
Barton Court			1				7															8
King Street	1			6																		7
John Street	1	2	1	3	3	1	2															13
Quiet Street	1	1	5																			7
Wood Street			1		1	2	2		1													7
Queen Square	1	2	1		1		1		2			6	10	5			3		1			32
Chappell Row		1	1	1	8																	11
Prince Street	3	3	2	3	3																	14
Beaufort Square		4	4	8	3																	19
St Johns Court		1			3	2	3															9

APPENDIX C

																			Total
Monmouth Street	2	9	7	2	4	1	1			2	2		1		1				32
Cross Lane	11	5		1	1														18
Charles Street			2	4	7	1													15
Kingsmead Street		6	14	19	10	8	1	1					1						60
Kingsmead Square		5	2		5	2	2		1										17
Avon Street	16	**40	41	3	4														104
TOTAL	37	93	97	58	81	24	47	11	9	29	1	19	10	32	1	8	1	2	560

* (+ Void 4)
** Includes 4 Poor (+ Void 5)
Total Void = 15

APPENDIX D

FOOD PRICE INDICES, BATH
1812–44

APPENDIX D

Food Price Indices, Bath 1812–44
(Average 1838=100)

	Bread Quarter				Food Prices* Quarter				Barley Quarter				Lowest meat price Quarter			
	1	2	3	4	1	2	3	4	1	2	3	4	1	2	3	4
1812	186	180	171	186	198	188	167	184	243	217	184	241	139	150	141	122
1813	135	121	123	138	148	123	119	144	117	107	104	155	133	124	113	121
1814	124	127	123	135	131	126	125	137	89	95	105	115	117	100	104	103
1815	104	120	141	108	113	120	143	118	84	100	113	95	83	81	83	87
1816	196	199	173	167	166	179	153	148	127	124	117	168	75	83	70	80
1817	151	149	139	150	142	142	141	135	119	131	138	115	89	100	100	75
1818	127	117	123	132	135	124	124	140	205	129	121	180	127	127	114	119
1819	119	118	119	121	125	122	123	123	107	108	106	117	125	124	124	124
1820	96	93	107	103	107	97	104	111	75	78	92	84	114	100	89	117
1821	115	106	94	124	105	102	106	114	58	57	64	80	75	72	73	87
1822	89	102	106	81	92	100	103	86	83	87	93	78	74	89	94	68
1823	116	115	108	103	110	112	106	100	93	99	100	91	83	91	100	88
1824	119	119	118	115	122	127	137	116	117	116	126	125	107	115	117	108
1825	110	103	100	116	118	108	116	127	117	110	111	122	119	103	103	117
1826	96	96	100	96	106	102	97	104	126	136	123	122	108	112	106	100
1827	96	96	103	100	101	95	98	103	94	98	100	98	111	108	106	104
1828	127	125	119	125	126	117	105	118	111	107	106	118	100	106	104	103
1829	102	106	110	105	108	113	120	121	80	81	92	107	83	83	83	100
1830	110	107	104	107	124	119	117	105	101	106	105	103	83	83	83	83
1831				103												

408

APPENDIX D

Year																
1832	102	96	96	91	96	89	91	91	107	102	99	95	83	83	83	83
1833	87	86	86	86	88	85	87	90	85	82	84	89	83	83	83	83
1834	86	86	86	82	88	85	86	82	84	86	92	94	83	83	83	83
1835	78	75	75	70	79	77	80	79	86	93	91	95	83	83	83	83
1836	72	85	86	93	82	91	91	99	95	95	95	99	83	86	100	100
1837	101	102	91	86	109	106	100	98	112	92	99	92	100	100	100	100
1838	86	96	108	110	97	95	102	105	88	96	109	107	100	100	100	100
1839	110	105	104	112	105	100	101	106	120	119	118	130	100	100	103	100
1840	112	110	107	100	108	106	107	106					106	108	103	114
1841	96	96	109	107	102	102	110	109					108	108	108	108
1842	103	102	94	85	106	104	96	85					108	108	101	92
1843	78	72	86	86	82	76	85	87					83	83	83	83
1844	86	90	86	80	87	86	82	81					83	83	83	83

*For composition see p. 419.

Source: *Bath and Cheltenham Gazette* 1812–44.

APPENDIX D

The price of the quartern wheaten loaf in the city of Bath 1800–1844
prices in pence

	Jan.	Feb.	Mar.	Apr.	May	June	July	Aug.	Sept.	Oct.	Nov.	Dec.	Average
1800								15	17	19	20	20	18
01	21¼	21	22½	22	19	17¾	17½	16	12¾	10	9½	10¼	16¾
02	10¼	10	9¼	9½	9¼	9	9¼	9½	9	9	8¾	8½	9¼
03	8½	8½	8½	8½	8	8	8½	8½	8¼	8¼	8¼	8¼	8½
04	8¼	8	7¼	7¼	7¼	7¼	7¼	8¾	9½	10	12	13	8¾
05	12	12½	12½	12½	12½	13	13½	14½	13	13	13	12	13
06	12	12	11½	11½	12½	12½	12	12	12	12	11½	11½	12
07	11	11	11	11	10½	10½	10	11	10½	10	10	10	10½
08	10½	10½	10	10¼	10½	11	11½	11½	12	13½	14	14	11½
09	13	13½	13½	13	12¾	12¼	12½	14	14½	15½	15	15½	13¾
1810	15¾	15	15¼	16	16	17¼	17½	17½	16¾	16	15½	15¼	16¼
11	15¼	14¾	14	13¼	13	13	13¼	13½	15	15½	15½	16¾	14½
12	16½	16¼	16	17½	18¾	19	19½	21	19¾	16¾	18¼	17¼	18¼
13	17¼	17½	17½	17	16½	17	16¾	16½	15	14½	12¾	11¾	15½
14	12½	13	12½	12	11	11	10½	11½	12½	13	12¾	12¼	12
15	11½	11½	11¾	12	12	11½	11½	12	11	10½	10	9¾	11¼
16	9½	9¾	10	10¼	11½	12	12	13¼	14	14	15¾	17	12½
17	18½	18½	18	18	18	19¾	18¼	16	14¼	13½	14	14½	16¾
18	14¼	14	14	14¾	14	13	13¼	12¾	13	13	12	12	13¼
19	11¾	12	12	11¼	11	10½	11½	11¼	11½	11½	11½	11	11½
1820	11	11	11½	11	11	11	11	11½	11	10	9¾	9¼	11
21	9	9	9	9	8½	8½	9	9½	11½	12	12	10¾	9¾
22	11	11	10¼	10	10	9¾	9½	9	8	7¾	7½	7½	9¼

23	8	8	9	9	9¾	10	10	10¼	9½	9½	9½	10	9¼
24	10½	11	11	11	10¾	10½	10½	10	9¾	10¼	11	11	10½
25	11	11	11½	11½	11	11	11	11	11	11	11	10½	11
26	10½	10½	10	10	9½	9½	9	9½	9½	9	9	9	9½
27	9	9	9	9	9	9	9	9½	9½	9½	9½	9	9
28	9	9	9	9	9	9	9	10	10	12	11½	11½	10
29	12	12	11½	11	12	12	11¾	11½	10*	10	10	9½	11¼
1830	9½	9½	9½	9¾	10	10	10½	10½	10	10	10	10	10
31	10	11	10	10	10	10	10	9¾	9½	9½	9½	9½	10
32	9½	9½	9½	9	9	9	9	9	9	8½	8½	8½	9
33	8½	8	8	8	8	8	8	8	8	8	8	8	8
34	8	8	8	8	8	8	8	8	8	8	7½	7½	8
35	7	7½	7½	7	7	7	7	7	7	6½	6½	6½	7
36	6½	6¾	7	7¾	8	8	8	8	8	8	8¾	9¼	8
37	9¼	9½	9½	9½	9½	9½	9½	8	8	8	8	8	9
38	8	8	8	9	9	9	9¼	10½	10	10	10½	10½	9½
39	10½	10½	10	10	10	9½	9½	9½	10¼	10½	10½	10½	10
1840	10½	10½	10½	10½	10½	10	10	10	10	9½	9½	9	10
41	9	9	9	9	9	9	9½	10½	10½	10	10	10	9½
42	10	9½	9½	9½	9½	9½	9½	9	7¾	8	8	7¾	9
43	7½	7	7½	6¼	6½	7½	8	8	8	8	8	8	7½
44	8	8	8¼	8¼	8½	8½	8½	8	7½	7½	7½	7½	8

*Loaf changed from quartern to regular 4lb. loaf there exaggerating the fall in price.

Source: *Bath Chronicle* and *Bath and Cheltenham Gazette*, 1800–44.

APPENDIX E

WAGES AND REAL WAGES IN BATH
1780–1814

APPENDIX E

I

Earnings of labourers in Bath, Somerset, Wiltshire and Gloucestershire in selected years, 1767–1860

Year	Bath*	Somerset †	Wiltshire †	Gloucestershire †
1767–70	—	6s. 5d.‡	7s.	6s. 9d.
1780	8s.	—	—	—
1790	7s. 7d.	—	—	7s.
1795	9s. 1d.	7s. 3d.	8s. 4d.	—
1801	9s. 6d.	—	—	—
1809	9s. 4d.	—	—	—
1824	—	8s. 2d.	7s. 6d.	9s. 3d.
1831	—	9s.	9s. 5d.	10s.
1832	7s. 6d.	8s. 6d.	9s. 1d.	9s. 6d.
1833	7s. 9d.	8s. 4d.	9s. 2d.	9s. 3d.
1834	7s. 2d.	—	—	—
1837	7s. 7d.	8s. 8d.	8s.	9s.
1840	10s. 3d.	—	—	—
1850	11s.	8s. 7d.‡	7s. 3d.	7s.
1860	—	9s. 10s.	8s. 6d.	9s. 6d.

* Account Books of Surveyor of Highways, Walcot Parish.
† A. L. Bowley, 'The Statistics of Wages in the U.K. During the last 100 Years', *J.R.S.S.* LXI, part IV, LXIII, part III of reprint.
‡ Interpolated.

APPENDIX E

Real wages of non-agricultural labourers in the city of Bath, 1780–1850

Year	Bath earnings/Schumpeter-Gilboy prices 1780=100	Bath earnings/Silberling prices 1838=100	Year	Bath earnings/Bath prices 1838=100	Bath earnings/Silberling prices 1838=100
1780	100	133	(1812)	64	77
1781	88	113			
1782	97	120	1816–17	85	—
1783	71	105			
1786	94	138	1832	104	104
1787	94	126	1833	113	108
1788	86	121	1834	101	100
1789	91	120	1835	120	112
1790	85	112	1836	108	101
1791	98	130	1837	92	101
1792	104	127	1838	98	98
1793	86	112	1839	102	99
1794	83	110	1840	122	125
1795	86	104	1841	123	130
1796	84	106	1842	138	149
			1843	161	167
			1844	163	170
1801	55	81	1845		163
1802	76	102	1846		162
1803	80	95	1847		134
1804	82	100	1848		166
1807	72	98	1849		194
1808	67	93	1850		195
1809	61	78			
1812	53	77			
1816–17	65	—			

Source: Account Books of Surveyor of Highways, Walcot Parish. Elizabeth Boody Schumpeter, 'English Prices and Public Finance 1660–1822; *Review of Economic Statistics*, xx (1938).

APPENDIX E

III

Average weekly earnings of labourers employed by the highway surveyors in the parish of Walcot in the city of Bath, 1780–1851

Year	First week in January		First week in May		First week in September		Year	First week in January		First week in May		First week in September	
	No. emp.*	Average earnings	No. emp.	Average earnings	No. emp.	Average earnings		No. emp.	Average earnings	No. emp.	Average earnings	No. emp.	Average earnings
		s. d.		s. d.		s. d.			s. d.		s. d.		s. d.
1780	1	8 –	1	8 –	1	8 –	1801	2	9 6	3	8 1	2	11 –†
1781	1	8 –	1	8 –	1	6 –							
1782	–	–	1	8 –	2	8 7	1803	–	–	–	–	2	9 6‡
1783	2	4 8	2	7 6	3	8 –	1804	2	9 6	2	9 6	2	9 6
							1807	–	–	–	–	2	9 7
1786	1	8 8	2	7 6	2	8 –	1808	4	10 –	3	10 –	3	10 –
1787	1	8 –	2	8 –	2	8 –	1809	4	10 –	3	10 –	3	8 1
1788	2	8 –	1	8 –	3	7 1	1816–17	4	8 11				
1789	1	8 –	2	7 2	2	8 –	1832	89	5 9	8	6 2	11	10 7
1790	2	7 8	3	8 5	5	6 7	1833	21	8 –	19	7 6	14	7 10
1791	2	8 –	3	9 –	3	9 –	1834	23	7 1	20	7 1	16	7 5
1792	3	8 –	7	9 8½	5	9 5½	1835	24	7 7	23	7 9	19	7 5
1793	3	6 6	4	9 –	5	8 8	1836	–	–	19	7 9	19	7 11½
1794	3	8 –	5	8 3	5	8 3	1837	21	7 5	18	7 9	18	7 7
1795	3	9 2½	3	9 2½	2	8 9	1838	22	7 7	20	7 10	18	8 –
1796	2	8 9	2	9 6	1	10 –	1839	22	7 10	7	9 5	6	9 11

APPENDIX E

Year	emp.*	s d	emp.†	s d	emp.‡	s d	Year	emp.*	s d	emp.†	s d	emp.‡	s d
1840	14	10 1	9	10 4	7	10 3	1846	7	11 5	4	10 10	4	11 –
1841	11	9 4	5	10 8	5	10 6	1847	7	10 4	4	10 4	4	11 1½
1842	9	10 11	5	10 6	4	10 10	1848	5	10 6	4	11 1½	4	11 1½
1843	6	10 3	6	11 1	4	10 10	1849	4	11 1½	4	11 8	4	11 6
1844	6	11 5	4	10 10	4	10 10	1850	6	11 5	5	11 4	4	10 1½
1845	4	10 10	3	10 8	3	10 8	1851	8	11 10	3	10 11	5	11 4

* emp. = employed.
† August
‡ October

Source: Account Books of the Surveyor of Highways

APPENDIX E

Prices, earnings and real wages of labourers in Bath
1809–51 (1838=100)

	Prices*	Earnings	Real wages	
1809	–	117	–	
1812	184	–	(64)	
1813	174	–	–	
1814	132	–	–	
1815	125	–	–	
1816	131	111	85	
1817	158	–	–	
1818	141	–	–	
1819	126	–	–	
1820	120	–	–	
1821	106	–	–	
1822	100	–	–	
1823	99	–	–	
1824	111	–	–	
1825	128	–	–	
1826	112	–	–	
1827	102	–	–	
1828	103	–	–	
1829	114	–	–	
1830	116	–	–	
1831	116	–	–	
1832	92	96	(106)	104
1833	86	97	(114)	113
1834	85	86	(105)	101
1835	79	95	(122)	120
1836	91	98	(109)	108
1837	103	95	(93)	92
1838	100	98	(98)	98
1839	103	103	(102)	100
1840	107	128	(122)	120
1841	106	127	(123)	120
1842	98	134	(138)	137
1843	83	134	(161)	161
1844	84	137	(163)	163
1845	–	134	–	
1846	–	138	–	
1847	–	132	–	
1848	–	136	–	
1849	–	142	–	
1850	–	137	–	
1851	–	141	–	

APPENDIX E

* Prices are the weighted arithmetic mean of the prices of bread, potatoes, butter, eggs, and the lowest price of mutton, pork, veal, lamb, and beef. The weights are: bread, 12; potatoes, 3; meat, 4; butter, 1; eggs, 1. The real wage figures in brackets are those originally published in the *Economic History Review*, 1966.

Source: *Bath and Cheltenham Gazette*, 1812–44. For earnings, Account Books of Surveyor of Highways, Walcot Parish and for 1816, Widcombe District Accounts, vol. 143.

APPENDIX F

MORTALITY IN BATH 1838–44, COMPARED WITH 21 HEALTHY AND 32 UNHEALTHY STATISTICAL DISTRICTS

APPENDIX F

Annual Mortality per cent during the seven years 1838-44, in 21 healthy statistical districts

Districts	0–5 Males	0–5 Females	10–15 Males	10–15 Females	35–45 Males	35–45 Females	45–55 Males	45–55 Females	55–65 Males	55–65 Females	65–75 Males	65–75 Females
Lewisham .... *London*	5.317	4.663	.357	.553	1.226	.988	1.849	1.646	3.711	2.512	5.756	6.260
Thanet, Eastry .... *Kent*	4.531	3.835	.485	.495	1.066	.916	1.286	1.173	2.399	2.290	5.963	4.402
Godstone, Reigate, Dorking *Surrey*	4.123	3.332	.318	.363	1.006	.949	1.174	1.215	2.283	3.087	6.359	5.655
Hendon, Barnet .... *Middlesex*	4.786	4.284	.307	.474	.885	.923	1.669	1.037	2.612	2.262	6.129	5.191
Blything, Mutford, Wangford *Suffolk*	4.827	3.920	.288	.374	.985	1.052	1.017	1.082	1.625	2.109	5.259	4.022
Bideford, Holsworthy .... *Devon*	3.936	3.286	.411	.516	.853	.793	1.202	1.146	2.076	1.702	4.667	4.201
S. Molton, Torrington, Crediton, Barnstaple .... *Devon*	3.993	3.384	.286	.382	.880	.824	1.185	.945	2.491	1.939	5.951	4.490
Wheatenhurst, Westbury-on-Severn .... *Gloucester*	4.862	3.992	.594	.436	.774	1.053	1.370	1.013	2.578	2.102	5.601	4.679
Tenbury, Martley, Upton-on-Severn .... *Worcester*	4.076	3.561	.398	.525	1.001	1.154	1.610	1.313	2.479	1.957	5.994	5.234
Risbridge, Sudbury .... *Suffolk*	5.619	4.625	.618	.730	1.119	1.331	1.221	1.244	2.594	2.472	5.919	5.184
East Retford, Workshop *Nottingham*	5.208	4.243	.395	.528	.866	.930	1.137	1.169	2.597	2.016	5.498	4.906
Ulverstone .... *Lancashire*	3.877	3.493	.304	.350	1.079	1.135	1.292	1.271	2.602	1.842	5.872	5.051
Fylde, Garstang, Clitheroe .... *Lancashire*	4.818	4.238	.500	.520	.894	1.249	1.205	1.294	2.341	2.340	5.873	5.304
Pocklington, Tadcaster .... *York*	4.881	4.250	.354	.426	.839	1.095	1.056	1.403	2.479	2.214	5.228	4.720
Glendale, Bellingham, Haltwhistle .... *Northumberland*	2.851	2.455	.345	.364	.654	.840	1.173	1.022	2.149	2.000	5.615	5.136

APPENDIX F

Morpeth, Rothbury, Alnwick, Belford .Northumberland	3.941	3.005	.388	.371	.878	.945	1.201	1.122	2.552	2.143	6.041	4.319
Brampton, Longtown .. Cumberland	3.900	3.337	.355	.383	.907	.788	1.043	1.245	2.364	2.013	5.795	4.638
Tregaron, Lampter, Newcastle-in-Emlyn .South Wales	3.752	2.755	.377	.475	.826	.941	1.176	1.034	2.097	1.860	5.696	4.497
Anglesey .... North Wales	3.617	3.501	.420	.436	.652	.782	1.062	.976	2.103	2.020	4.892	4.410
Aberyswith ....South Wales	4.201	3.681	.327	.478	.980	1.075	1.662	1.300	2.217	2.019	5.961	4.722
Dolgelly, Crowen Bala, Festiniog .... North Wales	3.665	3.020	.422	.487	.798	1.064	1.211	.963	1.957	1.857	4.727	3.754
Average	4.323	3.660	.393	.460	.913	.992	1.276	1.172	2.396	2.131	5.657	4.799

APPENDIX F

Annual Mortality per cent during the seven years 1838-44, in 33 unhealthy statistical districts

Districts		0–5		10–15		35–45		45–55		55–65		65–75	
		Males	Females	Males	Females	Males	Females	Males	Females	Males	Females	Males	Females
Saint Saviour, St Olave	London	11.273	10.150	.583	.459	2.164	1.535	3.211	2.345	4.977	3.812	9.019	8.061
Saint Luke	London	10.894	9.319	.482	.459	1.988	1.734	2.878	2.442	5.075	4.497	8.960	9.765
Whitechapel	London	11.437	10.116	.432	.319	2.118	1.631	3.259	2.657	5.736	4.466	10.907	8.954
Medway (excluding Military)	Kent	6.350	6.891	.470	.486	1.893	1.293	1.992	1.817	3.210	2.734	7.145	6.316
Canterbury	Kent	7.561	5.837	.372	.642	1.812	1.458	2.609	1.953	3.883	2.722	6.531	6.039
Maidstone	Kent	7.077	6.366	.606	.473	1.401	1.438	1.922	1.559	3.279	2.577	5.940	6.432
Bedford	Bedford	6.827	5.415	.609	.824	1.161	1.436	1.521	1.610	2.954	2.868	5.920	6.303
Ely, North Witchford, Whittesley, Wisbeach.	Cambridge	8.944	7.322	.678	.649	1.098	1.120	1.586	1.515	2.722	2.669	5.759	5.065
Northampton	Northampton	8.452	7.416	.489	.743	1.421	1.496	2.103	1.679	3.973	3.537	8.190	7.576
Ipswich	Suffolk	7.751	7.348	.525	.628	1.648	1.192	1.870	1.509	3.878	2.896	6.961	6.133
Colchester	Essex	8.659	7.060	.734	.655	1.677	1.328	2.190	1.880	3.081	3.236	8.411	6.312
Norwich	Norfolk	9.755	8.128	.567	.656	1.321	1.209	1.748	1.424	3.263	2.577	6.837	5.431
Bath	Somerset	8.588	7.340	.544	.590	1.644	1.396	2.518	1.897	4.031	3.174	7.960	6.807
Exeter	Devon	9.588	8.199	.444	.490	1.715	1.329	2.746	1.557	3.848	2.837	7.997	6.691
Salisbury	Wilts	7.927	7.619	.329	.686	1.632	1.345	2.509	1.835	4.147	3.563	8.089	6.463
Coventry	Warwick	9.334	7.620	.493	.642	1.326	1.182	1.917	1.618	3.496	3.636	7.138	7.232
Birmingham	Warwick	9.609	8.365	.539	.547	1.746	1.378	2.758	1.928	4.428	3.743	9.885	6.983
Stoke-on-Trent, Wolstanton	Stafford	8.692	7.305	.653	.742	1.537	1.561	2.352	2.122	4.792	3.348	8.971	7.061

APPENDIX F

Bristol .... Gloucester	10.698	9.234	.782	.667	2.210	1.446	2.880	2.094	4.993	3.419	9.184	7.341
Derby .... Derby	9.628	7.811	.519	.923	1.245	1.433	1.916	1.787	3.429	3.175	9.769	6.657
Leicester .... Leicester	11.080	8.790	.568	.699	1.491	1.399	2.174	1.949	3.834	3.188	6.911	6.941
Nottingham .... Nottingham	12.239	10.346	.437	.581	1.255	1.502	1.850	1.927	3.728	3.339	8.165	6.873
Salford .... Lancashire	12.062	10.586	.586	.560	1.498	1.557	2.345	2.028	4.820	3.724	9.546	7.426
Manchester .... Lancashire	13.660	12.158	.567	.681	1.984	1.780	3.040	2.831	5.247	4.466	10.149	8.647
Liverpool .... Lancashire	14.372	12.771	.631	.597	2.162	1.808	3.367	2.637	5.305	4.668	10.634	9.370
Leeds, Hunslet .... York	9.597	8.349	.621	.654	1.457	1.419	2.112	1.694	3.982	3.170	8.774	7.126
Sheffield .... York	10.364	8.600	.597	.574	1.658	1.329	2.397	1.850	4.781	3.641	8.756	7.205
Hull .... York	10.184	9.095	.544	.597	1.816	1.345	2.862	2.055	4.031	2.962	7.476	6.131
Gateshead .... Durham	8.107	6.958	.648	.528	1.603	1.553	1.986	1.754	3.597	2.990	8.182	6.858
Newcastle-on-Tyne . Northumberland	9.777	8.786	.597	.452	1.659	1.322	2.499	1.771	4.353	3.279	8.430	6.872
South Shields .... Durham	9.129	8.098	.708	.485	1.846	1.149	2.393	1.873	5.189	3.135	11.354	8.508
Abergavenny, Pontypool Monmouth	8.980	7.805	.776	.636	.912	1.189	1.596	1.432	3.333	2.686	6.418	5.549
Merthyr Tydfil .... South Wales	10.778	10.176	.735	.571	1.117	1.259	1.980	1.519	3.168	2.920	7.018	4.699
Average	9.678	8.405	.572	.603	1.613	1.411	2.336	1.895	4.078	3.323	8.224	6.964
Increase per cent. over 21 Healthy Districts	124	130	46	31	77	42	83	62	70	56	45	45

Source: Report of the Registrar-General on cholera in England, 1848–9.

APPENDIX G

RATIOS OF POOR LAW OFFENCES 1777, AND 1787–93

Ratios of Poor Law offences
1777, and 1787–93

	Settlement Examinations	Removals	Examination of passes	Bastardy Examinations
1777	1:225	1:900	—	1:945
1787	1:237	1:982	1:540	1:450
1788	1:191	1:1158	1:440	1:489
1789	1:210	1:1715	1:656	1:557
1790	1:193	1:1143	1:375	1:553
1791	1:308	1:2844	1:275	1:753
1792	1:350	1:1950	1:535	1:635
1793	1:252	1:784	1:2416	1:604

Source: *Business before the Mayor and Justices*, GAB.

APPENDIX H

ESTIMATED RENTAL OF HOUSES IN THE PARISH OF ST JAMES IN THE 1830s

APPENDIX H

Estimated rental of houses in the parish of St James in the 1830s

	10	20	30	40	50	60	70	80	90	100	150	200	250	Total
Bath Street						1			1					2
Stall Street		2	7	4	12	3	2	2						32
New Orchard Street			5	3		1								9
Southgate Street		4	15	17	7	6	1			1	4			55
Harris Court	13													13
Taylor's Court	11													11
Marchant's Passage	8	1	1											10
Howell's Court	7													7
Selden's Court	5					1								6
Somerset Street	4	9	4		1									18
Newark Street			1											1
Dorchester Street		2	5											7
Bean Street		1	2		1									4
Hot Bath Street		2	6	2										10
St James Parade		1	13	22	4									40
Peter Street	7	16	7		2									32
Wine Street	8	5												13
Amery Lane	6	7												13
St James Court	18													18
Corn Street	6	22	13	1										42
Brimble's Court	4	3												7
Bolwell's Court	4	3												7
Margarets Passage	6													6
Ambury	4	4												5
Broad Quay	7		2											9
Narrow Quay	5	4	1	1										11
Hacklebridge's Court	6													6
Little Corn Street	16		5											21
Back Street	18	1	3											22

APPENDIX H

Street														Total
St James Street	1	2	2	5	1						1			11
Abbeygate Street		2	2	1		2								7
Swallow Street		2	1											3
Abbey Green		2	4	2			1							9
Lilliput Alley		2	2	1										5
Abbey Street			1	5	2				1					9
Churchyard											1			3*
Abbey Passage	1	1	1	2									2	6*
The Walks		3	6	5	1	2			1					18*
Gallaway Buildings		2	5	1	2									10
North Parade				2	2	5	2			2	1		1	15*
Duke Street			3	5	2	1								11*
South Parade				1	4	4	1				2			14*
Pierrepoint Street		3	6	3	2	1	1						1	16*
Pierrepoint Place														3
Orchard Street	5	3	3								1	2		18
Henry Street		10	6	1	1									11
Philip Street			15	1		2								20
Behind End of Philip St	4	4	2	1										15
York Street	1	8	6	2	2		1							21
Total(1) (omits streets marked *)	171	127	139	37	15	4	3	8	2		1	4	576
Total(2)	172	131	152	51	29	6	8	4			5	8	659
Avon Street(3)	49	81	5	1									198
Milk Street(4)	43	14	3	2									
Total (1+3+4)	263	222	147	76	35	15	4	3	2		1	4	774

Source: *Rate Book for Cleansing and Lighting*, 1839; *Highway Rate Book, Walcot*, 1830, GAB.

APPENDIX I

POPULATION IN BATH AND ITS SURBURBAN PARISHES, 1801–51

Parish	1801	1811	1821	1831	1841	1851
St James (1)	3,962	5,253	6,278	5,848	6,194	5,861
St Michael (2)	3,700	2,916	3,462	3,526	3,336	3,022
St Peter and Paul (3)	2,465	2,767	3,025	2,666	2,574	2,764
Bathwick (4)	2,727	3,172	4,009	4,033	4,972	5,162
Lyncombe and Widcombe (5)	2,790	3,740	5,880	8,704	9,920	9,974
Walcot (6)	17,559	20,560	24,046	26,023	26,210	27,471
TOTAL	33,196	38,408	46,700	50,800	53,206	54,254
%	–	+15.7	+21.5	+8.7	+4.7	+1.9
Total for (1), (2) and (3)	10,127	10,936	12,765	12,040	12,104	11,647
% change	–	+8	+16.9	–5.7	+0.5	–3.8
Total for (4), (5) and (6)	23,060	27,472	33,935	38,760	41,102	42,607
% change	–	+19	+23.5	+14.1	+6	+3.6

Source: *Census of Population 1801–51.*

NOTES

Abbreviations used in the notes

AN	Avon Navigation
BEC	Bathwick Estate Collection
BM	British Museum (Library)
BRL	Bath Reference Library
CRO	County Record Office
GAB	Guildhall Archives Bath
MO	Montague Manuscripts
PEP	Pulteney Estate Papers
PRO	Public Record Office
PU	Pulteney Manuscripts
SCC	Somerset County Council
ST.	Stowe Collection
UNE	University of New England

Chapter 1 By way of introduction

1 Laurence Sterne, *The Life and Opinions of Tristram Shandy, Gentleman,* first published 1759–67, Penguin edition, 1967, p. 64.
2 Quoted in Manuel Castells, *The Urban Question, A Marxist Approach,* London, 1977, p. 452.

Chapter 2 The company and the size of the market

1 Anon., *A Step to the Bath with a Character of the Place*, 1700.
2 *The Correspondence of Alexander Pope*, ed. George Sherburn, Oxford, 1956, vol. 1, p. 260 (6 October 1714).
3 Mrs Mary Chandler, *The Description of Bath, A Poem*, Leake, Bath, 5th edition, 1741, p. 4.
4 Sarah Robinson to Matthew Robinson, 1 October 1749, MO 5160, Huntington Library, California.
5 William Oliver, *A Practical Dissertation on Bath Waters*, London, 1707, *passim*.
6 Robert Peirce, *Bath Memoirs: or Observations in Three and Forty Years Practice at the Bath*, Bath, 1697, pp. 192–3.
7 *Ibid.*
8 *Ibid.*
9 Elizabeth Montague to Sarah Scott (Robinson), 29 July 1760, MO 5785, *loc. cit.*
10 Sarah Scott (Robinson) to Elizabeth Montague, June 1720, MO 5281, *loc. cit.*
11 William Oliver, *op. cit.* p. 70.
12 Anon., *op. cit.*
13 Elizabeth Montague to the Duchess of Portland, 4 January 1740, MO 293, *loc. cit.*
14 Elizabeth Montague to the Duchess of Portland, January 1740, MO 293, *loc. cit.*
15 Elizabeth Montague to Sarah Scott (Robinson), August 1740, MO 5539, *loc. cit.*
16 *Ibid.*
17 Sarah Scott (Robinson) to Elizabeth Montague, 14 November 1743, MO 5179, *loc. cit.*
18 Sarah Scott (Robinson) to Elizabeth Montague, December 1743, MO 5181, *loc. cit.*
19 William Freind to Elizabeth Montague, 28 August 1740, M40, MO 979 and 22 November 1741, MO 984, *loc. cit.*
20 Sarah Scott (Robinson) to Elizabeth Montague, 1753, MO 5231, *loc. cit.*
21 Elizabeth Montague to Sarah Scott (Robinson), September 1752, MO 5729, *loc. cit.*
22 Philip Thicknesse to John Cooke, 10 November 1773, Th. 85, Huntington Library.
23 Elizabeth Montague to Sarah Scott (Robinson), September 1750, MO 5719, *loc. cit.*

24 John Beresford (ed.), *Diary of a Country Parson*, Oxford, 1926, vol. I, 1758–81, p. 114.
25 *Ibid.*, p. 258.
26 Howard Coombs and Arthur N. Bax, *Journal of a Somerset Rector 1772–1839*, London, 1930, p. 231.
27 Sarah Scott (Robinson) to Elizabeth Montague, 6 November 1755, MO 5251, *loc. cit.*
28 Richard Steele, *The Spectator.*
29 David Foxon, *Libertine Literature in England 1660–1745*, New York, 1965, pp. 15–17.
30 Thomas Stretzer, *A New Description of Merryland*, Bath, 1741, p. 26.
31 Foxon, *op. cit.*, pp. 15–17.
32 Thomas Stretzer, *Merryland Displayed or, Plagiarism, Ignorance and Impudence Detected. Being Observations upon a Pamphlet Intitled A New Description of Merryland*, Bath, 1741, p. 3.
33 *Ibid.*, p. 5.
34 Samuel Richardson, *A Collection of the Moral and Instructive Sentiments . . . Contained in the Histories of Pamela, Clarissa, and Sir Charles Grandison*, London, 1750, p. vi.
35 *The Orrery Papers, 1903*, vol. I, pp. 99–100, quoted in John Kite, 'Libraries in Bath 1618–1964', unpublished thesis, Bath Reference Library, 1966, p. 16. See also T. C. Duncan Eaves and Ben D. Kimpel, *Samuel Richardson – A Biography*, Clarendon Press, 1971.
36 Quoted in *ibid.*, p. 74.
37 Kite, *op. cit.*, pp. 39–45.
38 Lewis Melville, *Bath Under Beau Nash*, London, 1907, p. 50.
39 Robert Halsband (ed.), *Complete Letters of Lady Mary Wortley Montague*, Oxford, 1966, vol. II, p. 57, Lady Mary to Lady Mar, September 1725.
40 John Wood, *A Description of Bath*, 2nd edition, London, 1745, pp. 446–53. Also Lewis Melville, *op. cit.*, pp. 194–9.
41 Oliver Goldsmith, *The Life of Richard Nash*, London, 1762, p. iv. See also Lewis Melville, *Bath Under Beau Nash*, London, 1907.
42 Sarah Scott (Robinson) to Elizabeth Montague, 17 November 1754, MO 5245, *loc. cit.*
43 *Bath Quarter Sessions Books*, 1686–1723 and 1724–42, GAB.
44 Melville, *op. cit.*, p. 201.
45 *Business Before Mayor*, 1787, GAB.
46 Goldsmith, *op. cit.*, p. 127.
47 *John Wesley's Journal*, Everyman's Library Edition, vol. I, p. 413.
48 *Christianity in Somerset*, ed. Robert Dunning, SCC, 1976, p. 68.
49 Stephen Tuck, *Wesleyan Methodism in Frome*, Rylands Library Manchester, reference given to me by Jane Leiden, Bath.

50 Rev. Joseph Hunter, *The Connection of Bath with The Literature and Science of England*, Bath, 1853, p. 23.
51 G. Monkland, *The Literature and Literati of Bath*, Bath, 1854, p. 3.
52 A Barbeau, *Life and Letters at Bath in the Eighteenth Century*, London, 1904, p. 297.
53 Georges Lamoine, '*La Vie Littéraire De Bath et De Bristol 1750–1800*', Thesis, University of Paris III, 1975, p. 664.
54 *Ibid.*, p. 86.
55 Howard Erskine Hill, *The Social Milieu of Alexander Pope*, Yale, 1975, pp. 228, 233.
56 Ellis Waterhouse, 'Bath and Gainsborough', *Apollo*, November 1973, p. 362.
57 E. P. Thompson, 'Patrician society, Plebeian culture', *Journal of Social History*, vol. 7, 1974, pp. 382–405.
58 Tobias Smollett, *The Expedition of Humphrey Clinker* (1771), 1966 edition, Oxford, pp. 36–7.
59 Philip Thicknesse to John Cooke, 10 November 1773, Th. 85, Huntington Library.
60 Philip Thicknesse, *Valetudinarian's Bath Guide*, Bath, 1780, p. 16.
61 Philip Thicknesse to John Cooke, 1780 or 1783, Th. 194 and Th. 204, *loc. cit.*
62 George Lichtenberg to Friedrich Herschel, 12 January 1783, in G. C. Lichtenberg, *Briefe*, Leipzig, 1902, vol. II, p. 65 (reprint 1965). Reference and translation by Klaus Loewald, Department of History, UNE Armidale, NSW.
63 A. J. Turner, *Science and Music in Eighteenth Century Bath*, Bath, 1977, part iv.
64 Private communication from Hugh Torrens, Department of Geology, Keele University.
65 *The Works and Correspondence of David Ricardo*, ed., Piero Sraffa, Cambridge, 1933, vol. x, pp. 7, 35–6.
66 Clement Shorter, *Charlotte Bronte and her Circle*, p. 399.
67 Robert Halsband (ed.), *op. cit.*, vol. II, p. 84.
68 Wood, *op. cit.*, p. 446.
69 Barbeau, *op. cit.*, pp. 50, 308.
70 William Tyte, *Bath in the Eighteenth Century*, Bath, 1903, p. 28.
71 Private communication from Dr John Chartres, School of Economics, Leeds University.
72 James Brydges, Duke of Chandos. Four volumes of accounts with his brokers. Huntington Library, San Marino, California. ST. 12, vol. 1–4.
73 Sylvia McIntyre, 'Towns as Health and Pleasure Resorts: Bath, Scarborough and Weymouth, 1700–1815', unpublished D Phil thesis, Oxford, 1973.

NOTES TO PAGES 42–66

74 The Avon Navigation Accounts, AN 23/7, 8, 9, 10. British Transport Historical Records, London.
75 Bath Corporation Accounts, Bath City Rate Books, 1771–1800, GAB.
76 Alehouse Recognisance Books and Quarter Session Books, GAB.
77 Estimates of Value of Real Property, *Census of Population*, 1831.
78 Bernard Mandeville, *The Fable of The Bees: or Private Vices, Publick Benefits*, Penguin edition, 1970.

Chapter 3   The labouring population

1 Quoted in John Wood, *A Description of Bath*, 2nd edition, London, 1745.
2 The following discussion is based upon entries in *Inrolment of Apprentices Book 1706–1776*, in Box, *Merchant Tailors of Bath 1666–1878*, GAB.
3 *Sessions Books*, 233, GAB. See relevant years for quotations in this paragraph.
4 Benjamin Boyce, *The Benevolent Man*, Harvard, 1967; Bryan Little, *Bath Portrait*, Bristol, 1961; David Gadd, *Georgian Summer*, Bath, 1971, pp. 35–6. See also *Ralph Allen's Own Narrative*, ed. A. E. Hopkins, London, 1961, pp. 22–5.
5 The principal sources for the life and activities of Richard Marchant the elder and younger are: GAB, *Inrolment of Apprentices Book 1706–1776; Minute and Record Book of Merchant Taylors, 1666–1735; Freeman's Book, 1697–1775; Lunatics Estate Account; John Jeffrey's Account Books, 1751–1762;* British Museum, Egerton MS. 3647, fol. 136–7; *Bath Chronicle*, 4 August, 1774; *Chandos' Accounts with his Brokers*, vol. 4, ST. 12, Huntington Library, San Marino, California.
6 *A Brief Account of Many of the Prosecutions of the People Call'd Quakers*, London, 1736, pp. 102–4; William Sewel, *The History of The Rise, Increase and Progress of the Christian People Called Quakers*, 3rd edition, New Jersey, 1774, pp. 651–7.
7 Sir John Dalrymple, *Memoirs of Great Britain and Ireland*, London, 1753, part one, vol. 1, Appendix, p. 52.
8 British Museum, Egerton MS. 3647, fol. 105–11.
9 Mrs Frances Vaughan to John Sommerset, A1 983, BRL.
10 Robert Barclay, *An Apology for the True Christian Divinity*, 6th edition, London, 1736, pp. 536–9.
11 Egerton MS. 3647, fol. 111, *loc. cit.*
12 *Bath Chronicle*, 4 August 1774.
13 This account of the Company of Merchant Taylors is based on material contained in Box, *Merchant Tailors of Bath, 1666–1878*, GAB.
14 *Ibid.*, Merchant Taylors v Glazby.
15 *Ibid.*, Bundle 114.

16 *Ibid.*, Letter to Bath Corporation, September 1765.
17 *Bath Chronicle*, 11 May 1775.
18 Petition, February 1752. *Merchant Tailors of Bath, 1666–1878.*
19 *Quarter Sessions Records*, Box 1776–1824, 28 September 1784, GAB.
20 Based on *Examinations Before Justices of the Peace*, Bath, 1763 and 1772–4; Walcot, 1766–7 and 1816–20; St Michael, 1811–1920; St James, 1823.
21 J. Anthony Williams (ed.), *Post Reformation Catholicism in Bath*, Catholic Record Society, 1975, vol. I, pp. 75–80; vol. II, Registers, pp. 28–33.
22 *Bath Examinations*, 1774.
23 *St Michael's Examinations*, 1817.
24 *Sessions Book*, 1724–42; August 1725.
25 *St Michael's Examinations*, 1820.
26 *Walcot Examinations*, 1817.
27 St James Parish Records, *Apprenticeship Indentures and Orders of Removal*, GAB.
28 Wood, *op. cit.* and *Ralph Allen's Own Narrative* ed. A. E. Hopkins, London, 1961.
29 Based on R. S. Neale, 'The standard of living, 1780–1844; a regional and class study', *Economic History Review*, second series, vol. XIX, no. 3, 1966, and R. S. Neale, 'Economic Conditions and Working Class Movements in the City of Bath, 1800–50', MA thesis, Bristol, 1962. See, also, Appendices D and E.
30 *Bath Herald*, 24 February 1801.
31 *Bath Herald*, 11 July 1800.
32 *Bath Herald*, 18 March 1800.
33 *Committee Book, St Peter and Paul and St James Poor House*, 8 August 1800, GAB.
34 *Business Before the Mayor*, vol. 1, 1777–8, vol. 2, 1781–93, GAB.
35 *Quarter Sessions Records*, 17 July 1778, *loc. cit.*
36 Philip Thicknesse to John Cooke, 10 November 1773, Th.85, Huntington Library.
37 Williams, *op. cit.*, vol. 1, pp. 67–9 and *Examinations Before Coroner*, 12 June 1780, GAB.
38 *Quarter Sessions Records*, Presentment, 28 September 1784 and *Business Before Mayor*, 1790.
39 *Examinations Before Coroner*, GAB.
40 Quoted in William Tyte, *Bath in the Eighteenth Century*, Bath, 1903, p. 29.

Chapter 4   Landowners and peasants

1 Henry Chapman, *Thermae Redivivae: The City of Bath Described*, Bath, 1673.

2 'The History of the Desertion', in *Collection of State Tracts*, London, 1705, vol. 1, pp. 78–9. Other versions of the skirmish place the number of dead at fifteen, including only four on the King's side. However, the fact that thirty of the Prince's force fired at least four volleys almost point blank into the ranks of 120 horse packed into a narrow lane suggests that the number killed must have been rather more than four. I am indebted to the Rev. J. Everett of Wincanton for supplying me with a copy of G. Sweetman, *Wincanton during the Civil Wars*, n.d.

3 A. W. B. Simpson, *Introduction to the History of Land Law*, Oxford, 1961. Also Eugène Kamenka and R. S. Neale (eds), *Feudalism, Capitalism and Beyond*, London, 1975, pp. 94–100.

4 *Survey Book of the Lands of George Dodington Esq., in the County of Somerset*, 1713, ST. 173, and *An Estimate and Valuation of the Several MANORS and Estates belonging to his Grace the most noble James Duke of Chandos Situate in the County of Somerset, July 1773* and *Rodney Stoke, Calculation of Value in Fee*, December 1781, ST. Brydges, L8G5, Huntington Library, San Marino, California.

5 An Abstract of William Snygges Lease, DD/DT B x 3; *The Survey of Walcot, 1638*, B.R./Sb N68. Both in CRO, Taunton, Somerset. Also *Rodney Stoke, Calculation of Value in Fee*, December 1781, ST. Brydges, L8G5, *loc. cit.*

6 Indenture, 29 April 1745, DD/BR/PY Box 4, CRO, Taunton.

7 Index to the plan of Walcot parish drawn by Thomas Thorp, 1740. MS. no. 516, Walcot Estate Papers, BRL.

8 Private communication from Patricia Croot.

9 See below, chapter 4.

10 MS. 1809, Pulteney Estate Papers, BRL. Also Indenture, 4 May 1736, DD/BR rjf, CRO, Taunton.

11 Sylvia McIntyre, 'Towns as Health and Pleasure Resorts: Bath, Scarborough and Weymouth, 1700–1815', unpublished DPhil thesis, Oxford, 1973, p. 119.

12 Egerton MS. 3647, fol. 14 and fol. 113, BM; Indentures, 10–11 October 1726, 21 October 1726, 25–26 October 1726, ST. Brydges, L8H6, Huntington Library; Egerton MS. 3647, fol. 11–13, BM; Indenture, 31 March 1731, DD/ML 20, CRO, Taunton and Indenture, 10 October 1753, Box 1775–76, GAB.

13 Indenture, 19 April 1784, GAB.

14 John Wood, *A Description of Bath*, 2nd edition, London, 1745, p. 247. For the Corporation's opposition to Harrison's Assembly Rooms see McIntyre, *op. cit.*, p. 128.

15 Indenture, 25 December 1731, DD/X/OBN C243 Pt of 2, CRO, Taunton.

16 Indenture, 29 January 1745, 16 January 1767, 29 August 1785, DD/BR/PY Box 4, CRO, Taunton.
17 Indenture, 5 September 1700, 4 October 1720, 26 December 1768, 4 August 1779, DD/LO Box 4, CRO, Taunton.
18 Particulars of capital freehold and leasehold estates, Hensley Family Deeds, GAB.
19 Wood, *op. cit.*, pp. 316, 325, 334; Indenture, 31 March 1731, DD/ML 20, CRO, Taunton; Indenture 10 October 1753, Box 1775–6, GAB.
20 Indenture, 24 June 1761, DD/SAS C120 6, CRO, Taunton.

Chapter 5   Stockjobbers and entrepreneurs

1 T. S. Ashton, *Economic Fluctuations in England 1700–1800*, London, 1959, Statistical Table 23, J. Parry Lewis, *Building Cycles and Britain's Growth*, London, 1965, T. Machin, 'The great rebuilding: re-assessment', *Past and Present*, no. 77, November, 1977. The peaks in building identified by these authors are:

Ashton	Parry Lewis	Machin	Neale (Bath)
1701			
1707	1705	1703	1707
1716–18	1724	1714	1718
1730		1720–21	1732
1739	1736	1727	1743
1753	1753	1739	1755
1760		1754	1758–9
1776	1776	1758	1771
		1767	
		1774	

2 *Chamberlain's Accounts*, GAB.
3 An 23/4, British Transport Historical Records, London.
4 An 1/1A Minutes, 5 April 1725, *loc. cit.*
5 *Ibid.*, 18 February 1726.
6 *Ibid.*, 15 July 1727.
7 John Wood, *A Description of Bath*, 2nd edition, London, 1745, p. 241 and Chandos to Marchant, 6 February 1727, Brydges Correspondence, ST. 57, Huntington Library, California.
8 See C. H. Collins Baker and Muriel Baker, *James Brydges, First Duke of*

Chandos, Oxford, 1949. Also R. E. Scouller, *The Armies of Queen Anne*, Oxford, 1966, pp. 41, 42, 183.

9 *Report of a Committee appointed by the Commons to enquire into the State of the public accounts*, 4 April 1711, quoted in J. Robinson, *The Princely Chandos*, London, 1893, p. 12.

10 Godfrey Davies, 'The Seamy Side of Marlborough's Wars', *Huntington Library Quarterly*, vol. 15, 1951–2, pp. 21–44. Cadogan's letter dated 17–28 April 1707 quoted on p. 26 reads, 'I am persuaded this matter is so settled that we shall turn fifteen or sixteen thousand pund a month at 2 per cent, clear of all charges. I would not indicate a greater sum for these two reasons. First, I could not conveniently manage it; and in the second place, too great a sum would alarm Sir Harry Furness and Sweet.' See also H. L. Snyder (ed.), *Marlborough Godolphin Correspondence*, Oxford, 1975, pp. 568–609 *passim*, and H. T. Dickson, *Bolingbroke*, London, 1970, pp. 13, 46, 83.

11 All figures and calculations relating to Chandos's dealings with his brokers are from four volumes of his accounts held by the Huntington Library, San Marino, California, ST. 12, vols 1–4. Entries for specific brokers may be identified through the alphabetical index contained in each volume.

12 Alice Clare Carter, *Getting, Spending and Investing in Early Modern Times*, Van Goren, 1975. Analyses of public indebtedness in eighteenth-century England, pp. 11–19.

13 P. G. M. Dickson, *The Financial Revolution in England, A Study in the Development of Public Credit 1688–1756*, Macmillan, 1967, p. 138, referring to the *London Journal*, 20–27 February, 1720.

14 Chandos to Cantillon, 27 September 1720, Brydges Correspondence, ST. 57, Huntington Library, California.

15 Chandos's accounts under Pels et Fils.

16 Chandos to Henrick, 18 October 1720, Brydges Correspondence, *loc. cit.*

17 Chandos to Cantillon, 28 September 1720, Brydges Correspondence, *loc. cit.*

18 *Abstract of The Several Estates*, 1719–20, ST. 20, Huntington Library, California.

19 John Macky, *A Journey Through England*, London, 1722.

20 Young, *Imperium Pelagi*, London, 1730.

21 Baker and Baker, *op. cit.*, p. 299.

22 *Ibid.*, p. 299.

23 Chandos to Marchant, 29 June 1726, Brydges Correspondence, *loc. cit.*

24 Chandos to Marchant, 13 July 1726, Brydges Correspondence, *loc. cit.*

25 Indentures, 10–11 October 1726, 15–26 October 1726, 21 October 1727, in ST. Brydges Land Papers, L8H6 *loc. cit.*

26 *Ibid.*, also 19 November 1726 and a draft 1727, ST. 57, vol. 28, July

1726–July 1727 and ST. 12, vol. 4, Anne Phillips's and Charles Stuart's account with Chandos, *loc. cit.*
27 Chandos to Marchant, 30 July 1726, Brydges Correspondence, *loc. cit.*
28 Chandos to Wood, 24 May 1727, Brydges Correspondence, *loc. cit.*
29 Chandos to Wood, 19 August 1727, Brydges Correspondence, *loc. cit.*
30 Chandos to Wood, 29 December 1727, Brydges Correspondence, *loc. cit.*
31 Chandos to Wood, 16 December 1727, Brydges Correspondence, *loc. cit.*
32 Chandos to Wood, 20 September 1729, Brydges Correspondence, *loc. cit.*
33 Chandos to Wood, 21 December 1727, Brydges Correspondence, *loc. cit.*
34 Wood's account with Chandos, ST. 12, vol. 4, *loc. cit.*
35 *Ibid.*, Theobald's account with Chandos.
36 Chandos to Theobald, 1 July 1729, Brydges Correspondence, *loc. cit.*
37 Chandos to Wood, 23 November 1729, Brydges Correspondence, *loc. cit.*
38 Chandos to Theobald, 8 November 1728, Brydges Correspondence, *loc. cit.*
39 Benjamin Boyce, *The Benevolent Man, A Life of Ralph Allen of Bath*, Harvard, 1967, pp. 40–4 and, Allen to Tims, 26 June 1731 and 12 August 1732, St Bartholomew's Hospital Archives, Ha 19/29/12.
40 Anne Phillips's and Jane Degge's accounts with Chandos, ST. 12, vol. 4, *loc. cit.*. The total, £2,906, also includes payment of Mrs Tynte's annuity.
41 Chandos to Marchant, 6 February and 6 April 1727, Brydges Correspondence, *loc. cit.*
42 John Wood, *An Essay Toward a Description of Bath*, 2nd edition, London, 1765, part III, pp. 343–7.
43 Chandos to Henrick, 18 October 1720, Brydges Correspondence, *loc. cit.*
44 Particulars of fee farm rents and leasehold ground rents, 1787 and Indenture, 1 November 1754, GAB. Indenture, 30 April 1768, DD/BR/PY Box 4 and Indenture, 29 October 1767, CRO, Taunton. Indenture, 20 December 1766, Wood Bundle, BRL.
45 Indenture, 11 April 1771, GAB.
46 Indenture, 29 September, 21 December 1763, 24 December 1778 in Boxes 1754–61, 1763, 1778, and Bathwick Estate Records, GAB. See also C. W. Chalklin, *The Provincial Towns of Georgian England*, London, 1974.
47 Particulars of fee farm rents and leasehold ground rents, 1787, *loc. cit.* This source is the basis for the argument in this and the ensuing paragraph.
48 Chalklin, *op. cit.*, Appendix V.
49 Letters of Ralph Allen, 26 June 1731, 31 May 1732, 8 July 1732, 12 August 1732 and various bills and accounts in St Bartholomew's Hos-

pital Archives, Ha 19/1a, Ha 19/7, Ha 19/29, Ha 19/30. See also Sir D'Arcy Power, 'The rebuilding of the hospital in the eighteenth century', *St Bartholomew's Hospital Reports*, vol. LIX, 1926 and LX, 1927.
50 Banker's Draft Book for the year 1792, Stock no. 8112, Class B690. John Eveleigh's Capital Ledger No. 6. An Abstract of Mr Eveleigh's Accounts, Stock No. B690 BRL.
51 This account is based on, The account of all the estate of Richard Jones, Box 1768–72, GAB.
52 Benjamin Boyce, *The Benevolent Man*, Harvard, 1967, p. 46 and Ralph Allen and Buckeridge MS. p. 14, BRL.
53 Indentures, 29 October 1747 and 11 August 1748, Wood Box, GAB.
54 Indentures, 5 February 1757, 18 October 1759, 29 October 1763, 29 May 1765, 17 December 1768, 11 April 1771, 11 October 1771, and Draft Agreement 21 August 1770, Wood Box, GAB.
55 Indenture, 11 January 1771, GAB.
56 Indenture, 20 December 1766 referring to agreement on 22 September 1764 and John Wood to John Jeffreys, 21 May 1770, Walcot Estate Papers, BRL.
57 James Rivers to William Drake, 25 July 1771, Walcot Estate Papers, AL1672, *loc. cit.*
58 The main source for Jeffrey's activities is his Account Book, 1751–62, GAB. But he is also referred to in many indentures relating to John Wood, particularly in Box 1780, GAB and in the Walcot Estate Papers.
59 Indenture, 25 February 1781, Box 1780, GAB.
60 Indentures, 5 July 1772 and 30 March 1773, GAB.
61 Indentures, 29 December 1807 and 3 November 1813, DD/BR/MMD C/1232, CRO, Taunton.
62 Chalklin *op. cit.* p. 183, footnote 100, also Fielder and Beale's Valuation of Houses, n.d., relating to the claims of the parishioners of St Michael's versus the city of Bath (1780s), GAB.
63 A further discussion of interest rates is in R. S. Neale, 'Society, belief and the building of Bath, 1700–1793' in C. W. Chalklin and M. A. Havinden, *Rural Change and Urban Growth 1500–1800*, London, 1974. See also appendix B.

Chapter 6 Ideology and Utopia

1 Manuel Castells, *The Urban Question, A Marxist Approach*, London, 1977, p. 430.
2 Some authors expressing views about Bath are: Walter Ison, *The Georgian Buildings of Bath from 1700 to 1830*, London, 1948; John Summerson, *Architecture in Britain, 1530–1830*, Harmondsworth, 1953; Nikolaus Pev-

sner, *An Outline of European Architecture*, Harmondsworth, 1960, p. 581; John Fleming, Hugh Honour and Nikolaus Pevsner, *The Penguin Dictionary of Architecture*, Harmondsworth, 1966, p. 242; Fritz Baumgat, *A History of Architectural Styles*, London, 1970, pp. 255–6; Colin and Rose Bell, *City Fathers: The Early History of Town Planning in Britain*, Harmondsworth, 1972.
3   Karl Mannheim, *Ideology and Utopia: An Introduction to the Sociology of Knowledge*, London, 1972, pp. 49–87.
4   *Quarter Sessions Book 233* (inside of back cover), GAB, also Sylvia McIntyre, 'Towns as Health and Pleasure Resorts: Bath, Scarborough and Weymouth, 1700–1815', unpublished DPhil thesis, Oxford, 1973, p. 38.
5   *Quarter Sessions Book 233*, May 1709.
6   *Chamberlain's Accounts*, GAB, loc. cit.
7   *Minute Books of Bath Corporation*, GAB.
8   Ison, *op. cit.*, p. 152.
9   Indenture, 31 August 1765, Box 1764–67, GAB.
10 John Wood, *An Essay Towards a Description of Bath*, 2nd edition, London, 1765, p. 353.
11 Jean Duvignaud, *The Sociology of Art*, London, 1972, p. 51.
12 A dialect version was included in an appendix to Guidott, *Collection of Treatises*. Another version was inscribed on Gilmore's map of Bath and there was an inscription on a tablet in the Hot Bath. See especially, H. C. Lewis, *Bladud of Bath*, first printed 1919, reprinted by West Country editions, Bath, 1973.
13 Wood, *op. cit.*, p. 40.
14 *Ibid.*, p. 54.
15 *Ibid.*, p. 48.
16 *Ibid.*, p. 57.
17 *Ibid.*, p. 121.
18 *Ibid.*, p. 125.
19 *Ibid.*, p. 53.
20 *Ibid.*, pp. 56–7.
21 Erwin Panofsky, *Renaissance and Renascences in Western Art*, London, 1970, p. 84.
22 Advertisement for *The Origin of Building: or, The Plagiarism of the Heathens Detected*, London and Bath, 1741, in *A Description of the Exchange at Bristol*, Bath, 1745, p. 37.
23 *Origin*, p. 71.
24 Wood, *op. cit.*, p. 238.
25 *Ibid.*, p. 240.
26 John Wood, *A Dissertation Upon The Orders of Columns*, London, 1750, p. 27.
27 *Ibid.*, p. 30.

28 Wood, *Essay*, p. 345.
29 *Ibid.*, p. 351.
30 Inigo Jones, *Stonheng – Restored*, London, 1655, p. 11.
31 *Ibid.*, p. 67.
32 Webb, *Stonheng Restored with the Chorea Gigantum or Stoneheng restored to the Danes*, 2nd edition, London, 1725, pl. 38.
33 Wood, *Essay*, p. 240.
34 Summerson, *op. cit.*, p. 30.
35 Anon., *Bath, – A Simile*, 1779.
36 *Ibid.*
37 Indenture, 5 January 1749, GAB.
38 Indenture, 29 October 1767, DD/X/STU, CRO, Taunton.
39 William Tyte, *Bath in the Eighteenth Century*, Bath, 1903, pp. 28–9.
40 *The Correspondence of Jonathan Swift*, ed. Harold Williams, Oxford, 1965, vol. IV, p. 475, 22 April 1736.
41 *Sessions Record Books, passim*, GAB.
42 *Ibid.*, 1756.
43 30Geo II C65.
44 *Sessions Record Book*, June 1755. For the distribution of alehouses see Alehouse Recognisance Books, GAB.
45 J. Mansford to Improvement Commissioners, January 1786, Improvement Commission Records, GAB.
46 *Bath Chronicle*, November 1764 to August 1765, *passim*.
47 *Ibid.*, 6 December 1764.
48 *Ibid.*, 10 November 1774.
49 *Ibid.*, 17 November 1774.
50 *Ibid.*, 8 December 1774.

Chapter 7 Property and absolute self-interest

1 Bathwick Estate Company Papers, Indenture, 12 March 1757, GAB.
2 Sir John Sinclair quoted in L.T.C. Rolt, *Thomas Telford*, London, 1958, p. 17.
3 *Ibid.*, p. 17.
4 George Dempster to William Pulteney, 2 October 1764, PU 143, Huntington Library, California.
5 MS. 1809, *Pulteney Estate Papers*, Bundle 6, BRL.
6 *Ibid.*
7 AL 1788, PEP, 23 August 1769, *loc. cit.*
8 Private Act of Parliament, 1769.
9 AL 1788, *loc. cit.*
10 *Ibid.*

11 *Ibid.*
12 Preamble to Private Act 1774 and Indenture 2 June 1770, PEP.
13 MS. 1806 and 1807 and Private Act 1772, PEP.
14 MS. 1806 and 1807, PEP.
15 MS. 1820, PEP.
16 James Adam to William Pulteney, 31 July 1770, PU 4, Huntington Library, California.
17 MS. 1813, Agreement dated 17 May 1771, PEP.
18 Preamble to the Private Act of 1772.
19 See Note 16.
20 Mayor, Alderman and Common Council to William Pulteney, n.d., PU 57, Huntington Library, California.
21 Letter to William Pulteney, 24 August 1770, PU 8, Huntington Library, California.
22 Petition re Pulteney Bridge, 4 July 1777 with seventeen signatures, *Quarter Sessions* Box, 1776–1824, GAB.
23 *Bath Chronicle*, 13 January – 8 September 1774, *passim*.
24 *Council Minutes*, February 1771, p. 181.
25 *Bath Turnpike Records*, 12 January 1771, vol. 2 of Minutes 1770–1776, D/T/6a7, CRO, Taunton.
26 *Council Minutes*, 1774, vol. 9, pp. 324–6, *Bath Turnpike Records*, 21 January to 3 March 1774, D/T/6a7, CRO, Taunton. Also Pulteney's letter to Turnpike Commissioners, 22 February 1774, same location.
27 Indenture, 26 March 1788, BEC in GAB.
28 Indenture with William Hulance, March 1790, BEC in GAB.
29 Various Indentures, BEC in GAB, especially 1 April 1788 with William Matthews, George Clark and William Phillips.
30 *Ibid.*
31 Indentures 6 June 1794, Bundle no. 2, Acc. 44, BEC in GAB. and 21 April 1791, DD/X/SAL C1537, CRO, Taunton.
32 Petition from Sir James Pulteney and Henrietta Pulteney 1798, PU 1436, Huntington Library, California.
33 Nathaniel Bayley to Sir James Pulteney, 30 July 1802, PU 65, Huntington Library, California.
34 John Eveleigh, Ledger no. 6, p. 91, BRL.
35 *Ibid.*
36 Articles of Agreement, 4 August 1794 in my possession. See R. S. Neale, 'An equitable trust in the building industry in 1794', *Business History*, vol. VII, no. 2, July 1965.
37 John Eveleigh's Ledger, no. 6, and Abstract of Mr Eveleigh's Account, Stock No. B690, BRL.
38 Indentures, 10 March 1792, 14 October 1792, 24 October 1792, 6 November 1792, 19 November 1792, BRL.

39 Bankers Draft Book, Stock no. 8112, Class B690, BRL.
40 Long Acre Institute and Deeds 2561, GAB.
41 Indenture, 8 July 1795, Long Acre Institute and Deeds, GAB.
42 A. G. E. Jones, 'The Banks of Bath', *Notes and Queries*, July 1958, pp. 277–83.
43 Complaint of John Lowder v Charles Spackman and Charles Phillot, 29 November 1794, C12 202/30, PRO.
44 John Symons, *Reasons for removing private property from the Hot Baths*, 1783, and another letter, Improvement Commissioners Records, GAB.
45 *Ibid.*
46 *Council Minutes*, 27 September 1784.
47 *Ibid.*, 3 October 1785.
48 *Ibid.*, 6 October 1785.
49 *Ibid.*, 13 March 1788 and Improvement Act, 1789.
50 *Bath Chronicle*, 9 April 1789, 7 May 1789, 21 May 1789, and *Bath Journal*, 6 April 1789. See also *Minutes of Trustees of Bath Turnpike* March to April 1789, D/T/ba8, CRO, Taunton.
51 A View of Bath, *Hunt Pamphlets*, vol. 12, BRL.
52 *Minutes of Improvement Commissioners*, 6 November 1789, GAB.
53 *Ibid.*, 20 May 1791, 15 August 1798, 5 November 1801, 14 April 1802 and a printed proposal dated 3 February 1802, Improvement Commissioners Records, GAB.
54 *Ibid.*, 6 January 1792, 3 February 1792, 23 March 1792.
55 *Report Book 1794–1837*, reports by Telford and Montague in 1825, GAB.
56 C. W. Chalklin, *The Provincial Towns of Georgian England*, London, 1974, pp. 79–80.
57 *Bath Journal*, 8 October 1792.
58 PRO B1 89 fol. 53.
59 W. Bailey, *A List of Bankrupts 1786–1806*, London, 1806. This reference was given to me by Professor L. S. Presnell.
60 *Bath Journal*, 18 March 1793.
61 *Bath Journal*, 7 January 1793, 11 March 1793, 1 April 1793.
Bath Chronicle, 21 March 1793, 4 April 1793, 23 May 1793, 30 May 1793, 6 June 1793, 13 June 1793, 8 August 1793, 5 September 1793, 10 October 1793.
62 Neale, 'An equitable trust in the building industry in 1794'.
63 Improvement Commissioner's Records.
64 A. B. Granville, *The Spas of England, Southern Spas*, London, 1841, pp. 375–431.

Chapter 8 Social structure and economic welfare

1 *Egan's Walks*, 1st edition, 1819, p. 74.
2 *Bath and Cheltenham Gazette*, 12 January 1830.
3 Based on *Census of Population, 1801–51* as analysed in R. S. Neale, 'Economic Conditions and Working Class Movements in the City of Bath, 1800–1850', MA thesis, Bristol, 1963.
4 Overseers copy of list forwarded to the central government, St James parish records, GAB.
5 *Bath Chronicle*, 26 April 1802, 3 May 1802, 1 April 1813; *Bath and Cheltenham Gazette*, 17 May 1813; *Bath Journal* 5 May 1813.
6 *Bath Chronicle*, 25 April 1805, 2 May 1805; *Bath Journal*, 6 May 1805; *Bath Chronicle*, 25 February 1805, 17 April 1813; *Bath and Cheltenham Gazette*, 7 April 1824, 24 May 1825; *Bath Chronicle*, 17 April 1845; also A. Aspinall, *The Early English Trade Unions*, London, 1949, pp. 75–90.
7 R. S. Neale, 'The industries of the city of Bath in the first half of the nineteenth century', *Proceedings of Somersetshire Archaeological and Natural History Society*, 1964, pp. 132–44 and Rate Books for Cleansing and Lighting, St James Parish, 1839.
8 Hugh Torrens, *Stotherts of Bath*, Bath, 1978, and *ibid*.
9 Highway Rate Book, Walcot, 1839.
10 Neale, 'Economic Conditions...', pp. 17–18.
11 *Bath and Cheltenham Gazette*, 5 November 1817.
12 *Ibid.*, 11 October 1815.
13 Quoted in Dorothy George, *London Life in the Eighteenth Century*, London, 1925, p. 200.
14 Briefs, St James, 48381, St James Box, 1809, BRL.
15 *Bath and Cheltenham Gazette*, 21 February 1837.
16 *Ibid.*, 17 February 1819.
17 Briefs, St James, 48381, Cases and Opinions 48389, BRL.
18 Report of the Committee of Investigation on The Bath United Hospital 1866, *Bath Pamphlets*, vol. VI.
19 *Bath and Cheltenham Gazette*, 21 February 1837.
20 R. S. Neale, 'The standard of living 1780–1844; a regional and class study', *Economic History Review*, 2nd series, vol. XIX, number 3, 1966.
21 *Bath Journal*, 17 January 1831.
22 *Bath and Cheltenham Gazette*, 12 January 1841.
23 *Ibid.*, 22 February 1844.
24 Second report of the chairman of the Bath Union (Thomas Spencer) 1 August 1836.
25 *Bath and Cheltenham Gazette*, 4 October 1841.
26 H. A. Bruce (ed.), *Life of Sir William Napier*, London, 1864, p. 404.
27 Bath Vagrancy, *The Bathonian*, February 1849.

28 *Ibid.*
29 *Bath and Cheltenham Gazette*, 1 September 1840.
30 *Report on the Sanitary Condition of the Labouring Population of Great Britain*, 1842, p. 169.
31 *Ibid.*
32 *Ibid.*
33 *Ibid.*, p. 170.
34 *Ibid.*
35 R. Warner, *History of Bath*, Bath, 1801, p. 344.
36 Sylvia McIntyre, 'Towns as Health and Pleasure Resorts: Bath, Scarborough and Weymouth, 1700–1815', unpublished DPhil thesis, Oxford, 1793.
37 Articles of Agreement, 23 March 1767, BRL.
38 R. S. Neale, 'An equitable trust in the building industry in 1794', *Business History*, vol. VII, no. 2, July 1965 and Articles of Agreement, 4 August 1794, author's collection.

Chapter 9 *The consciousness of the people: 1680–1815*

1 I. Anthony Williams (ed.), *Post Reformation Catholicism in Bath*, Catholic Record Society, 1975, Vol. I, p. 38.
2 Charles Tench, *The Western Rising*, London, 1969, pp. 161–80, *passim*.
3 Peter Earle, *Monmouth Rebels*, London, 1977, pp. 175–7; Also J. G. Muddiman (ed.), *The Bloody Assizes*, London, 1929.
4 *A View of Bath, Historical, Political and Chronological, 1813*, Hunt Pamphlets, vol. 12, BRL.
5 Muddiman, *op. cit.*, p. 40.
6 Williams (ed.), *op. cit.*, p. 40.
7 *Ibid.*, p. 43.
8 *Ibid.*, p. 44.
9 John Cannon, 'Bath politics in the eighteenth century', *Somersetshire Archaeological and Natural History Society Proceedings*, 1960–1, vol. 105, pp. 87–105 and Sylvia McIntyre, 'Towns as Health and Pleasure Resorts: Bath, Scarborough and Weymouth, 1700–1815', unpublished DPhil thesis, Oxford 1973, pp. 80–2.
10 Richard Jones, *Life*, p. 23, BRL.
11 Eugène Kamenka and R. S. Neale (eds), *Feudalism, Capitalism and Beyond*, pp. 3–27, 93–102.
12 J. H. Plumb, *The Growth of Political Stability in England 1675–1725*, and 'The growth of the electorate in England from 1600–1715', *Past and Present* no. 45, November 1969.
13 George Rudé, *The Crowd in History, 1730–1848*, London, 1964, p. 59.

14 John Brewer to Sir Stonier Porter, PRO, SP 37/20/362, 15 November 1780.
15 *Bath Chronicle*, 15 June 1780.
16 Williams (ed.) *op. cit.*, p. 70.
17 *Ibid.*, p. 67.
18 J. Caldwell to Secretary of State, PRO, SP 37/21/68–71, 11 June 1780.
19 John Jeffreys to Rt Hon. Earl Hillsborough. PRO, SP 37/21/125–6, 18 June 1780.
20 *Striking Events in the History of Bath*, newspaper cuttings, n.d., BRL.
21 Francis Bennett to the Mayor of Bath, July 1780, PRO, SO 37/21/229. Others found the execution of Butler an unpleasant experience. The Bath Chronicle reported, 'The water drinkers, by whom more than half the inhabitants get their bread, declare they will leave the place for ever, if any more circumstances of horror happen in consequence of the riot.' Quoted in *Striking Events, op. cit.*
22 *Bath Journal*, 12 December 1792; Also the signature book in BRL.
23 Presentment, 30 November 1793, *Quarter Sessions*, Box 1776–1824, GAB.
24 Presentment, 12 August 1794, *loc. cit.*
25 *Ibid*; Also John Trew, who on 8 January 1798 was charged with a breach of the peace and damning the King. He was discharged for want of prosecution. *Quarter Sessions*, 8 January 1798, GAB.
26 *Bath Journal*, 10 December 1792.
27 *Politics for the People*, Pt II, no. IX, 1794.
   Tree of Liberty
In the days of Alfred, we read of the whole
nation reposing under its branches.
28 Philip Thicknesse, *Valetudinarian's Bath Guide*, Bath, 1780.
29 A. Barbeau, *Life and Letters of Bath in the Eighteenth Century*, London, 1904, p. 164.
30 *A Description of Millenium Hall, by a Gentleman on His Travels*, Dublin, 1763. Oliver Goldsmith appears as the nominal author. However, see Elizabeth Mavor, *The Ladies of Llangollen*, London, 1971.
31 *Ibid.*, p. 83.
32 *Ibid.*, p. 83.
33 *Ibid.*
34 *Ibid.*, p. 152.
35 *Ibid.*, p. 160.
36 *Ibid.*, the full title of the book is, *A Description of Millenium Hall As May excite in the Readers proper Sentiments of Humanity, and lead the Mind to the Love of Virtue.*
37 William Ogilvie, *An Essay on the Right of Property in Land*, London, 1782, p. 9.

38 Charles Hall, *The Effects of Civilisation on the People in the European States*, London, 1805.
39 *Ibid.*, pp. 75–6.
40 *Ibid.*, p. 129.
41 *Ibid.*, p. 301.
42 *Ibid.*, p. 170.
43 Charles Hall to Thomas Spence quoted in Olive B. Rudkin, *Thomas Spence and His Connections*, London, 1927, p. 133.
44 *Bath and Cheltenham Gazette*, 22 June 1814. In 1809 there had been 33 societies with a membership of 2,487, *Bath Chronicle*, 26 October 1809.
45 *Bath Chronicle*, 23 March 1775, 13 April 1775, 11 May 1775, 18 May 1775.
46 *Ibid.*, 13 April 1775.
47 Above, Chapter 2, Note 19 and *Bath Chronicle*, 26 April 1802 and 3 May 1802.
48 *Bath Chronicle*, 23 March 1809.
49 *Bath Journal*, 2 July 1792.
50 *Bath and Cheltenham Gazette*, 30 August 1825, 11 October 1825.
51 *Ibid.*, 30 August 1825.
52 *Ibid.*, 30 October 1838, 6 November 1838, 11 December 1838, 3 July 1844; *Bath Chronicle*, 24 July 1845.
53 Record of Convictions and Acquittals, 1724–1812, 1735, GAB.
54 *Bath Journal*, 12 March 1792.
55 *Ibid.*
56 *Quarter Sessions Records*, 19 April 1798, GAB.
57 A. Aspinall, *Early English Trade Unions*, London, 1949.
58 R. S. Neale, 'Economic Conditions and Working Class Movements in the City of Bath, 1800–1850', MA thesis, Bristol, 1963, pp. 170–4. Also Chapter 7, Note 6, and A. Aspinall, *op. cit.*, pp. 75–90.

Chapter 10 A radical Utopia: 1812–47

1 *A View of Bath, Hunt Pamphlets*, vol. 12.
2 *Ibid.*, Frontispiece.
3 *Bath and Cheltenham Gazette*, 28 October 1812.
4 *Ibid.*
5 *Ibid.*
6 *Ibid.*, 28 October 1812.
7 *Ibid.*, 24 February 1812.
8 *Memoirs of Henry Hunt*, London, 1820, vol. 3, pp. 327–420; E. P. Thompson, *The Making of the English Working Class*, London, 1963, pp. 631–7;

The Resolutions and Petitions of the Freeholders, Householders, and Inhabitants of the City of Bath and the Vicinity, 6 January 1817, BRL.
9 Henry Hunt, *op. cit.*
10 *Bath and Cheltenham Gazette*, 16 March 1820.
11 *Ibid.*
12 *Bath Journal*, 12 June 1826.
13 *Ibid.*
14 *Bath and Cheltenham Gazette*, 7 August 1816.
15 R. S. Neale, 'Economic Conditions and Working Class Movements in the City of Bath, 1800–1850', MA thesis, Bristol, 1963, pp. 155–60.
16 *Bath and Cheltenham Gazette*, 18 October 1831.
17 *Ibid.*
18 *Ibid.*
19 *Ibid.*
20 *Ibid.*
21 *Bath Journal*, October to November 1831; *Bath Chronicle*, 3 November 1831; *Bath and Cheltenham Gazette*, November 1831 and 28 August 1832.
22 *Bath and Cheltenham Gazette*, 10 January 1832, 3 April 1832.
23 *Ibid.*, 8 November 1831 and A citizen, *The Bristol Riots*, 2 vols Bristol, 1832, p. 43.
24 *Ibid.*
25 *Ibid.*
26 *Ibid.*
27 *Bath Chronicle*, 17 November 1831.
28 *Bath and Cheltenham Gazette*, 15 May 1832.
29 *Ibid.*
30 *Ibid.*
31 *Ibid.*
32 *Bath Elections*, A collection of newspaper cuttings, pamphlets and posters relating to the 1832 election compiled by Thomas Falconer, p. 10, BRL.
33 *Bath Journal*, 6 July 1832, *Bath and Cheltenham Gazette*, 3 July 1832.
34 *Ibid.*
35 *Bath Elections*, handbill, p. 12.
36 *Ibid.*; *The Times*, 20 September 1832; *Bath and Cheltenham Gazette*, 25 September, 1832; *Examiner* 30 September 1832.
37 R. Eadon Leader, *Autobiography of the Rt. Hon. J. A. Roebuck*, London, 1897, p. 31.
38 *The Times*, 20 September 1832.
39 *Bath Elections* and *Bath and Cheltenham Gazette*, 18 September 1832.
40 *Bath Chronicle*, 13 September 1832.
41 *Bath Elections*, election posters.
42 *Ibid.*
43 *Bath Poll Books*, 1832.

44 *Pamphlets for the People*, no. 22. See also R. S. Neale, *Class and Ideology in The Nineteenth Century*, London, 1972, pp. 75–96 and 'Roebuck's constitution and The Durham proposals', *Historical Studies Australia and New Zealand*, vol. 14, no. 56 (April 1971).
45 *Bath and Cheltenham Gazette*, 31 May 1836.
46 *Bath Chronicle*, 8 July 1841.
47 H. S. Chapman, 'Decay of Whiggism – public opinion in Bath', *Pamphlets for the People*, no. 23.
48 Article on Charles Buller in DNB.
49 H. S. Chapman, 'The people are not to blame', *Pamphlets for the People*, no. 23.
50 *Bath Chronicle*, 12 January 1837.
51 *Bath and Cheltenham Gazette*, 29 December 1835 and *Bath Poll Books*, 1832, 1834, 1837.
52 Tom Paine, *Commonsense*, 1776.
53 *Bath and Cheltenham Gazette*, 28 March 1837; *Bath Chronicle*, 2 March 1837, 9 February 1837, 23 March 1837.
54 William Napier, *Life of General Sir Charles Napier*, London, vol. I, p. 466.
55 Robert G. Gammage, *History of the Chartist Movement*, London, 1894, p. 11.
56 Leader, *op. cit.*, p. 126.
57 *Bath and Cheltenham Gazette*, 17 October 1837.
58 *Ibid.*, 19 December 1837.
59 R. S. Neale, *Class and Ideology in the Nineteenth Century*, London, 1972, pp. 75–96.
60 *Bath Chronicle*, 21 September 1838.
61 *Western Vindicator*, 9 March 1839.
62 *Ibid.*, 24 August 1839.
63 *Bath and Cheltenham Gazette*, 12 November 1839.
64 *Ibid.*, 11 December 1844, and *Bath Chronicle*, 5 December 1844.
65 *Bath Chronicle*, 23 October 1845.
66 *Ibid.*, 22 July 1847.
67 *Ibid.*, 8 July 1847.
68 *Ibid.*
69 *Ibid.*, 5 August 1847.
70 *Ibid.*, 16 March 1848.
71 *Ibid.*, 26 December 1850.

NAME INDEX

*Names of men and women
referred to in the text who were alive
during the period 1680 – 1850*

For other persons see Subject index

Abraham, Martha (servant), 73, 172, 279
Ackersley, John Hawksey (gentleman), 336, 341
Adam, Robert (architect), 221, 232, 237
Adams, Ann (butterseller), 82
Adderley, Edward (billbroker), 123, 125
Allen, George (gentleman), 251
Allen, John (gentleman), 330–4, 342, 344–5, 347, 365
Allen, Ralph (gentleman), 5–6, 24, 31, 56, 58, 69–70, 79, 93–4, 98, 111, 117, 136, 141, 148, 150, 155, 157, 158; as builder, 161, 171, 176, 272, 294, 297, 307
Allen, Ralph (gentleman), 237
Amey, John (lifeholder), 103
Ancaster, Duke of, 20
Anderdon, Edward (banker), 257
Anne, Queen, 16
Ansty, Francis (distiller), 221
Arbuthnot, Doctor, 38
Arundel, Lord, 311
Ashley, Lord ((later Shaftesbury), MP for Bath), 356–8, 362, 376–8
Aston, Toney (gambler), 28
Attwood, James (overseer of the poor), 83
Attwood, Thomas (plumber and glazier), 98, 117
Attwood, Thomas (baker), 52
Atwood, Richard (banker), 256
Atwood, Thomas Warr (builder and banker), 243, 249, 298
Austen, Jane (writer), 9, 30, 36
Axford, ? (gentleman), 98

Baily, ? (billbroker), 140
Baker, Thomas (joiner), 53
Baker, Walter (rebel), 304
Baker, William (schoolmaster), 306

Baldwin, Thomas (architect), 238, 242, 251, 256–7
Bally, John (chairman), 75
Bamford, Mr (clothier), 76
Banks, Mary (servant), 74, 279
Barker, Benjamin (painter), 30
Barker, Thomas (painter), 30
Bartlett, George (shoemaker), 375
Bath, Marquis of, 330, 335
Bayly, Nathaniel (banker), 260, 261
Bayly, Zachariah (banker), 256, 261
Beatrice, Maria, Queen, 16, 305
Bedford, Duke of, 241
Bennet, Isaac (carpenter), 247
Bennett, Francis (linendraper and Mayor), 311–12
Bennett, William (tailor), 69
Berkeley, George (moral philosopher), 36
Bertie, Lady Jane, 20
Best, Elizabeth (pauper), 72
Beswick, Mrs (gentlewoman), 21
Biggs, Charles (gentleman), 164
Biggs, Harry (apothecary), 111
Biggs, Richard (foreman), 158
Bishop, Samuel (gentleman), 227
Blair, William (gentleman), 377
Blathwayt, William (secretary at war, MP for Bath), 39, 177, 307
Blount, Martha (gentlewoman), 12
Body, Henry (rebel), 304
Bolton, Duke of, 21
Bolwell, George (waggoner), 76
Bolwell, Thomas (shoemaker, president WMA), 369, 372, 375, 376–8
Boswell, James (writer), 30
Bowsher, Richard (attorney), 260, 262
Braddock, Miss (gentlewoman and decoy), 5, 26, 36, 39
Bradley, Moses (gentleman), 161

453

NAME INDEX

Brecknock, Lord, 335, 337
Brooke, Arthur (rioter), 91
Bronte, Charlotte (writer), 36
Brown, Daniel (carpenter), 183
Brown, James (gentleman), 39
Brown, Prudence (servant), 6, 73, 172
Brown, Thomas (carpenter), 183
Browne, James (gentleman), 62
Bruges, Ludlow (gentleman, MP for Bath), 363, 369
Bryant, Gerard (seaman and rebel), 304
Bryant, John (soapboiler), 74
Brydges, James, First Duke of Chandos, 7, 40, 61, 107; relationship between Brydges and Wood, 118–51; a millionaire, 127–8, 166, 171, 205, 210, 227, 238, 308
Brydges, Cassandra (Chandos's second wife, gentlewoman), 131
Brydges, Mary (née Lake) (Chandos's first wife, gentlewoman), 119
Buckeridge, Anthony (gentleman), 111
Buckeridge, Mrs (gentlewoman), 161
Buckingham, Duchess of, 315–16
Bull, Benjamin (tailor), 313, 315
Buller, Charles (gentleman, MP), 363
Burdett, Sir Frances (MP), 334, 345
Burke, Edmund (MP), 30
Burton, Bishop, 36
Burton, John (gentleman), 232
Burton, Leonard (gentleman), 232
Butler, John (footman and rioter), 311
Butler, John (tailor), 65

Cadogan, Lord, 221
Cadogan, William (quarter-master general), 120
Camden, Lord (Lord lieutenant of Somerset), 221, 334, 335
Cantillon, Richard (banker and bill broker), 123, 125–7
Carnarvon, Marquis of, 222
Carne, Frances (schoolmaster, theatre proprietor), 306–7
Carter, John (rebel), 304
Cartwright, Major John, 329, 334
Chadwick, Edwin (gentleman), 280, 287, 293
Chandler, Mary (poet), 13, 24, 31
Chandos, Duke of, *see* Brydges, James
Chapman, Henry (gentleman), 15, 95, 98, 115
Chapman, Henry Samuel (lawyer), 355, 363, 371
Chapman, Walter, Rev., 62
Chapman, William (city chamberlain), 180
Chesterfield, Earl of, 28, 30
Cheyne (doctor of physick), 24
Churchill, John, Duke of Marlborough, 99, 149
Clatworthy, Thomas (rebel), 304

Clutterbuck, Lewis (gentleman), 161, 162, 166
Cobbett, William (writer), 334, 343
Codrington, Colonel John (MP for Bath), 307
Cogswell, James (billbroker), 158, 167–8, 246, 248
Coles, Mrs (gentlewoman), 19
Collens, Thomas (rebel), 304
Collibee, Ann (?), 106
Collibee, Edward (gentleman), 230
Collins, John (apprentice baker), 52
Collins, Samuel (labourer), 76
Collett, Thomas (apprentice carpenter), 73
Congreve, William (playwright), 36
Combes, Richard (apprentice farrier), 53
Cooper, J. (master shoemaker), 270, 327
Coram, Thomas (sea captain), 2
Cosgrove, John (tailor), 66, 69
Cottle, ? (carpenter), 333
Coward, Mr (gentleman), 257
Cox, ? (chairman), 331
Cox, George (master hatter), 270, 298, 342, 344–5, 347, 364, 366
Crisp, James (master hatter, president Bath Political Union), 342–5, 347, 364, 368, 369, 372, 377
Crook, Charles (gentleman), 257
Cross, James (banker), 261
Cross, James the younger (banker), 261

Davis, George (attorney and banker), 262
Decker, Matthew, Sir (director East India Company), 123, 125
Defoe, Daniel (writer), 188
Degge, Jane (lodging house keeper), 39, 141, 147
Delaney, Mrs (gentlewoman), 31
Demster, George (gentleman), 228
Derrick, Samuel (master of ceremonies), 93
Ditcher, John (gambler), 27
Ditcher, Philip (gambler), 27
Dixon, Henry (shopkeeper), 62
Doddington, George (gentleman), 101
Drake, William (gentleman), 163
Drummond, Andrew (banker), 123, 141
Duncan, Lord (MP for Bath), 363

Edridge, Love (widow, gentlewoman), 162
Edwards, John (railway labourer), 283
Elkington, Samuel (tailor), 67
Elwin, Rev. (rapporteur on sanitary state of Bath), 287–94
Essex, Earl of, 106
Eveleigh, John (architect), 155, 207, 209, 242–6, 248, 262, 299, 312
Evill, George (tailor), 67

Falconer, Alexander (gentleman), 347
Falconer, Henrietta (gentlewoman), 347

NAME INDEX

Falconer, Thomas (lawyer), 346–7
Falconer, Dr Thomas, 347
Fergusson, Walter (land agent), 141
Fisher, Mr (gentleman), 21
Fielding, Henry (writer), 5, 30, 56
Fielding, Sarah (writer), 30
Fisher, Henry (mason), 159–60
Fisher, James (merchant), 232
Ford, Richard (apothecary), 114

Gainsborough, Thomas (painter), 30, 31, 294
Galloway, William (gentleman), 205
Garrard, Sir Benet (gentleman), 151, 162, 207, 220
Garrard, Margaret (gentlewoman), 162, 205
Gammage, Robert (historian), 369
Garrick, Richard (actor), 18, 30
Gay, Robert (gentleman, MP for Bath), 98, 104, 111–12, 151, 169, 171, 307
George I, King, 16
George II, King, 128
George, Philip (attorney), 164, 257
Gibson, Thomas (billbroker), 140, 149
Gilbert, Thomas (lead miner), 131
Giles, John (carver and dealer), 247–8
Gilmore, Joseph (teacher of mathematics), 96
Glazby, William (tailor), 66–7, 79
Goldsmith, Oliver (writer), 27, 30
Gore-Langton, William (gentleman), 252
Granville, A. B. (writer), 263–4
Grote, Sir Francis (MP), 363
Groves, Colleton (gentleman), 76
Groves, George (labourer), 331
Guidott, Thomas (doctor of physick), 15
Gutch, Robert (banker), 261

Hale, William (?), 73
Hall, Charles (doctor and radical writer), 320–3
Hall, John (gentleman), 58, 107
Hancock, Sarah (servant), 279
Handel, George (composer), 128
Harford, Richard (woollen draper), 111
Harrington, Henry (doctor and mayor), 251, 256–7
Harrison, Thomas (gentleman), 107, 150
Hart, Moses (billbroker), 123, 125
Haynes, Lovelace (gentleman), 112, 114–15
Hayward, Robert (licensee Assembly Rooms), 221
Henley, Anthony, Sir, 20–1
Hensley, John (builder), 155–7, 171
Herschel, William (musician and natural philosopher), 30, 34, 38
Hervey, Lord John, 36, 220
Hewlett, Richard (builder), 243
Hickes, Walter (alderman), 304
Hillary, Andrew (farmer), 76
Hoare, John (surveyor), 117

Hoare, William (painter), 30
Hobbs, John (timber merchant), 149
Hobhouse, John Cam (MP), 35, 345
Hobhouse, W. H. (banker), 345, 347–8, 350–4
Hogarth, William (painter), 2, 36
Holloway, Benjamin (builder), 113, 134
Holloway, Stephen (victualler), 113
Hooper, Nicholas (yeoman), 103, 107, 111–12
Hornby, Caleb (draper), 298
Howse, (gentleman), 98
Hulance, William (builder), 246
Hume, David (moral philosopher), 36
Hume, Joseph (MP), 346
Hunt, Henry (farmer/orator), 333–4
Hunt, William (gentleman), 347
Hunter, Joseph, Rev., 30
Huntingdon, Selina, Countess of, 5, 315–17

Idle, John (tailor), 67, 69

James, Alexander (gentleman), 62
James II, King, 16, 58, 99, 306
Janssen, Theodore, Sir (banker and billbroker), 120, 123, 149
Jeffreys, John (attorney and Town Clerk), 163, 165–7, 171, 237, 255
Jeffreys, Judge, 304
Jelly, Thomas (carpenter and builder), 73, 159–60, 182, 210
Johnson, Dr Samuel (wit), 30
Johnson, Thomas (painter), 13
Jolly, Mr (draper), 371
Jones, Inigo (architect), 50, 199, 201
Jones, Mrs (milliner), 277, 295
Jones, Richard (ironmonger and deal merchant), 62
Jones (colonel), 344
Jones, William (tailor), 69

Keene, J. (gentleman, editor of *Bath Journal*), 341
Kemp, William (banker and dealer), 298
Killigrew, William (architect), 134
King, Gregory (government officer), 41
Kingston, Duke of, 59, 61–2, 98, 107, 111–12, 219
Kingston, Countess of, 107
Kissock, Mr (alderman), 373
Knight, Charles (tailor), 64

Lacy, Elizabeth (gentlewoman), 76
Ladd, Lady, 222
Laguerre, Louis (painter), 205
Langton, Mrs (gentlewoman), 16
Lansdown, Samuel (banker), 51
Lawrence, Thomas, Sir (painter), 30
Leake, James (printer and bookseller), 23–4, 27, 31, 35

NAME INDEX

Leake, John (printer and bookseller), 23
Lechmere, Lady, 25
Lichtenberg, George (professor of physics), 33–4, 36
Lightholer, Thomas (architect), 229
Ligonier, Sir John (MP for Bath), 180
Lindsey, Dame (Assembly Room proprietor), 6, 26
Linley, Elizabeth, Miss (singer), 30
Lloyd, Harford (banker), 62, 163, 166
Locke, John (moral philosopher), 36, 99, 100, 187
Lockyer, John (?), 216
Lowder, John (banker), 248
Lowther, Mr (builder), 232
Lowes, Mr (?), 20
Lyttleton, Mrs (?), 21

Mainwaring, Captain (?), 338
Maitland, William (billbroker), 123
Malthus, Thomas, Rev. (political economist), 30
Mandeville, Bernard (pamphleteer), 48, 321
Marchant, Edward (rough mason), 117, 118
Marchant, Richard, the elder (merchant tailor), 58–61, 98–9, 103–4, 111–15
Marchant, Richard, the younger (banker), 6, 58–64, 69–70, 73, 94, 100, 103, 111–12, 132–4, 136, 140, 160, 162–3, 165–7, 169, 171, 188, 307–8
Margerum, Christopher (victualler), 75
Marlborough, Duchess of, 36
Marye, James (billbroker), 121, 123
Matthews, Mr (?), 21
Matthews, William (miller and builder), 239–40
McDougall, James (apprentice victualler), 51
Mead, John (goldsmith banker), 120, 123–4
Metford, W. (gentleman), 341
Mill, John Stuart (political economist), 346
Miller, Sir John Riggs, 256
Milsom, Charles (winecooper), 182–3
Milsom, Daniel (schoolmaster), 111, 181–2
Mitchell, Priscilla (wife of corporal Mitchell), 77
Mitchell, William (labourer), 172
Monkland, G. (gentleman), 30, 36
Montague, Lady Barbara, 317
Montague, Elizabeth (née Robinson) (gentlewoman), 12, 16, 17–22, 36, 171
Montague, Lady Mary Wortley, 25, 36
Monmouth, Duke of, 304, 306, 311
Moore, A. (master shoemaker) 299
Moore, Arthur (gentleman), 120
Moxham, Robert (carpenter), 247
Mullaway, James (wine merchant), 74, 93

Nalder, ? (billbroker), 140
Napier, Charles (general), 370
Napier, William (colonel), 285, 287, 344

Nash, Beau (master of ceremonies), 5, 26–9, 58; Nash and the Corporation, 176–7, 220
Newton, John (natural philosopher), 29, 36
Nichols, Morgan (gentleman), 256
Nightingale, Mr (?), 74
Noel, Lord and Lady, 20
Norfolk, Duke of, 311
Northumberland, Lord, 222

Ogilvie, William (professor of humanity), 320
Oliver, William (doctor of physick), 13, 15, 17
Orange, William, Duke of, 6, 98, 119, 305, 306; with Mary, 305–6
Orrery, Earl of, 141
Oxford, Earl of, 141

Pain, Elizabeth (servant), 279
Paine, Thomas (writer), 315, 366
Painter, Lawrence (labourer), 76
Palmer, John (architect), 207, 248–9, 257, 299
Palmer, John (gentleman, MP Bath), 330
Palmer, John (major general, MP for Bath), 330, 334–5, 337, 339, 344–7, 350
Palmer, Thomas (glazier), 182
Palmerston, Viscount, 344
Parker, Richard (builder), 164
Parkes, Joseph (lawyer), 364
Paty, Mr (architect), 231–2
Pearson, Joseph (draper), 299
Peirce, Robert (doctor of physick), 15–16
Pels, André (banker and billbroker), 123, 127
Pepys, Elizabeth (gentlewoman), 39, 40
Pepys, Samuel (secretary to the Admiralty), 39, 40, 95
Percival, William (solicitor), 257
Pescod, Mr (attorney), 130
Phillips, Anne (lodging house keeper), 38, 40, 131, 137, 141, 147
Phillips, William (carpenter), 238–9
Phillott, Charles (innholder), 255–6
Phillott, Henry (innholder), 254
Phillott, Joseph (innholder and mayor), 51, 255–6
Philp, Mr (?), 375
Phipps, Mr (master shoemaker), 327
Phrips (sea captain), 130
Pitt, Isabella (gentlewoman), 232
Pitt, William (gentleman, MP for Bath), 308
Pitts, Thomas (billbroker), 158
Place, Frances (breechesmaker), 278
Pocock (colonel), 307
Pope, Alexander (poet), 5, 12–13, 29, 30–1, 36, 56
Portland, Duchess of, 12, 18
Powell, Mr (Bristol Political Union), 342
Powerscourt, Lord (MP for Bath), 363, 370

456

NAME INDEX

Price, Mary (laundress), 280
Priestly, Joseph, Dr (natural philosopher), 34
Pulteney, Frances (wife of William Johnstone, gentlewoman) 227–8, 240
Pulteney, General, 227–8
Pulteney, Henrietta, Laura (gentlewoman), 228, 238
Pulteney, Sir James, 241
Pulteney, William Johnstone (?) 106, 150, 171, 219, 221; development of Bathwick 226–46, 249, 252, 262; as financier, 238–40
Pulteney, William, Earl of Bath, 98, 106, 111–12, 149, 171, 240, 303

Quin, James (actor), 18, 30

Rack, Edmund (gentleman), 34
Randell, Mr (gentleman), 257
Reynolds, Joshua, Sir (painter), 31
Ricardo, David (banker and political economist), 35
Ricardo, Moses (gentleman), 35
Ricardo, Mrs (gentlewoman), 35
Richards (sawyer and rioter), 341
Richardson, Samuel (writer), 24, 56
Rick, Lady, 36
Ricketts, John (builder), 240
Ried, Mr (builder), 232
Rivers, James (gentleman), 163
Roberts, Thomas (ironfounder), 6, 76–7, 80, 172
Roberts, W. P. (solicitor), 366, 368, 372–3
Robin, Rev. Thomas (minister of religion), 247
Robins, Thomas (gentleman), 104
Roebuck, J. A. (MP for Bath), 10, 346–72, 376–9
Rogers, S. (master shoemaker), 270
Rowlandson, Thomas (painter), 32
Ryan, Daniel (tailor), 69

Sanders (widow, lifeholder), 103, 106, 172
Sandford, E. A. (gentleman, MP for Somerset), 339
Saunders, John (gentleman, Mayor of Bath), 98, 114, 117, 176
Saunders, William (gentleman), 103, 111
Scott, Sarah (née Robinson) (gentlewoman), 5, 17–23, 27, 171, 220, 317, 319
Scott, Walter (writer), 30
Scott, Sir William (lawyer), 334
Selby, Margaret (pauper), 73
Selden, William (mason), 155, 157, 171
Senserf, Walter (banker and billbroker), 123
Seymour, Lord Webb, 252
Shaftesbury, First Earl of, 303
Shaftesbury (Anthony Ashley Cooper), Third Earl of, 36, 185, 319
Shenstone, William (gentleman), 325, 368
Sheridan, Richard (playwright), 30

Shell, Samuel (pauper), 77
Shergold, Richard (billbroker), 123
Sherlock, George (billbroker), 158
Siddons, Mrs (actress), 30
Sims, William (soldier), 77
Skeet, Denham (gentleman), 158, 243
Sloan, William (tailor), 69
Smith (fish and oysterseller and rioter), 341
Smith, Adam (professor of moral philosophy), 35, 185, 222
Smith, Henry (land surveyor, chairman Bath Political Union), 347
Smith, Joseph (builder), 240
Smith, Mrs (milliner), 277, 295
Smith, William (surveyor), 34
Smollett, Tobias (writer), 30, 32, 204
Snygges, William (gentleman), 101
Sommerset, John (?), 59
Southwell, Lord, 221
Spackman, Charles (builder), 248
Spence, Thomas (radical writer), 320, 323
Spencer, Rev. Thomas, 375
Sproule, Andrew (gentleman), 155, 157
Stagg, John (gentleman), 115
Staples, Elizabeth (banker), 158, 247–8
Staples, Moses (banker), 158, 247–8
Steele, Richard (writer), 22
Sterne, Laurence (writer), 2
Stevens, George (carpenter), 113
St John, Henry, Lord Bolingbroke, 120
St John, Thomas (shoemaker), 326
Stone, Hester (?), 106
Stourton, Lord, 311
Strahan, John (architect), 149, 193, 205
Stothert, George, Senior (ironmonger), 81, 270, 271
Stothert, George, Junior (ironfounder), 271
Stothert, Henry (ironfounder), 299, 347
Stretzer, Thomas (writer), 23–4
Stuart, Charles (doctor of physick and billbroker), 134
Sturge, Joseph (gentleman), 374
Swift, Jonathan (writer), 206
Symons, John (surgeon and mayor), 250, 251, 257

Telford, Thomas (surveyor), 227, 240
Thayer, Humphrey (apothecary and commissioner of excise), 136, 148, 161, 166
Theobald, James (timber merchant and billbroker), 134; intermediary between Wood and Chandos, 136–50, 158–9, 161, 166
Thicknesse (née Ford), Mrs (gentlewoman), 31
Thicknesse, Philip (writer), 5, 32, 91, 315
Thornburgh, John (gentleman), 114–15, 121
Thynn, William (lead miner), 131
Thynne, Lord John (MP for Bath), 331, 335, 337
Tirrell, Thomas (gaming house keeper), 27

457

NAME INDEX

Thomas, William (apprentice surgeon), 51
Towers, Elizabeth (widow, gentlewoman), 161–2
Townsend, John (silversmith), 243
Townsend, William (silversmith), 243
Trease, Constant (tailor), 104, 111
Trymme, George (gentleman clothier), 7, 58, 63, 104, 112–15, 176
Turner, Betty (gentlewoman's companion), 39, 40
Twycross, Mr (gaming house keeper), 28, 46
Tynte, Susanna (gentlewoman), 134

Uphill, Robert (coroner), 347
Upton, Richard (carpenter), 157, 164, 171

Vaughan, Frances, Mrs (gentlewoman), 59, 150
Vincent, Henry (compositor), 369–70, 372–5
Vincent, John (cuckold), 91

Wade, Major General (MP for Bath), 307
Wade, William (master of ceremonies), 221
Walcott, John (natural philosopher), 34
Walpole, Horace (writer), 30
Walters, Joseph (?), 111
Warburton, Bishop, 24
Warburton, ? (gentleman), 20, 21
Warner, Rev. Richard (historian of Bath), 293
Waters, Charles (apprentice barber), 51
Watson, Mrs, 73

Watson, William (gentleman), 256
Watts, Thomas (billbroker), 123, 140, 149
Wayte, Elizabeth (gentlewoman), 15–16
Webb, Ann (widow, gentlewoman), 161
Webster, Captain (master of ceremonies), 26
Wells, Thomas (banker), 261
Wesley, John, Rev., 5, 29, 315
West, Joseph (porter), 284
Wetenhall, Mr (gaming house keeper), 28, 46
Wheeler, Sarah (servant), 73
White, James (mason), 76
Wilkins, Captain (clothier), 340–1, 368
Wiltshire, Walter (gentleman), 180
Wiltshire, William (gentleman and mayor), 256
Whitfield, George, Rev., 29, 315
Wordsworth, William (poet), 30
Wood, John, the elder (architect), 7–8, 26, 36, 47, 56, 58, 61, 69–70, 79, 93, 104, 108, 110, 117–19, 161, 169, 171, 260, 264, 298, 315, 317, 319, 344; and Chandos, 129–51, 158–61, 165; and the social organisation of space, 173–226, *passim*; as town planner, 173, 199
Wood, John, the younger (architect), 7, 62, 161–9, 171, 206–9, 220, 237–8, 298
Woodforde, James, Rev., 21
Wright, Henry (surgeon), 51
Wylde, Thomas (labourer), 313

Zollicoffre, Bartholomew (banker), 123

SUBJECT INDEX

Abaris, *see* Bladud and the Brittanic Myth
Abbey Church, 50, 210
Abbey House, 107
Absolute property, 7, 9, 10, 100, 115, 174, 218; in Bathwick, 241, 263, 297, 380; rights claimed in relation to Assembly Rooms, 222, 224, 225
absolute self interest, 9, 11, 174, 218, 224, 226-63 *passim*, 297
Acts of Parliament: against gambling (1739), (1740), (1745), 28; Avon Navigation Act (1711), 117, 309; Black Act (1723), 309; Brown Bread Act (1801), 82; Bubble Act (1720), 297; Combination Laws (1799), 326, 327, 358; Compulsory Powers in Acts of 1707, 1711, 1766, 178-9, 183, 184, 219, 288, 308; Improvement Acts (1720), (1739), 178; Improvement Act (1757), 178, 214; Improvement Act (1766), 110, 183, 184, 210, 214, 217, 219, 230, 249, 288, 309; Improvement Act (1789), 251-9; Municipal Corporations Act (1835), 302, 364; Poor Law (1602), 75; Poor Law (1834), 364; Private Acts for Pulteney Bridge (1769), (1772), (1774), (1800), 229, 230, 232, 234, 241; Property Qualification Act, 309; Reform Act (1832), 302, 337-44, 362, 364, 367; Septennial Act, 309, 345, 348; Six Acts, 348; Test Act, 58; Turnpike and Improvement Act (1707), 177-8, 214, 309
alehouses; 46, 47, 74, 93; a public nuisance, 216, 217, 220
America, 70, 237
annuities, 134
Anti-Corn Law League, 374
apprentices/apprenticeship, 51-6; pauper, 77;

proportions in different trades, 63-4, 67, 70; supervision of, 87-90, 336
architect(s), 1, 4, 8, 172; God as Divine, 190-2; *see* under Name index
architecture, 1, 9, 18; architectural history, 119, 172, 204; as art, 172; columns in, 191-3, 242; meaning in, 172-4; Palladian, 191, 201; 204, 207, 242; and urban landscape, 169, 172, 204; *see* social organisation of space
Arminius, 29
army: reduction in expenditure on, 348; standing, reduction in, 344
art, 35; history of, 8
assault, rate of, 87-94
Assembly Rooms, 5, 21, 28, 48, 93, 113, 116, 136, 220, 230; competition between, 220-5, 248, 251, 263, 294; New, 9, 33, 34; *see also* building developments
Assize of Bread, 79, 82
Avon Navigation, 7, 28, 42; destruction of locks on, 310; tolls on, 87; traffic on, 259, 261; use of Black Act by, 309; work on, 117-19, 134, 178, 215
Avon River, 50, 93, 96, 117, 118, 210, 226, 228, 235, 239, 241, 271

Bailbrook House, 295
ballot, secret, 345, 348, 349, 355, 370, 371; Victorian, 1856, 371; votes on in Parliament, 363
bank stock, 120-1
banks, in Bath: Bath Bank (Cam and Co.), 247; Bath City Bank (Bayly, Gutch and Cross), 245, 255, 259-61, cash ratio, 260, failure, 261; Bath and Somersetshire, failure of, 261; Bladud Bank (Atwood and Co.), 158, 243; Bridge Street Bank, failure

459

SUBJECT INDEX

of, 261; High Street Bank, 245; Sherlock and Mortimer, 239; Union Bank, 247
banks, other: Bank of England, 150, 348; Barry and Death, Chippenham, 245; Bristol Old Bank, 62, 162, 166; Dumfries Bank, 227; Elizabeth and Moses Staples, London, 158, 246; goldsmith bank, 120, London Banks, 261
Barbeau, A., 30
Bath, amusements at, 12–38, 73–4
Bath: Baths at, 38, 48, 50, 230; Cross Bath, 16, 131, 132, 210, 247, 306; King's Bath, 13; Queen's Bath, 13
Bath, company at, 12, 47, 49, 296, 309; decline of, 260–2, 274; paid for city improvement, 258
Bath, constables of, 305
Bath, corporation of, 7, 8, 9, 28, 50, 58, 63, 65, 67–9, 98, 104; corporation and development, 175–84, 220; *see also* building developments, Bathwick; Bridge, opposition to Mr Pulteney's, 232–5; corporation, expenditure and debt, 178–80; corporation and political power, 302–36 *passim*, 364; Corporatism, 8; economic corporatism, 175–7, 180–3, 184, 185, 218; end of Corporation scheme, 260; as landowner, 107–10, 117, 133, 169, 207, 297; need for extraordinary income, 181, 257; social corporatism, 175, 218, 219, 309
Bath, election of Councillors in, 364, 365
Bath, emigrants from, 77
Bath, executions at, 304–6, 311; reference to in 1812, 332
Bath, freedom of, 51, 58, 59, 64–7, 68, 108, 175, 180
Bath, Freemen, 98, 104, 108, 175; claims against Corporation, 253, 259; and election of 1812, 330–3; petitions against Corporation, 302, 308, 328, 329; share in government, 350
Bath, gaol, 230, 237
Bath, hospitals: Bath General Hospital, 60; United Hospital, 264; servants attending, 279
Bath, house rents in, 38, 41, 106; house values, 157–9, 164–6
Bath, immigrants to, 6, 51, 70–9, 89, 245, 309
Bath, industries: Bamford and Co., textile mill, 84; Brass Foundry, 269; Breweries, 269; Brough and Deveralls Steam Engine Manufactory, 269; Cut-Glass Factory, 269; Gaslight and Coke Company, 265; George Cox Hatting Business, 269; Pin Factory, 269; Wilkins' Woollen Mills, 340
Bath, income in, 39–41
Bath, medical treatment at, 13–16
Bath, parishes (at census 1801): Bathwick, 6, 9, 42, 82, 96, 104, 106, 107, 112; development in, 226–49 *passim*, 265, 267–300 *passim*, 303; Boundaries re-drawn into wards, 364; Lyncombe and Widcombe, 42, 47, 96, 111, 112, 206, 259, 261, 266, 267–300 *passim*, 333; political allegiance in all parishes, 350–67; St James, 50, 61, 73–4, 77, 83, 91, 98, 104, 153, 177, 210, conditions of housing in, 211–20, 257, 265, 266, 269–300 *passim*, 313, 333, 338, radicalism in, 339, 342–67; St Michael, 74, 75, 111, 181, 211, 266–300 *passim*, radicalism in, 343; St Peter and St Paul, 50, 83, 111, 181, 215, 216, 241, 266–300 *passim*; Walcot, 6, 41, 47, 65, 74, 80, 83, 96, 104, 106, 107, 108, 111, 112, 210, 214, 215, 216, 226, 227, 246, 259, 265, 266–300 *passim*, 303, 313
Bath, population of, 40, 42, 48, 87; economic importance of, 298; intercensal rates of change in, 267, 268, 275; role of in the decline of Bath, 265; tenfold increase in, 266
Bath, poverty in, 279–95; absolute poverty, 283, 284, 291; *see also* Poor Law; wages
Bath, prices in, 5, 38–40, 79–85, 92, 282, 286, 374
Bath chair(s), 10; chairmen's influence, 108, 110, 175, 380
Bath Literary and Philosophical Association, 30
Bath Literary Club, 30
Bath Philosophical Society, 34, 38
Bath Provision Committee, 84–5
Bath Turnpike, 26, 42, 60; opposition to Improvement Act, 252; opposition to Pulteney's turnpike proposal, 235, 236, 241; *see also* Acts of Parliament
Bath volunteers, 91
Bath waters, 13, 18; their influence on fertility, 15–17, 305
Batheaston, 65, 75, 164, 266, 317
Bathford, 73, 236, 237, 241
Bathampton, 33
Bathwick Estate/Manor, 106, 111, 226–45, 248, 259
Beckington, 39
Berkshire, 114
Bill of Exchange, 60, 61, 63, 120, 129, 130, 134, 136–50 *passim*
Bills in circulation, 150, 243; Cogswell, discounter of bills, 246, 261, 308
Bill-brokers, 120–9, 134–70 *passim*, 262
Birmingham, 34, 47, 270, 366
Bladud and the Brittania Myth, Wood's version of, 186–90, 196–9, 315
Blenheim Palace, Laguerre's designs for, 205
bookshops, 24–5
Borja, Jordis, 5
Box, 254
Bradford-on-Avon, 58, 177
bridges: Cleveland, 265; Mr Pulteney's,

460

SUBJECT INDEX

development of, 227–37, proposed bridge at Bathford, 237, opposition to, 232–7, 250, 338; North Bridge, Edinburgh, 231, 234; North Parade, 265; The Old, 50, 96, 214; Samuel Bishop's proposal, 227; Tay Bridge, 234; Victoria, 270
Bridgwater, Urban Development at, 130, 131; Chandos's estate at, 134, 140, 149, 157, 261
Brighton, 17, 72, 263
Bristol, 39, 42, 47, 70, 77, 79, 117, 167, 177, 187, 246, 261, 265, 266, 267, 270, 271, 325, 333, 334, 339
Bristol Avon, 49
Bristol Brass Company, 63
Bristol Exchange Building, 185
building booms and slumps, 9, 42–6, 53, 61, 89, 90, 110, 113–19 *passim*; building booms and interest rates, 168, 182–3, 211, 226, 228, 235, 237, 238, 242, 246, 249, 250, 251; of 1789–92, 260–3, 265, 270, 282
building developments: Ambury, 159–60, 183, 184, 210; Bathwick, 153, 158, 218, 226–46; Bazaar Rooms, 265; Beauford Square, 149, 193, 205; Camden Crescent, 242, 263; Catherine Place, 206; Cavendish Crescent, 265; Chandos Buildings (Chandos/Wood Development), 40–1, 132–50; Cleveland Place, 265; Corridor, The, 265; Galloways Buildings, 110, 205, 210, 214, 272, 372, 375; Gravel Walks, 113; Grand Parade and South Parade, 38, 61, 110, 153, 155, 156, 161, 162, 166, 176, 185, 196, 205, 210, 214, 227; Great Pulteney Street, 239, 240, 242, 260, 265, 316, 338; Grosvenor Place and Gardens, 242, 243, 262, 297, 299; Hooper's Court, 111; King's Circus, 38, 62, 110, 153, 155, 162, 165, 183, 196, 199, 204, 205, 207, 210, 224, 272, 346, 347, 361–2, 367; Kingsmead Square, 114, 149, 205, 211; Kingston Buildings, 108; Lansdown Crescent, 248; Laura Place, 238, 239, 246; Norfolk Crescent, 260, 262; Princes Buildings, 110; Queen's Parade, 161, 165; Queen Square, 7, 26, 110, 139, 148, 151–3, 158, 160–1, 164–6, 176, 183–5, 192–6, 199, 207, 210, 220, 238, 265, 338, 367, 372; Royal Crescent, 38, 62, 91, 156, 157, 164, 165, 176, 207–9, 242, 263; St James Square, 206, 248; Sion Hill Place, 265; Somerset Place, 207, 242; 248; Somersetshire Buildings, 112, 183; Southcot Place, 206; Sydney Place and Gardens, 242, 271, 338, 341; Trymme Street, 114, 115, 116, 117, 275; West Gate Buildings, 184, 270; working class, 157, 209–17, 246, 247, 269
building developments, by corporation: Bladud's Buildings, 110, 181–3, 207; High Street, 50, 211, 215, 219, 230, 294; Milsom Street and Edgar's Buildings, 153, 155, 183, 184, 207, 210, 219, 229, 265, 294, 338; Paragon Buildings, 183; re-building of city centre (Pump Room and environs), 248–59, paid for by tolls on visiting company, 253, 263, 330
building developments, capital in, 116, 153–70; in Bathwick, 230–5, 240; in city redevelopment, 251, 253–5, 257–9; return on investment in, 147, 165; see also finance and financial institutions
building leases, examples of, 107–9, 182, 238; in Bathwick, 237–40; breaking of covenants in, 239; Corporation's lease to Milsom, 181–8; importance of for urban development, 112, 162, 167; made to John Wood, 150–3
Burford, 73

Calne, 34
Cameron, 22
canals/canal building, 260; Kennet and Avon, 266, 271, 286
Cannons, Edgeware, Chandos's house at, 119, 128
capital: in Assembly Rooms, 221; in Bridgwater, 130; in building, 6, *see also* building developments; in cotton, 6; shortage, 139, 148, 185
capitalism: 3; advance of, 169; agrarian, 169, 176, 189; capitalist agriculture, 100; capitalists in Bath, 267; corporate, 221, dynamic of, 260, 263; early stages of, 309
Carey's wine vaults, 40, 147
Castle Cary, 22
chapels: Argyle, 316; Chapel Royal, imitation of, 128; Countess of Huntingdon's, 5, 29, 316; Octagon, 229; Roman Catholic, 91, 92; St John's, 134; St Mary's, 196; The Tabernacle, 316
charities, Bath:- Black Alms, 84–5; Bellott's Hospital, 85; Bluecoat School, 134; Charitable School, Batheaston, 317–18; Free School (King Edwards), 8, 172, 306; Monmouth Street Society, 283, 285; Refuge for Destitute, 80, 217; St John's Hospital, 107, 131, 132, 134; Society for Relief of Lying in Women, 85; Stranger's Friend Society, 85; London:- Charitable Society, The, 127
Charter, Bath (1590), 302
Charter, The, 355, 370; introduced to Bath, 371; the Radical, 355, 362, 370, 379
Chartists/Chartism, 367, 370–9
Charterhouse, 161
Cheltenham, 263
Chester, 270
Chew Magna, 73–4, 93
Chippenham, 161, 166
church rates, action against, 366, 367

461

SUBJECT INDEX

Cirencester, 22
City gates and Burrough Walls, destruction of, 113, 181-3, 184
city/cities: pre-industrial, 3, 37, 46; production of, 5
civil society, 7, 169, 174, 185; a frame around, 193
Clapham, 161
class(es), 3, 4, 10, 37-8, 171, 172, 173; areas of settlement for, 209-18, 266-75; and Assembly Rooms, 222; distribution of stratum, 264-80; Elwin's analysis of class and space, 287-90; lumpen proletariat, 217, 275; middle-class reformers, 341ff, political abdication of, 341; middling-class, 296-8, 349, 359, 371, 373, 375, 378-9
class consciousness, 4, 10, 298; radical, 329-80 *passim*, overtaken by events, 379; reform and, 339; trade union, 329; working, 300, 303-28 *passim*, not Marxian, 374; *see also* radicalism; Roebuck, J. A.; space
coach services, 41-2, 46, 263, 330
Coalbrookdale works, 271
Combe Down, 93, 118
Communist Manifesto, The, 378
companies: British Fishery Company, 240; formed at Bath, 65, 108, 175; Merchant Taylors Bath, 58, 61, 63-70, action against interlopers, 64, 65-8, 98, 132, 184; Scottish Fishery Company, 131
conflict, 85; Hobbesian, 318
Consols, yield on, 147, 168
consumption, 11; a factor in the growth of Bath, 149
contraception, 23
Corn Laws, revision of, 345; abolition of, 348, 373
Corporation Bonds, 147, 168
Coventry, 47, 270
credit, 7, 9, 11, 115-19, 123; creditmen, 130, 136, 140, 148; a factor in Bath's growth, 148, 261; web of credit, 128-30, 140, 148
crime, 86-94, 217, 219; murder, 92, 93
Croot, Patricia, 104

Declaration of Indulgence, 58
Denmark, 70
Devizes, 58
Devon, 56, 232
Dewall, 119
disease: Bath claimed exceptionally healthy, 286-8; cholera, 217, 259, 289, 290, 338; diarrhoea, 290, 291; infant mortality, 292-4 mortality, 287-95; smallpox, 290, 291
Ditcheat, 76
Doddington Survey, 101-2
Dorset, 51, 270
duels, 26, 38
Durham proposals, 355

East Indies, 130
East Penhard, 76
economics, 35
Edinburgh, 193, 231, 234; New Town, 187, 270
education: by Chartists, 374; at Millenium Hall, 317, 319; sectarian control of, 375, 379; *see also* apprenticeship
Elfege, Abbott, 30
English Channel, 70
Englishcombe, 82
entrepreneurs, 7, 9, 116-68, 171, 177
Equitable Trust in, 297-8, 308, equity of redemption, 308
Essex, 51
Exclusion Crisis, 303
Exeter, 99

field and rural place names: Ambury, the, 159, 160, 188; Barton Farm, 6, 96, 101, 103, 104, 111, 151, Gay's crucial decision on, 169, 307; Bathwick Down, 239; Beacon Hill, 49, 96; Beechen Cliff, 49, 132, 199; Cockey's Garden, 182; Dolmeads, the, 118, 217, 260, 273, 291; Ham, the, 58, 59, 60, 61, 106, 107, 112, 188, 196; Hayes Lower Furlong, 207; Kingsmead, 96, 114, 132, 205, 216; Hedgemead, 218, Upper Hedgemead, 218; Kingsmead Furlong, 207; Little Kingsmead, 114; Lansdown, 8, 49, 96, 207, 248; Milsom's Garden, 181, 183; Rack Close, 98, 183; Solsbury Hill, 196; Town Acre, 98, 181, 183; Town Common, 96, 108, 112, 176, 253, 259, 268; Town Garden, 98; Vineyards, 316
Financial institutions in Bath's growth, 149, 167, 242; new force in Bath, 248; large scale ventures, 266; Tontine in Assembly Rooms, 220-1
floods/flooding, 235, 241, 259, 272; Council inaction over, 365
Freshford, 344
Frome, 373

gambling, 25-8, 39; on the outcome of military campaigns, 120, 217; revenue from cards and dice, 117
geology, 34
Glastonbury, 177
Gloucestershire, 51, 70, 72, 77, 94, 177, 178, 247
Gloucester, 211
Guildhall (town hall), built by Inigo Jones, 50, 91; New, 180, 182, 183, 219, 230, 249, 251, 331, 340, 372

Hampshire, 73
Hertfordshire, 111, 166
Herefordshire, 119, 128
Hinton Charterhouse, 76, 375

SUBJECT INDEX

Homecounties, 70
Hull, 270
Hull, Gloucestershire, 247

ideology, 8, 11, 169, 171–25 *passim*; *see also* class; radicalism
Ilchester gaol, 331
Improvement Commissioners, *see* building developments by Corporation; re-building of city centre
infanticide, 92, 93
inns, 39, 40, 41, 48; description of, 50
Insurance: Bath Fire Office, 255, 297; Sun Fire Office, 61, 131, 134
Interest rates, 168, instability of, 260
Ireland, 71; justice for, 345; no religious coercion, 379
Irish, 71, 91
Ison, Walter, 8

Jacobites/Jacobitism, 16, 306; Jacobite rising (1715), 307, (1745), 307
John Warren's Mill, 238

Kahnweiler, Daniel-Henry, 2
Keynsham, 101
kings, *see under* Name index

labour: 6, 11, 47, 49; deficiency, 185; efficient use of, 79, 118; enticement of, 68, 69; troubles of Wood, 135
labourers, urban, 6; average age of death, 223; families of, 279–85; living standards, 85–7, 172, 280–300
labouring population, 6, 9, 10, 49–94 *passim*; consciousness of, 303–28 *passim*, 339, 340; depressed conditions of, 260; effect on townscape, 264ff; excluded from political community, 368; increase of, 265; pleasures of, 93; political aspirations blocked, 379
Lamoine, Georges, 35
land, 7, 11; birthright in, 320, 332; nationalisation of, 322
landowners/landlords, 6, 95–115, 171, 265; and control over corporation, 329–36
land tenure: corporation as trustees, 98, power to draw 42-year leases, 133; freeholders, 97, 103, 104; leaseholders, 97; lifehold tenancies/lifeholder, 7, 100–9, 133, 176, 240; life tenants, 100, 240; military tenures, 99; mortgagors an estate in land, 100; rack rents, 101, 151; settled estates, 100, 228
land values, 61; in Bathwick, 106, 107, 227, 237, 240; custom for estimating capital values, 100, 101–4; land sales, 111–12, 115; in Walcot, 151, 163, 182, 253
Larkhall, 82
law: administration of at Quarter Sessions,

85–90; compulsory powers in Acts of Parliament, 178, 308; as condition for economic development, 303; equality before, 349, 367, 379; of mortgages, 100; of property, 169, 308; riotous assembly, 340; suits in Chancery, 253, 256, 330; trials, for sedition, 313, conspiracy, 326; used against customary rights, 308
law, cases: Glazby v. Merchant Taylors, 66–9, 79, 169, 220; Nicholas Hyde's Award (1619), 96–7; at Wells Assizes, 311
Leicester, 47, 51
leisure, 3, 9, 38, 46
Lewes, 325
libraries, circulating, 24, 25, 35, 38
literature, 30, 35; labourers in, 85; literary history, 119
Liverpool, 47, 269
Llangollen, Ladies of, 317
lodgings/lodging houses: Bath's houses as, 173; description of, 50, 131; fitting and furnishing, 141, 147; rent of, 38–40, 141–8
London, 12, 25, 42, 49, 59, 70, 76, 77, 81, 96, 111, 114, 129; Cavendish Square, 130, 162, 166; East London Democratic Association, 369; Freemason's Tavern, 346; Spa Fields, 333, 334
London money market, 140, 166, 168
Loretto, 2
Lydney, 77

Manchester, 47
market/markets, 180, 183, 219, 230, 372
Market Harborough, 28
marriage, 15, 18: wardship and marriage, 99
Marshfield, 72
Marx/Marxist, 35, 136, 303, 374
Mechanics Institute, 325, 337
Mendips, 101, 104
Meso America, 3
Mesopotamia, 3
Midford, 34–5
Millenium Hall, description of, 317–21
monied interest, 128, 166, 171, 176, 184–5
mortgages, 153–70 *passim*, money transferred by bills, 247

National Debt, 121, 129, 168
nature, excluded from Wood's buildings, 193
Nempnett, 134
Netherlands, towns in, 120, 121, 129, 131
New Sarum, 73
Newspaper Stamp (taxes on knowledge), fight against, 355, 362, 379
Northampton, 232
Norwich, 232

Oldland Common, journeyman hatters in, 339, 343
Oxford, 21, 177, 211; New College, 119

SUBJECT INDEX

Oxfordshire, 73

Paisley, 47
parliaments, triennial, 345
peasantry, 6, 95–115; destruction of, 265
Pensford, 99
Picasso, Pablo, 2
Poldens, 104
police, 373; problem of, 366
political economy, 35
political organisations: Association for Preserving Liberty, Property and the Constitution of Great Britain Against Republicans and Levellers, 313; Bath Complete Suffrage Association, 375; Conservative Association, 378; Independent Association, 346–7, 349, 362; Liberal Association, 378; Tradesmen and Operatives Conservative Association, 376; Working Men's Association, 370, 371, London, 370
political unions: Bath, 342, artisan-controlled, 342, 343, 344, 345–6, 348, 362, 368; Birmingham, 341; Bristol, outgrowth of Union of Trades, 341, working-class, 442; Frome, 343; Holt, 343; Trowbridge, 343
Poor Laws: bastardy, 75, 88, 89, 92, 262; examinations, 70–9, 87–90, 361; Irish, 358, 375; New Poor Law (1834), 365, 368, 375, Bath Union, 282, 283, opposition to, 80, 374; poor house, 111, 181–2, pauper diet in, 282; regulation of, 219; relief, 83, 85; removals, 88, 89, 262
pornography, 22–4, 31
Portsmouth, 325
post office/postal service, 56, 141, 166
power, 174, 219, 302–28 *passim*; Radical stand on, 367
Prior Park, 31
production, 11
promissory notes, 137, 261
property, 9, 11, 99; consolidation of rights, 168, 175, secured by law, 309; described by Hall, 320–3; division of rights, 108, 167; and urban development, 115, 149; *see also* absolute property
prostitution, 17, 22, 23, 39, 217, 272
Pump Room, 29, 48, 113, 117, 180, 230; halt in work on, 261; new, 249–60 *passim*

Quantocks, 101
Quarter Sessions, 27, 28, 51; business at, 85–90, 214, 219

railways: construction of GWR, 286; speculation about, 266
radicals/radicalism, 10, 304, 329–80 *passim*; differences with Liberals, 344; Movement, 363, 371, 379, 380; Philosophic, 10, 346,

348, 362; radical programme, 332, 333, 344, 348, 349; Ultra, 371
Rebellion, Monmouth's, 304–5
religion, 8, 29, 193; in Ireland, 379; religious belief and class, 320; religious influence and Mechanics Institute, 337; religious liberty, 349; religious meaning in architecture, 174; *see also* architecture; Bladud; space
religious denominations: Anglicans, 304, 306, 316, Church of England, 358; Arminians/Arminianism, 29, 316; Baptists, 93, 317, 342, 358; Calvinism, 29, 316; Catholics/Catholicism, 71, 91, 304, 306, 310–12, Catholic College at Maynooth, 358, 375; Methodists/Methodism, 93, 216, 310, 315, 316, Primitive, 316, 358; Moravians, 29; Quakers, 58, 60, 63, 132, 307, 310; Wesleyans, 29
Responsible Government, 362, 379
Revolutions: American, 366; Bath described as revolutionary, 329, 363, 378; Revolution (1688), 99, 100, 175, 305–6, 308; Revolutionary Settlement (1689), 306, 308, 310, in Canada, 362–3, 371, in France, 378; and shoemakers, 373
riots, 82, 90–2, 310; Bristol riots, 339–42, 350; anti-Catholic, 362; Chartist, 372, 378; Church and King, 379–80; Gordon Riots, 91, 93, 246, 310–13; other trade riots, 328; by Wiltshire shearmen, 328; in 1812, 331–2
Rodney Stoke, 101, 102, 103
Rome, 2

Salisbury, 99, 177
Saltford, 101
Saxon myth, 315, 332
Scarborough, 28
science, 30, 34
Scotland, 70
Scotland Yard timber wharf, 131, 136
servants, 10, 39, 70–6; expectations of, 318–19, 378; origins of, 71–6, 82, 172, 269, 276, 279, 310
sewers/sewerage, 136, 158, 160; cleansing and lighting, 177, 178, 182, 217, 238
sexual life at Bath, 17–24, 26, 30, 33
Shaftesbury, 270
Shepton Mallet, 271
Shropshire, 227
slavery/slave trade, 127, 128, 129, 162, 166, 188; abolition of, 345, 348, 349
social critics, eighteenth century, 320
social history, 1, 5, 11
social movements, 1, 5, 309–80 *passim*
social structure, 4, 6, 7, 9, 10; transformation of, 106, 264–300 *passim*, 330, 379
socialism, Owenite, 375
Somerset, 51, 58, 70, 72, 77, 94, 99, 101, 106,

464

SUBJECT INDEX

134, 177, 178, 261, 267; Sheriff of, 305; Somerset Militia, 304
South Carolina, 51
South Mims, farm at, 139
South Sea Bubble, 123, 125, 127, 130;
South Sea Company and stock, 115, Chandos's dealings in, 121–9
space, social organisation of, 1, 4, 8, 9, 26, 47, 98, 110–11; in Bathwick, 242; in city centre, 253ff, 258, 265; influence on political consciousness, 350–5; influence of traffic routes and alehouses on, 211–18; organisation of space and health, 287–94; place of Assembly Rooms in, 219–25; role of Corporation in, 175–84, 219; the role of credit in, 168, 171–4, 183, 206, 209; space and welfare, 292; structured by class relations, 300, 310; unintended, 237, 241; urban ecology and political consciousness, enjoyment of in nineteenth century, 380; use of, by labouring population, 339; use of space by different classes, 268–75; *see also*, architecture
Spain, 120; towns in, 129
Spring Gardens, 226, 237
Staffordshire, 131
St Bartholomew's Hospital, 141, 150, 157
St George's, Hanover Square, 47
Stanton Drew, 187, 190
state, coercive power of, 304, 307, 308, 367, 373
stockjobbers, 7, 9, 61, 116–70 *passim*
Stockport, 47
stone: export of, 118, 239; supply of, 118
Stonehenge, 199, 201
Stratton-on-Fosse, 255
Street, 161, 166
streets/roads/places: Abbey Churchyard, 295; Abbey Green, 107, 136; Abbey Street, 210; Ainslie's Belvedere, 277, 295; Alfred Street, 155, 315; Avon Street, 29, 73, 76, 80, 93, 149, 183, 184, problem of, 211–16 *passim*, 223, 224, 225, 259, 269, 271, 275, 289, 290; Ballance Street, 218, 272; Bath Street, 257, 260, 327; Beau Street, 254; Bennett Street, 155, 162; Bridge Street, 234, 249, 262; Bristol Road, 114, 214, 217, 311, 340; Broad Street, 50, 114, 155, 211, 215; Broad Quay, 81, 270; Brock Street, 153, 162, 207; Burlington Street, 112; Burrough Walls, 7, 108, 110, 113, 114, 135, 176, 183, 184, 206, 215; Chapel Street, 275; Cheap Street, 49, 214, 215, 256, 338; Cheapside, 158, 246; Chelsea Buildings, 247; Church Street, 210, 375; Corn Street, 217, 266, 270, 277, 295; Cross Bath Street, 254; Dorchester Street, 270; Dover Street, 218, 247, 272; East Gate, 214; Gay Street, 38, 153, 162, 183, 206, 207; George Street, 338; Half Moon Street, 158, 247; High Street, 50, 211, 215, 230, 338; Holloway, 217, 259, 272; Horse Street (Southgate Street), 50, 108, 211, 214, 215; Hot Bath Street, 254, 256; James Buildings, 218; Johnson Street, 158, 246; Kingsmead Street, 215, 217; Kingston Street, 210; Ladymead, 65, 74, 155, 211; Lampards Buildings, 218; Lansdown Road, 155; Laura Place, 158; London Road, 241; Lower Camden Place, 362; Marchant's Court, 61; Marchant's Passage, 59, 211; Margaret's Buildings, 327; Margaret's Hill, 211; Market Place, 307; Market Street, 215; Miles' Court, 162; Milk Street, 211, 217, 272; Monmouth Street, 215; Morford Street, 218, 272, 316, 341; Nash Street, 254; Newark Street, 270; New Bond Street, 277, 295; North Gate, 113, 114, 211, 214; Northgate Street, 215; Northumberland Buildings, 372; Orange Grove, 26, 215, 230, 295; Orchard Street, 74, 221; Peter Street, 311; Pierrepoint Street, 161; Phillip Street, 333; Quay, 211, 215; Quiet Street, 215; St James Parade, 91, 310, 311; St John's Place, 217; Saville Row, 155; Snow Hill, 247, 265, 269, 272, 291; South Gate, 113, 210, 214; Stall Street, 58, 91, 214, 215, 221, 373; Terrace Walk, 24, 35; Thomas Street (St James Street), 159, 205, 210, 214; Trymme Street, 58, 114, 134; Union Street, 254, 255, 256, 333; Wade's Passage, 210; Walcot Street, 50, 74, 155, 215, 242, 272; Wells Road, 00; West Gate, 114, 214; Westgate Street, 49, 214, 215; *see also* building developments
strikes, 69, 70, 225, 270, 325–8
suffrage: extension of, 349, 355, effect of extension of, 345; Freemen and, 330, 332; taxpayer, 333, 334, 348; universal, 334, 355, 371, 378
suicide, 26, 39, 92, 93
Sunderland, 47
Sussex, 72
Swansea, 47

Taunton, 271
taxation, 129; assessed taxes, repeal of, 336, 345, 348, 349, 366; cuts in, 365
temperance, 374, 375
Ten Hour Movement, 375, 377
Tennis Court, 341, 342
theatre, 13, 32, 48, 93
Theatre Royal, 38; rebuilt, 265
Titanbarrow, Logia, 192
trades, 50–6; Benefit Societies among, 324; combinations in, tailors, 69, 70, 76, 91, 225, 269, 324; condition of, 294; distribution of trades, 267–300 *passim*; shoemakers, account of 277, 288, the

SUBJECT INDEX

lowest class, 223, numbers of, 268, 276; and radicalism, 337–40; and voting behaviour, 355–7
trade unions; cordwainers, 269, 310; shoemakers, 326–7; shop assistants, 325; trade unionists, 373
traffic routes, 211–18, 220; traffic problems in Bathwick, 241–2, 250, 268, 289
traffic free areas, 214
tramway(s), 56, 118, 272
Trowbridge, 331
Tunbridge Wells, 16
Turkey Company, 119
Twerton, 76, 107, 117, 272, 340, 372

unemployment, 77, 283, 285; measures against, 336
urban growth and development, 8, 10, 63; in Bridgwater, 130, 131, 149; cautious investment in, 116; early in century, 115; planned, 104; problems of urban centres, 320
utopia, 8, 9, 10, 171–225 *passim*, 286; in Millenium Hall, 315–20; a radical utopia, 329–80

vagrancy, 87
venereal disease, 17
Victoria Park, 176, 253, 260; *see also* field names; Town Common
Victoria, State of, 371
voting behaviour: according to value of houses, 357–62; occupational analysis of, 355–7
Vitruvian figure, 191, 193, 196

wages, 39, 77–81, 83; real wages, 87–9, 262, 279, 281–2, 282–7; rise in, 285

wage fixing, 66, 68, 69
Walcot Lordship, 6, 95, 103, 106, 111
Walcot survey, 101–4
Wales, 70
Wallington, 114
war, Marlborough's, 25, 128; Office, 39, 40, 41
war economy, 81; with America, 237, 250; and the building of Bath, 167; the burden of, 322; with France, 262, 312; funds accumulated through, 129; history of Peninsular Wars, 345; in Ireland, 306; profit from, 119, 120–1; *see also* Wincanton, battle of
Ware, 111
Warleigh, 73
Warminster, 261
water closets, 135, 137
water supply, 117, 133, 158, 178, 288; for houses, 216; regulation of, 219; water rights (in Bathwick), 229, 230, 250, 365
welfare, economic, 10, 264–300 *passim*
Wells, 96, 104, 246, 261, 286, 311
Westerhall, 227
Western Vindicator, 372, 373
Weston, 372
Wiltshire, 51, 70, 72, 77, 94, 177, 178, 255; shearmen, 328
Weston, 30, 101
Wincanton, 6, 76; battle of, 98, 100, 306
Winchester, 130
women, distribution and employment, 72–6, 275–81; Millenium Hall, a model for women, 317–19; mortality of, 292; widows and deserted wives, 280–3

Yeomanry, North Somerset, 82, 339, 372
York, 270
York Building Company, 127, 140